RISING TIDE

Is Growth in Emerging Economies Good for the United States?

RISING
TIDE

Is Growth in Emerging Economies Good for the United States?

Lawrence Edwards and Robert Z. Lawrence

PETERSON INSTITUTE FOR INTERNATIONAL ECONOMICS

Washington, DC
February 2013

Lawrence Edwards is a professor at the School of Economics, University of Cape Town, and research associate at the South African Labor and Development Research Unit (SALDRU) and Policy Research on International Services and Manufacturing (PRISM). His research interests focus on the effects of international trade on labor, determinants of trade flows, and trade policy. He has published in *World Development, Journal of International Development, Economics of Transition, Harvard Business Review,* and *South African Journal of Economics.* He has consulted widely on trade policy issues for the World Bank, African Development Bank, International Growth Centre, the Organization for Economic Cooperation and Development, the Southern African Development Community Secretariat, and various governments in Africa, including South Africa, Swaziland, Lesotho, and Zambia. He was an associate editor of the *South African Journal of Economics* and *South African Journal of Economics and Management Studies.* He is a graduate of the University of Cape Town, where he completed his PhD, the London School of Economics and Political Science, and Rhodes University.

Robert Z. Lawrence, senior fellow at the Peterson Institute for International Economics since 2001, is the Albert L. Williams Professor of Trade and Investment at the John F. Kennedy School of Government at Harvard University and a research associate at the National Bureau of Economic Research. He was appointed by President Clinton to serve as a member of his Council of Economic Advisers in 1999. He held the New Century Chair as a nonresident senior fellow at the Brookings Institution and founded and edited the *Brookings Trade Forum.* Lawrence has been a senior fellow in the Economic Studies Program at Brookings (1983–91), a professorial lecturer at the Johns Hopkins School of Advanced International Studies (1978–81), and an instructor at Yale University (1975). He has served as a consultant to the Federal Reserve Bank of New York, the World Bank, the Organization for Economic Cooperation and Development, and the United Nations Conference on Trade and Development. He has written over 100 papers and articles on international economics, particularly on global integration, trade in the Middle East, and the impact of trade on the labor market. He is also the author or coauthor of several books, including *Blue-Collar Blues: Is Trade to Blame for Rising US Income Inequality?* (2008), *Case Studies in US Trade Negotiation* (2006), *Anchoring Reform with a US-Egypt Free Trade Agreement* (2005), *Has Globalization Gone Far Enough? The Costs of Fragmented Markets* (2004), *Crimes and Punishment? Retaliation under the WTO* (2003), and *Globaphobia: Confronting Fears about Open Trade* (Brookings Institution Press, 1998).

**PETERSON INSTITUTE FOR
INTERNATIONAL ECONOMICS**
1750 Massachusetts Avenue, NW
Washington, DC 20036-1903
(202) 328-9000   FAX: (202) 659-3225
www.piie.com

Adam S. Posen, *President*
Edward A. Tureen, *Director of Marketing
  and Publications*

Typesetting by BMWW
Cover design by Richard Fletcher—Fletcher Design
Cover photos by Thinkstock
Printing by United Book Press, Inc.

Printed in the United States of America
15   14   13   5   4   3   2   1

Library of Congress Cataloging-in-Publication Data
Edwards, Lawrence.
  Rising tide: is growth in emerging economies good for the united states? / Lawrence Edwards and Robert Z. Lawrence.
    p. cm.
  Includes bibliographical references and index.
  ISBN 978-0-88132-500-3
  1. Developing countries—Economic conditions.   2. Economic development—Developing countries.   3. United States—Economic conditions—21st century.   4. Developed countries—Economic conditions.   I. Lawrence, Robert Z., 1949– II. Title.
  HC59.7.E326 2013
  330.9172'4—dc23

                          2012045670

For
Anna and Nicole with love and gratitude

Contents

Preface   xiii

Acknowledgments   xix

Introduction   1
The Public's Concerns: Jobs   4
The Economists' Concerns: Welfare and Inequality   6
Study Findings   10
Study Outline   13
Scope of the Study   26

I   Trade and Jobs: Exploring the Public's Concerns   29

1   Trade and (Total) Jobs   33
    Arithmetic versus Behavior   34
    Trade Agreements   42
    Fiscal and Macroeconomic Policies   42

2   Imports and Lost Jobs and Wages   45
    Imports and Gross Job Losses   47
    Imports and Specific Wages   52
    Implications   54

3 "Good Jobs"—Trade and US Manufacturing Employment   57

   Closing of the US Labor Market   60
   Manufacturing Employment: Tracking the Decline   63
   Explaining Deindustrialization   67
   Did the Manufacturing Trade Deficit Play a Large Role in   79
      Manufacturing Employment Losses?
   Offshoring   84
   Conclusions   84

II Competitiveness, Welfare, and Inequality: 87
    Exploring the Concerns With Detailed Data

4 Do Developed and Developing Countries Compete   91
   Head to Head?

   Export Overlap   94
   Technological Sophistication   103
   Price Dispersion by Technology Classification   115
   Intermediate Inputs versus Finished Products   118
   The Question of Quality   120
   Conclusions   122
   Appendix 4A   Quality Measurement   125

III Trade and Welfare: Exploring the Economists'   133
     Concerns

5 Developing-Country Growth and US Welfare   135
   Theory, Foreign Growth, and Welfare   136
   Hicks' Conjecture   139
   Gains from US Trade with Emerging-Market Economies   149

6 US Welfare and the Trade Balance   153
   The Trade Deficit   154
   Correcting for the Trade Deficit   157
   Graphical Analysis of the Relationship between Terms of Trade   162
      and Trade Balance
   Welfare   165

7 Oil   171
   Oil Price Fluctuations and the US Economy   172
   Explaining the Recent Oil Price Boom   174
   The Future   179
   Conclusions   183

IV Trade and Wage Inequality: Exploring the Economists' Concerns   185

8 Developing-Country Trade and US Wages: Theoretical Perspectives   187
Restrictive Assumptions: Nonspecialization and Perfect Labor Mobility   190
Other Theories   195

9 Trade and the US Skill Premium   199
Recent Developments   202
Studies of Recent Data   210
Analysis of Prices   212
Conclusions   218
Appendix 9A   Are Developing-Country Manufactured Imports Intensive in Unskilled Labor?   221
Appendix 9B   Measurement Error in the Price Data   227
Appendix 9C   Isolating the Role of Trade with Mandated Wage Regressions   231

10 Conclusions and Policy Implications   235
What Do These Findings Imply for Policy?   238
Conclusions   251

References   253

Index   269

Tables
3.1   Share of employment in manufacturing, 1973–2010   67
3.2   Growth of employment, output, and labor productivity, 1960–2007   69
3.3   Manufacturing employment content of the manufacturing trade deficit, 1990, 2000, and 2010   83
4.1   Export similarity indices for manufactured goods, ranked by similarity with high-income OECD countries in 2006   96
4.2   Cumulative shares of manufactured exports to the United States relative to China, 2006   98
4.3   Average unit values relative to OECD exports to the United States and aggregate US exports, ranked by price relative to the OECD countries in 2006   101
4.4   Lall (2000) technology classification of exports   105
4.5   Share structure of US manufacturing imports by technology classification, 1990 and 2006   106

4.6 Comparison of average relative import unit values by technology classification using log mean share weights, 1990–2006   114

4.7 Weighted-average unit values of developing-country exports relative to OECD exports, 1990–2006   119

4A.1 Summary statistics of relative quality regression estimated at the SITC 4-digit level   128

4A.2 Indicators of quality differentiation by technology classification, manufacturing sectors only   129

5.1 Purchasing-power-parity-converted GDP per capita relative to the United States at current prices, 1950–2009   141

5.2 Gains from trade in manufactured goods, 1998–2009   151

7.1 Sources of oil market supply and demand pressure   175

7.2 International crude oil and liquid fuel supply, 2000 and 2008   177

7.3 Energy Information Administration scenario projections for liquid fuels   180

9.1 Weighted relative effective prices, 4-digit NAICS industries, 1987–2006   214

9A.1 Composition of US manufacturing imports from developed and developing countries by industries ranked by employment skill intensity, 1997–2007   222

9A.2 Manufacturing payroll and employment shares using nonproduction worker and college education measures to define skilled workers (average for 1997, 2002, and 2007)   223

9B.1 Weighted relative effective domestic prices without computers, 4-digit NAICS industries excluding NAICS 334, 1987–2006   229

Figures

1.1 Association between US employment and import growth, 1991–2011   36

3.1 Manufacturing and nonfarm employment, 1990–2011   58

3.2 Sector share in total employment, 1929–2009   61

3.3 Manufacturing share in total nonfarm employment, 1961–2010   64

3.4 International comparison of share of employment in manufacturing, 1973–2008   66

3.5 Measures of relative manufacturing productivity and prices, 1960–2007   71

3.6 US spending on goods relative to services, 1960–2010   76

3.7 Spending on equipment relative to total and services spending, 1960–2010   78

3.8 Manufacturing employment, actual and adjusted for manufacturing trade deficit, 1990–2010   81

3.9   Manufacturing job (full-time equivalent) content of   82
manufacturing trade deficit, actual productivity versus 1990
productivity, 1990–2010

4.1   Weighted-average import unit values relative to US export   102
unit values, 1990–2006

4.2   China's export unit values relative to US export unit values,   107
1990–2006

4.3   Developing-country export unit values relative to US export   108
unit values, 1990–2006

4.4   High-income OECD export unit values relative to US export   109
unit values, 1990–2006

4.5   Cross-country dispersion of US import unit values by   116
technology classification, 2006

4.6   Identifying relative quality from relative prices and relative   121
quantity, data processing machines, 2006

4.7   Average relative product quality by technology classification   123
for developed and developing countries, 1991–2006

4A.1 Average product-level relative quality for selected countries,   130
1991–2006

5.1   US terms of trade (goods and services), 1950–2010   142

5.2   US merchandise imports, 1978–2008   144

5.3   Ratios of US nonagricultural export prices to prices of   145
manufactured goods imports from developed and developing
countries, 1990–2008

5.4   US nonagricultural export prices relative to Chinese   146
manufactured import prices, 2003–11

5.5   Manufacturing terms of trade, 1996–2009   146

5.6   US terms of trade, 1980–2010   147

6.1   US nominal trade balance as a share of GDP, 1980–2010   155

6.2   US nominal bilateral merchandise trade balance as a share   156
of GDP, 1980–2010

6.3   How shifts in the transfer schedule provide a measure of   161
trade performance

6.4   Nominal trade balance in goods and services and lagged   163
terms of trade, 1990–2009

6.5   Nominal nonpetroleum trade balance and lagged terms of   164
trade, 1990–2009

7.1   US petroleum imports as share of GDP, 1969–2011   173

9.1   Ratio of import prices of manufactured goods from   203
developing countries to import prices of manufactured goods
from developed countries, 1990–2008

9.2   Full-time wages relative to high-school graduates, 1975–2008   204

9.3   Share of US manufactured imports from developing   208
countries in 6-digit NAICS industries ranked by skill intensity,
1997–2007

9.4 Domestic effective prices weighted by import shares and   215
    production and nonproduction employment, 1987–2006

Boxes

1.1 Multipliers   39
3.1 The manufacturing employment multiplier   59
3.2 Productivity and real wages   74
4.1 The United States and China: A disaggregated analysis   111
9.1 Defining skilled and unskilled labor   207

Preface

Many Americans view the rise of emerging-market economies with ambivalence. Principal concerns of a large share of the US public are about jobs and wages, especially at a time of high unemployment and slow income growth. Imports and offshoring by US firms to emerging-market economies such as India and China are often named in popular surveys as the most important reason for US job loss, especially in manufacturing. As a result of this not necessarily well-founded view, public opinion has been highly skeptical about the benefits of open trade and trade agreements.

These public concerns have been reinforced of late by several prominent economists, who have made more serious arguments considering the possibility that emerging-market-economy growth has or could reduce US living standards, lower US wages, and increase wage inequality (although none of these economists support a protectionist response).

If these concerns were valid, the implications would be serious. Overall US international economic policy since World War II has been based on the premise that foreign economic growth is in America's economic, as well as political and security, self-interest. Confronting these fears with the data is an imperative to inform our economic policymaking and public debate.

In this study, Lawrence Edwards and Robert Lawrence do just that. They undertake an extensive survey of the empirical literature to date and more importantly conduct their own indepth analyses of the evidence. Their conclusions contradict several popular theories about the negative impact of US trade with developing countries. Edwards and Lawrence demonstrate that trade has been tagged a villain far out of proportion to its actual impact on America's problems of slow income growth and rising inequality. To be sure, imports have caused some localized harm, such as when trade-related job losses hurt specific communities and prove to be costly for displaced workers, as long acknowledged to be inevitable. That does not justify the many exaggerations surrounding trade's role in the US income distribution. Indeed, the authors conclude that growth in emerging-market economies is part of the solution to America's current economic problems, rather than their source.

In particular, Edwards and Lawrence find that the decline in manufacturing's contribution to employment in the United States is driven by the combination of a shift in domestic demand away from spending on goods and faster productivity growth in manufacturing—not by imports and US trade policy, in contrast to received wisdom. This is borne out by the fact that the United States is not alone in experiencing these shifts—all industrial countries experienced a decline in their share of employment in manufacturing, even those with large trade surpluses.

For these reasons, even if the United States had recorded balanced trade over the past two decades, the share of manufacturing employment would have fallen by about as much as it did. The link between the rising US trade deficit since 2000 and the absolute decline in the level of manufacturing employment is more apparent than real. The increasing growth observed in US labor productivity implies that the imputed job content of the manufacturing trade deficit did not change over the past decade. Further, the authors find that that the association between *overall* US employment growth and import growth has been strikingly *positive*. Trade has actually boosted US employment in downturns because the country's recessions have originated domestically, and employment growth in the aftermath of major trade agreements has actually been robust. This finding is a sharp contradiction to the common view that imports and offshoring have been an important source of aggregate employment loss, especially during the most recent recession.

Edwards and Lawrence also find that trade with emerging-market economies has improved America's nonoil terms of trade and increased its product choices, thereby improving consumers' purchasing power. For example, they estimate that in 2008 this trade boosted US incomes by an average of $500 per person. As theory and common sense predict, developing-country growth provides US exporters with larger markets and US producers with cheaper and more varied inputs. In addition, while some emerging-market imports have caused dislocation, most are low-value-added finished and intermediate products that the United States no longer produces at home and would not produce at its current income levels. Most US producers are thus not adversely affected by these imports from emerging-market economies, while US buyers—consumers and downstream producers—enjoy lower prices and more choice. These results cast serious doubt on claims that increased competition by emerging-market countries has reduced US economic welfare.

Oil is an exception. There is evidence that demand generated by developing-country growth has played a role in boosting oil prices. But again misperceptions exaggerate the impact of countries such as India and China. The primary responsibility for the shortfall between supply and demand that caused oil prices to soar between 2000 and 2008 actually rests with the developed countries, whose own oil production failed to keep up with their demand. There is also evidence that with anticipated increases in US domestic energy supplies, this concern will become less important over time (as Trevor Houser projects in a forthcoming study for the Peterson Institute).

The past decade has seen an increase in overall income inequality in the United States with larger shares of income going to profits than to wages and to the super-rich than to everyone else. Using a variety of methodologies, however, the authors do not find that emerging-market-economy trade has had a substantial impact on economywide wage growth of workers with different levels of skill and education.

All told, the authors conclude that the premise that economic growth in emerging-market economies is in American self-interest will remain appropriate as a guide for US international economic policy in general and US trade policy in particular. In the aggregate, Americans benefit from growth in developing countries, and the effects on economywide wage inequality in the United States are relatively modest. Though there will continue to be some displacement and specific wage loss, those also take place in the process of industrial change within the United States and all capitalist economies. The ability of developing countries to meet the commonly made optimistic growth projections is by no means assured. But since this growth provides larger markets for US exports and improves America's terms of trade, it helps the United States undertake its own internal adjustment challenges. Indeed, slower growth in emerging-market economies would likely present the United States and its citizens with far greater economic problems than rapid growth.

The Peterson Institute for International Economics is a private, nonprofit institution for rigorous, intellectually open, and honest study and discussion of international economic policy. Its purpose is to identify and analyze important issues to making globalization beneficial and sustainable for the people of the United States and the world and then to develop and communicate practical new approaches for dealing with them. The Institute is completely nonpartisan.

The Institute's work is funded by a highly diverse group of philanthropic foundations, private corporations, and interested individuals, as well as by income on its capital fund. About 35 percent of the Institute's resources in our latest fiscal year were provided by contributors from outside the United States. The Alfred P. Sloan Foundation and Toyota Motor Corporation provided generous support for this study.

The Executive Committee of the Institute's Board of Directors bears overall responsibility for the Institute's direction, gives general guidance and approval to its research program, and evaluates its performance in pursuit of its mission. The Institute's President is responsible for the identification of topics that are likely to become important over the medium term (one to three years) and that should be addressed by Institute scholars. This rolling agenda is set in close consultation with the Institute's research staff, Board of Directors, and its Academic and Corporate Advisory Committees, as well as other stakeholders.

The President makes the final decision to publish any individual Institute study, following independent internal and external review of the work.

The Institute hopes that its research and other activities will contribute to building a stronger foundation for international economic policy around the world. We invite readers of these publications to let us know how they think we can best accomplish this objective.

ADAM S. POSEN
President
February 2013

Acknowledgments

We thank the Alfred P. Sloan Foundation, the Center for International Development at Harvard University, Economic Research Southern Africa (ERSA), and the National Research Foundation of South Africa for financial support. We are indebted for research assistance to Pandey Bibek, Sounman Hong, Natasha Lawrence, Ryan Mills, and Ivana Zecevic. We are especially grateful for comments from Martin Baily, Richard Cooper, Suzanne Cooper, Joseph Gagnon, Jonathan Haskel, J. Bradford Jensen, Marcus Noland, David Richardson, Dani Rodrik, Howard Rosen, Lawrence Summers, and three anonymous referees as well as participants at seminars held at Harvard Kennedy School, the Peterson Institute for International Economics, and the University of Stellenbosch. We thank Madona Devasahayam for managing the editing of the manuscript and Susann Luetjen for managing the production and cover design.

Introduction

As they say on my own Cape Cod, a rising tide lifts all the boats. And a partnership, by definition, serves both partners, without domination or unfair advantage.

—US President John F. Kennedy in an address
in Frankfurt, Germany, on June 25, 1963

Perceptions about the benefits of global trade have undergone radical changes in recent years. In 2000, the conventional wisdom was that trade had been good for developed countries such as the United States and a few countries in Asia such as China and India but bad for developing countries, especially those in Africa and Latin America that had experienced two decades of economic stagnation. Partly in response to this view, a new round of multilateral trade negotiations dubbed the Doha Development Agenda was launched in 2001 with the principal goal of creating a trading system that would be more beneficial to developing countries. Ironically, subsequent global growth in emerging markets was robust and concentrated. Not only did China and India sustain their rapid growth but also growth was strong in Africa, the Middle East, Latin America, and the rest of Asia. By contrast, after 2000, US economic performance was modest. The longest US postwar expansion lasted from 1991 to 2000, but it ended rudely with the bursting of the speculative dot. com bubble in the stock market, which led to falling investment in capital goods and a recession during which the US manufacturing sector lost almost 3 million jobs. Although the economy recovered after 2003, manufacturing employment remained stagnant and GDP growth averaged just 2.3 percent between 2000 and 2007.

The difference between US and foreign economic performance during the period from 2000 to 2007 was striking. The US share in the world economy had declined between 1950 and 1980 as Western Europe and Japan converged toward US income levels. But between 1980 and 2000, the United States had actually grown about as rapidly as the rest of the world—a remarkable achievement for the world's richest economy.

Between 2000 and 2007, however, the combination of weak US growth and rapid growth in emerging-market economies reduced the US share in global GDP by about 10 percent.[1] Moreover, the gains from this tepid growth were not widely shared. Although the top 1 percent of US income earners did well and corporate profits reached the highest share of national income in 80 years, wage growth for most Americans was slow and real median household income actually fell.

In the face of this slow income growth, Americans had to resort to borrowing in order to continue to increase their spending—a response made possible by low interest rates and strong housing and equity prices. This increased borrowing led to large current account deficits, and thus the disappointing US growth performance was associated with large trade deficits and a rapid increase in imports from developing countries, especially China.

It was not surprising, then, that even prior to the global financial crisis, Americans had become increasingly disillusioned with international trade and particularly concerned about America's ability to compete with emerging-market economies. The coincidence of trade deficits and increased imports from developing countries with several years of sluggish real wage growth, growing income inequality, and declining manufacturing employment all contributed to these attitudes. In addition, the rapid growth in the offshoring of business services sparked by the internet added to the worries. By 2004, in the face of slow employment growth, it was hard to open a US newspaper without reading stories about jobs going to India. Alarm bells rang as more educated Americans who thought their jobs were safe suddenly discovered that they too might have to engage in international competition with low-wage countries. Strikingly, the stories about India disappeared from the headlines when employment recovered, and it turned out that the number of jobs that had migrated there had been modest. Nonetheless, it was clear that the concerns had struck a chord with the public and helped contribute to fears about the potential for greater disruption in the future.

A poll by *Fortune* magazine in January 2008 reflected these negative views. The poll found that 63 percent of US respondents indicated that "trade had made matters worse for the United States as a whole," 78 percent felt it "made things worse for US workers," and 55 percent said it "made things worse for US business." Finally, 68 percent said that "the benefits of trade to other countries were greater than those for the United States."[2] A CBS News Poll in 2008 found similar sentiments when it asked the question "Do you think the recent economic expansion in countries like China and India has been generally good

1. According to the International Monetary Fund, the United States averaged 3.3 percent real GDP growth in both the 1980s and 1990s, while the rest of the world grew at annual rates of 3.1 and 2.8 percent, respectively. The US share of world GDP (based on purchasing power parity valuations) fell from 23.4 percent in 2000 to 21.3 percent in 2007.

2. "Recession Near, or Already Here," *Fortune,* January 2008. http://money.cnn.com/magazines/fortune/electionpoll/2008/pollresults.html (accessed on November 1, 2012).

for the US economy, or bad for the US economy, or had no effect on the US economy?" Fourteen percent of respondents said good, 62 percent said bad, 10 percent said there was no effect, and 14 percent were unsure.[3] Finally, a Rasmussen poll in September 2009 found that 14 percent of Americans said what is good for the world economy is always good for the United States, while 75 percent disagreed with that statement.[4]

The global financial crisis further influenced these views. While no country was spared the effects of the crisis, economies like China and India, though adversely affected, were able to maintain positive growth and then recover quickly. With their relatively isolated financial sectors, low inflation rates, and large holdings of foreign exchange reserves, many developing countries were able to adopt stimulatory domestic policies. Such actions in turn bolstered primary commodity markets, helping other troubled developing-country producers. In the developed countries, however, the slump was steep and deep. In the United States, the unemployment rate breached 10 percent, and between 2007 and 2009 an additional 2 million jobs were lost in manufacturing. The International Monetary Fund (IMF) forecasts in 2010 suggested emerging-market economies would achieve growth rates close to the rapid rates they had recorded prior to the crisis. Longer-term projections by other research organizations presented a similar outlook (Lawrence 2011). By contrast, the advanced economies were expected to grow far more slowly. The US share in global output would decline, and if current trends continued China would eventually surpass the United States as the world's largest economy.

It was again not surprising that the US public's view on trade appeared to sour even further. In October 2010, the *Wall Street Journal* reported that Americans believed that "free-trade pacts had hurt the United States."[5] Remarkably, over 50 percent of well-educated and upper-income Americans—those earning $75,000 a year or more, a group that had previously strongly supported new trade agreements—now concurred with this view.[6] Partly in response to this inhospitable environment, the trade policies of the Obama administration were initially lethargic. The Doha Round was left to linger without US leadership and free trade agreements that had been signed by the Bush administration with Korea, Colombia, and Panama were presented to Congress for ratification only in late 2011. And it was not until 2012 that the administration became active in negotiating new agreements.

---

3. CBS News Poll, July 31–August 5, 2008, www.pollingreport.com/trade.htm (accessed on November 1, 2012).

4. "60% Favor Less International Economic Oversight, Not More," Rasmussen Reports, October 1, 2009, www.rasmussenreports.com/public_content/politics/general_politics/september_2009/60_favor_less_international_economic_oversight_not_more (accessed on November 1, 2012).

5. "Americans Sour on Trade," *Wall Street Journal,* October 4, 2010, 1.

6. In 1999, only 24 percent of Americans earning more than $75,000 were skeptical about trade's benefits.

The Public's Concerns: Jobs

While Americans appreciate that imports provide them with cheaper products, their principal concerns about trade relate to jobs. In the aforementioned *Fortune* poll in early 2008, for example, only 30 percent of respondents felt that the statement "International trade is good for the United States because it leads to lower prices for consumers" was closest to their views. More than twice that share—63 percent—identified more closely with the view that "International trade is bad for the US because it results in the loss of jobs and lower wages."[7]

The United States has implemented numerous trade agreements over the past two decades. These include the North American Free Trade Agreement (NAFTA) with Mexico and Canada in 1994, the Uruguay Round that established the World Trade Organization (WTO) in the same year, and the granting of China permanent most favored nation status in 2000 that allowed its accession to the WTO the following year. But the *Fortune* poll also indicated that a majority of Americans believe that these agreements have cost US jobs while providing other countries with considerably more benefits than those obtained by the United States.

The job concerns are especially focused on manufacturing. In 1970, 24 percent of US workers on nonagricultural payrolls were employed in manufacturing. By 2010, that share had dwindled to just 9 percent. Manufacturing has historically been an important provider of high-quality jobs, especially for men with relatively low educational levels. Henry Farber (2009, 2) of Princeton University puts it well:

> The concern about job quality is based in part on the fact that the share of employment that is in manufacturing has been declining over a long period of time. This has led to the view that as high-quality manufacturing jobs are lost, perhaps to import competition, they are being replaced by low-quality service sector jobs (so-called hamburger-flipping jobs). The high-quality jobs are characterized by relatively high wages, full-time employment, substantial fringe benefits, and, perhaps most importantly, substantial job security (low rates of turnover). The low-quality jobs are characterized disproportionately by relatively low wages, part-time employment, an absence of fringe benefits, and low job security (high rates of turnover).

There are other concerns about the erosion of manufacturing. Manufacturing commands a disproportionately large share of spending on research and development, accounts for a disproportionately large share of productivity growth, and has been pivotal in the economies of major regions in the United States such as the Midwest. Manufacturing also plays an important role in international trade. Almost 60 percent of US exports of goods and services and 70 percent of imports are manufactured goods. Indeed, this tradability is a special source of concern when it comes to manufacturing because, as indicated in

---

7. "Recession Near, or Already Here," *Fortune,* January 2008, http://money.cnn.com/magazines/fortune/electionpoll/2008/pollresults.html (accessed on November 1, 2012).

Farber's comments, many believe that America's trade performance is the most important reason for manufacturing's declining role in the economy.

What explains the trade deficits in manufacturing? Many claim they reflect a decline in US international competitiveness. Some fault poor management (e.g., auto manufacturers), others fault unions for burdening their employers with costly benefit packages. But much of the blame is focused on US government policies. Frequently cited are corporate taxes (too high), regulatory and skilled-worker immigration policies (too restrictive), and an education system especially weak in math and science (Liveris 2010, chapter 6). Others point to unfair foreign practices and what they see as the toothless responses to these by the United States (Brown 2004, Fletcher 2009). Some castigate American policymakers for these policies and ascribe them to misguided beliefs in laissez-faire economics (Choate 2008). Articles on this theme often excoriate economists in particular for their cavalier attitude toward manufacturing.[8]

There have therefore been numerous calls for new trade and industrial policies. Prominent leaders from the business community have advocated new policies to encourage firms to "Make It in America"—the title of one such book by Andrew Liveris, the chairman and CEO of the Dow Chemical Company (Liveris 2010).[9] Warren Buffett, CEO of Berkshire-Hathaway, has a plan to guarantee balanced US trade by rationing the right to import using vouchers earned by exporting.[10] Ralph Gomory, former director of research at IBM, has endorsed Buffett's proposal and advocated new tax breaks for firms that produce output with "high-value-added-per-US-employee."[11] Andy Grove, former CEO of the Intel Corporation, would like to "tax the products of off-shored labor."[12]

As the economy recovered from the global financial crisis, there were numerous reports about the possibilities of manufacturing jobs returning to the United States due to higher wage costs in China and discoveries of new technologies in the production of energy. Nonetheless, whatever the specific prescriptions and prospects, there is a widespread view that the key to creating more jobs and preserving those that still exist in the US industries that

---

8. For example, Alan Blinder of Princeton University has been pilloried for suggesting that the United States is better off when more standardized products are produced elsewhere. (Blinder was referring to televisions.) Michael Boskin of Stanford University has been criticized for allegedly saying "Computer chips, potato chips, what's the difference?" And Gregory Mankiw, chairman of President George W. Bush's Council of Economic Advisors, almost lost his job for saying that outsourcing would prove to be a "plus for the economy in the long run" and was simply "a new way of doing international trade."

9. An earlier work making similar arguments was Cohen and Zysman (1988).

10. Warren E. Buffett and Carol J. Loomis, "America's Growing Trade Deficit Is Selling the Nation Out from Under Us. Here's a Way to Fix the Problem—And We Need to Do It Now," *Fortune*, November 10, 2003.

11. Ralph Gomory, "A Time for Action, Jobs, Prosperity and National Goals," *Huffington Post*, January 25, 2010. www.huffingtonpost.com/ralph-gomory/a-time-for-action-jobs-pr_b_434698.html (accessed on November 1, 2012).

12. Andy Grove, "How America Can Create Jobs," *Business Week*, July 1, 2010.

produce tradable goods lies in policies that promote more innovation and enhanced productivity growth at home, and in adopting a more aggressive stance abroad toward the emerging-market economies.

The Economists' Concerns: Welfare and Inequality

It is not only the public at large that has negative views about developing-country growth and its impact on the United States through trade. Some very prominent economists have also voiced their doubts. While the public's concern is mainly about jobs—and while some economists have raised questions about the impact of trade on employment in sectors producing goods and services that are actually or potentially tradable (Spence 2011, Blinder 2006)— the issues raised by economists are for the most part different, although their arguments resonate with the broader public's worries. Emblematic of these views was an op-ed in the *Financial Times* in April 2008 by former US Treasury Secretary Lawrence Summers, who was also the director of the National Economic Council during the first two years of the Obama administration.[13] Summers raised several concerns, as outlined in the next two sections.[14]

Aggregate Welfare

First, Summers invoked the authority of Nobel Laureate Paul Samuelson, who in a widely quoted article published in 2004 had used the classical trade model originally developed by David Ricardo to point out that growth in developing countries does not necessarily improve welfare in the United States.[15] Summers was not alone in agreeing with Samuelson. In her 2008 campaign for the US presidency, Hillary Clinton referred to Samuelson's argument as providing support for her position that the United States call a "time out" on negotiating any new trade agreements in order to reconsider whether these were in America's interest.[16]

In his paper, Samuelson had presented three scenarios. Two supported the conventional view that the United States could gain from growth abroad through cheaper imports and larger export markets. But in a third scenario he demonstrated the possibility that the United States could lose if foreigners emerged as stronger competitors for US exports (Samuelson 2004). Summers added to Samuelson's argument by pointing out that in addition to such

---

13. Lawrence Summers, "America Needs to Make a New Case for Trade," *Financial Times*, April 27, 2008.

14. Summers made several observations about US multinational firms that are evaluated in Moran (2009, 2010).

15. For a presentation of the model, see Krugman and Obstfeld (2003, chapter 2).

16. Edward Luce, "Clinton Doubts Benefits of Doha Revival," *Financial Times*, December 2, 2007. Senator Clinton was quoted as saying "I agree with Paul Samuelson, the very famous economist, who has recently spoken and written about how comparative advantage, as it is classically understood, may not be descriptive of the 21st century economy in which we find ourselves."

competition with the United States in export markets, faster growth in oil-importing countries like China could increase the world price of oil and thus reduce US welfare by raising US import costs.[17]

Winners and Losers

Summers also observed that while global growth might benefit Americans who were already highly paid for intellectual creations by providing them with large markets, it could also put downward pressure on US wages in industries such as computers that the United States produces on a significant scale. Again Summers was not alone. In making this claim, he was joining another Nobel Laureate, Paul Krugman, who had raised alarms that US trade with developing countries had become an important reason for increased US wage inequality and slow real wage growth. Krugman also argued on the basis of another widely used classical trade model that "growing US trade with third world countries reduces the real wages of many and perhaps most workers in this country."[18]

The concerns raised by these prominent economists about lower US welfare, increased inequality, and lower real wages for most US workers are especially troubling because they relate to the long-run impact of trade. If true, they would not be mitigated by the passage of time and would be present even if the US economy returned to full employment.

Some of the public's fears are well founded and recognized. Some (but not all) increased trade certainly could cause short-term pain in the form of job losses, lower profits, and the dislocation of people and communities. In addition, in the context of the other downward pressures on US manufacturing employment due to sluggish demand and rapid productivity growth, these adverse effects of trade on US blue-collar workers have been especially painful. Nonetheless, the justification for open trade is that even if there are adjustment costs, they will be more than offset by eventual gains from improved resource allocation and enhanced productivity once those who lose their jobs are reemployed, even taking into account the costs to those who are not.[19]

---

17. In the *Financial Times* article (see footnote 13), Summers wrote, "As Paul Samuelson pointed out several years ago, the valid proposition that trade barriers hurt an economy does not imply the corollary that it necessarily benefits from the economic success of its trading partners. . . . When other countries develop, American producers benefit from having larger markets to sell into but are challenged by more formidable competition. Which effect predominates cannot be judged a priori. But there are reasons to think that economic success abroad will be more problematic for American workers in the future."

18. Paul R. Krugman, "The Trouble with Trade; Keep Our Markets Open but Protect Those Who Get Hurt," *Pittsburgh Post-Gazette*, December 29, 2007, B-7.

19. Stephen Magee (1972), for example, estimated that the benefits from a five-year phaseout of all US trade restrictions in 1971 would be 100 times greater than the wages that would be lost during the transitional unemployment required for displaced workers to find new jobs. A more detailed follow-up study concluded that the overall gains from trade liberalization were 20 times the overall adjustment costs (Baldwin, Mutti, and Richardson 1980). See also Autor, Dorn, and Hanson (2012) for a cost-benefit analysis of Chinese imports.

These prominent economists are challenging the view that these net benefits exist for the US economy as a whole (in the case of Samuelson and Summers) and for most American workers, even those not directly engaged in international competition (in the case of Krugman).

Support for free trade is widespread among economists. Accustomed to being berated, free-trade skeptics relish the sight of apparent cracks in the foundation on which that support rests. When those in the highest ranks of the economics profession raise questions about the benefits of trade, they attract lots of attention.[20] But the high priests of the economics profession making these arguments are not apostates who advocate protectionism. Indeed, Samuelson, Summers, and Krugman have all made clear their opposition to higher trade barriers. Nor are they challenging conventional trade theory and agreeing with those who claim that the theory requires outdated assumptions that are inappropriate for "new realities."[21] Instead, they are actually *invoking* standard trade theory to make empirical claims about the impact of foreign growth that are familiar to anyone who has taken an undergraduate course in international economics. The textbooks for these courses do demonstrate how trade can be more beneficial than self-sufficiency, but they also explain that (1) these benefits could shrink or grow as a result of developments abroad, and (2) trade can create winners and losers within nations. The fact that the most basic conventional economic theory could be used to support the broader concerns of the US public about trade and foreign growth may come as a surprise to some, but it underscores the fact that the concerns could rest on solid ground and therefore merit serious consideration.

Implications

If the economists' concerns are valid, the implications for US policies could be profound. The downward pressures on US living standards from developing-country growth would be occurring at a particularly inopportune time, since Americans are already being forced to tighten their belts because of the global financial crisis. The US spending binge has proven to be unsustainable. In the late 1990s, US households became increasingly indebted as their homes and stocks appreciated and credit was available at low real interest rates. Because home and equity prices declined precipitously when the financial crisis erupted, however, it seems reasonable now to foresee a period in which American households increase their savings and rebuild their wealth. More US growth will therefore have to come from foreign demand and less from domestic private and government spending. It is likely that whatever the trend effects of growth in emerging-market economies, the adjustment process will entail a weaker dollar and the downward pressures it could exert on living

---

20. These reactions are documented by Jagdish Bhagwati (2009).

21. See Charles Schumer and Paul Craig Roberts, "Second Thoughts on Free Trade," *New York Times,* January 6, 2004. See also the comments by Hillary Clinton cited in footnote 16.

standards through a worsening of America's terms of trade (Obstfeld and Rogoff 2004, Cline and Williamson 2012).

The US economy initially responded to the recession caused by the global financial crisis with expansionary monetary and fiscal policies. But over time the country has become increasingly dependent on foreign growth to maintain the recovery. This can be seen in President Barack Obama's pledge in his 2010 State of the Union address to double US exports in five years. US exports are fundamentally driven by growth in foreign demand, and, according to IMF projections in April 2012, emerging-market economies will account on a purchasing power basis for two-thirds of global income growth between 2012 and 2017.[22] If the critics are correct, however, the United States is caught between a rock and a hard place. On the one hand, it needs foreign growth to maintain demand and increase US exports; on the other, the costs of this dependence could rise if such growth imposes additional burdens on US living standards.

US foreign policy might also be affected. As exemplified by the Marshall Plan after World War II, and reiterated by John F. Kennedy in his words cited at the opening of this Introduction, American global economic leadership has been predicated on the view that a "rising tide lifts all boats." The American case for a liberal economic order is that it is "win-win." Open markets are conducive to growth in foreign economies, and that growth is in America's economic interest. But the claim that the United States is hurt by developing-country growth could provide an economic rationale for policies that would seek to preserve US incomes by keeping the rest of the world poor. Given the emergence of countries such as China and India as major global players, an American repositioning on this issue and the policies that might follow could seriously threaten the current global order that is increasingly centered on the G-20, which gives more decision-making power to developing countries.[23] It could, of course, still be in America's interest to foster foreign economic growth, because of either altruism or noneconomic benefits such as greater stability and peace. But the case for doing so is much stronger if foreign growth also provides material advantages for Americans.

Even if growth in developing countries does benefit the United States as a whole, there could be reasons for concern if it also harms large numbers of US workers, especially at a time of slow real wage growth and high unemployment. If American workers were generally doing well, some pressures on US wages because of trade might be acceptable. But in a context of stagnant compensation, rising income inequality, and high unemployment, such pressures could engender more powerful protectionist responses. The conventional nostrum—adjustment assistance for workers displaced by trade—is of no help

---

22. IMF, *World Economic Outlook* database, www.imf.org/external/pubs/ft/weo/2012/01/weodata/index.aspx (accessed on November 1, 2012).

23. At the Pittsburgh Summit in September 2009, it was decided to designate the G-20 to be the premier forum for international economic cooperation.

to workers who remain employed but experience real wage reductions because of trade.[24] A response that could help would be more progressive tax and transfer policies to redistribute gains from winners to losers. In practice, however, it is politically difficult to raise taxes on the rich, and workers have justifiable reasons for skepticism that they will be fully compensated. As Paul Samuelson (2004, 144) observed, "Marie Antoinette said, 'Let them eat cake,' but history records no transfer of sugar and flour to her peasant subjects."

The implications of higher oil prices are also significant. Growth in China and India has been robust. As their middle classes grow, increased spending on transportation (automobiles) and power could put upward pressure on global oil prices. America's urban geography and transportation system are premised on abundant and inexpensive gasoline. Oil is also the most important reason for the strategic significance of the Middle East, because even though that region's share of US oil imports has declined from its 60 percent peak in 2005, the United States in 2011 still imported about 50 percent of its oil, and the prospects are that it will continue to import a substantial share for the foreseeable future.[25] The price of oil influences politics among both US allies and adversaries. The impact of developing-country growth on oil prices influences both America's domestic lifestyle and its foreign policies.[26]

This study, therefore, explores concerns about developing-country growth raised by the public and by economists. What impact has trade had on jobs in the United States? Has growth in developing countries reduced US welfare by providing increased competition in export markets and sparking higher oil prices? Has it significantly increased wage inequality and depressed wages? This study attempts to answer these questions and draw policy implications. In the sections below we summarize our arguments and findings and then make some qualifying comments about the scope of the study.

Study Findings

This study challenges many of the perceptions about US trade with emerging-market economies. In several cases, these perceptions are derived from theoretical preconceptions or the use of data that point to conclusions that, while plausible, turn out to be either incomplete or wrong. Several of the findings in the study contradict widely held public views about the effects of trade with emerging-market economies on US employment and demonstrate that trade has often been assigned a role in America's economic difficulties that far exceeds its impact.

---

24. For discussions of trade adjustment assistance, see Kletzer and Litan (2001) and Rosen (2008).

25. For projections, see EIA (2012).

26. Developing-country growth will also affect the United States through its impact on global CO_2 emissions. For discussions of this issue, see Cline (1992), Victor (2004), Hufbauer, Charnovitz, and Kim (2009), and Houser et al. (2008).

In contrast to the view that trade is the dominant source of declining US manufacturing employment, for example, we argue that the trend is driven by the combination of a shift in domestic demand away from spending on goods and faster productivity growth in manufacturing—a trend that is evident in all industrial countries, even those with large trade surpluses. While the rising trade deficit after 2000 does correspond with an absolute decline in the level of manufacturing employment, rising productivity implies that the imputed job content of the manufacturing trade deficit did not change over the decade. Even if the United States had recorded balanced trade over the past two decades, the share of manufacturing employment would have fallen considerably.

In contrast to the view that imports and offshoring have been an important source of aggregate employment loss, especially during the most recent recession, we find that the association between employment growth and import growth has been strikingly positive and that trade has actually boosted US employment in downturns because the country's recessions have originated domestically.

These findings do not mean that some imports have not been disruptive. While its impact on net employment growth has been modest, international competition *has* been a source of job and wage loss for individual workers that should not be minimized. At times this loss has damaged communities, put downward pressure on local and occupational wages, and been especially costly for workers who are displaced. But again, in contrast to widely held views, trade accounts for just a small part of overall worker displacement in an economy that is quite volatile.

We also cast doubt on several of the claims made by some economists. We do not find that manufacturing competition with developing countries has reduced US living standards. On the contrary, such trade has improved America's nonoil terms of trade and increased its product choices. Developing-country growth provides US exporters with larger markets and US producers with cheaper and more varied inputs, albeit with some exceptions, as most developing countries are not yet major competitors for US exports. In addition, while some imports have been disruptive, close substitutes for many of the finished and intermediate products the United States imports are no longer produced at home. US producers are thus not adversely affected by these imports, while US buyers enjoy lower prices and more choice. Although international trade has resulted in lower and lost wages for some workers, trade with developing countries over the past decade has not exacerbated economywide US wage inequality along the lines of skill or education. The core reason why trade has improved welfare without worsening wage inequality is that the United States and developing countries have become specialized in very different products and processes, which makes much of their growth complementary rather than competitive.

The classical models used by Samuelson and Krugman are elegant and their predictions powerful and plausible, but the frameworks oversimplify the world by assuming that (1) products, factors, and industries are standardized and homogeneous, in other words, that competition is perfect; (2) factors of production are completely mobile within countries; and (3) the United States and developing countries still produce the same products. In reality, most products are differentiated by variety and quality, factors of production are often used only for specific tasks, many shocks primarily impact particular communities, and many products exported by developing countries are no longer produced in the United States. These differences help explain why our findings contradict the economists' predictions.

Oil is an exception to the favorable impact on the terms of trade of developing-country growth. There is evidence that supports Summers' argument that the purchases of developed and developing oil-importing countries compete with each other, and large differences in world oil prices can be occasioned by relatively small changes in the world oil supply-demand balance. In this regard, demand generated by developing-country growth has played a role in boosting oil prices. But again there are misperceptions that exaggerate the impact of countries such as India and China. The primary responsibility for the shortfall between supply and demand that caused oil prices to soar between 2000 and 2008 actually rests with the developed countries, whose oil production failed to keep up with their demand. The contribution of the United States to higher global prices over this period was actually as important as that of China. Since 2008, China's role has increased, while that of the United States has declined, but upward pressures on prices from advanced economies still account for two-thirds of the price rise between 2000 and 2011. There is also evidence that with anticipated increases in US domestic energy supplies, this concern will become less important over time.

In our view, the maxim that a rising tide raises all boats will remain appropriate for some time in the future as a guide for US international economic policy in general and trade policy in particular. In the decades ahead, firms in developing countries could become more formidable competitors for US exporters, but by and large these pressures are not yet present. This does not mean that import competition has not been disruptive, and that it might not continue to induce some displacement and specific wage loss in the future. However, in the aggregate, Americans benefit from growth in developing countries, and the effects on economywide wage inequality in the United States are relatively modest.

In sum, the United States would not be better served by erecting new barriers at home or viewing foreign growth as damaging to its economic interests. Indeed, growth in developing economies is part of the solution to America's current economic difficulties, and not the major reason for its problems. The ability of developing countries to meet the optimistic growth projections that are commonly made is by no means assured. But since this growth provides larger markets for US exports and improves America's terms of trade, it helps the United States address its adjustment challenges.

Despite these relatively optimistic conclusions about emerging-market-economy growth, policy challenges most certainly remain for the United States. There is considerable scope for improved policies that diminish international imbalances, reduce foreign barriers to US exports, limit US oil imports, protect US intellectual property, revitalize the country's industrial base, and provide US firms and workers with the tools they need to adjust and compete.

Study Outline

The three chapters in part I focus on the public's concerns about trade and jobs. We do not contest the validity of those concerns. Indeed, we discuss how increased imports could inhibit recovery, especially through higher oil prices; present evidence that some import competition has led to job dislocation and wage losses; and quantify the employment content of the trade deficit in manufacturing. But we also argue that public understanding is lacking and has overlooked more important reasons behind unemployment, job loss, and deindustrialization.

Total Employment

Chapter 1 discusses aggregate employment—that is, "total jobs." Public accounts and analyses by some think tanks reflect the presumption that increased imports (or larger trade deficits) lead automatically to aggregate job loss. But this presumption is not always warranted. While trade flows obviously do affect employment, the relationships between trade and employment are complex. Trade flows are not independent "causes" of change but rather are outcomes of a number of factors, making it perilous to make causal inferences and quantitative estimates about the impact of "trade" using data after the fact.

From the standpoint of employment creation, all import growth is not created equal. Some import growth does reflect offshoring and the loss of sales by domestic firms to foreign producers, but imports can also result from more domestic growth and indeed can facilitate it. Thus, concerns that imports reduce employment may sometimes be warranted. But more commonly, because domestic spending has been the primary driver of import growth, faster growth in imports in recent US history has generally been associated with increased employment.

Similarly, larger US trade deficits typically have been the result of an expansion in domestic spending and production, rather than associated with economic contraction. Increased trade deficits do not necessarily indicate that trade is, on balance, reducing aggregate employment. Nor does the emergence of larger trade deficits during an expansion preclude recovery. The specific reasons for the larger deficits need to be understood. Even when deficits are growing, it is quite possible that they simply are the result of a recovery in domestic spending that leads to more imports, and that increased export growth is actually further boosting employment.

Over the past two decades, fluctuations in import volumes have not been the major driver of aggregate changes in employment. Neither the rapid rise in imports from developing countries nor the declining share of employment in manufacturing prevented the US economy from achieving virtually full employment in the late 1990s and mid-2000s. Employment growth has actually been strong in the years following major trade agreements such as NAFTA, the founding of the WTO, and China's WTO accession. This suggests that, whatever their individual net employment effects, these agreements have had only a modest impact on overall unemployment.

When unemployment reflects insufficient aggregate demand, trade *can* have an impact on aggregate demand and thus employment. For example, with the need for smaller budget deficits constraining fiscal policy during the US expansion for the foreseeable future, increased exports and import substitution can play a role in restoring full employment. Exports can be stimulated by foreign growth, and that stimulus can give rise to additional domestic multiplier effects on spending. A weaker dollar can assist both exporters and domestic firms that compete with imports. Lower world oil prices and increased oil conservation can keep more purchasing power at home. Thus forces operating through trade can make a contribution to recovery.

Displacement

Chapter 2 considers lost jobs and wages. Several studies have found that import competition from developing countries has led to worker dislocation. Some also report that import competition has damaged local economies and exerted downward pressure on local industrial and occupational wages. In addition, displaced workers draw unemployment benefits. Many experience significant wage losses once they find new employment, some workers draw disability benefits, and others permanently withdraw from the labor force. However, increased imports do not always lead to job loss. Studies report cases where no job loss is found and cases where the association between imported inputs and domestic production has actually been positive.

Whether negative or positive, these effects need to be viewed in perspective. Import competition is by no means the most important source of displacement or wage pressures in the economy. A growing majority of US workers experience little direct international competition. Moreover, the US labor market is quite volatile for many reasons that have little to do with trade. Indeed, by all accounts, job losses due to imports have accounted for a small percentage of gross job losses in the United States. This does not mean that the jobs lost because of trade are insignificant, or that the pressures on those remaining employed in the tradable sector are not substantial. But it suggests the need for policies that assist worker adjustment to all forms of displacement rather than displacement focused narrowly on trade.

Manufacturing Employment

Chapter 3 explores declining manufacturing employment. Remarkably, given today's powerful forces of globalization, the US labor market is actually becoming more closed. The long-run decline in the manufacturing share of employment has been so pronounced that even when the increase in tradable services is taken into account, a smaller share of Americans in 2010 worked in industries that are exposed to international competition than in 1990. This deindustrialization of the United States is not due only to trade. Indeed, it is primarily "made in America" and reflects in part American spending decisions. Relatively rapid productivity growth has led to lower prices for goods, but US demand has been insufficiently responsive to prevent the declining trend in manufacturing employment. The driving force behind the shrinking employment share in manufacturing is thus quite similar to the earlier forces that reduced employment in agriculture. Faster productivity growth allowed the United States to meet its growing need for food (and the needs of many foreigners) while at the same time redeploying workers to other parts of the economy and allocating smaller shares of spending to food. The same is true for manufactured goods.

To explain the decline in manufacturing's employment share, popular accounts typically stress the effects of the emergence of China and India, offshoring through global supply chains, and US trade deficits. But these accounts overlook the far more powerful forces that have been operating for some time, long before imports from emerging-market economies were a concern. Between 2000 and 2010, the share of manufacturing in total employment did decline by about 0.4 percentage points per year. But this is almost exactly the same annual rate of decline in the share over the prior 40 years from 1960 to 2000. Likewise, the decline in manufacturing employment between 2000 and 2010 is precisely what would have been predicted given the sluggish behavior of aggregate employment and the relationships between manufacturing and aggregate employment changes that were typical prior to 2000.

But what about the manufacturing trade deficits? We estimate that in 2010, the manufacturing employment content of the US manufacturing trade deficit was equal to 22 percent of overall manufacturing employment. But surprisingly, we find that the manufacturing job content of the manufacturing trade deficit has not changed much over the past decade as a whole. In both 1998 and 2010, the manufacturing employment equivalence of the manufacturing trade deficit was about 2.5 million jobs. This is a surprise, because measured in current dollars the manufacturing trade deficit more than doubled over this period. But the explanation is faster manufacturing labor productivity growth. While the nominal manufacturing trade deficit was two and a half times as large in 2010 as it was in 1998, (nominal) output per worker soared, so the job content of each dollar of deficit fell.

Reducing or closing the trade deficit through increased exports could provide a boost to employment in manufacturing or at least delay its decline, but it would be like taking a few upward steps on an escalator moving downwards. There is a limit to the extent the deficit could fall (or even turn into a surplus), and thus the respite is likely to be temporary. The decline in manufacturing employment shares in other countries with large trade surpluses has been very similar to that in the United States. Eventually, as their experience indicates, the long-run relationships will again dominate and the descending trend will likely resume.

Head-to-Head Competition

In part II the study turns to the concerns about competitiveness and inequality. In chapter 4 we undertake a detailed investigation using highly disaggregated trade data to (1) explore concerns about US competitiveness and (2) set the scene for our consideration of the economists' concerns about the aggregate welfare and distributional impacts of trade with developing countries. The argument voiced by Samuelson (2004) that emerging-market economies are becoming increasingly competitive with US exports seems to be supported by the large trade deficits the United States has been running in high-tech products. The argument by Krugman[27] that unskilled-labor-intensive exports from developing countries have put downward pressures on the relative wages of unskilled US workers seems to be supported by the declining prices of manufactured imports from developing countries. But both concerns implicitly reflect the assumption that goods produced in the United States and developing countries are close substitutes. To the contrary, chapter 4 shows that there are distinctive patterns of international specialization and that developed and developing countries export fundamentally different products, especially those classified as high-tech.

Although they have become more similar over time as judged by export shares, the United States and developing countries specialize in product categories that for the most part do not overlap. Moreover, even when exports are classified in the same category, there are large and systematic differences in unit values (average prices) that suggest the products made by developed and developing countries are not very close substitutes—developed-country products are far more sophisticated. This finding cannot be dismissed as simply the result of developing countries producing more intermediate products in each category—in other words, as simply reflecting global supply chains. We find it holds as well in categories that include only finished goods. These differences in prices are not apparent for all types of products, however. Export prices of developed and developing countries of primary-commodity-intensive products are typically quite similar. Think steel or copper. Prices of standardized (low-tech) manufactured products exported by developed and developing

---

27. Krugman, "The Trouble with Trade; Keep Our Markets Open but Protect Those Who Get Hurt."

countries are somewhat similar. Think clothing. By contrast, the medium- and high-tech manufactured exports of developed and developing countries differ greatly. Think autos, pharmaceuticals, and electronics.

High-tech products are characterized by a greater scope for product differentiation, enabling US producers in these sectors to better insulate themselves from foreign competition from emerging-market exporters. Further, as we demonstrate, the average quality of developing-country exports is low compared to exports from high-income countries, particularly in high-tech products. Therefore, not only are the prices of developing-country exports on average low, but the quality of these exports is relatively low too. Moreover, the average gap in quality between the exports of developing countries as a group and US exports has not narrowed over time.

These findings shed light on the paradoxical finding, exemplified by computers and electronics, that US-manufactured imports from developing countries are concentrated in US industries that employ relatively high shares of skilled American workers. They help explain why America's nonoil terms of trade have improved and suggest that recently declining relative import prices from developing countries may not all produce significant wage inequality in the United States. Finally, the findings suggest that inferring competitive trends based on trade balances in products classified as high-tech or advanced technology can be highly misleading.

Trade and Welfare

Part III then explores whether trade with developing countries has improved US welfare. As outlined in chapter 5, in the core trade models, these gains depend on the volume of trade and the rate at which the United States can exchange the goods and services it exports for the goods and services it imports—the terms of trade, which are the ratio of export to import prices. Samuelson's basic point is that foreign growth could reduce US welfare by having an adverse impact on its terms of trade and reducing the volume of trade (Samuelson 2004). In principle, as Samuelson proves, the impact of foreign growth on the terms of trade is ambiguous. He shows in a Ricardian model that the United States will enjoy additional gains with productivity growth in foreign export industries. This expands trade and improves America's real rate of exchange. But if foreign productivity growth occurs only in industries that compete with their imports from the United States—import-biased growth—then the United States could lose because foreigners emerge as competitors in export markets and substitute their domestic products for imports. In this case, America's export prices fall relative to its import prices and trade contracts.

As Samuelson himself stresses, and as has long been recognized in the international trade literature, the proposition that foreign growth has an ambiguous impact on domestic welfare emerges in conventional trade theory frameworks other than the one he uses. This means that empirical investigation is required to resolve the issue. But we can make presumptions on a priori grounds. John Hicks (1953) conjectured, for example, that in their early stages of development, countries are most likely to experience rapid productivity growth in the industries in which they have a comparative advantage. Such "export-biased" growth will improve the terms of trade of their more developed trading partners. Hicks plausibly suggested that the negative case for the rich countries, in which developing-country growth is biased toward their imports, is likely to occur only when they come closer to developed-country income levels. This view that specialization patterns will be correlated with incomes emerges in many other frameworks that explain patterns of trade based on factor endowments (richer countries have relatively more skilled labor and capital), technology (richer countries are more advanced), and demand patterns (richer-country tastes lead them to develop high-end products).

After laying out the theory in chapter 5, we explore the behavior of the US terms of trade. There is considerable support for Hicks' conjectures. From 1950 until the late 1960s, when today's developed countries started relatively far behind the United States, the US terms of trade had a strong upward trend. In the 1970s, as he predicted, the improvement was more than reversed as Japan and Europe converged more closely to US productivity levels. More recently, countries such as China and Mexico, which currently have around one-fifth of US productivity levels, have become increasingly more important US trading partners. Again, as Hicks would have anticipated, a trend of improving terms of trade has been apparent. Between 1993 and 2010, the US manufacturing (and nonoil goods and services) terms of trade steadily improved primarily because the relative prices of US manufactured imports from developing countries declined. Between 1995 and 2009, Germany also experienced a strong rising trend in its manufacturing terms of trade, while Japan experienced such a trend through 2005.

Looking at the data, the fact that the (nonoil) US terms of trade have improved is suggestive. But to attribute causation to growth in emerging-market economies, we need to control for other influences. This has been done by Chang-Tai Hsieh and Ralph Ossa (2011) in a simulation study that finds a positive impact of Chinese productivity growth on the United States.

Using new methods for estimating trade gains developed by Costas Arkolakis, Arnaud Costinot, and Andrés Rodríguez-Clare (2010), we are able to estimate the welfare contribution of US manufacturing trade in finished and intermediate goods. The approach takes account of the costs not only of reduced specialization but also of reduced available product variety and of losses from reducing output in relatively more productive firms. We find that by 2008 these annual gains from US manufactured goods trade amounted to $337.8 billion, or about $1,000 per person. About half of these gains—an amount equal to 1.2 percent of US GDP—was accounted for by manufactured trade with emerging-market economies, and a quarter—or about $250 per person—to trade with China alone. We also find that the implied gains have grown steadily since the mid-1990s.

Impact of Trade Deficits

As in most classical trade models, Samuelson (2004) assumes that trade is balanced. However, to test the validity of his concern, we also need to take account of the fact that the United States has been running larger trade deficits. This is necessary because the trade balance is likely to be associated with an independent and systematic influence on the terms of trade. As explained in chapter 6, if consumption patterns are biased toward domestic goods and services, and/or many goods and services are not tradable, adjustment of US trade balances back to levels sustained in the early 1990s, for example, is likely to require lower terms of trade. The relevant question to ask is what the US terms of trade would be if the *current* trade balance were to return to the levels of the early 1990s.

We use three methods to answer this question. First, we simply chart the relationship between the trade balance and the terms of trade. Using data from 1990 through 2003, we find a negative association that is consistent with our theoretical expectations: a decline in the trade balance is associated with an improvement in the terms of trade of goods and services. After 2003, the relationship shifts downward and lower terms of trade are consistent with any given trade balance. However, this shift is entirely due to oil. Once oil is excluded, after 2004, the relationship of the (nonoil) terms of trade for any given (nonoil) trade balance in goods and services actually shifts *upward*, leaving the US economy with an 8.5 percent higher nonoil terms of trade in 2009 than 1990, even after adjusting for the increase in the trade deficit. This is contrary to what we would expect if Samuelson's concerns about import-biased growth in developing countries were increasingly relevant. Instead, the data point to strong export-biased growth in foreign countries.

Second, we cite simulation studies that have used theoretically grounded structural models to explore the implications for the terms of trade of restoring balance to the current account. These studies indicate that, although quite substantial changes in the real exchange rate (and relative US wages) are required to eliminate a deficit equal to 5 percent of GDP, the terms of trade changes are relatively small—on the order of 5 to 7 percent. An implication of these simulation results is that restoring balance to the 3.6 percent of GDP current account deficit in 2010 would not offset the nonoil terms of trade gains in recent years.

Third, we come to a similar conclusion when we use our own model based on estimated trade equations to simulate the impact of a restoration of the US nonoil trade balance from 2007 to 1990 levels. According to these estimates, to induce a lower deficit would require a depreciation of 15 percent in the real dollar exchange rate. Nonetheless, after taking account of the pass-through of this depreciation into export and import prices, this would still leave the United States with a 5 log-point (percent) improvement in the nonoil terms of trade over 1990 levels.

Thus, the three approaches we present reinforce each other. They indicate that the US nonoil terms of trade have improved since the early 1990s, even after adjusting for the impact of larger trade deficits. Contrary to Samuelson's concerns, therefore, foreign growth has contributed toward improvements in US welfare, as measured by the nonoil terms of trade.

The estimates of the structural trade model also point to additional sources of welfare gains for the United States. China's peg to the dollar over much of the post-2000 period has disciplined the pricing behavior of other exporters and restrained their ability to pass on their higher dollar costs to US consumers when their currencies appreciate. An important consequence arising from this is that an appreciation of the renminbi could lead to a more sizable decline in the US terms of trade as other developing countries raise their own export prices.

We find that growth in foreign income raises US export volumes, but also raises US import demand in the form of new varieties. The net effect on the trade balance, however, is positive. Developing-country growth has therefore contributed toward faster US export growth, an increase in the variety of imports available to Americans, and higher terms of trade associated with any given trade balance.

Oil Prices

Despite the improvement in the manufacturing terms of trade, the aggregate US terms of trade in 2008 were lower than in the mid-1990s. As discussed in chapter 7, higher oil import prices account for the difference. We analyze the contributions of supply and demand in both developed and developing countries in driving oil prices higher between 2000 and 2008, when they averaged $95 a barrel. While attention has been focused on the contribution of demand growth in China and other emerging markets, the role of slow production growth in developed countries was far more important. Ex ante demand by Organization for Economic Cooperation and Development countries increased by 6.7 percent between 2000 and 2008, but their oil production declined by 9 percent. This shortfall explains 81 percent of the price rise over the same period. The increase in net Chinese demand can explain 34 percent of the price rise, but increased supplies in other developing countries offset 15 percentage points, so that overall developing countries accounted for just 19 percent of the rise. The net-supply shortfalls created by the United States alone, where production fell by 6 percent over the period, were actually quite similar to those created by China. Even taking into account reduced oil demand by developed countries due to the global slowdown in 2008–09, we still find that the developed countries are responsible for two-thirds of the price increases between 2000 and 2011.

Holding oil supply constant, faster growth in emerging-market economies does lead to higher oil prices and has adverse effects on US welfare. However, the size of the effect that operates through this mechanism is modest. Each

1 percent faster growth in emerging-market economies as a whole reduces US real incomes by less than one-tenth of a percent by inducing higher oil prices. Further, emerging-market-economy growth in the future is only one of many factors that will affect oil prices. Future outcomes are extremely sensitive to both supply growth and conservation trends. Scenarios projected by the US Energy Information Agency, for example, suggest that increased global supplies or reduced demand of just 0.8 percent per year could reduce oil prices in 2035 to $50 in 2009 dollars—that is, by 75 percent compared with what they would otherwise be (EIA 2011). There is growing evidence that over time this concern will diminish in importance as the US becomes more self-sufficient in energy (IEA 2012).

Wage Inequality

The study then turns to the topic of wages. While improvements in the US terms of trade from trade with developing countries are good for national welfare, they may nevertheless be associated with rising wage inequality within the United States. Chapter 8 explicates the theory. Orthodox trade theory that assumes labor is mobile and homogeneous assigns a key role to changes in the relative prices of skilled- and unskilled-labor-intensive traded goods in wage determination. Cheaper exports produced by developing countries could, according to this theory, increase wage inequality throughout the US economy by reducing the prices of unskilled-labor-intensive traded goods produced in the United States. It could also make unskilled workers absolutely worse off.

This theory has served as the basis for many studies of the effects of trade on the relative wages of US workers with easily identifiable general skills such as those workers with college rather than high school degrees. However, to link changes in relative imported goods prices directly to changes in economywide relative wages requires assuming that imports and domestic products are perfect substitutes, and that labor is homogeneous and mobile. We found reasons in chapter 4 to question the perfect substitute assumption, and if the United States and developing countries do not compete directly in making products similar to imports, for example, lower-priced imports from developing countries could actually raise the real wages of less skilled US workers by increasing their purchasing power.

It is also possible, however, that even if the US economy were fully specialized, specialization patterns could change and wage inequality could rise if some relatively unskilled-labor-intensive production were shifted from the United States to emerging markets. This occurs because the relative wages of unskilled workers need to fall to induce other industries to employ them. However, with both incomplete and complete specialization, if wages reflect specific attributes of workers, the adverse impact on workers competing with imports might not be fully reflected in the wages of workers elsewhere in the economy.

Wage Inequality: Evidence

Chapter 9 considers the evidence behind the issues raised in the previous chapter. We note that in the 1980s, increased wage inequality was pervasive, with skill premiums rising all along the wage distribution. Orthodox theory that linked rising wage inequality to increased price competition from developing countries in low-skill US industries offered a potential explanation. Since the mid-1990s, however, applying the standard two-factor theory confronts major challenges. The nature of wage inequality has changed. In particular, while wages at the very top of the distribution have continued to grow relatively rapidly, those at the bottom have not always fared poorly relative to those in the middle.

The composition of imports from developing countries has also changed and is no longer concentrated in low-skill US industries. Indeed, appendix 9A shows that US manufacturing imports from developing countries are no more concentrated in low-skill US manufacturing industries than US imports from developed countries. The computer and electronics industry (NAICS 334) is emblematic of this paradox.[28] Developing countries account for three-quarters of US imports in the sector, yet the US industry employs very high shares of skilled workers and the pace of its productivity growth and price declines reflect rapid technological change. Viewed through the prism of conventional trade theory in which specialization is assumed to be incomplete, the computer and electronics sector is an anomaly. But assuming intraindustry specialization allows us to explain that the products from developing countries are different and less skill-intensive than those still made in the United States.

As with our consideration of aggregate welfare, we use several different methods to consider the impact of trade on recent US wage inequality. All indicate that it has not been large. First, we cite estimates that use measures of the skilled- and unskilled-labor content of US exports and imports (the so-called net factor content of trade). These do not indicate that displacement due to trade has disproportionately affected unskilled US workers and in fact indicate almost no impact. However, these estimates have been criticized for being too aggregated to detect increased specialization within industries.

We then cite estimates that employ a simulation model that uses assumed skill intensities and is therefore not subject to such "aggregation bias." This approach suggests that trade with emerging-market economies might have increased the skill premium between 1995 and 2006 by about 2 percent. These models are informative, as they can indicate the impact of developing-country trade on wage inequality that operates either through the conventional price channel or by changing specialization patterns.

While small, the 2 percent estimate obtained from the model is likely to be an upper bound because the model (1) assumes that all import growth occurs in products that compete directly with US production, whereas many imports are no longer produced locally, and (2) ignores the share of the value added in

---

28. NAICS stands for the North American Industry Classification System.

imports from developing countries that, because of global supply chains, actually comes from more advanced countries (e.g., Japanese and US components in Chinese imports).

Third, we explore industry price and productivity data and find no evidence that the prices, adjusted for the productivity of unskilled labor products, have fallen. Fourth, we (and others) reach similar conclusions by using the two-stage approach that first estimates the impact of changes in product prices associated with trade due to offshoring and then considers the changes in the skill premium that are mandated by such price changes. All told, therefore, there is little support for the conventional (Stolper and Samuelson 1941) theory in recent US data. Based on our own econometric estimates and numerous studies using a variety of methods, we conclude that imports from developing countries have not mandated increases in wage inequality along the lines of skill.

However, this does not mean that trade has had no impact on wages. Instead, as the studies we surveyed in chapter 2 suggest, the effects appear to be better captured by models that explore the effects on the specific returns to working in particular firms, industries, occupations, and regions than by models that assume labor is homogeneous and fully mobile. Trade with developing countries has therefore had some adverse effects on particular workers, but it does not appear to have played an important role in recent economywide inequality that reflects skills, education, or reduced incomes of all low-skilled workers in the United States.

Policy Implications

Chapter 10 concludes and draws some policy implications. We note that the large emerging-market economies are expected to continue to converge toward US per capita incomes. Nonetheless, for the next two decades, even forecasts that are optimistic about their prospects imply that income levels in China and India will still lag far behind those of the United States. So while these economies are likely to compete head to head with the United States in export markets at some time in the future, their growth for the foreseeable future is likely to be concentrated in the kinds of goods and services the United States imports. Moreover, even if China and India do compete head to head with the United States, the beneficial impact of increased varieties could offset some or all of the downward pressures on the US terms of trade. This pattern of growth should provide the United States not only with larger export markets but also improved terms of trade at any given trade balance.

Growth along such lines could be especially helpful, given America's adjustment and employment challenges. The United States economy has to grow faster than its long-run potential for several years to absorb its high levels of unemployment. Yet at the same time it has to increase national saving by reducing the federal budget deficit and consumer debt. As Americans spend less of their incomes, more of the demand for their production has to come through exports. This implies a key role for trade with emerging-market economies in facilitating American adjustment.

If Americans save more, the replacement demand for US goods and services can be generated in a number of ways. These include exporting to larger foreign markets, reducing foreign current account surpluses, producing cheaper or more innovative US goods and services, and facilitating more open foreign markets. Consensus projections suggest that even if the other advanced economies can achieve their full potential growth rates, the emerging-market economies will contribute almost 70 percent of global growth over the next 20 years. This growth should stimulate US exports and reduce the need for adjustment by making US goods and services cheaper (through devaluation) or more attractive (through innovation). In addition, numerous countries, especially China, have large current account surpluses. Reducing these surpluses involves increased spending relative to incomes, which also boosts US exports.

There is no free lunch. Americans will have to reduce their spending relative to their incomes. But in addition, real exchange rate depreciation is likely to be required to facilitate this adjustment (Cline and Williamson 2012). Our regression analysis in background work for this study indicates that most of the adjustment in the value of the trade balance to exchange rates comes through increased export values. We have also found that, for the most part, US exports compete with exports from other developed countries. This implies that movements in the dollar with respect to other developed-country currencies (the euro, yen, sterling, and Canadian dollar) are especially important. However, adjustment in China and other developing countries toward smaller current surpluses would also boost US exports and is likely to be accompanied by appreciation of their currencies.

In addition to the pain of belt-tightening associated with reducing foreign borrowing, US living standards could be further reduced by the adverse impact of a weaker dollar on America's buying power. Fortunately, however, this study and others that we cite have found that the required terms of trade and real wage declines that are likely to be associated with dollar depreciation are modest. For example, we estimate that restoring the trade deficit in goods and services to its 1990 levels would reduce the terms of trade by just 5 percent and lower real incomes by about one-tenth of a percent of GDP.

Rather than stimulating US exports and reducing imports through a weaker dollar, it would be preferable and less costly if US goods and services were to become more attractive to foreigners. If the United States can stimulate demand for American products through increased innovation and quality improvements, the exchange rate adjustments required to achieve any given trade balance will be smaller. This underscores the important role that can be played by improvements in regulatory, tax, and other policies that enhance innovation and make the United States a more attractive location for production.

Industrial policies and exchange rate adjustments are substitutes. The United States should not be stampeded into adopting new industrial policies on the grounds it has no alternative but to copy others. Instead, the benchmark against which such policies should be judged is whether they can do better than the default adjustment mechanism that operates through changes in exchange rates and lower relative prices for US goods and services. This requires concentrating on cases where the government is likely to be able to compensate for market failures.

An active US trade policy can reduce the costs of adjustment by lowering foreign barriers to US exports and enhancing the protection of US intellectual property abroad. On average, the tariffs faced by American exporters are among the highest faced by any country because other countries have been more active in negotiating access and granting preferential market access to each other. The Trans-Pacific Partnership and efforts to capture some gains from the Doha Round through partial or plurilateral agreements merit serious attention (Hufbauer and Schott 2012).

The US position is changing in the world, and over time the country's ability to influence events will diminish. Sharing leadership will not be easy, but retreat or relying purely on bilateral approaches is likely to be increasingly less effective. An emphasis on the multilateral trading system is particularly important, given the patterns of growth that are likely in the future. The WTO is the major vehicle for improving US access to large emerging-market economies and ensuring that these countries adhere to the trade rules.

Even if the United States is successful in creating new jobs through policies to boost exports, challenges will remain at home. Even if the United States does reduce its trade deficit and raise manufacturing employment, the impact is likely to be a one-off change that will not permanently offset the declining trend in the manufacturing employment share. Ultimately, Americans need to be trained and educated for the jobs of the future. And absent a change in American spending patterns, these are increasingly unlikely to involve the production of goods.

Growth in emerging markets may be beneficial overall, but it will continue to be associated with increased import penetration and job displacement in the United States. This highlights the need for policies that assist displaced workers through improved unemployment and healthcare benefits, training and reemployment assistance, and wage-loss insurance for workers who find new jobs at lower wages. Income inequality has increased in the United States, but trade with developing countries is a modest contributor. The appropriate policy response in any case is not trade protection but income redistribution through taxes and transfers.

Finally, the United States is vulnerable to higher oil prices, and especially to the macroeconomic effects of large oil import volumes. Stimulating conservation as well as the production of energy supplies both at home and abroad deserves policy attention. Variable import levies or taxes that raise and maintain a high domestic price for oil could play a vital role in reducing that dependence.

Scope of the Study

Rapid growth in emerging-market economies affects the United States through many channels besides trade. Some relate to politics and the environment, others are economic and relate to the diffusion of ideas, capital flows, people, and finance. But in this study, for reasons of tractability (and competence), we focus on trade.

We are aware that there are major political implications that also need to be weighed in a more complete account of the effects of emerging-market-economy growth. Economists typically focus on measures of absolute welfare, but relative incomes have important effects on power and influence. When historians speak of Britain's decline, they do not mean it became poorer, but rather that it failed to maintain its lead as others became richer. As populous nations such as China and India grow, rival, and even surpass the United States in economic size, they could dramatically affect the global balance of power and America's leadership role.[29] We have already seen the transformation of the G-8 into the G-20 as the steering committee of the world economy, and in the coming decades global governance will undoubtedly continue to evolve toward giving emerging-market economies a greater say.

In addition, there are serious implications for the environment. Developing-country growth will have a major impact on greenhouse gas emissions, and friction over costs and obligations is bound to grow. Without meaningful action by developing countries, costly conservation efforts by developed countries might do little to prevent global warming. The great challenge in this area, therefore, is how to reconcile developing-country growth with effective action on climate change.

These other serious challenges notwithstanding, we concentrate in this study on economic effects, and even in this regard we are constrained. We emphasize trade. Four important economic effects will not be evaluated.[30] The first is technological diffusion. There are benefits from directly adopting the ideas and innovations of others. Developing countries have traditionally enjoyed what have been called "the benefits of relative backwardness" by adopting innovations made in the West. But if those countries increasingly create knowledge, the United States will benefit from a reverse flow through the diffusion of foreign discoveries and innovations. A second economic effect is international capital flows. Foreign growth can boost the profits of US-owned firms located in emerging-market economies. It also increases the returns to US citizens who invest in these countries and who share in the value

---

29. See Subramanian (2011) for a discussion of these implications. A similar debate over the implications of Japan's rise occurred in the late 1980s—see Kennedy (1989) and Nye (1991). Fallows (2010) is an excellent recent discussion of the Chinese challenge to the United States.

30. See Subramanian (2011) for a broader economic perspective on the implications of Chinese growth.

added in their exports.[31] In addition, such growth can lead to increased foreign investment in the United States, which could increase capital formation and improve technology and thereby raise US output.

A third effect comes through migration. The United States has derived great benefits by being a magnet for migrants seeking a better life. Faster growth abroad could reduce these flows, especially if more educated foreigners find better opportunities at home. And finally, the United States has enjoyed supremacy—"an exorbitant privilege" in the words of Charles de Gaulle—as the center of the global monetary system with the dollar playing a central role as a reserve currency. Developments in foreign financial centers could erode this position.

We thus concentrate in this study on the economic effects of developing-country growth that operate directly through trade. Wherever possible we focus on trade in both goods and services. But in some cases, because of data availability and the context of the arguments being considered, we concentrate even more narrowly on the manufacturing sector. In addition, we operate for the most part at a fairly aggregated level, using growth and other measures for emerging-market economies as a whole, and thereby submerging some distinctions among these countries that could lead to a more nuanced approach. We, however, pay particular attention to China and India.

31. In fact, this was another concern expressed by Lawrence Summers, who noted that as US multinationals earn more of their profits abroad, they become detached from their interests in the United States. Lawrence Summers, "America Needs to Make a New Case for Trade," *Financial Times,* April 27, 2008.

TRADE AND JOBS: EXPLORING THE PUBLIC'S CONCERNS

The next three chapters appraise the public's concerns about trade and its effect on employment. Before we proceed, however, we need to be clear what we mean by "trade and jobs." When the subject is discussed, three interrelated but distinct concerns are often conflated, but they need to be distinguished because they relate to different time dimensions and call for very different policy responses.

Total Jobs

The first concern is high unemployment, which relates to the role of import competition in preventing the economy from achieving full employment. This is a cyclical concern that has emerged when recoveries are viewed as too slow or "jobless." In this context, imports and larger trade deficits are seen as draining purchasing power from the domestic economy in the face of recovery. Such sentiments have been apparent after each of the past three recessions. They were expressed in 1991–92 when the recovery took a while to gain speed; they arose again in 2003–04 when the media was filled with reports that services jobs were being offshored to India in large numbers; and they have surfaced more recently in the face of the very high unemployment rates following the global financial crisis, when there have been claims that absent an increase in US manufacturing jobs (Liveris 2010) or tradable goods employment (Spence and Hlatshwayo 2011), the economy will not be able to recover fully. We call this concern "total jobs."

Lost Jobs

The second concern is job loss—that is, displacement due to trade and the associated effects on wages. This relates to the short-run impact of trade. It is about workers who are laid off and have to find new jobs because their employers have either lost sales to imports or have decided to move abroad. Such job changes can be costly for workers, even when unemployment rates are low, because of the time they spend out of work, the costs of finding new jobs, and the (sometimes lower) wages they receive in their new jobs. We call this concern "lost jobs."

Good Jobs

The third concern is the disappearance of good jobs. This reflects the view that international competition has played a major role in eroding the US industrial base and caused a substantial loss of high-paying, steady jobs in sectors that produce tradable goods and services, especially manufacturing. These jobs have been particularly important for blue-collar male workers without college degrees. This is a long-run concern about the structure of the economy and we label it "good jobs."

Conceptualizing Trade and Jobs

These three concerns can be illustrated with an analogy. Imagine the US economy as a large version of the game of musical chairs in which each chair represents a job opportunity and some chairs are more comfortable than others. While the music plays the participants must keep moving from chair to chair, alternately standing, moving, and sitting. But when the music stops, some participants find themselves unable to sit down because the number of chairs is less than the number of players. Others choose not to sit down because they cannot find comfortable chairs. The concern about "total jobs" relates to the relationship between the number of participants and the number of chairs. The fear is that imports reduce the overall number of chairs available. "Total jobs" is thus a net employment concept and relates to the number of positions (chairs) available.

The concern about "lost jobs," by contrast, is a gross jobs concept. It relates to how many times people must move to change chairs. Because one person could have occupied several chairs in any round, and similarly one person could have several spells of unemployment and work in a year, gross jobs can be far larger than net jobs. The fear is that imports result in too many such episodes.

Finally, the concern about "good jobs" relates to the share of chairs that are comfortable. It is also a "net jobs" concept. The fear is that imports (or the trade deficit) result in fewer comfortable chairs or available positions in manufacturing.

Policies

Obviously these concerns are interrelated. When the aggregate number of positions is small and good jobs are in short supply, job loss can be more costly. But they may also require quite different policy responses. High overall unemployment, the problem of total jobs, suggests the need for macroeconomic policies to stimulate aggregate demand (using fiscal and tax cuts and more government spending) and monetary policy (interest rates) or supply-side policies that improve people's abilities to search more effectively and find jobs. High rates of displacement—lost jobs—suggest a need for policies that reduce the costs of adjustment (unemployment insurance, training, job search assistance, wage insurance) or slow it down (trade protection, rules on firing). Devising policies to deal with the erosion of manufacturing employment presents a complex challenge. Manufacturing employment could be boosted if the trade deficit were reduced through a combination of policies that alter expenditure patterns and switch more spending toward goods produced in the United States. This suggests combining measures that increase national saving relative to investment so that the United States can borrow less from foreigners with measures that improve the nation's competitiveness as a location for manufacturing production (e.g., a more competitive exchange rate, lower corporate taxes, and improved industrial policies). But the links between smaller trade deficits in manufacturing and increased employment are quite complex, and while enhanced US productivity could make its products more attractive and lead to smaller current account deficits, it could also lead to less employment in tradable goods by requiring fewer workers.

1

Trade and (Total) Jobs

At a time of high unemployment, concerns about trade often focus on the perceived impact on the total number of jobs in the economy, that is, aggregate employment. One concern in the United States is that import growth is a significant factor in generating high unemployment. Such import growth is often blamed on (1) defective trade policies, such as the implementation of free trade agreements or the failure to deal with unfair foreign trade practices; (2) competition from emerging-market economies, especially China and Mexico; and (3) decisions by US-based firms to offshore their production. A second concern relates to the role of trade in economic recovery. While export growth is viewed as favorable—it is indeed especially important when fiscal policy is encumbered with large budget deficits—the fear is that unless such growth is more rapid than import growth, a deteriorating trade balance could prevent recovery.

This chapter argues that while trade flows obviously do affect employment, the relationships between trade and employment are complex. In particular, we emphasize the need to recognize that trade flows are not independent "causes" of change but rather are outcomes of influences, making it extremely perilous and often misleading to make causal inferences and quantitative estimates about the impact of trade using data after the fact.

Causation between trade and growth runs in both directions. Higher imports and larger trade deficits can cause slower growth, but faster growth can cause higher imports and larger deficits. From the standpoint of employment creation, therefore, all import growth is not created equal. Sometimes, the concerns that imports reduce employment may be warranted, but more commonly, especially in recent US history, import growth has been associated with increased employment at home. Similarly, larger trade deficits have typically been the result of robust domestic growth, leading to greater import demand, rather than economic contraction. The emergence of larger trade deficits during an expansion certainly does not preclude recovery. Moreover, increased deficits do not necessarily indicate that trade is, on balance, reducing aggregate employment. It is possible that larger deficits during a recovery reflect a combination of two forces, both of which are increasing aggregate employment: (1) a recovery in domestic spending, which aids recovery even as it induces larger trade deficits by raising import demand; and (2) increased export growth that also boosts employment but does not fully offset the effects of increased domestic spending on the trade deficit.

Over the long run, employment in the economy will reflect the growth in the labor supply and the "structural" rate of unemployment required to allow people to change jobs and firms to search for workers.[1] In frameworks appropriate for long time horizons, therefore, the volume of trade is generally not thought to be a significant determinant of total employment. Some more-sophisticated theories take into account how trade might affect the structural rate by influencing incentives for job searches and hiring. But commonly, long-run models of trade simply assume "full" employment and focus on the effects of trade on resource allocation and the composition rather than the amount of employment.

Arithmetic versus Behavior

In the short run, the phenomenon of "involuntary" unemployment—when people who are willing to work at the going wage rate cannot find jobs—can be significant. To explain it, macroeconomists often point to insufficient aggregate demand. Since exports and imports both contribute to aggregate demand, their behavior is likely to impact employment, but as with the other components of demand such as consumption, investment, and government expenditures, attributing causation to their behavior must be done carefully.[2]

In explaining the components of demand (such as consumption, investment, exports, and imports), economists since John Maynard Keynes have found it useful to distinguish between the parts of such demand that are "autonomous" and result from influences such as interest rates, price levels, wealth, and exchange rates, and the parts that are "induced" by changes in

---

1. Sophisticated economic theories have been developed to explain the unemployment rate associated with full employment (or the so-called natural rate of unemployment). These include search theory and efficiency wage theory. Economists have integrated the effects of trade into these frameworks. One example is the work of Elhanan Helpman, Oleg Itskhoki, and Stephen Redding (2010), whose theory combines search frictions, wage bargaining, and firm heterogeneity and shows how openness to trade, while beneficial, could nonetheless increase frictional unemployment. Another important and eloquent exploration of these issues is Davidson and Matusz (2009).

2. For a discussion of income determination in the open economy, see Mankiw (2012, 390–95).

income. To the degree that the components of demand are affected by changes in income, a change in any one of the variables that constitute demand is likely to affect all the others. Thus the assumption that spending $(C + I + G)$ will not change—which is required for the statement "imports or higher trade deficits reduce employment" to necessarily describe behavior—is implausible. In particular, since changes in exports and imports will change income, and since C, I, and G are all likely to be affected by income, changes in the trade variables are likely to change the other components of spending. Therefore, in the identity $Y = C + I + G + X - M$, causation is likely to run in both directions.

Unfortunately, however, it is very common for commentators to talk about the links between trade and aggregate employment in simplistic terms and to ignore the interactive nature in which aggregate demand is determined. Exports, however generated, are viewed as automatically adding to total jobs; imports to reducing them; and larger trade deficits presumed necessarily to be associated with less demand and increased unemployment. To quantify these influences, estimates of the employment content of imports (using input-output and other methods) are sometimes presented as if they indicate the number of jobs that have actually been lost due to imports and estimates of the employment content of the trade deficit used to indicate the employment that would be added if the deficit were closed. For example, Robert Scott (2010, 2), an economist at the Economic Policy Institute, writes that "While it is true that exports support jobs in the United States, it is equally true that imports displace them. . . . The net effect of trade flows on employment is determined by changes in the trade balance."[3]

In a purely arithmetic sense these statements are correct. It is an accounting identity that GDP (Y) is equal to consumption (C) plus investment (I) plus government spending (G) plus exports (X) – imports (M), i.e., $Y = C + I + G + X - M$. Thus, given spending $(C + I + G)$, a larger trade surplus $(X - M)$ implies that output and thus employment will be larger. Similarly, arithmetically, income Y and thus employment will rise if X is larger or M is smaller, all else being equal. But if propositions such as "exports support jobs," "imports displace them," and "the trade balance determines the net effect of trade flows on employment" are claims about behavior, these statements could be seriously erroneous. The assumption that we can take consumption, investment, and government spending as given when we change exports and imports is utterly implausible. Thus the volume of imports, for example, is an outcome rather than a cause, and the association between imports and employment is not invariant to the reasons imports are changing.[4]

Figure 1.1 plots import growth on the left scale and employment growth on the right scale. If all import growth necessarily is associated with job

3. See also C. Fred Bergsten, "An Overlooked Way to Create Jobs," *New York Times*, September 28, 2011.

4. Technically, imports, exports, and the trade balance are all endogenous variables, and only exogenous variables can be said to be causes.

Figure 1.1 Association between US employment and import growth, 1991–2011 (annual growth rates in percent)

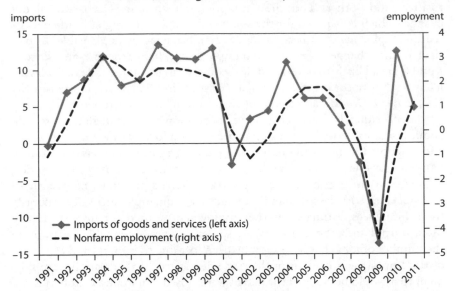

Sources: Bureau of Economic Analysis, www.bea.gov/national/nipaweb (accessed on November 1, 2012); Bureau of Labor Statistics, http://data.bls.gov/pdq/SurveyOutputServlet (accessed on November 1, 2012).

loss, we would expect a negative relationship between these two variables. Yet clearly what is remarkable in the figure is the strong positive correlation between the two variables. The changes in imports are about five times more volatile (left scale) than changes in total employment (right scale), but the two series move in tandem. To explain this paradox and expose the flawed thinking that lies behind these estimates we need to think carefully about what determines import behavior.

Imports change for numerous reasons, and it is especially important to distinguish the import growth that is induced by higher domestic spending (and output) from the import growth that reflects other autonomous factors. Typically, to make this distinction clear, the simplest mathematical formulations that capture the behavior of the volume of imports (M) represent imports as the sum of an "autonomous" variable (MA) and a response that depends on income. Thus, $M = MA + mY$, where MA (the autonomous component) may be affected by relative prices and exchange rates, decisions to offshore, etc., whereas m is the marginal propensity to import and depends on income. The expression mY captures the fact that as income rises, people demand more of everything, including domestically produced goods and services *and* imports.[5]

---

5. The size of the marginal propensity to import will reflect consumption preferences (for imported versus domestic products) as well as the use of imported intermediates in domestic production.

If this function reflects behavior, therefore, after the fact we cannot tell if the changes we actually see in the import data are due to the income component or the autonomous component. Yet making this distinction is crucial for assigning causation and predicting the association between import and employment growth.[6] If import growth is due to changes in the autonomous component and attributable to lower foreign prices or increased offshoring, spending could shift away from domestic and toward imported goods and services, and employment could fall. In these cases, the negative relationship between import growth and employment that is often assumed in popular discussions *would* occur. However, if import growth is due to the changes in the induced component and attributable, for example, to higher domestic spending on investment, consumption, or government services, or to imports of parts required for expanding domestic production, there need be no job loss. Imports can rise even as income and employment rise, and in fact as a result of the expanded income. In these cases, the relationship between imports and employment would be positive.

A similar logic applies to changes in total employment that will be associated with changes in the trade balance. These too could be positive or negative. Recall that the trade balance equals the differences between exports and imports. If the trade balance moves into surplus because of increased exports, for example, it would be associated with growing employment not only because exports give rise to more employment, but because those who now earn more income will further spend their money on additional goods and services. However, if the balance moves toward surplus because of reduced domestic spending on both domestic and foreign goods and services, imports will fall, and thus larger surpluses could be associated with declining employment as the economy contracts and further import declines are induced. Similarly, larger trade deficits could be part and parcel of an economic recovery if they reflect strongly rising domestic expenditures and increasing demand for both domestic and foreign goods and services. On the other hand, larger deficits could reflect forces that are responsible for a contraction if they are caused by losses of exports or increases in the autonomous component of imports.

This analysis points to three important results for our purposes. First, in making statements about causality we should only consider sources of change that are independent or exogenous. It does not make sense to refer to endogenous or derived variables such as imports or the trade balance as if they are causes. Second, under conditions of excess capacity in the economy, the job content of the initial (autonomous) increases in exports or imports will underestimate the total employment effects because there will be additional activity generated through multiplier effects. And third, the initial changes in exports (or imports) will not fully indicate the long-run impact on the trade balance because they will give rise to induced effects on imports that will affect

---

6. This is something Scott (2011, 2010) fails to do. He implicitly assumes all imports result from autonomous changes.

the ultimate outcome on the trade balance. This means that estimates of the job content of an ex post trade balance would underestimate the employment impact of the autonomous increase in exports.[7]

It is also an implication of this discussion that output (and employment) can increase even if the trade balance is getting worse. This occurs when an expansion is being driven by increases in the autonomous domestic components of expenditure and causing income and employment to rise, even though at the same time they are inducing import growth.

We should note that we have chosen to present this argument using the very simplest multiplier framework (box 1.1). For greater realism, the effects we have emphasized need to be embedded in more complex models that incorporate capital flows, the response of monetary authorities, price changes, and the influence of exchange and interest rates on key economic variables. But for our purposes this version's simplicity is useful, because it demonstrates that to understand the role played by trade in affecting employment we cannot simply use after-the-fact measures of trade flows and balances. Instead, we need to be able to disentangle the changes that reflect shocks due to shifts in the autonomous components of demand from those that are induced.

We can now understand what was happening in figure 1.1 when we found such a positive relationship between import growth and employment growth. This is because the most important drivers of both total US employment and imports are domestic spending and production—the autonomous determinants of domestic US spending (that affect consumption, investment, and government expenditures) have generally been far larger than the autonomous changes in imports (such as offshoring). It is not surprising that fluctuations in aggregate US domestic demand and production dominate US employment growth. After all, 85 percent of the goods and services that Americans buy are still made at home, and an even higher percentage of the goods and services that are produced at home are not exported but are consumed at home. Normally, therefore, US economic expansions and contractions have been driven by changes in domestic spending. When Americans spent more, they simultaneously bought more imported products and they created more jobs at home. Moreover, imports include not only final products but also key inputs of goods and services that are required for domestic

---

7. Indeed, consider a special case that we could call the balanced trade deficit multiplier. Consider what would happen if exports increased by $1 billion and $s = 0$ and $m = 0.25$. In this case, the multiplier would be $1/m = 4$. Assume that trade originally was balanced. With a multiplier of 4, an increase in exports of $1 billion would raise income by $4 billion. Employment would therefore increase to produce the additional income. But with $m = 0.25$, the rise in income of $4 billion would raise imports by $1 billion and the trade balance would thus return to zero, yet income, exports, and imports would all be much higher. In this case, the absence of changes in the trade balance ex post would be an extremely misleading indicator of the actual stimulus to employment that had been provided by the increased exports. Although the trade balance would not have changed at all, income and employment would be much higher, and increased exports would be the cause.

Box 1.1 Multipliers

After-the-fact numbers on trade flows and trade balances are poor indicators of the total number of jobs that trade flows have actually caused. Not only is there the problem of distinguishing between the autonomous and induced components of import demand, but a further complication arises through what is known as the multiplier—that is, the effect such changes have by leading to additional expenditure and thus employment.[1]

Suppose, for example, that exports rise by $1 billion in an economy with unemployed resources. Assume further that all prices and interest rates are unchanged and that consumers have a marginal propensity to save (s) and import (m) that are fixed shares of their additional incomes. Initially, the exports would boost demand and income by $1 billion and employment would increase by the number of jobs required to produce that additional output. But this would not be the full impact because some of the additional income created would also be spent and thus induce more employment. To derive the total impact we need to distinguish between the additional income that is spent at home and income that will be withdrawn from domestic income creation either because it is saved or because it is spent on imports. The domestic spending share of the initial increase in exports would be equal to $(1 - s - m)$. This spending would in turn create a second round of effects and in this case the additional spending in the second round would be $(1 - s - m)^2 \times \$1$ billion. Thus the total amount of increased demand is equal to a sequence of spending decisions each getting smaller, i.e., $(1 + (1 - s - m) + (1 - s - m)^2 + (1 - s - m)^3 + \ldots) \times \$1$ billion. (Here the "...." represents an infinite series.) This expression is an infinite geometric series—each term involves multiplication by the prior term, and in standard algebra it can be shown that when x is between -1 and $+1$, the sum of an infinite series $1 + x + x^2 + x^3 + \ldots$ will be equal to $1/(1 - x)$. In this case $x = (1 - s - m)$, thus the multiplier will equal $1/(1 - s - m)$. This means that the overall impact on demand will equal $\$1$ billion $\times (1/(1 - s - m))$.[2]

This is the so-called open economy multiplier. If s and m were both .25, for example, the open economy multiplier would be equal to 2, i.e., $(1/(1 - (.25 + .25)) = 1/(0.5)$. Ultimately, therefore, income would rise by twice the original increase in exports. This suggests that far more jobs would be created than only those directly associated with producing the exports.

Since higher incomes also induce more spending on imports, while the trade balance would improve as a result of the higher exports, it would only improve by half of the increase in exports. Since with a multiplier of two income ultimately rises by $2 billion, with a marginal propensity to import of 0.25, imports will rise by $500 million and thus the trade balance would improve by $500 million. Using

(box continues next page)

production and exports. When Americans produce more at home, therefore, they simultaneously import more inputs from abroad.

Because final demand for imports is dominated by the induced impact of domestic spending, the US trade balance will move toward deficits in expansions and toward surplus during contractions.[8] This suggests that imports tend to stabilize the economy during US downturns, because purchases of foreign goods and services decline more rapidly than goods and services produced at home and the trade deficit typically gets smaller in contraction. This is especially evident in the shrinking trade deficit in the aftermath of the global financial crisis in 2008. Thus, contrary to popular belief that plants moving abroad and offshoring have been dominant sources of recent US recessions, fluctuations in imports that reflect domestic spending have actually stabilized the economy, making recessions that have stemmed mainly from

---

8. Econometric estimates of the import-demand relationship presented in a background paper for this study (Edwards and Lawrence 2012) indicate that for each 1 percent change in domestic spending, the quantity of imports changes by 2 percent.

domestic sources, such as the dot.com bust in 2001 and the financial crisis in 2008, less severe in the United States than they might otherwise have been.[9]

The relationship is symmetric on the upside, and, typically, when domestic spending grows rapidly, the trade balance moves into deficit. If the marginal propensity to import is lower, spending on domestic goods is greater, and in this sense import growth can slow a recovery in its initial stages. But it also implies that the marginal propensity to import can help sustain recoveries longer by preventing the economy from overheating as it moves toward full employment.[10]

We should caution that this strong ex post correlation does not rule out the other possibility we have considered, i.e., job loss through autonomous increases in imports due to causes such as outward shifts in foreign supplies, decisions to offshore, or inelastic demand, as is the case with oil prices, by draining buying power from the domestic economy. However, it does suggest that in practice the dominant impact has come through induced import growth and that great caution is required in assuming that the employment effects of increased imports are automatically negative.

Concerns about imports are greatest when unemployment is high and the public becomes impatient about the pace of job creation. But we can trace the growth in employment and imports using figure 1.1 to provide an account of the past 15 years and show that import growth has not prevented recovery— indeed it has been part of recovery. Following the recession in 1991, for example, the expansion was initially quite sluggish and was dubbed a "jobless recovery." In 1992, employment growth was barely 1 percent. Fortunately, however, after about 18 months, the recovery matured and ushered in the longest and most robust expansion in the postwar period. Annual job growth averaged over 2 percent and as a result unemployment levels fell to below 4 percent by the late 1990s. This employment growth took place despite a rapid acceleration in imports from developing countries led by growth in imports from Mexico after NAFTA, which came into effect in 1995.

As a result of the US recession in 2001 following the bursting of the dot. com bubble, aggregate employment fell, led by a precipitous decline in manufacturing employment. But the volume of imports fell even more rapidly and again helped stabilize the economy. Employment growth also was initially weak in the aftermath of that recession. Again, some observers pointed to im-

---

9. Countries in the rest of the world have a different opinion of these two major US disturbances: The more open they were to international finance, the greater the shocks they were forced to contend with. Theory suggests that if shocks stem from domestic disturbances, more open countries could be more stable by spreading the disturbances abroad. On the other hand, if shocks originate abroad it might be better to be more isolated.

10. Paul Bergin, Robert Feenstra, and Gordon Hanson (2007) point out that production in Mexican maquiladoras is much less stable than in the United States. They develop a model that shows how a shock in the United States is amplified in its transmission abroad. Volatility is higher in the foreign country owing to the fact that firms there specialize entirely in the variable-cost activity. The corollary, however, is that the home country becomes more stable.

ports as the reason. This time the focus was on the offshoring of services jobs to India. Indeed, in 2003 and 2004, it was hard to open a newspaper without reading a story about this threat to recovery. But these fears, too, proved to be unfounded, and despite strong import growth, this time led by Chinese imports, the unemployment rate fell to 4.7 percent in 2007.

As a result of the financial crisis in 2008, US unemployment rates soared to over 10 percent. While there was a recovery in growth, the recovery in employment was again exasperatingly slow. By contrast, after a short downturn, in 2009 large emerging-market economies such as China and India renewed their rapid growth. Some look at this contrasting experience and argue that part of the US problem is that it has been losing sales to these competitors. But in fact emerging-market growth is generally good news for US exporters. As reported in the background paper for this study (Edwards and Lawrence 2012), all else being equal, each 1 percent increase in foreign growth raises US exports by 2 percent. Robust foreign growth can help stabilize the US economy when it is in recession. Indeed, as the United States takes steps to reduce its budget deficits, the role of exports in assisting recovery becomes increasingly important if domestic spending on housing, investment, and consumption remain weak.

Trade Agreements

As we noted in the Introduction to this study, it has been common to blame trade agreements for high unemployment. Indeed, NAFTA and its impact on aggregate employment was a major issue in the 2008 elections. But the United States signed NAFTA and helped found the WTO in the mid-1990s. Whether or not on balance these agreements led to more job opportunities continues to be debated,[11] but what is not debatable is that their implementation did not prevent a massive expansion that saw substantial aggregate employment growth, positive manufacturing employment growth, and full employment for the overall economy. Moreover, it is utterly implausible that agreements in effect for many years suddenly led to the slumps in 2001 and 2008. The much simpler explanation for those recessions was the drop in domestic demand. Similarly, China joined the WTO in November 2001 when the United States was already in recession. Imports from China grew rapidly during the subsequent recovery, but again, the economy reached close to full employment in 2007 despite that import growth (and a large current deficit).

Fiscal and Macroeconomic Policies

This account of the relationship between economic growth, employment, and the trade balance has important policy implications. It underscores the role

---

11. For discussions of NAFTA, see Burfisher, Robinson, and Thierfelder (2001), Caliendo and Parro (2009), Romalis (2007), McLaren and Hakobyan (2012), and Hufbauer and Schott (2005).

of macroeconomic policies such as fiscal and monetary policies rather than trade policies as the most important instruments in the government's toolkit to reduce short-run unemployment. These are the policies the government should use to generate increases in the autonomous components of spending.

The main points made in this chapter are analogous to the more familiar discussions about fiscal policy relating to the stimulus package. First, the ex post budget deficit is a poor indicator of the amount of stimulus being provided to the economy by a tax cut, because it reflects not only the loss of revenues due to the tax cut, but the increased revenues that result from the higher incomes the tax cut itself generates. To measure fiscal stimulus properly, therefore, we need to distinguish between the (autonomous) policy changes and the induced effects. In the same way, we have argued here, the autonomous and induced parts of import growth need to be distinguished.

Second, in addition to the effects of such a policy, the eventual outcome in the economy will reflect many nonpolicy-related shocks. After the fact, therefore, it would be wrong to conclude that the stimulus package did not work simply because the economy deteriorated. The counterfactual could have been that without the policy the deterioration would have been even larger (Blinder and Zandi 2010). In the same way, we have argued here, just because after-the-fact imports rose by more than exports, it would be wrong to conclude that an export program failed to stimulate the economy or led to a trade deficit that was smaller than it otherwise would have been.

Third, the expansionary effects of increased government spending or tax cuts are highly contingent on how the monetary authorities choose to react. Monetary policy often constrains demand expansion, reacting to what the central bank views as excessive or potentially inflationary demand growth stemming from either government or private behavior by raising interest rates. Under normal circumstances, for example, fiscal policy has been considered to be a weak instrument, with low multipliers, because increases in government spending and/or tax cuts give rise to offsetting behavior by the central bank (higher interest rates) or the exchange rate (by attracting capital inflows). But under conditions in which unemployment is very high, interest rates are kept close to zero, and exchange rates prevented from appreciating, fiscal multipliers can be much larger (DeLong and Summers 2012). Under these conditions, for similar reasons, the multiplier effects of export growth are likely to be significant. The same would hold true of demand generated by exports under these circumstances.

In sum, unless the autonomous and induced components of expenditure are differentiated, the causal contributions of trade flows to employment are likely to be misunderstood. From the standpoint of stimulating or reducing domestic demand, imports are not all created equal. In the short run, if the problem is inadequate demand, imports that result from autonomous shocks (such as higher oil prices or increased offshoring) could further depress employment. But imports that reflect increased domestic expenditures and production are actually part of the solution rather than the problem.

2

Imports and Lost Jobs and Wages

What exactly do the public mean when they voice concerns about the effects of trade on jobs? One concern, which we considered in the previous chapter, is aggregate employment. But a second, which we consider in this chapter, is the actual loss of jobs, i.e., the experience of dislocation. This is clearly reflected in the polls cited in the Introduction to this study, that indicate that Americans believe that import competition in general and offshoring in particular are especially important sources of job loss. But to test the validity of this belief it is necessary to isolate trade-related hiring and firing empirically and then compare it with other sources of change. If our concern is to establish the relative importance of import competition as a source of job loss, we need to estimate the number of workers displaced because of trade and compare this with the number of workers who are displaced because of other reasons. To do this, we should compare our findings on worker displacements not with the total net number of jobs created in the economy as a whole but rather with the total number of unemployment experiences.

In the introduction to part I we used the analogy of a game of musical chairs in which workers are continuously moving between chairs while the music plays. Over a period of time, each chair could be occupied by many workers, and thus it is important to distinguish between the number of positions (chairs) that are available and the number of chair "sittings" people actually experience. There is a difference therefore between the (net) number of jobs created and the (gross) number of jobs lost.

Some studies ignore this distinction and estimate what they call "the employment impact of trade" by using the Input-Output Tables to calculate the number of jobs it takes to produce a given quantity of exports and the number of jobs that would be required if imports were actually produced at home.[1] These estimates are sometimes presented and interpreted as if they indicate actual job losses. But what such calculations provide are the ex post measures of changes in net job opportunities associated with trade (a net jobs concept) rather than the role of trade in actually inducing job losses and gains (a gross jobs concept).

To investigate the actual displacement due to import competition, some method for isolating the causes of job loss is required. This chapter reports on several studies that have used econometric techniques to do this. We also explore what we can learn from survey data, but it suffices to say that different methodological approaches are required for estimating lost jobs or actual displacement—and total jobs or good jobs (net jobs)—that reflect changes in employment structure.

The importance of distinguishing between such net and gross job flows emerges clearly if we consider surveys of the US labor market. Even when the unemployment rate is low and the economy is at (close to) full employment, the labor market is in a constant state of flux, with large numbers of workers changing their jobs both willingly and unwillingly.

A picture of this astounding volatility can be seen in surveys that are regularly conducted by the US Department of Labor. In 2007, for example, aggregate private sector payroll employment increased by just over 2 million: from 137.329 million in January to 139.495 million in December. One would say, therefore, that over the year, the US economy "created an additional two million jobs." But more precisely, we should say it created 2 million more job opportunities or positions. And this is the sense in which the Input-Output studies are measuring the employment impact of trade. But it turns out that this relatively small net increase in employment was accompanied by gross employment changes that were orders of magnitude bigger.

The Bureau of Labor Statistics' (BLS) Business Employment Dynamics Survey provides a quarterly series of gross job gains and gross job losses at the level of establishments.[2] Since this survey defines employment differently from the payroll survey, it differs somewhat in the estimates it provides on net gains in employment growth. But this survey provides some insights into the behavior of firms. It indicates that over the course of 2007, establishments added slightly over 30 million jobs, which takes into account those establishments that expanded their payrolls and those that were newly created. Conversely, establishments that were contracting their payrolls and those that went out of business reduced employment by nearly 29.3 million jobs.

But even these data fail to capture the full extent of the changes, because they only look at what happened across establishments and do not consider

---

1. A prominent practitioner of this approach is Robert Scott at the Economic Policy Institute. See Scott (2011).

2. Bureau of Labor Statistics, Business Employment Dynamics Survey, www.bls.gov/bdm (accessed on November 1, 2012).

what is going on within them. Even if a firm's total employment was unchanged, it could still have fired a bunch of workers and replaced them with others. According to a second BLS survey, the Job Opening and Labor Turnover Survey, which tracks individuals rather than firms, the actual number of *individual* hires and separations in 2007 was almost twice as large as the net additions and subtractions from firm payrolls. There were 57.8 million new additions to payrolls and 54.6 million separations.[3] While a majority of the separations were due to voluntary departures, 19.7 million—almost 40 percent—were involuntary, that is, the result of discharges and layoffs.

Is this a reasonable estimate of involuntary separations? Workers need to be laid off to qualify for unemployment insurance. In a typical week in 2011, there were around 430,000 additions to unemployment insurance. This translates into almost 23 million a year—a number that is the same order of magnitude reported by the Job Opening and Labor Turnover Survey. Thus, if we are really concerned about the impact of trade on people losing jobs and not simply the total number of jobs available in the economy, we need to look at the gross gains and losses due to trade as a share of overall gross gains and losses. And that is much harder to do, since it is generally difficult to know precisely why people are losing their jobs.

Imports and Gross Job Losses

Let us begin with some back-of-the-envelope calculations as to the order of magnitude of gross gains and losses due to trade as a share of overall gross gains and losses. Between 2000 and 2009, the value of US imports of goods and services measured in 2005 dollars increased by $368 billion. In 2005, output (GDP) per worker in the United States was $100,000. This gives a ratio of 10 workers for each $1 million of output. An extreme assumption would be that all of these imports displaced US workers producing output of equal value, and that all of these increased imports resulted in involuntary displacement rather than voluntary attrition. This would mean that 3.68 million US workers lost their jobs over the nine-year period because of imports. If we assume that the 19.7 million number for 2007 cited in the previous section is typical of the number of workers who are involuntarily discharged annually, we would obtain 9×19.7, i.e., 177 million discharges over the nine years. This implies that, at most, imports could be responsible for 3.68/177, i.e., just over 2 percent of all involuntary displacements.

We should note that this calculation could understate the role of imports in displacements by failing to capture the possibility that import levels could fluctuate and result in additional hires (when imports fall) and additional fires (when they expand again). In addition, displacement rates are generally lower in manufacturing, which accounts for over half of all trade. Nonetheless,

---

3. Bureau of Labor Statistics, Job Opening and Labor Turnover Survey, www.bls.gov/jlt (accessed on November 1, 2012).

the estimate does suggest that import displacement is likely to be very small compared to other reasons for involuntary job loss. Indeed, this view is supported by studies that have tried to establish reasons for job loss. Research on US manufacturing plants by Steven Davis, John Haltiwanger, and Scott Schuh (1996), for example, found that most job creation and destruction in plants was the result of idiosyncratic plant-specific shocks (reorganization, adoption of new technologies, new firm strategies, and outsourcing to other US firms) rather than broader forces such as trade flows.

Survey Evidence

Support for this view also emerges from surveys of the BLS on extended mass layoffs.[4] Not unexpectedly given the financial crisis, the number of mass layoff events and the number of worker separations associated with them in 2009 registered their highest levels since annual data became available in 1996. In 2009, employers laid off 2.1 million workers. Respondents to the survey (employers) are asked to choose from a number of reasons for the layoffs. Remarkably, of these 2.1 million separations only 3,000 were explicitly attributed to "import competition." This was actually less than the similarly minute numbers attributed to import competition in surveys for the previous two years (11,500 in 2007 and 6,800 in 2008). Cited as far more important reasons were "slack work/insufficient demand/nonseasonal business slowdown," "organizational changes," and "financial difficulties." Imports could contribute indirectly to some of these other factors, but if this is the case, it underscores that import competition is just one of a host of reasons why people actually lose their jobs.

Because of concerns about offshoring, especially to India, the BLS added a question to the survey in 2004 to explore the role in mass layoffs of movements of jobs either abroad or to other locations in the United States. In a report published by the BLS on what had occurred between January and September 2004, the respondents reported that just 10,772 of the 469,000 "mass-layoff separations" over the period involved movement of work out of the country. Again, this points to the small contribution of offshoring to overall displacement.

Finally the US Department of Labor has a Trade Adjustment Assistance (TAA) Program that specifically identifies and helps workers who have lost their jobs due to trade. While many eligible workers do not apply for such assistance, the program does provide another piece of evidence. Between October 2009 and October 2010, 282,000 workers were certified eligible for the program. (Between 2002–03 and 2006–07 the average number was 145,000

---

4. Bureau of Labor Statistics, Mass Layoff Statistics, www.bls.gov/mls (accessed on November 1, 2012). The BLS defines "mass layoffs" as events of at least 31 days' duration that involve the filing of initial claims for unemployment insurance by 50 or more individuals from a single establishment during a period of five consecutive weeks.

workers.) Given that the average number of discharges (i.e., involuntary lay-offs) was typically around 1.6 million per month over that 2009–10 period, this implies that workers who subsequently received TAA accounted for about 1 percent of the involuntary layoffs in the economy.

In pointing out that import competition explains a small share of job loss, we do not mean to minimize its importance or the costs to those affected.[5] Indeed, it is of little comfort for people who contract a rare but damaging disease to be told that their disease accounts for just a small share of all the people who are suffering from diseases. Given the massive churning (and firings) that take place in the US labor market even at the best of times, workers are legitimately anxious about change. And when these concerns are compounded by high unemployment rates and declining opportunities in manufacturing, it is not surprising that employment considerations dominate their thinking about trade.

Indeed, worker insecurity has been rising over time. Despite the long economic expansion of the 1990s, US workers during that decade reported feeling more pessimistic about losing their jobs than in the 1980s (Schmidt 1999). More generally, risks have been passed from the government to individuals (Hacker 2006, Gosselin 2008). There is evidence that the expansion of international trade and investment in particular raises worker insecurity in tradable goods sectors.[6] According to Kenneth Scheve and Matthew Slaughter (2004), for example, workers in the United Kingdom who work in sectors with high levels of foreign direct investment are much more likely to report greater perceptions of economic insecurity. Similarly, Richard Anderson and Charles Gascon (2007) find that US workers in services activities and occupations that are potentially tradable report both greater insecurity and a stronger desire for a government safety net.[7]

Unemployment, when involuntary, is an extremely painful and costly experience, and for many people directly involved in competing with imports, competition is threatening because they fear it could result in job loss.

---

5. See Scheve and Slaughter (2004) for evidence on worker insecurity with respect to the globalization of production.

6. Are globally engaged firms and industries likely to be less stable than those that are not? Theory suggests the answer could go either way. Firms participating in global production networks are more responsive to costs of all kinds, including wage costs. This greater cost sensitivity can result in more volatile employment and wage outcomes for workers by making labor demand more elastic—a point stressed by Dani Rodrik (1997). Globalization can also change the incentives for firms to provide risk insurance in the form of explicit or implicit wage contracts for their employees (Karabay and McLaren 2009). Paul Bergin, Robert Feenstra, and Gordon Hanson (2007) argue that offshoring reduces the volatility of domestic demand (by concentrating fixed costs at home) while increasing volatility abroad (by locating more variable costs abroad).

7. Bradford Jensen and Lori Kletzer (2005) find that jobs in occupations and industries in services that are potentially tradable (both domestically and internationally) have been more prone to lead to displacement. From 2001 to 2003, annual job loss rates in their sample of displaced workers were 12.8 percent for those working in tradable services versus just 7.3 percent for those in nontradable services.

Research on worker mobility confirms that these fears are well founded. Human capital is partly specific to firms, industries, and occupations.[8] This implies that it can be destroyed or depreciated if workers are forced to change firms, industries, or occupations because of import competition (or for any other reason). Workers displaced by such developments often experience permanent losses; some never return to the labor force while others are forced to take new jobs at lower wages (Kletzer 2001, Farber 2005). Henry Farber (2005) has examined displacement from manufacturing and reports that about two-thirds of displaced workers find new full-time jobs—but at an average wage loss of 13 percent (the cost is 17 percent if one accounts for forgone wage growth during the unemployment transition). This average disguises a range of experiences: 36 percent gained reemployment at or above previous earnings, whereas 25 percent suffered earnings losses of 30 percent or more.

Empirical Studies of Imports and Employment

As already noted in chapter 1, imports do not necessarily lead to job loss. In principle, displacement will depend on why imports have increased. On the one hand, imports could rise because of an outward shift in the foreign supply curve (an example of a shift in the autonomous component of the import equation we described in chapter 1). In this case, given domestic demand, domestic producers might indeed lose sales and workers could be displaced. On the other hand, imports could rise because domestic demand for importable products increases (because of a shift in the induced component), and in response to this outward shift in the demand curve, imports and domestic production and employment of similar products could both increase

Similar distinctions should be made when it comes to import growth of offshored components. On the one hand, the initial movement of production abroad could be associated with the displacement of workers who produced the components at home. On the other hand, the ability to obtain cheap inputs could assist domestic firms in becoming more competitive and help boost their sales and employment. If firms that use imported components expand production, we might find a positive association between their employment numbers and the growth in imported components.

The links between US imports and domestic employment have been explored in several recent studies using data from the BLS Current Population Survey on individual workers and the industries and/or occupations in which they are employed.[9] The most convincing of these have developed a method of isolating the reasons for import growth. Avraham Ebenstein et al. (2009) implicitly control for demand by using changes in import shares as their demand variable. David Autor, David Dorn, and Gordon Hanson (2012) use

---

8. See Jacobson, LaLonde, and Sullivan (1993), Neal (1995), and Kambourov and Manovskii (2009).

9. Bureau of Labor Statistics, Labor Force Statistics from the Current Population Survey, www. bls.gov/cps (accessed on November 1, 2012).

Chinese exports to other markets to identify imports into the United States that are most likely due to Chinese supply expansion, while John McLaren and Shushanik Hakobyan (2012) use the reduction in NAFTA tariffs to isolate import-supply shocks.

These studies all find that import growth can reduce employment. Autor, Dorn, and Hanson find economically and statistically significant evidence of job loss in manufacturing employment in regions that compete heavily with Chinese imports, although they have trouble isolating the impact of imports from Mexico and other lower-wage countries. They find only small and inconsistently signed effects of imports from all other medium- and high-income countries.[10] McLaren and Hakobyan, however, obtain negative effects on manufacturing employment in industries and locations affected by Mexican imports. Ebenstein at al. conclude that between 1982 and 2002, the 8 percentage point increase in import penetration (from 8 to 16 percent) can explain a 5 percent reduction in manufacturing employment (opportunities).[11]

Other studies that explicitly consider offshoring by firms obtain mixed results, although all suggest the effects are small. Some find that offshoring activities by US multinationals actually boost domestic employment (Borga 2006; Brainard and Riker 1997; Desai, Foley, and Hines 2005; Slaughter 2000). Others find negative effects (Hanson, Mataloni, and Slaughter 2003; Harrison and McMillan 2006; Harrison, McMillan, and Null 2007; Muendler and Becker 2006). Ebenstein et al. (2009) find that effects are positive with respect to offshoring to high-wage countries and negative for offshoring to low-wage countries. All in all, this literature confirms that in some cases (such as circumstances involving foreign supply growth and trade agreements), imports can adversely affect employment, but it also shows that in other cases the effects could be neutral or even positive.[12]

Services

The most comprehensive analysis of the services issue is by Runjuan Liu and Daniel Trefler (2008).[13] They consider both the effects of outsourcing of traded services between unaffiliated buyers to India and China and the services exports to these countries from the United States. Their results are summarized by the

---

10. Autor, Dorn, and Hanson show that the job loss due to Chinese imports not only is costly for the displaced workers but also increases the public costs associated with dislocation by raising payments for unemployment and worker disability. This does not mean that over the long run there are not aggregate gains to the United States from such trade, but it does indicate that the adjustment can be painful and costly.

11. In addition, the coefficients are the largest and most negative (and significant) for US workers with a high school education or less. The point estimate for workers with a high school education is –0.85, indicating that the average 8 percentage point increase in import penetration was associated with a reduction in employment of high school graduates by nearly 7 percent.

12. See also van Welsum and Reif (2006).

13. See also Dickens and Rose (2007), Crino (2010), and Sethupathy (2009).

provocative title of their paper: "Much Ado About Nothing." They consider the effects on (1) occupation and industry switching, (2) weeks spent unemployed as a share of weeks in the labor force, and (3) earnings. They find small negative effects or zero effects of offshore outsourcing on all outcomes, and the negative effects of outsourcing are more than offset by the small positive effects of inshoring.[14] They also undertake an interesting analysis of the impact going forward by assuming that growth rates between 2006 and 2011 match those achieved between 1996 and 2005. They find that over the nine years, workers in occupations exposed to inshoring and offshore outsourcing would (1) switch 4-digit occupations 2 percent less often, (2) spend 0.1 percent less time unemployed, and (3) earn 1.5 percent more. They conclude that "Since the small effects are precisely estimated we can say with confidence that even if services trade with China and India grows at its current clip, the labor-market implications will be small" (Liu and Trefler 2008, 3).

Imports and Specific Wages

A second reason for the public's concern about import competition is the impact on wages. There is a widespread view that workers with high wages in developed countries cannot compete with workers in emerging-market economies who earn low wages. Indeed, this view was famously reflected in Ross Perot's argument against concluding a free trade agreement with Mexico on the grounds that it would automatically lead to a "giant sucking sound" as the jobs all moved to Mexico in search of lower wages. The result of such competition according to this logic must be either high unemployment or wages adjusted to foreign levels.

The flaw in such reasoning, however, is a failure to recognize that ultimately firms will decide where to locate not on the basis of wages but on the basis of the costs of production. And costs will reflect not only wage levels but also productivity levels. If American workers are seven times as productive as workers in Mexico, for example, there is no reason why their wages cannot be seven times higher and still be competitive. Indeed, the reason wages are higher in the United States than in Mexico is because on average US workers are far more productive for a number of reasons. These include superior technology, the use of more plant and equipment, and superior public infrastructure and other public goods such as legal and social institutions.

If foreign workers were on average really as productive as American workers, their wages would likely rise to US levels. This was the experience as Europe and Japan converged toward US productivity levels during the postwar period. And while Chinese wages remain far below wages in the United States, we have recently seen substantial increases in Chinese wages as average productivity there has increased. Of course, the fact that wages on average reflect

---

14. They find some small negative impacts on the wages of less educated workers in industries exposed to services imports and to workers in less skilled white-collar jobs.

productivity does not imply that if they have to pay average wages, all industries will be competitive. There could be some activities in which differences in technology and other contributing factors to costs might be insufficient to offset the differences in wages, and the US industry might be uncompetitive.[15]

In evaluating this concern, again we need to be clear on what we mean. In practice it is likely that the wages of any particular worker will reflect some combination of returns to the worker's mobile human capital—for example, level of education—and specific returns to the worker's particular work. Economic theory suggests that the wage effects of international competition will depend on the degree to which workers are mobile. If workers are homogeneous and fully mobile, workers with the same general skills—for example, college or high school education—should all earn the same wages. Thus, the effects of imports on the wages of workers with general skills will be felt throughout the economy, and not confined or even related to the firms or industries in which particular individuals are employed. We describe the testing methods and consider the evidence on economywide effects in chapter 9. However, several theories assume wages also have a dimension that includes rewards for skills that are immobile and specific to particular firms, occupations, and industries. When researchers explore whether increased import penetration in a particular industry has an effect on the wages of individual workers employed in that industry, they are implicitly testing for the impact of trade on the specific component. Another dimension of specificity is location. When workers are immobile, the negative effects of trade could affect other workers in the same community.[16]

As surveyed comprehensively by Anne Harrison, John McLaren, and Margaret McMillan (2010) there has been a large amount of empirical research devoted to tracing the impact of trade on wages at the firm and industry levels based on the specific-factors model as well as on new theories assuming heterogeneous firms and workers. Most of the studies have been applied to countries other than the United States.[17] However, a number have used US data. Autor, Dorn, and Hanson (2012) do not find that wages decline for those who remain employed in industries experiencing job loss due to manufactured imports from China, but they do find that such loss lowers local wages more generally. They estimate that local wages in regions subject to Chinese competition fell by about 2 percent over a 17-year period. They also find adverse

---

15. For example, Stephen Golub (1998) compares US wages and productivity in manufacturing with a range of developing economies.

16. As noted by Autor, Dorn, and Hanson (2012, 4), "The literature on regional adjustment to labor-market shocks suggests that mobility responses to labor demand shocks across US cities and states are slow and incomplete. . . . Mobility is lowest for non-college workers, who are overrepresented in manufacturing. . . ." For excellent discussions of the importance of local labor markets, see Moretti (2010, 2012).

17. Countries with empirical studies using these approaches have included Mexico (Verhoogen 2008), Indonesia (Amiti and Davis 2008), Denmark (Hummels et al. 2010), Argentina (Bustos 2007), and Brazil (Brambilla, Lederman, and Porto 2010).

effects that operate through decreased labor force participation, and increased use of disability and other transfer benefits.

Ebenstein et al. (2009) also find no impact of imports on industry wages but do find a depressing impact on occupational wages and on earnings of workers who are displaced from manufacturing and forced to find work in other sectors. One interesting byproduct of their analysis is their calculations of the degree to which occupations are exposed to trade. While they find that exposure to import and export competition is quite high for several occupations relating to footwear, clothing, and machinery, a large number of US occupations—they list about 150—are not exposed at all, and the average US occupation in 2002 had an exposure to both exports and imports of just 3 percent of all its sales. This suggests that while some shocks have had significant and substantial effects on the returns to specific factors, they are unlikely to have had a major impact on the overall variance in US wages.

McLaren and Hakobyan (2012) find that wages of unskilled workers are depressed in domestic industries that compete with NAFTA imports and in local labor markets (even in services industries in affected localities).[18] They write:

> To put it in concrete terms, the effect of the NAFTA on most workers and on the average worker is likely close to zero, but for an important minority of workers the effects are very negative. A high-school dropout living in an apparel and footwear dependent small town in South Carolina, even if she is employed in the non-traded sector such as in a diner where she would appear to be immune to trade shocks, would see substantially lower wage growth from 1990 to 2000 than if she were in, for example, College Park, Maryland, as the local workers in tradable sectors that do compete with Mexico start seeking jobs in the non-traded sectors. (McLaren and Hakobyan 2012, 4)

All told, we conclude that while there is mixed evidence of some wage-loss impact on other workers, especially those who are unskilled and share an occupation, industry, or location with workers who are displaced by imports, most of the wage costs of imports are borne by the job losers.

Implications

The evidence on employment and wages paints a consistent picture. The anxieties of workers in tradable industries are rational. Job loss is painful and costly for workers who experience it and imports are a source of job loss. Imports induced by increases in foreign supplies can also have adverse effects on wages in specific locations, occupations, and industries. But there are many reasons for job loss, and the effects of import competition on the wages of workers who do not lose their jobs appear modest. This suggests that policy responses to these concerns should be focused on assisting displaced workers,

---

18. Wage growth in the most protected industries that lost their protection quickly because of NAFTA fell relative to industries that were unprotected to begin with. (These industry effects are, however, sensitive to small changes in specification.)

with the benefits provided regardless of the reasons they have been displaced. This could involve general measures that (1) cushion the blow of unemployment (unemployment insurance that includes both wages and health benefits), (2) assist with the job search, (3) assist with training, (4) compensate for losses due to job change (wage-loss insurance), and (5) assist communities that experience sudden erosions of their tax base (Deep and Lawrence 2008).

3

"Good Jobs"—Trade and US Manufacturing Employment

The manufacturing sector has historically played an important role in providing employment opportunities for less educated workers, especially men. Many Americans were able to join the middle class and live well in blue-collar jobs in industries such as automobiles and steel that are especially remunerative. Thus, expanding manufacturing employment is often viewed as the key to creating "good jobs." Manufacturing has also played a pivotal role in many regional economies, and its decline has adversely affected many towns and cities. Its revitalization is also seen as important for urban renewal.

But since 2000, manufacturing employment has plummeted.[1] As shown in figure 3.1, employment in manufacturing in the 1990s remained fairly constant (right scale) while overall employment grew rapidly (left scale). By 2011, however, manufacturing employment had been reduced by almost 6 million—a 35 percent decline from the 17.3 million jobs that existed in 2000—to just 11.6 million. This more than accounted for the 1.5 million overall decline in employment over the same period.

Manufactured products are highly tradable, and between 1998 and 2010 the US trade deficit in manufactured goods doubled.[2] It is no surprise, then, that America's trade competition with emerging-market economies in Asia and the development of international supply chains are frequently cited as the reasons for manufacturing's weak employment growth. These forces have in-

1. For an excellent discussion of the hardships this has created, see Longworth (2008).

2. As an example of the tradability of manufactured products, in 2008 they made up 64 percent of US imports of goods and services (78 percent of goods imports) and 54 percent of US exports of goods and services (85 percent of goods exports).

Figure 3.1 Manufacturing and nonfarm employment, 1990–2011

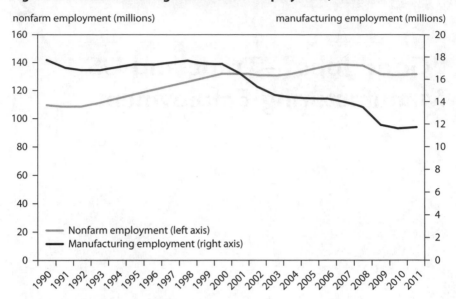

nonfarm employment (millions)   manufacturing employment (millions)

— Nonfarm employment (left axis)
— Manufacturing employment (right axis)

Source: Bureau of Labor Statistics.

deed contributed to the decline, but this chapter shows that domestic forces are primarily responsible for manufacturing's recent employment performance.

In this chapter, we first place our discussion in context by demonstrating that, surprisingly, the share of total employment represented by Americans working in sectors producing tradable goods and tradable services combined has been declining. While a higher share of US workers has become exposed to international services trade because of improvements in communications technology along with trade liberalization, this increased international exposure of services has been more than offset by the shrinking share of workers employed in producing tradable goods. Manufacturing plays the largest role in this declining share and this chapter demonstrates the remarkably persistent links between declining manufacturing employment and total employment over time.

We also show that this development in the United States is very similar to that in other industrial countries—suggesting that those blaming US policies and performance are ignoring something more fundamental and pervasive. We then consider both the domestic and international factors that explain manufacturing employment. We find that the most important reason for the declining share of manufacturing employment has been the combination of relatively rapid productivity growth and relatively unresponsive demand. Surprisingly, we find that because of faster productivity growth, between 1998 and 2010 the employment content of the trade deficit in manufacturing barely changed (box 3.1).

Box 3.1 The manufacturing employment multiplier

A common argument in favoring the promotion of manufacturing is the claim that such activity has a high employment multiplier. Reports from the National Association of Manufacturing (NAM) indicate that each dollar's worth of manufactured goods creates another $1.43 of activity in other sectors, twice the $0.71 multiplier for services (NAM 2010). The impression sometimes given by such claims is that a dollar spent on manufacturing will "create" more employment opportunities than a dollar spent on services.

It is certainly the case that when manufactured goods finally reach consumers, they are likely to contain value added from a variety of sectors of the economy. For example, autos purchased by consumers contain not only value added by auto assembly firms but also value added that can be ascribed to raw materials (iron ore, glass, rubber, etc.), transportation, and additional services such as banking, accounting, advertising, and wholesale and retail distribution. And it may well be the case, by contrast, that a much higher share of the value of certain services (haircuts, for example) is added in the haircut industry and therefore haircuts have a smaller multiplier in this sense. But before we jump to conclusions about employment, caution is in order.

First, ultimately what matters for total employment in any production process is the overall value of that product divided by average labor productivity. To simplify, assume that output per hour is $40 in every industry in the economy. How many hours of work would be created by the final sale of $10,000 worth of haircuts? Let's say 250 hours of work—almost all in the haircut industry. How many jobs would benefit from the final sale of $10,000 worth of autos? Again the total would be 250 hours of work, some in assembly, but many hours as well in a variety of sectors. If we assume that all the value added for haircuts was added by hairdressers, the haircut multiplier would be zero. If we assume that of the 250 hours it took to make autos, 100 occurred in auto production and the rest in other parts of the value chain, the auto multiplier would be 2.5. Thus, even though haircuts have a "multiplier" of one and manufacturing a multiplier of 2.5, the $10,000 in spending on each would give rise to exactly the same number of jobs. In practice, in fact, because such activity is capital intensive, value added per worker could well be higher in manufacturing than services, in which case actually fewer jobs would be created.

A second issue relates to the location of the jobs. The US Input-Output Tables on which these multiplier estimates are based actually assume all production in the value chain takes place in the United States. But in reality the raw materials, transportation, and other intermediate inputs used in manufacturing need not be

(box continues next page)

Box 3.1   The manufacturing employment multiplier
(continued)

produced within the same country. Thus, the multiplier does not necessarily refer to domestic jobs. Indeed, the domestic jobs may depend on access to imported inputs in order to be competitive. And even when finished manufactured products are imported they are still associated with domestic employment in the distribution sector. Actually, since services generally contain much smaller shares of imports, the domestic employment impact of a final dollar's worth of spending on services is actually likely to give rise to more domestic employment than spending on manufacturing of equal value.

A third issue relates to the quite arbitrary allocation of activities and value added to manufacturing. Research and development, for example, can be performed in universities and laboratories and thus represent services, or within manufacturing firms and thus be counted as manufacturing value added. The same is true for many other services—janitorial, data processing, accounting, marketing, advertising, legal, etc.

All told, the implication is that these multipliers do not warrant the causal significance often attributed to them. Thus we draw conclusions about employment using them at our peril.

Closing of the US Labor Market

It is often taken as given that the US economy has become more open and globalized, and indeed international competition is increasingly important for US goods producers both at home and abroad. In 1960, only 7 percent of all US goods purchases were imports; by 2010 this share had increased to almost 40 percent. In 1960, exports accounted for 9.2 percent of overall goods output in GDP, while they were 27 percent of goods output in GDP in 2010. In most manufacturing industries, therefore, domestic producers face more intense foreign competition at home and are relatively more dependent on foreign sales.

But the globalization of the US labor market has been offset by a more powerful force, namely the shift by larger shares of workers into nontradable sectors. Figure 3.2 presents the share of employment in agriculture, mining, and manufacturing in total employment. These sectors represent a rough measure of tradable goods.[3]

---

3. The GDP accounts report full- and part-time employment going back to 1929, but use four different classification systems over the period, according to the Bureau of Economic Analysis (available at www.bea.gov/iTable/iTable.cfm?ReqID=9&step=1). Nonetheless we have spliced these series together as a rough measure of tradable goods.

Figure 3.2   Sector share in total employment, 1929–2009

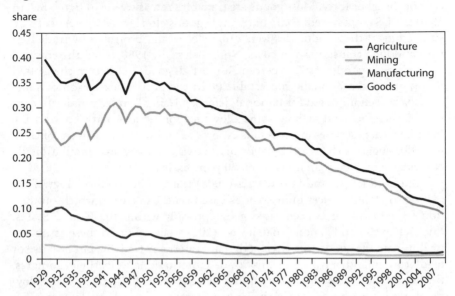

Source: Bureau of Economic Analysis.

The strength of the trends in the declining share of employment in US goods-producing industries is remarkable. Until 1950, manufacturing's employment share increased but was offset by declining shares in agriculture and mining. In the early 1950s, the manufacturing share was fairly constant, but thereafter the share began to decline. In combination with the declining shares in agriculture and mining, there is a consistently strong downward trend in the manufacturing goods employment share for the subsequent 60 years, reaching just 10 percent of the labor force by 2010. However we also need to take into account international trade in services. Advances in communications technology along with deregulation and privatization around the world have also made services more tradable and the economy more open. Yet, even the inclusion of employment in tradable services is not sufficient to offset the overall decline in the share of Americans employed in tradable sectors. This conclusion emerges when using either of the two leading methodologies to measure the tradability of services.

Alan Blinder (2006) has examined occupational data to distinguish all the jobs that can potentially be offshored.[4] He identifies these jobs based on two criteria. Either the output produced through the job can be delivered to a remote location, or the job itself need not be undertaken in a particular US location. Thus, his definition includes all potentially tradable goods and services. He estimates that in the mid-2000s, the share of such jobs in the United

---

4. See also Bhagwati and Blinder (2009).

States was between 22.2 and 29 percent with a midrange estimate of 25.6 percent of the labor force. Most goods are tradable. Yet, as we see in figure 3.2, in 1950 the US employment share in tradable goods alone was 35 percent. To be sure, many of these industries were quite closed and protected by trade barriers and high transportation costs. Nonetheless, by 1980, when the employment share in goods was 23.7 percent, almost all goods markets in the United States were internationally contestable (with the possible exception of some aerospace spending used for national defense). Using Blinder's mid-range estimate, therefore, and making some allowance for services that were tradable in earlier years—services imports plus exports were equal to 3.7 percent of GDP in 1980—suggests that the US labor market was actually less internationally contestable in 2006 than it had been 30 years earlier.

Bradford Jensen and Lori Kletzer (2005) use another methodology. They identify tradable services industry jobs based on the degree to which production in industries is concentrated geographically within the United States. Michael Spence and Sandile Hlatshwayo (2011) have adjusted these estimates to eliminate the goods and services that are internally tradable but because of regulatory and other reasons are not traded internationally. By their estimates, the Jensen and Kletzer approach implies that between 1990 and 2008, employment in the tradable sectors in the United States fell from 27 to 23 percent—a figure that is close to Blinder's midrange number.[5] Our data indicate that over the same period, the employment share of tradable goods (manufacturing, agriculture, and mining) fell from 18.4 to 10.3 percent. This implies that the employment share in tradable services increased from 8.6 to 12.6 percent.[6] Thus the increased share of employment in services that are potentially internationally tradable has been insufficient to offset the declines in the share of employment in tradable goods.[7]

The finding that the share of Americans employed in all tradable sectors has been falling has important implications for concerns about unemployment, job losses, and wages that we consider in the following chapters. As we have noted and will discuss in some detail in chapter 9, some theories (such as Stolper-Samuelson) that explain how trade affects factor prices assume that factors of production are homogeneous and mobile and that specialization is incomplete. If these conditions hold, the size of the tradable sectors does not matter because trade affects wages and other factor prices throughout the economy. But other theories assume that factors are industry-, firm-, and

---

5. Spence (2011) claims that declining employment in tradables is due to global production chains and also argues that the decline is responsible for growing US wage inequality.

6. Bureau of Economic Analysis, "National Income and Product Account Table 6.4, Full-Time and Part-Time Employees by Industry," www.bea.gov/iTable/iTable.cfm?ReqID=9&step=1 (accessed on November 1, 2012).

7. Indeed, the 23 percent employment share estimated by these authors in 2008 for tradable goods and services is roughly equal to the 23.6 share of tradable goods *alone* in 1980 employment, and the 27.1 share accounted for by goods alone in 1970 is the same as the share of the whole tradable sector employment share for goods and services that they estimate for 1990.

occupation-specific (immobile), and some allow for complete specialization. If these conditions hold, the size of tradables will influence the importance of shocks transmitted through trade in economywide measures such as wage inequality and aggregate job loss.

In addition, our evidence points to two contrasting political implications: on the one hand, global competition has become more intense for those workers who are employed in tradable goods and services, and indeed there is evidence these workers are more anxious about trade (Scheve and Slaughter 2004, Anderson and Gascon 2007). On the other hand, international competition is becoming less relevant for a growing share of American workers over time. Thus, while in some locations trade concerns could become more important, in the economy as a whole the salience of trade as a political issue could diminish over time. Indeed, Craig Van Grasstek (2011) produces considerable evidence that policy attention to trade has declined.

Manufacturing Employment: Tracking the Decline

The definition of the industries included in manufacturing has changed several times over the years, and it is hard to come by a consistent time series of employment or output over the long term. However, establishment data are available for manufacturing and nonfarm employment on a consistent basis since 1961 and are therefore suitable for a regression analysis. Figure 3.3 plots the manufacturing share of nonfarm employment against time. The dramatic decline in the share of manufacturing employment in total nonfarm employment is clear. In 1961, manufacturing accounted for 27.7 percent of nonfarm employment; by 2010, this share had fallen to just 8.9 percent. Most remarkable, however, is the persistence and stability of the relationship, irrespective of the changing trends in trade flows and other factors during this period. To illustrate this, a regression line has been fitted to the data from 1961 and 1980 and then extrapolated through 2010. Using the relationship from 1961 to 1980, a forecaster in 1980, knowing that in 2010 total nonfarm employment would be 129 million, would have predicted manufacturing employment in 2010 within 25,000 of its level of 11.524 million, that is, with an error of less than 1 percent.

We have also split the sample period from 1961 to 2010 into two periods and regressed the manufacturing employment share against time. The trend coefficients in both periods are very similar and reveal an annual decline in the manufacturing employment share of about four-tenths of one percentage point.[8] This fairly constant shift in the US employment share is similar to that of sand falling through an hourglass. While the same amount of sand moves from the top to the bottom, it represents an increasing share of the sand at the top and a decreasing share at the bottom. Similarly, this coefficient implies

---

8. Splitting the 50-year sample in half, we obtain very similar coefficients: .0043 per year prior to 1985 and .0037 per year from 1985 through 2010.

Figure 3.3   Manufacturing share in total nonfarm employment, 1961–2010

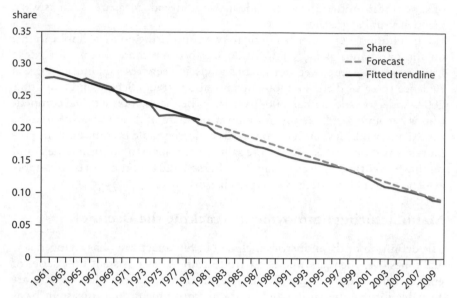

Source: Bureau of Labor Statistics.

that over time, the declining share of employment in manufacturing is an ever greater percentage of the jobs that remain in manufacturing employment, but a smaller percentage addition to employment in the rest of the economy.[9]

The 2 Percent Solution

The decade between 2000 and 2010 was unusual not because the share of manufacturing declined but because there was an absolute decline in manufacturing employment. Yet this too would have been predicted on the basis of historic relationships between manufacturing employment growth and employment growth in the rest of the economy.[10] We capture this relationship

---

9. If we assume that over time manufacturing employs a higher share of unskilled workers than the rest of the economy, and that a constant fraction of job opportunities in manufacturing disappears, the share of unskilled workers employed in other sectors of the economy will have to increase. However, if the elasticity of substitution between skilled and unskilled workers is constant, since the nonmanufacturing sector is growing over time, the downward pressure on the relative wages of unskilled workers that results from these diminished opportunities will decline. If the least skilled workers are the first who are displaced, the impact on wage inequality will diminish even faster.

10. The Bureau of Labor Statistics has two major surveys that provide employment data. The Current Employment Statistics (CES) Survey, which is obtained by surveying firms (establish-

by relating annual percentage changes in manufacturing establishment employment (%ΔM) to annual percentage changes in establishment employment (%ΔE).[11] The equation we obtain explains manufacturing employment growth very accurately. It accounts for 91 percent of the overall variance. The average prediction error (root mean squared error) is just 1.1 percent and both coefficients are highly significant.

The coefficient on the growth in employment highlights the sensitivity of manufacturing employment to overall economic conditions. The equation indicates that if there is no overall employment growth, employment will fall by 3.74 percent (the negative constant term in the regression).[12] However, for each percentage increase/decrease in employment, manufacturing employment will grow/fall by 1.8 percent. Thus, manufacturing employment falls unless employment in the economy grows at a rate that exceeds 2 percent per year (i.e., 3.74/1.89).

This relationship can be seen back in figure 3.1. When employment in the rest of the economy was expanding through the 1990s at an average of around 2 percent, manufacturing employment basically remained constant. But when aggregate employment stagnated after 2000, manufacturing employment fell rapidly. This decline in manufacturing employment after 2000 is well predicted by the simple regression model. If we forecast manufacturing employment growth using an equation estimated over the period from 1961 to 2000, we predict an annual average decline over the decade of 4.05 percent—almost exactly the 3.9 percent average annual decline that actually occurred.[13]

Therefore, as with the trend regression in figure 3.1, there is little to suggest that something fundamental has changed recently in the relationship between manufacturing employment growth and employment growth in the economy as a whole.

The regression results we have just reported are not carefully constructed structural models. In fact, they are simply statistical summaries of the relationship between two (endogenous) variables that are each affected by the numerous causes that determine the level and composition of output and employment. In a complete account these links should all be modeled in a general equilibrium setting. Nonetheless, given the complexity of forces that link them, the stability of the comovement of these variables is remarkable

---

ments), and the Current Population Survey, which surveys households. We use the CES (establishment) data for our measure of manufacturing employment.

11. The regression we obtain is:

Period 1962 to 2010 (t statistics in parentheses)

$$\%\Delta M = -3.74 + 1.80 \times \%\Delta E$$
$$\quad\quad (17.5) \quad (22.26)$$

12. This is indicated by the constant term in the regression.

13. Period 1961 through 2000:

$$\%\Delta M = -3.81 + 1.81\% \,\Delta E \quad\quad RMSE = .011$$
$$\quad\quad (t = 12.5) \quad (t = 17.0)$$

Figure 3.4   International comparison of share of employment in manufacturing, 1973–2008

percent

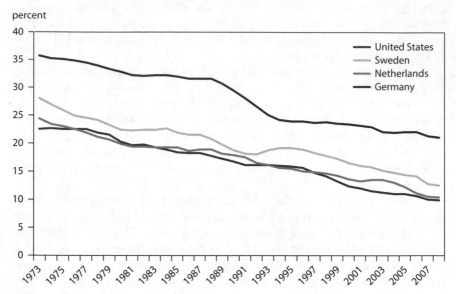

Source: Bureau of Labor Statistics.

and suggests that while recent shocks may have affected employment, something far more persistent is driving the declining share of manufacturing employment.

International Comparisons

Before we explain these more fundamental forces, we briefly point to the international experience. Much of the discussion about deindustrialization in the United States focuses on policies and practices that are specifically American, with the presumption that had these been different, the United States might have avoided the shrinking share of manufacturing employment. It is useful therefore to compare the US experience with that of other industrial countries. Data on the share of manufacturing employment for industrial countries going back to 1973 have been assembled by the Bureau of Labor Statistics (BLS).[14] As illustrated in figure 3.4 we select industrial countries with large manufacturing trade surpluses and compare them with the United States. The trends in these other industrial countries are actually remarkably similar. While the share of manufacturing employment in Germany in 2010

14. When developing countries are included in the sample, the share of industry in the economy rises with incomes at low levels of income, but then reaches a peak and falls as incomes rise further. See Herrendorf, Rogerson, and Valentini (2011).

Table 3.1   Share of employment in manufacturing, 1973–2010 (percent)

Country	1973 (1)	1990 (2)	2000 (3)	2010 (4)	Change (4) – (1)
United States	24.8	18.0	14.4	10.1	–14.7
Canada	22.0	15.8	15.3	10.3	–11.7
Australia	23.3	14.4	12.0	8.9	–14.4
Japan	27.8	24.3	20.7	16.9	–10.9
France	28.8	21.0	17.6	13.1	–15.7
Germany	36.7	31.6	23.9	21.2	–15.5
Italy	27.9	22.6	23.6	18.8	–9.1
Netherlands	25.3	19.1	14.8	10.6	–14.7
Sweden	27.6	21.0	18.0	12.7	–14.9
United Kingdom	32.3	22.4	16.2	10.0	–22.3

Source: Bureau of Labor Statistics.

(21 percent) was twice as high as in the United States, the downward slope in a trendline fitted to the data is –0.46 percent per year. This is actually larger than the US trendline coefficient of –0.39 percent. Moreover, this US trend is very similar to the Netherlands (–0.36) and Sweden (–0.38).

Table 3.1, which includes additional countries, shows that in 2010 the US employment share in manufacturing was actually quite typical of an industrial country. It was the same as the United Kingdom (10 percent), Canada (10.3), and the Netherlands (10.6), somewhat higher than Australia (8.9), and lower than Sweden (12.7) and France (13.1). The range of declines in the shares over the period is also very similar and typically on the order of 15 percentage points over the 37-year period. It is also noteworthy that several of these countries on average ran large trade surpluses in their goods trade between 2000 and 2010: the Netherlands (7 percent of GDP), Sweden (5.4 percent), Germany (6.2 percent), and Canada (4 percent). As shown in figure 3.4, these surpluses have not mitigated these countries' declining trends in manufacturing employment. These data suggest a cause that is common, pervasive, and not closely related to the size of the trade balance. And we argue that the cause is found in the interaction between productivity growth and demand patterns.

Explaining Deindustrialization

The debate over the declining share of manufacturing employment often focuses on the relative importance of two forces: international trade and technological change. On one side are those who point to the offshoring of production by US companies and on the other are those who emphasize the role of automation and advances in technology in displacing workers—especially those who are relatively unskilled (McAfee and Brynjolfsson 2011). While both these forces undoubtedly contribute to the decline, economists since Alfred Marshall have focused on supply *and* demand in determining output. Yet, automation and offshoring are supply factors, and conspicuously missing from most explanations is attention to the role played by demand. This is a problem because ultimately it will be the response of demand to these supply shocks that determines whether offshoring or automation leads to fewer or more manufacturing jobs.

The sections that follow explore these supply and demand forces. We start by comparing measures of productivity growth in manufacturing with measures for the economy as a whole, noting that productivity growth in manufacturing has persistently been relatively faster than in the economy as a whole. Next we point out that these productivity differentials have resulted in similarly persistent declines in the relative prices of manufactured products. Finally, we turn to demand and explore how final spending on goods has responded to the declining relative prices.

Productivity, Output, and Employment in Manufacturing

Trends in manufacturing employment are a combination of two components: changes in labor productivity and changes in output. Improvements in productivity increase the output produced by each worker. With fixed quantities of output, therefore, this would reduce manufacturing employment. However, faster productivity growth does not necessarily mean less employment, since higher productivity growth could enhance profitability and increase supply. In response, prices would fall, and induce more demand. If demand is very responsive, therefore, the induced expansion and consequent increase in demand for workers could more than offset the effects of the decline in the employment intensity of output. In addition to the impact of these price changes, the demand for manufacturing output will be affected by changes in income and in tastes. Thus in some cases, employment could grow despite rapid productivity growth, while in other cases it could fall.[15]

Which case pertains to the United States? Table 3.2 draws on a time series database developed by Dale Jorgenson, Mun Ho, and Jon Samuels (2010) to present average annual growth (log change) in real value added, employment, and labor productivity (value added per person employed) in US manufacturing and the total economy for periods from 1960 to 2007. As shown in the table and discussed earlier, employment in manufacturing experienced a long-term decline relative to total employment. However, the source of this deindustrialization is not a decline in real manufacturing value added (output). Real growth in manufacturing value added was actually remarkably similar to growth in the economy as a whole and averaged 3.1 percent per year over the

---

15. Total employment in manufacturing (E^M) = $n_m Q^M$, where (n_m) is the employment intensity of output and Q^M the level of manufacturing output. This relationship also holds for total employment (E^T). We can therefore decompose changes in the manufactured goods share of total employment into changes in the employment intensity of production (commonly referred to as technological change) in manufacturing relative to the entire economy ($dln\left(\frac{n_m}{n_T}\right)$) as well as changes in the relative quantity of output ($dln\left(\frac{Q^M}{Q^T}\right)$) as follows:

$$dln\left(\frac{E^M}{E^T}\right) = \left(dln\left(\frac{n_m}{n_T}\right)\right) + \left(dln\left(\frac{Q^M}{Q^T}\right)\right).$$

Table 3.2   Growth of employment, output, and labor productivity, 1960–2007 (percent)

Indicator	1960–2007	1960–79	1980–99	2000–2007
Employment (BEA data)				
Manufacturing	–0.3	1.1	–0.5	–3.1
Total	1.6	2.0	1.6	0.5
Output (real value added)				
Manufacturing	3.1	3.9	3.5	0.7
Total	3.2	3.8	3.2	2.3
Output per person employed				
Manufacturing	3.3	2.8	4.0	3.8
Total	1.6	1.8	1.6	1.7

Source: Authors' calculations using data from the Bureau of Economic Analysis (BEA) and the World KLEMS Database, www.worldklems.net/data/index.htm (accessed on November 1, 2012).

period from 1960 to 2007. The share of manufacturing in real value added in 2007, at 16 percent, hardly differed from its share in 1960, at 17 percent. The deindustrialization of the US economy is therefore not a symptom of the failure of the US economy to grow its manufacturing sector.[16]

The proximate source of the decline in the manufacturing share of employment is labor productivity growth. In most periods, the productivity differentials between manufacturing and the overall economy have dominated the differences in real output growth between the sectors. Value added per person employed grew by 3.3 percent per year from 1960 to 2007 in manufacturing, compared to only 1.6 percent per year for the economy as a whole. The implication is that the amount of labor required to produce a real dollar of manufacturing value added fell by 1.7 percent (3.3 – 1.6) per year relative to the economy as a whole. Consequently, for the manufacturing share of total employment to have remained constant or grown over this period, growth in real value added in manufacturing would have had to exceed that of the overall economy by at least 1.7 percent per year. But, since growth in manufacturing only equaled that of the economy as a whole, it led to the secular decline in the share of manufacturing in employment shown in figure 3.3.

This decomposition is not a causal explanation of the sources of employment change. Changes in labor productivity and output growth are not independent of each other and are themselves outcomes of many changes in the economy, including total factor productivity (TFP) growth, international competition, industrial restructuring, labor supply, and domestic and foreign demand. We do not try to isolate the exact contribution of these many factors in driving the sources of growth in labor productivity and output. We do, however, concentrate on the contribution of TFP in driving both labor productivity and demand for manufactured output.

16. This point is made by Robert Rowthorn and Ramana Ramaswamy (1997) in their cross-country comparison of deindustrialization in advanced economies.

Jorgenson, Ho, and Samuels (2010) have developed time series estimates of TFP growth for the period from 1960 to 2007 using a consistent classification system.[17] We use their data in figure 3.5 to plot TFP and labor productivity (real value added per person employed) in manufacturing relative to these variables for the economy as a whole. We also plot the ratio of GDP prices (deflators) to those for manufacturing. What is striking is that the series track each other fairly closely.

The most comprehensive productivity measure is TFP, which is designed to capture improvements in technical efficiency by taking account of all the inputs (i.e., capital and labor used in production). By contrast, the amount of output produced by each person employed (labor productivity growth) will be influenced not only by changes in technical efficiency but also by the skills of workers and the available stock of capital. TFP appears to be the driving factor differentiating labor productivity in manufacturing compared to the rest of the economy, since the differences between these measures for manufacturing and the economy as a whole are quite similar. For example, over the period 1960–2007, TFP grew by 1.18 percent per year faster in manufacturing than in the economy as a whole, while over the same period labor productivity growth in manufacturing increased 1.51 percent per year more rapidly than labor productivity growth in the economy. The faster growth in relative labor productivity can be attributed to a gradual increase in the capital intensity of production in manufacturing compared to the rest of the economy.[18]

The data therefore suggest that close to 80 percent of the long-term differential in labor productivity growth between manufacturing and the economy as a whole is explained by faster TFP growth in manufacturing. This changes little if we look over the more recent period: In all periods, relative TFP growth accounts for a substantial portion of the relatively faster growth in labor productivity in manufacturing. It turns out, therefore, that relatively fast TFP growth in manufacturing plays a substantial role in explaining the deindustrialization of the US economy.

Why has productivity growth generally been so much faster in manufacturing? One explanation is that the sector accounts for the vast majority of research and development spending. Presumably, this spending is not exogenous but actually indicates the greater potential for innovation in this sector. By contrast, it seems more difficult to improve productivity growth in services. Indeed, the relatively slow productivity growth in services is sometimes described as "Baumol's cost disease" after William Baumol, who with William Bowen first pointed out the inherent limitations on productivity growth in some services (Baumol and Bowen 1965). In the 1960s, they studied the performing arts and observed

---

17. They use the US North American Industry Classification System (NAICS).

18. In 1960, capital services (1995 prices) per employed person in manufacturing equaled $391,000 and $647,000 in the economy as a whole. By 2007, manufacturing had become more capital intensive than the rest of the economy. Real capital services per worker in the total economy rose to $2.83 million, whereas in manufacturing it rose to $3.76 million.

Figure 3.5 Measures of relative manufacturing productivity and prices, 1960–2007

index (1995 = 1)

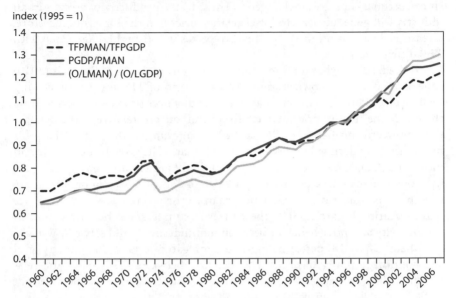

TFP = total factor productivity; MAN = manufacturing; GDP = gross domestic product; P = price;
O/L = output per worker

Source: Jorgenson, Ho, and Samuels (2010).

that the same number of musicians are needed to play a Beethoven string quartet today as were needed in the 19th century; that is, the productivity of classical performance has not increased.[19] Baumol has explored this theme with various coauthors in later work. However, it could also be the case that improvements in services are inherently more difficult to measure.[20]

This differential productivity growth between manufactures and services will affect relative demand through the impact on product prices. In a competitive market, if productivity increases in an industry, eventually its prices will fall. Assuming given input costs, if this were not the case and prices did not fall, firms would be earning excess profits and over time new entrants would increase supply. Thus, ultimately, competitive pressures should ensure that

---

19. These are cited by William Nordhaus (2006), who also presents an overview of the evidence on this issue. We should note that Nordhaus (2005) presents evidence based on pooled samples of manufacturing industries and finds that the demand for manufactured goods is actually slightly price elastic. This leads him to give greater weight to international competition as a source of deindustrialization, especially between 1998 and 2004. See, however, the final section of this chapter in which we estimate the employment impact attributable to trade. In addition, Nordhaus' more recent data could be influenced by the association between the rapid productivity growth in computers after 1995 together with the dot.com boost in demand.

20. For a discussion of measurement issues, see Bosworth and Triplett (2003).

relative price changes reflect relative productivity changes. In noncompetitive markets, a similar result occurs in the face of constant demand elasticity, since cost markups are unchanged.[21] Thus, faster productivity growth in an industry will generally lead to lower relative prices. In the long run, therefore, a reasonable assumption is that relative prices will (roughly) keep step with TFP differentials.[22]

Indeed, this is what we find using the Jorgenson, Ho, and Samuels (2010) time-series data. As shown in figure 3.5, the ratio of TFP for manufacturing relative to TFP in the economy has risen steadily over time, roughly matching the rise in the relative price deflator for overall output relative to the deflator for manufacturing. Between 1960 and 2007, for example, the price deflator for manufacturing declined by 1.42 percent per year relative to the deflator for all industries (GDP) over the period. Similarly, TFP growth and labor productivity growth increased, respectively, by 1.2 percent and 1.5 percent per year more rapidly in manufacturing production than in the economy as a whole. Since manufacturing is part of GDP, these measures understate the differentials in productivity and price behavior between manufacturing and services. William Nordhaus (2006, 18) performs more disaggregated tests at the industry level and confirms a powerful negative association between TFP growth and relative prices. For industries with well-measured data the summary coefficient of −0.965 is not significantly different from one.[23]

Price Effects

The net response of industry employment to productivity changes will depend on the responsiveness of demand to these price changes. If demand is elastic, i.e., if the percentage increase in the quantity demanded is greater than the percentage decline in price, lower prices could raise demand sufficiently to increase the demand for inputs. However, if demand is inelastic, fewer inputs may ultimately be required. Offshoring some parts of the manufacturing production process, for example, could similarly reduce the prices and thus increase the demand for the final goods that embody these services, and thus in theory, the demand for those employed in the remaining activities onshore could actually increase. Ultimately, therefore, the employment implications

---

21. The markup is generally a function of demand elasticity. As long as demand elasticity does not change, markups will be constant.

22. Actually, this assumes (Hicks) neutral productivity growth and that factor shares are the same in manufacturing and other sectors of the economy. More generally the definition of TFP in the dual is a share-weighted average of changes in factor prices minus product prices. Thus when there are two factors, labor L and capital K (both in logs) with wages W and rental rate R, $TFP = (S_l dW + S_k dR) - dP$, where d denotes marginal change, P is product price (in logs), S_l and S_k are the shares of labor and capital in costs, respectively, and $S_l + S_k = 1$. This implies that changes in product price $dP = TFP - (S_l dW + S_k dR)$. See, for example, Feenstra (2004, 125).

23. But he reaches different conclusions from ours about manufacturing.

of lower prices that reflect productivity improvements will depend on how spending responds.

Income Effects

We should note that productivity-driven changes in the employment intensity of production are only one side of the story explaining the declining share of manufacturing in total employment. Productivity growth raises national income and through this the demand for goods and services. And this increased expenditure is not necessarily allocated in the same proportions as the products already consumed. As economies grow, patterns of demand could shift and thus affect the composition of production and employment. For example, shifts in the pattern of demand from agricultural products to manufactured products and services during the industrialization stage of development in advanced economies contributed toward the movement of employment from agriculture to industry—known as Engel's law.[24] On the whole, however, differences in the income elasticity of demand for manufactures and services appear to be less of a consideration in explaining the decline in the share of manufacturing in employment. Cross-country estimates of the income elasticity of demand for services are close to unity (Falvey and Gemmel 1996). All else being constant, income growth alone should result in a constant share of services in expenditure (box 3.2).

Domestic Spending

We now shift our focus to the demand side of the ledger and consider what has happened to overall US spending on goods. While there is considerable debate about American prowess when it comes to production, no one doubts the ability of Americans to spend. Thus it is informative to ask how they have allocated their spending between goods and services.

To do this we have developed measures of total US spending on goods and services in both nominal and real terms. These measures reflect spending on finished goods by final purchasers and thus include more than just value added in US manufacturing and represent the variables that ultimately drive manufacturing employment. When they buy finished manufactured goods in the United States, consumers, for example, have to pay not only for manufacturing but also for the raw materials that are embodied in these goods and the distribution services required to bring the goods to markets. Moreover, they will buy not only goods that are produced in the United States but also those imported from the rest of the world.

The national income accounts data allow us to develop separate measures of US spending on goods and on services. We determine national expenditure on goods (i.e., $C + I + G$) by totaling the line items that are reported for

---

24. See Rowthorn and Wells (1987) and Rowthorn and Ramaswamy (1997).

Box 3.2 Productivity and real wages

We have shown that productivity growth has been relatively rapid in manufacturing and that this has for the most part been reflected in declining relative prices of manufactured goods. Michael Spence (2011) has claimed that this difference in labor productivity growth, which he ascribes to global supply chains, is an important driver of income inequality in the United States. But as one of us argued in Lawrence (2011), Spence's argument is seriously flawed and confuses product wages (i.e., wages in terms of what workers produce) with consumption wages (wages in terms of general buying power). Most of the additional productivity gains in US manufacturing did not take the form of higher wages or profits in manufacturing, which might cause inequality but instead were passed through to consumers in the form of lower prices. This means that while product wages increased more in manufacturing, consumption wages did not.

We do generally expect that wages measured in terms of what workers produce will increase with value added per worker. And in this sense, Spence is right. For example, if the price of computers falls rapidly because of improvements in productivity in the computer industry, the wages of workers in the computer industry measured in terms of computers will rise. But this change will not lead to increased wage inequality because the wages of workers who do not work in computers—say, hairdressers—will *also* rise in terms of computers. Indeed, since the invention of the scissors there has probably been no increase in the real value added per worker among hairdressers, but that has not stopped their real wages from rising together with similar workers employed elsewhere. This is basically the reason for Baumol's cost disease discussed in the main text, since it means that industries with slow productivity growth experience relative cost increases. We would expect that, especially over periods of more than a decade, workers with roughly similar general skills would tend to earn similar wages regardless of where they work. Using the data in Jorgenson, Ho, and Samuels (2010), we find that between 1960 and 2007 nominal value added per worker in the United States increased by 6 percent and 5.6 percent in manufacturing and the economy as a whole, respectively. This difference of 0.4 percent annually is considerably smaller than the 1.5 percent difference in the growth of real value added per worker in manufacturing and in the economy as a whole over the same period. And it should be noted that between 1960 and 2007, real value added per hour increased by 3.5 and 1.9 percent in manufacturing and the overall economy, respectively.[1]

---

1. William Nordhaus (2006, 19) similarly explores the relationship between productivity growth and wages in disaggregated industry data and finds effects that are either very small or negligible.

(1) personal consumption expenditure on goods, (2) private and government investment expenditure on equipment (and software), and (3) government consumption expenditure on goods.[25] Most of this spending on goods reflects personal consumption—on average, personal consumption expenditure accounted for 73.4 percent of overall US spending on goods between 1969 and 2010. We measure services expenditure by aggregating personal and government consumption expenditure on services. These measures of US domestic spending are thus inclusive of imports, but exclude exports.[26]

As illustrated in figure 3.6, there are powerful trends in the data. The top line shows the dramatic decline in the prices of goods relative to services over the period—by 100 log points over the 50 years or 1.95 percent per year.[27] If relative price changes for goods do move in line with relative changes in TFP, as is suggested by our earlier analysis, the quantity of goods grows at the same rate as the quantity of services, and if the United States were a closed economy or imports a constant share of value-added goods, this would imply a reduction in the relative demand for labor in the production of consumption and investment goods relative to services of around 1.95 percent per year. However,

---

25. In the national accounts, government consumption expenditures are services (such as education and national defense) produced by government. One approach is therefore to treat all government consumption expenditure as a service. Our interest is to obtain the closest link between expenditure on goods and the production of goods. We therefore use Bureau of Economic Analysis (BEA) Table 3.10 and its subtables on Government Consumption Expenditures and General Government Gross Output to identify intermediate goods and services purchased as part of government consumption expenditure. The value-added component of producing government consumption expenditure is omitted, implying that our total measure of government consumption and investment expenditure is less (by value-added amount) than total government consumption and gross investment expenditure provided in the national accounts data. The BEA's Table 3.9 and its subtables are used to obtain government investment expenditure on equipment and software. Private and government investment expenditures on nonresidential and residential structures are excluded. Real values of aggregate expenditure on goods and services are constructed by deflating the nominal value with a share-weighted average price index constructed using the subcomponents of each expenditure item. See www.bea.gov (accessed on November 1, 2012).

26. US spending is on final goods and services. Spending on domestic final goods is therefore not equivalent to US production of goods. Goods produced by US firms are used as intermediate inputs in the production of final goods in other sectors of the economy, including services. For example, coal output is used in the production of electricity—a service. There is no direct expenditure by consumers or government on coal. Demand for US coal production is indirect through demand for electricity. In our analysis we use US spending on final goods relative to final services as a measure of relative demand for manufacturing production to services production. This could be problematic insofar as manufacturing inputs are used to produce services. However, according to the total requirement matrices of the 2005 US Input-Output Tables, the value added in manufacturing associated with $1 of US spending on final goods is 5.5 times higher than $1 of spending on services.

27. The goods prices relevant for *final* goods demand are not only those for the value added in the manufacturing process, but also the costs of wholesale and retail distribution and those of the primary commodity and services inputs that are used in goods production. Given the final demand for goods, therefore, the demand for manufactured goods will thus also reflect any changes in distribution margins.

Figure 3.6　US spending on goods relative to services, 1960–2010

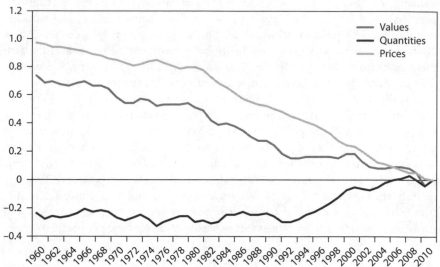

log scale (2010 = 0)

Source: Bureau of Economic Analysis, www.bea.gov/iTable/index_nipa.cfm (accessed on November 1, 2012).

the quantity of goods consumed relative to services responded in part to these falling prices. As shown in the bottom line in the figure, while remaining flat until about 1992 and rising thereafter, the quantity of goods consumed relative to the quantity of services consumed increased over the period as a whole, but by only 24 log points (0.5 percent per year). The labor demand effect of the increase in quantity of goods consumed relative to services was therefore insufficient to offset the decline in relative labor demand associated with the relatively strong productivity growth in the goods sector.

All told, therefore, as captured by the middle line in the figure, dollar spending on goods relative to services has a strong downward trend. In combination, consumers, government, and investors have been devoting declining shares of nominal spending to goods relative to services.[28] In 1960, for example, US consumers were allocating half of all their spending on consumption to goods—50.3 percent. By 2010 that share had fallen to 33 percent. Similarly, US government consumption and investment expenditure on goods made up 61 percent of expenditure in 1960, but by 2010 this had fallen to 42 percent.[29]

---

28. Thus, even if the demand for goods is elastic, as found by Nordhaus (2005), if the income demand elasticity is less than one, the share in overall spending on goods and employment could fall over time.

29. Note that these shares are calculated using government investment expenditure on equipment and software and the intermediate goods and services purchased as part of government consumption expenditure.

The overall impact, inclusive of investment expenditure on equipment and software, was a decline in US spending on goods relative to services by 1.47 log points per year over the entire period.

This sluggish increase in the relative volume of goods purchased in the face of relatively rapid growth in productivity in manufacturing and declining relative prices implies that even if the US economy had had no trade, the share of employment in the production of goods would have fallen relative to employment in the production of services.

Investment

While the big picture is one of falling prices of goods and insufficient responses in quantities demanded to prevent expenditure shares from declining, this is not true of all periods, especially when it comes to investment spending. As shown in figure 3.6, in the 1970s, relative goods prices declined more slowly, and in the 1990s there were increases in the relative quantities of goods demanded. Indeed, for three-quarters of the 1990s, growth in the demand for goods relative to services was more than sufficient to offset the decline in the price of goods relative to services.

This can be attributed to investment expenditure on equipment and software in what became the dot.com boom. As can be seen in figure 3.7, an important source of this behavior is equipment spending, which is much more volatile than other spending. There were actually some periods when there were strong upward trends in relative spending on equipment—these took place in the 1970s and the 1990s and bolstered overall spending on goods in those periods. In the 1990s, spending on computers and other forms of information technology was especially strong, indicating that innovation can indeed spur demand sufficiently for employment creation. But even in the investment category overall between 1960 and 2010, a declining share of spending was allocated to goods. Over these 50 years, the drop in nominal spending by government and private investors on equipment relative to overall services expenditures was about 0.9 percent per year, and since 2000 and the bursting of the dot.com bubble spending on equipment has been particularly weak—its share in overall US spending fell by close to a half.

While these final spending numbers are indicative of the powerful role played by demand, the precise numbers we derive need to be treated with some caution. First, trade *has* taken its toll since the United States has had a growing deficit in merchandise (and manufacturing) trade in recent years. In addition, our use of final goods measures has not explicitly considered the role of distribution services in addition to manufacturing and raw materials production. Further, the relatively rapid growth in productivity in manufacturing could itself be related to increased import competition.[30] Without

---

30. Trade-induced changes in the composition of firms within industries, for example, have been an important source of overall productivity gains in US manufacturing sectors. See Bernard, Jensen, and Schott (2006).

Figure 3.7   Spending on equipment relative to total and services spending, 1960–2010

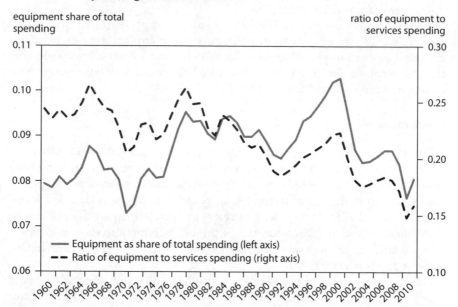

equipment share of total spending

ratio of equipment to services spending

—— Equipment as share of total spending (left axis)
– – Ratio of equipment to services spending (right axis)

Note: Total spending is calculated as GDP + imports – exports.

Source: Bureau of Economic Analysis, GDP accounts data, www.bea.gov/iTable/index_nipa.cfm (accessed on November 1, 2012).

import competition, productivity growth in manufacturing may have been slower, which could have attenuated the decline in the share of manufacturing in total employment. But even this cursory look at the data points to a dominant role for demand patterns in explaining the decline in employment in goods in general and manufacturing in particular. Unless these spending patterns change dramatically, long-run trends in relative productivity growth will inexorably lead to the deindustrialization of the US economy in terms of employment.

In sum, by looking at spending on goods rather than production we have seen that an important reason for the declining share of manufacturing in the United States is that Americans have increasingly chosen to allocate smaller shares of their spending to goods. We have not attempted to estimate price and income elasticities or to explore the role of changes in distribution margins, but we can conclude from this evidence that in combination, spending responses to higher incomes and faster productivity growth have played a powerful role in US deindustrialization.

We should emphasize that by pointing to the role of inelastic demand and productivity growth we are not arguing that trade has played no role at all. The declines in manufacturing employment relative to services employment since 1980 have been about 2.7 percent per year. Thus there is room for trade to have played some role, but the productivity/demand story is significant, and even if trade had been balanced, the forces driving reduced demand for goods would have been powerful.

Finally, we should also observe that as our data on equipment and computers indicated, there have been some periods when the share of spending on goods has increased. Typically these spurts have been associated with the diffusion of new technologies. Thus another key lesson is that innovation in new products that consumers and firms want to buy could be important in forestalling or reversing declines in demand.

Did the Manufacturing Trade Deficit Play a Large Role in Manufacturing Employment Losses?

So far we have tracked US spending on goods of various kinds, i.e., $C + I + G$. But ultimately employment in manufacturing depends not only on employment due to domestic spending ($C + I + G$) but also on employment due to the trade balance ($X - M$). In what follows, therefore, we calculate the employment equivalence of the manufacturing trade deficit.

There is a widespread view that the dominant reason for declining manufacturing employment after 2000 was the growing trade deficit and jobs going abroad, so it is revealing to obtain a measure of the employment content of the manufacturing trade deficit. These estimates need to be treated with great care. This is an arithmetic exercise rather than a simulation with an economic model. We provide it simply to give a sense of the order of magnitude of the jobs embodied in the manufacturing trade balance.[31] As our discussion in chapter 1 emphasized, the trade deficit is an outcome, not a cause. And thus the estimates we obtain here only indicate after the fact the manufacturing employment equivalence of the manufacturing trade deficit and do not accurately capture the number of manufacturing jobs that might be added if the deficit was actually to be closed in one way or another.

Indeed, in practice the impact on manufacturing employment would depend on exactly how the deficit was reduced. We can give two examples with very different implications. First, assume there is a recession in the United States that reduces manufacturing imports and thus the employment content of the smaller trade deficit. If the recession was caused by less US spending on manufactured goods, even though the "contribution" of the trade deficit would now be smaller, this might be more than offset by the negative contribution of domestic spending, and thus overall manufacturing employment might fall. Second, assume the manufacturing deficit declined because exports increased due to faster foreign growth, for example. In this case, total manufacturing employment would rise not only because of the direct impact

---

31. An earlier calculation along these lines is provided by Martin Baily and Robert Lawrence (2004).

of more exports but also because of the additional domestic spending due to the multiplier effect. Moreover, since such spending would also increase imports, the changed employment equivalence of the trade deficit after the fact could seriously underestimate the impact of "trade," i.e., the impact of export growth on employment.

To carry out the estimation we assume that in the industries in which the United States ran trade deficits domestic expenditure is reoriented toward domestic products such that the deficit is eliminated. Similarly we assume that in industries in which the United States ran trade surpluses, exports and domestic production would have been reduced so that they matched imports. We thus add the employment content of the trade balances in the manufacturing industries in which the United States had deficits and subtract the employment content of the trade balances in industries in which the United States had surpluses. We also assume that labor productivity growth would have been the same as was actually experienced in each industry (and those that supply it).

To undertake this analysis we use the annual Input-Output Tables produced by the US Bureau of Economic Analysis to link the changes in US spending to production (value added) in the US manufacturing sector. We use the tables to take account of not only the direct output effects of eliminating the deficits (or surpluses) in manufacturing, but also the indirect effects on output in other manufacturing sectors. Given the changes in sector output we can then estimate the employment equivalence using the nominal employment/output ratios in each year.[32]

Figure 3.8 shows actual manufacturing employment and an employment series that adds back the employment equivalence of the manufacturing trade deficit over the period from 1990 to 2010. This period coincides with a strong increase in the manufacturing trade deficit up to 2006/2007, a narrowing of the deficit during the global financial crisis of 2008 and 2009, and a rise as the economy began to recover in 2010. In 1990, the manufacturing trade deficit was equivalent (both directly and indirectly) to 1.65 million full-time equivalent jobs in manufacturing. This rose to 3.3 million jobs in 2000 with the

---

32. To develop the calculations, we construct nominal net export values for 19 manufacturing sectors using export and import values obtained from the annual Input-Output Tables (after redefinitions) for 1998–2009. Trade data from 1990 to 1997 are obtained from Feenstra, Romalis, and Schott (2002) and for 2010 from the US International Trade Commission. These data are adjusted to the equivalent prices in the Input-Output Tables using the implicit margins derived from the input-output-based trade data. The manufacturing GDP content of net trade in manufacturing is then calculated using the Input-Output Tables for 2005. To capture the indirect effects, we construct a domestic use table using the Total Requirements Table for 2005 and the Use and Make Tables. We do not use the total output requirements matrix, which estimates the total goods and services required from both domestic and foreign sources adjusted to meet final demand, because we are interested in the impact on US production only. Finally, the employment content is calculated using nominal GDP per worker obtained from the BEA GDP by Industry Data Tables, www.bea.gov/industry/gdpbyind_data.htm (accessed on November 1, 2012).

Figure 3.8 Manufacturing employment, actual and adjusted for manufacturing trade deficit, 1990–2010

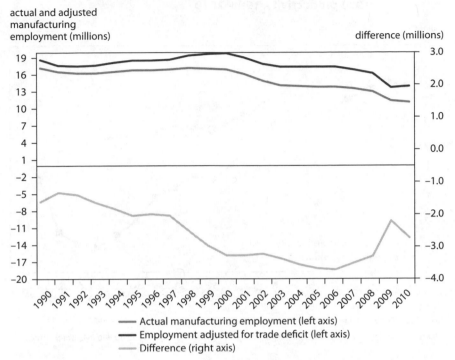

actual and adjusted
manufacturing
employment (millions)   difference (millions)

——— Actual manufacturing employment (left axis)
——— Employment adjusted for trade deficit (left axis)
——— Difference (right axis)

Note: Estimates include the direct and indirect employment (full-time equivalent) effects in manufacturing, calculated using the 2005 Make and Use Tables of the Bureau of Economic Analysis, www.bea.gov/iTable/index_nipa.cfm (accessed on November 1, 2012).

Source: Authors' calculations using data from the Bureau of Economic Analysis and Bureau of Labor Statistics.

sharp increases in the manufacturing trade deficit. As a percentage of actual manufacturing employment, adding the jobs equivalent to the deficit raises manufacturing employment by 10.4 percent in 1990, 20 percent in 2000, 26 percent in 2007 just prior to the financial crisis, 20 percent in 2009, and 26 percent in 2010 as the economy began to recover.

However, another revealing feature of the series is that the rise in the manufacturing trade deficit basically had very little impact on the total job equivalence of the trade deficit between 1998–99 and 2010. This conclusion is surprising. After all, despite the recession, the trade deficit in manufactured goods in 2010 of $644 billion was far more than twice the $256 billion deficit in 1998. But the manufacturing employment equivalence of the $256 billion deficit in 1998 was 2.5 million, whereas the employment equivalence of the $644 billion deficit in 2010 was only marginally higher at 2.7 million.

Figure 3.9 Manufacturing job (full-time equivalent) content of manufacturing trade deficit, actual productivity versus 1990 productivity, 1990–2010

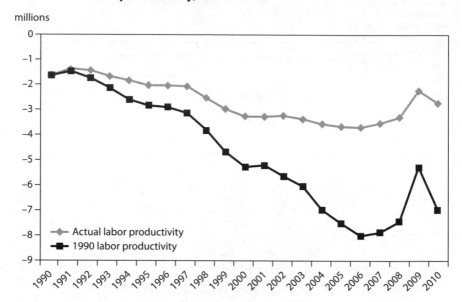

millions

Note: The 1990 value added per worker is adjusted for inflation using the sectoral GDP deflator.

Source: Authors' calculation using data from the Bureau of Economic Analysis and Bureau of Labor Statistics.

The explanation for this paradox is that productivity growth in manufacturing was extraordinarily rapid over this period. Thus, over time any given trade balance translates into fewer jobs. As shown in figure 3.9, which compares the manufacturing job content of the manufacturing trade deficit using actual labor productivity and constant 1990 labor productivity, faster productivity growth (real GDP per worker) had a very large impact on the employment equivalence of the manufacturing trade deficit over time. Indeed, at 1990 productivity levels the deficit in 2007 would have represented about 8 million jobs.

Two other interesting results are revealed by the data. First, while manufacturing employment is higher if the jobs embodied in the deficit are added to domestic production, the trends and timing of changes in manufacturing employment growth over the past decade are not very different. Both series indicate large drops in employment between 2000 and 2003 and between 2007 and 2009, demonstrating the powerful role of recessions rather than trade deficits as the major reason for the timing of the job loss. Clearly both series are heavily influenced by the combination of domestic demand and productivity growth that we identified earlier.

Table 3.3 Manufacturing employment content of the manufacturing trade deficit, 1990, 2000, and 2010 (thousands)

Category	1990	2000	2010
Wood products	30	112	62
Nonmetallic mineral products	46	79	65
Primary metals	109	209	177
Fabricated metal products	82	190	200
Machinery	20	63	13
Computer and electronic products	130	500	375
Electrical equipment, appliances, and components	34	110	127
Motor vehicles, bodies and trailers, and parts	294	371	422
Other transportation equipment	−181	−109	−156
Furniture and related products	46	120	115
Miscellaneous manufacturing	171	256	162
Food and beverage and tobacco products	10	33	45
Textile mills and textile product mills	104	166	177
Apparel and leather and allied products	672	950	751
Paper products	38	46	26
Printing and related support activities	3	16	18
Petroleum and coal products	7	21	5
Chemical products	0	98	90
Plastic and rubber products	44	79	94
Total	1,660	3,312	2,770

Note: The figures refer to full-time employment content of net exports in manufacturing. Trade data from 1990 to 2006 are obtained from Feenstra, Romalis, and Schott (2002). Estimates include the direct and indirect employment effects in manufacturing, calculated using the 2005 Make and Use Tables obtained from the Bureau of Economic Analysis. The results for 2010 are not presented as the sector-level employment data are not available. The total figures do not equal the sum of the components due to rounding.

Source: Authors' calculations using data from the Bureau of Economic Analysis and Bureau of Labor Statistics.

Second, after 2006 the gap between the two series—shown as a third line at the bottom of figure 3.8—narrowed considerably from 3.7 million in 2006 to 2.3 million in 2009. This suggests that "trade" actually boosted rather than reduced manufacturing employment opportunities during the 2008–09 recession. With recovery in 2010, the difference increased again back to about 2.7 million but still remained 1 million below the 2006 peak.

We also calculate the effects across sectors—these results are presented in table 3.3. There are substantial differences in the levels and trends of the sectoral trade balances over the period. The rise in the deficit in apparel was particularly high. If the employment content of the apparel trade deficit had been added back, employment in this sector would have been 950,000 higher in 2000 and 751,000 higher in 2010.

Another sector driving the overall trend in the manufacturing trade balance is computer and electronic products, where balancing of trade would have raised employment by approximately 500,000 jobs in 2000, but because of rapid productivity gains a lower 375,000 jobs in 2010. In other sectors, the employment equivalence of the manufacturing trade deficit in 2010 was equal to 177,000 in both textiles and primary metals, 422,000 in motor vehicles, 200,000 in fabricated metal products, and 162,000 in miscellaneous manufacturing. In many sectors, however, labor productivity growth exceeded the growth in the trade deficit, leading to a decline in the manufacturing employment content of the deficit from 2000 to 2010. The overall employment content of the deficit in 2010 was therefore lower than that of 2000.

Offshoring

In US policy discussions, the offshoring of US jobs by multinational companies is often given considerable attention and widely believed to be a major reason for declining US employment in manufacturing—especially since 2000. Indeed, offshoring was an important focus of the 2012 presidential campaign.[33] But how significant has the relocation of US manufacturing jobs to the foreign plants of US-owned firms actually been as a reason for declining US manufacturing employment? It requires an extensive study. But as a starting point, we can use the data on employment in the foreign affiliates of US-owned manufacturing multinationals.

According to the Bureau of Economic Analysis, which surveys US multinationals, between 1999 and 2009, employment in majority-owned foreign manufacturing affiliates increased from 4.58 million to 5.22 million—by 638,000—most of which was added in Asia and the Pacific.[34] In 2009, according to the same survey, in the United States, employment in the manufacturing parents of these affiliates amounted to 6.898 million.[35] In other words, even if every job added abroad since 2000 had instead been added in the United States, employment in these companies would have been only 9.25 percent higher than it actually was. Indeed, the additional 638,000 jobs amount to 11 percent of the overall loss in manufacturing employment between 1999 and 2009. Moreover, this is surely an upper-bound estimate of the jobs that were actually lost because (1) typically US workers are more productive than workers in developing countries and thus fewer workers would have been required to produce the same amount of sales; and (2) some of the jobs that were added abroad were devoted to servicing foreign markets that could not have been serviced by producing in the United States.

Conclusions

In sum, over the past decade, the decline in US manufacturing employment has been rapid, but it has been roughly in line with what would have been

---

33. See, for example, www.factcheck.org/2012/10/talking-tax-breaks-for-offshoring.

34. See Barefoot and Mataloni (2011, 35, table 4).

35. See Barefoot and Mataloni (2011, 39, table 6).

expected, given the slow overall employment growth. Even though productivity growth has been relatively rapid in manufacturing and goods have become cheaper, Americans (and consumers in other industrialized countries) have allocated ever smaller shares of their income growth to buying consumer goods and equipment. At times larger manufacturing deficits have contributed to lower manufacturing employment, but manufacturing's declining share in the economy reflects a particular combination of domestic demand patterns and productivity growth rather than a major role for trade. Rapid productivity growth in manufacturing implies that over time, the job equivalence of any given trade deficit declines.

It seems appropriate to end this chapter with another metaphor—that of an escalator. Boosting US employment in manufacturing by closing the trade deficit is like trying to walk up an escalator that is moving down. Closing the trade deficit—say, by increasing US exports of manufactured goods—would provide a one-time boost to manufacturing employment. But eventually, if the past is prologue, the combination of strong productivity growth and the income- and price-inelastic demand for goods would take over and the share of employment in manufacturing would likely resume its decline.

This is what we have seen happen even in the industrial countries with large trade surpluses, such as Germany. So while manufacturing employment growth may be required for a robust US recovery, over the long run US demand and productivity patterns are unlikely to change. Thus, unless the United States runs ever larger trade surpluses, or there is a fundamental change in demand and productivity patterns, the declining trend in the share of manufacturing employment is likely to continue. The only way to permanently reverse these trends would be to continuously come up with new innovative products that consumers and purchasers of equipment wish to buy. But absent this, Americans seeking good jobs will increasingly have to find them in sectors other than manufacturing.

There are claims that the United States will not be able to achieve full employment unless it creates more jobs in manufacturing. Spence (2011), for example, suggests the constraint will be insufficient domestic demand for services. Andrew Liveris (2010) claims the services sector alone cannot create enough jobs. But recent history is different. Demand has shifted increasingly to services, and while some rise in manufacturing employment is likely to accompany a rebound in aggregate employment, over the longer run it is likely that the contribution of manufacturing to overall employment growth will be modest. As has been the case in the recent past, most of the jobs of the future will be in the services economy.

COMPETITIVENESS, WELFARE, AND INEQUALITY: EXPLORING THE CONCERNS WITH DETAILED DATA

Chapter 4 serves as a segue between the public's concerns and those of economists, since the evidence it presents is relevant to both. The public's concerns are focused on jobs, but imbedded in those concerns is a lack of confidence in America's ability to compete, especially in relatively sophisticated products. As we discuss in greater detail, the economists' concerns also relate to the effects of competition between the United States and developing countries. On the one hand, Paul Samuelson (2004) has argued that growth in developing countries such as China could reduce America's gains from trade if these countries move up the technology ladder and provide important competition for US exports. On the other hand, Paul Krugman[1] is concerned that growing trade with developing countries exerts downward pressure on the wages of unskilled US workers who make similar products. The issues raised by Samuelson and Krugman are quite different,[2] but in both cases they reflect the presumption that the United States and developing countries compete head to head, i.e., that the products made by developed and developing countries are close substitutes.

---

1. Paul R. Krugman, "The Trouble with Trade; Keep Our Markets Open but Protect Those Who Get Hurt," *Pittsburgh Post-Gazette*, December 29, 2007, B-7.

2. Actually, in the conventional two-by-two Heckscher-Ohlin trade theory framework, Samuelson and Krugman cannot both be correct. If Samuelson's concern is valid and the United States specializes in skill-intensive products, declining US export prices will reduce skill premiums and lead to more equal wages. Conversely, if Krugman is correct and US imports of unskilled-labor-intensive products from developing countries become cheaper, the US terms of trade would improve and lead to greater aggregate welfare gains.

Support for Samuelson's contention and the more general public concern that US competitiveness has declined seems to come from the data on trade in high-technology products. These data are reported annually by the US National Science Foundation (NSF) in its Science Indicators and monthly by the US Department of Commerce in its report on trade in advanced technology products. Both reports show major declines in the world export market share of the United States in these products. The NSF data, for example, indicate that the US market share in global high-technology exports fell from 22 percent in the mid-1990s to 15 percent in 2010. This primarily reflects losses by industries producing communications equipment and office machinery and computers. By contrast, China's share in high-tech exports rose from 6 to 22 percent over the same period, making it by far the world's largest exporter of these products. In addition, America's historically strong trade balance in advanced technology products shifted from surplus to deficit in 2002, driven by US trade with developing countries such as China, Mexico, Malaysia, and Indonesia (NSF 2010).

Proponents of the view that US competitiveness has been seriously eroded, such as Clyde Prestowitz (2010), point to the US trade deficit of $100 billion in high-technology goods, especially with respect to China, as particularly disturbing. Similarly, others claim that China has surged ahead technologically and now poses a major threat to US commercial and security interests (Preeg 2004, McMillon 2007).[3]

In addition to these trade data other evidence bolsters claims of Chinese technological prowess. The Chinese have been investing very heavily in important product areas and have clearly achieved technological excellence. Two examples often cited are alternative energy products such as solar energy, emphasized by complaints at the World Trade Organization (WTO) that China has been unfairly subsidizing its efforts, and high-speed trains and railroads, emphasized by reports that California is looking to China to upgrade its system.[4] In addition, while they do not quite go as far as to suggest that China has reached America's levels of technology, research supports the view that Chinese products are unusually sophisticated. Peter Schott (2008) finds that China's export overlap with exports from Organization for Economic Cooperation and Development (OECD) countries is much greater than one would predict given its low income levels.[5] And similarly, Dani Rodrik (2006) finds that the composition of China's exports is associated with a productivity level that is higher than what would be expected given its income.

---

3. This is, of course, a repetition of the US debate over the need for a new industrial policy when similar fears arose with respect to Japan. See Wachter and Wachter (1981) and Lawrence (1984).

4. Nonetheless, it should be recalled that Japan, too, reached excellence in high-speed railroads in the early 1960s, several decades before it moved close to the global technological frontier in other areas. And it is to be expected that developing countries making large investments in basic capacity and infrastructure could well leapfrog more outdated technologies in some areas.

5. Kozo Kiyota (2008) compares US, EU, and Chinese exports with Japan.

Support for Krugman's view on wages seems to come from the data that show a rapid decline in the prices of manufactured imports from developing countries relative to those of imports from developed countries. If these goods are intensive in the use of unskilled labor, it could imply that these imports have placed downward pressures on the prices of similar goods produced in the United States. This could in turn reduce relative and absolute wages of unskilled US workers.

Chapter 4 drills down deeper into these issues using the most detailed data available. Both Samuelson's and Krugman's concerns rest on the assumption that developing-country imports are close substitutes for US-produced goods. The use of disaggregated data allows us to interrogate these assumptions in more depth. Our interest in this chapter in particular is whether developed and developing countries compete head to head in export markets.

4

Do Developed and Developing Countries Compete Head to Head?

In this chapter, we show that as an indicator of head-to-head competition in export markets, the data on high-technology products are insufficiently discriminating and thus seriously misleading. In fact, the United States remains a strong competitor in the most sophisticated (high unit value) high-technology products. By contrast, developing countries such as China generally export very different products, and where developing-country export products overlap with US exports, they are typically much cheaper and of lower quality. More generally, we demonstrate that even the most disaggregated data available—the 10-digit Harmonized Tariff Schedule (HTS) classification data—can be misleading because the products exported by developed and developing countries in these categories are fundamentally different. This is especially the case for products classified as high-technology because the scope for differentiating these products is much greater than for products in which technological inputs are less important.

We start by using disaggregated data to explore whether developed and developing countries export similar manufactured products. We calculate a similarity index that captures the degree to which exports share the same classification categories. This allows us to explore across-product specialization in exports. Fortunately, we can compile very fine-grained measures of similarity because the United States reports trade data in highly disaggregated 6- and 10-digit HTS categories. For example, the 10-digit HTS import category number 6103106030 contains values of "cotton waistcoats imported as parts of suits."

However, even at the 10-digit HTS level, the data still reflect an aggregation of products of different quality. For example, all cotton waistcoats that are parts of suits are not created equal. Indeed, some may be of much better quality and have different product attributes (e.g., silver versus gold buttons) than others. We therefore explore additional measures of within-product specialization. First, we compare price differences within detailed categories by examining average unit values at the most disaggregated level available (typically either the HTS 10- or 6-digit levels). Second, we report on additional tests in which we distinguish products according to both their technological intensity and whether they are finished products or intermediate inputs. And third, we report on the results of tests that reveal quality differences, even when goods have the same price. We also investigate the possibility that the classification system itself could bias the result.

Our tests all lead to a central conclusion. There are distinctive patterns of international specialization, and developed and developing countries export fundamentally different manufactured products. Judged by export shares, the United States and developing countries specialize in quite different product categories that for the most part do not overlap. Even when they do overlap and exports are classified in the same category, there are large systematic differences in unit values that suggest the products exported by developed and developing countries are not very close substitutes—developed-country products are far more sophisticated.

We find that per capita incomes are a powerful predictor of relative unit values—a result we draw on later in this study. It is generally possible, with a fairly high degree of accuracy, to rank relative export unit values from different countries and deduce their per capita income rankings. This finding is important because it suggests that developing economies will become serious head-to-head competitors with the United States in export markets only when their per capita incomes are much closer to US levels.

Nonetheless, these statements about prices do not hold to the same degree for all types of products. We find that the scope for price differentiation is far higher in what are called high-technology products than in primary-commodity-intensive products or manufactured products classified as "low-tech." Indeed, export prices for commodity-intensive products from developed and developing countries—think copper or steel—are typically not very different. Likewise, prices from developed and developing countries for low-tech products—think clothing—are often fairly close. (Although not all, of course—try comparing Italian and Brazilian shoes.) In these areas, therefore, head-to-head competition does exist. But when it comes to medium- and high-tech products, developing-country products are located much further down a much larger price spectrum. Moreover, there is little evidence of substantial price convergence over time. Especially in high-tech, therefore, developed and developing countries are not competing by exporting goods that are close substitutes.

To justify our conclusion that these goods are not substitutes we also consider and rule out two other interpretations of the results showing large price differences. The first is that the products reflect different stages of vertical integration because even these most disaggregated data do not distinguish sufficiently between finished goods and intermediate inputs. For example, exports from China and the United States might both fall in a category that is labeled as "audio parts," but the Chinese exports could be less finished parts (e.g., chips used in radio volume controls) while the US exports could be more finished products (e.g., completed volume control panels that contain chips). We carry out the analysis using only those end-use categories specifically identified as finished goods. While we do find the price differences are slightly smaller when we consider only high-tech finished goods, we again find that these differences are very large and persistent.

If products are homogeneous and of similar quality, the cheapest will capture the entire market, but if they are differentiated, price differences for similar products could coexist. A second concern, therefore, is that the lower prices of developing-country exports could simply indicate that they are selling fairly similar products at much lower prices rather than products that are fundamentally different from those sold by developed countries. We deal with this objection using a technique developed in the literature to distinguish quality differences. This approach uses the insight that if two similar but differentiated products have the same price, the one with higher quality will capture a larger market share. We report on a regression analysis that allows us to deduce product quality from the residuals of a regression that explains market shares controlling for price and variety. Our findings confirm that in terms of high-tech products, developing countries specialize in products that not only have lower prices but also, given these prices, lower quality.

These findings are particularly strong, as many of the goods imported by the United States from China and other developing countries actually contain high shares of value that was added in other countries that are more advanced than China. Global supply chains in which China adds assembly services to more sophisticated inputs bias the data toward suggesting China is more advanced than it actually is. Thus, the results show how seriously trade data in products classified as high-tech and advanced technology can mislead.

All told, our results point to the pitfalls of data aggregation in a world with a high degree of specialization within industries and narrow product categories. Developing countries have increasingly moved into the product categories in which developed countries also export. However, they have primarily moved into the low end of these categories, and there has not been a convergence in relative unit values over time.

Many years ago, Raymond Vernon (1966) wrote about a product cycle that is characteristic of trade in high-tech products. He argued that new products would initially be produced and exported by advanced countries, but later, as the new products became less novel and their production processes more standardized, production would eventually move to less developed countries. Our findings provide considerable confirmation for his view.[1] The anomalous findings that developing countries seem to be exporting technologically intensive products can be explained if it is recognized that the versions of these

---

1. See Zhu (2005) for a more recent application of product-cycle theory.

products that are made by these countries have become sufficiently standard-ized to no longer qualify as high-tech.

We are not the first researchers to argue that relative factor endowments provide poor explanations for specialization when aggregate industry data are used. We owe this insight to Peter Schott (2004), who concluded that the conventional Heckscher-Ohlin theory still explains trade patterns, but only when more disaggregated data are used to measure the factor intensity of products. However, the systematic relationships we find between the scope for differentiation and technological intensity could suggest that in addi-tion to endowments, technologies are fundamentally different in developed and developing countries. Indeed, part of the reason developed countries are richer is that they have invested more in developing technologies that are more advanced. Support for this view is provided by the work of Daron Acemoglu (1998, 2003), who argues that skill-abundant countries are likely to develop skill-biased technologies.

In the chapters that follow we refer back to these results because they help us explain how the US manufacturing terms of trade have improved strongly, despite the apparent loss of comparative advantage in high-tech products, and how the effective (productivity-adjusted) prices of manufactured prices of goods produced in the United States have not reduced the relative wage of unskilled US workers.

Export Overlap

We first explore the overlap between US manufactured exports and foreign exports to the United States using the data on commodity shares for 1990, 2000, and 2006. We concentrate on US trade in manufactured goods (NAICS 331–333),[2] dropping refined petroleum products from the data. We use the US trade data provided by Robert Feenstra, John Romalis, and Peter Schott (2002) and the United States International Trade Commission. The data are highly disaggregated. There are about 9,000 export codes and approximately 12,000 import codes.

To exploit the US data we assume that the goods foreigners export to the United States are representative of the goods they generally export to the rest of the world. This allows us to base our comparison of trade flows using the most disaggregated trade data available—namely the 10-digit HTS level. Schott (2008) pursues a similar approach in his analysis of the sophistica-tion of Chinese exports. Further, other research using much more aggregated 6-digit export data corroborates the findings presented in this chapter.[3]

---

2. NAICS is the North American Industry Classification System.

3. See the very detailed study by Lionel Fontagné, Guillaume Gaulier, and Soledad Zignago (2008), who find a high degree of international specialization within products, especially for trade between advanced and emerging-market economies. Andre Frauenknecht (2009) compares US and Chinese exports to 10 EU countries and six emerging Asian economies at the 6-digit level of the Harmo-

The overlap between US manufactured exports and foreign exports is calculated using an export similarity index. The similarity index involves (1) calculating shares of each commodity, (2) summing the absolute difference in these shares, (3) dividing the result by two, and (4) subtracting that result from unity.[4] If X_i is the share of commodity i in imports from country X and Y_i the share of commodity i in imports from country Y, then the absolute difference in the share of each commodity is first calculated.

$$|X_i - Y_i|. \tag{4.1}$$

The sum of these differences is then divided by two and subtracted from one to provide a similarity index SI_{XY} between X and Y that equals zero when the two series are completely different and one when they are completely similar.

$$SI_{XY} = 1 - \Sigma_i |X_i - Y_i|/2. \tag{4.2}$$

Consider, for example, if there were just two commodities and two countries. If each fully specialized in exporting one of the products, and both exported the same product, the second part of this expression would equal zero and thus subtracting zero from one would give us one, perfect overlap. If each exported a different product, the value of the second half would equal one, which subtracted from one would equal zero, indicating no overlap.

One weakness in the measure is that it is sensitive to the level of disaggregation. Accordingly, we have calculated these indices at the most disaggregated level possible, the 10-digit HTS level when comparing imports and the 6-digit level of the Harmonized System (HS) when analyzing US exports.[5]

Table 4.1 reports the various export similarity indices for a selection of developed and developing countries in 1990, 2000, and 2006. "Developing countries" here include all low- and middle-income economies defined according to the World Bank Income Classification System of 2007. Developed countries cover high-income economies.[6] The left side of the table compares

nized System (HS). He finds an increased overlap between Chinese and US exports to these regions, but also considerable overlap within product specialization. The mean unit value of US exports at the 6-digit level exceeds that of China's by a factor of 2–3 over the 1996 to 2006 period. Zhou Liu (2006) reaches similar conclusions.

4. An alternative approach developed by Michael Finger and Mordechai Kreinen (1979) sums the minimum share for each commodity and produces an index in which 100 implies complete similarity and zero no overlap. See also Sun and Ng (2000).

5. The HTS classification has been revised on numerous occasions to reflect the development of new products. To ensure comparability across time, we convert all the 10-digit HTS data to a time-consistent code using the concordance map developed by Justin Pierce and Peter Schott (2009). For similar reasons, the 6-digit HS code is converted to the 1988/92 revision.

6. Countries are divided among income groups according to 2006 gross national income per capita. The groups are low-income, $905 or less; lower-middle-income, $906–$3,595; upper-middle-income, $3,596–$11,115; and high-income, $11,116 or more. The high-income OECD category includes all OECD members prior to 2009, excluding Mexico, Poland, Slovakia, and Turkey.

Table 4.1   Export similarity indices for manufactured goods, ranked by similarity with high-income OECD countries in 2006

Country	Export similarity with high-income OECD country exports to the United States, 10-digit HTS level data				Export similarity with US exports, 6-digit HS level data			
	1990	2000	2006	Change, 1990–2006	1990	2000	2006	Change, 1990–2006
Vietnam	n.a.	0.03	0.08	n.a.	n.a.	0.04	0.07	n.a.
Hong Kong	0.22	0.19	0.18	−0.04	0.21	0.21	0.20	−0.01
India	0.08	0.13	0.18	0.10	0.09	0.15	0.21	0.12
Singapore	0.18	0.18	0.19	0.01	0.22	0.24	0.24	0.02
ASEAN 4	0.18	0.23	0.19	0.01	0.17	0.26	0.24	0.07
China	0.15	0.25	0.25	0.10	0.11	0.24	0.26	0.15
Taiwan	0.27	0.28	0.26	−0.01	0.27	0.33	0.31	0.04
Other developing	0.22	0.24	0.26	0.04	0.22	0.23	0.27	0.05
France	0.31	0.33	0.32	0.01	0.38	0.39	0.40	0.02
Mexico	0.33	0.41	0.39	0.06	0.30	0.37	0.37	0.07
United Kingdom	0.41	0.44	0.43	0.02	0.45	0.47	0.43	−0.02
Korea	0.28	0.34	0.44	0.16	0.23	0.30	0.34	0.11
Other developed	0.49	0.51	0.54	0.06	0.41	0.43	0.45	0.04
Japan	0.61	0.60	0.55	−0.06	0.42	0.46	0.40	−0.02
Germany	0.50	0.54	0.56	0.06	0.41	0.47	0.47	0.06
Canada	0.53	0.55	0.56	0.04	0.39	0.43	0.45	0.06

n.a. = not available

OECD = Organization for Economic Cooperation and Development; ASEAN = Association of Southeast Asian Nations

Note: Zero is completely different; higher numbers imply greater similarity. Processed petroleum products are excluded. The similarity indices based on high-income OECD countries use a time-consistent Harmonized Tariff Schedule (HTS) 10-digit code while the indices based on US exports use a time-consistent Harmonized System (HS) 6-digit code based on the 1988/92 revision of the HS. ASEAN 4 consists of Indonesia, Malaysia, the Philippines, and Thailand. The other developing countries category consists of the remaining low- and middle-income countries. The OECD category includes all OECD members prior to 2009 excluding Mexico, Poland, Slovakia, and Turkey.

Source: Authors' calculations based on US trade data obtained from Feenstra, Romalis, and Schott (2002).

US imports from these countries with US imports from high-income OECD countries. The right side compares the similarity of US imports with aggregate US exports.

The two different comparisons yield remarkably similar results in terms of both the level and trend of the indices. Focusing first on 2006, it is clear that among the sample of countries Vietnamese exports are the most different from those of the United States and high-income OECD countries. Next most different are those from Hong Kong and then India. China and the category of other developing countries occupy intermediate positions, while developed countries such as Germany, Japan, and the category of other developed countries have the most similar structure to US exports.

The ordering of export similarity is broadly consistent with GDP per capita. Exports from low-income countries display the least overlap with OECD exports and aggregate US exports, but exceptions are evident.[7] Surprisingly, perhaps, Hong Kong's export similarity with the OECD countries and the United States was very low in 2006 despite its high-income per capita status. This is consistent with Hong Kong specializing in the more sophisticated parts of global supply chains that produce labor-intensive products, e.g., contributing services like design and marketing to clothing and electronics produced in China. The composition of Korea's and Mexico's exports to the United States was more similar to aggregate OECD exports than France's export bundle (and the United Kingdom in the case of Korea) in 2006, but this ordering is reversed in the comparison with aggregate US exports.

The change in similarity over time is also interesting. The export similarity of China, India, and Korea with the OECD countries and the United States rose from 1990 to 2006. China, for example, rose from a low similarity position in 1990 to an intermediate position in 2006, but remains more similar to other developing economies than to developed countries, including the United States. A further observation is that almost the entire increase in China's export similarity took place between 1990 and 2000, with very little change in similarity from 2000 to 2006, a period when US imports from China rose dramatically.[8] Exports from Korea and India, in contrast, showed a steady increase in similarity with OECD and aggregate US exports in both periods.

Overall, the indices reveal a rising export similarity between many developing countries and the OECD and the United States, but the overlap remains low. The rising similarity is broadly consistent with improvements in per capita growth in these countries and does not necessarily reflect exceptional increases in competition with US exports in recent years. Further, developing-country export similarity with the United States continues to be far lower than for developed countries. Even developed countries show a high degree of dissimilarity with US exports (typically around 0.5).

A comparison of cumulative export shares to the United States in table 4.2 corroborates this finding. China has been the focus of considerable attention in the debate on the effect of emerging-market economies on US welfare. We have therefore ranked manufactured products according to their share in Chi-

---

7. Econometric estimates by Schott (2008) reveal a statistically significant association between GDP per capita and export similarity with the OECD. In Schott's simple regressions, China's export similarity to the OECD is greater than what would be predicted on the basis of its income per capita. However, China is no longer found to be an outlier after jointly controlling for size and level of development.

8. This is consistent with the findings in Amiti and Freund (2010) that most of China's export growth has taken place along the intensive margin.

Table 4.2 Cumulative shares of manufactured exports to the United States relative to China, 2006 (percent)

	Developing-country exports to the United States						High-income Asian country exports to the United States				Other high-income exporters	
China	ASEAN 4	Mexico	India	Vietnam	Other		Korea	Hong Kong	Singapore	Taiwan	OECD exports to the United States	US exports
5	10	0	0	0	0		0	0	1	1	0	0
10	13	2	0	0	0		13	1	4	5	2	1
15	21	3	0	3	1		19	2	20	14	3	2
20	24	12	1	3	1		21	3	20	19	4	2
25	25	15	1	11	2		21	3	21	19	4	3
30	32	15	1	12	2		22	5	39	20	4	4
35	38	17	3	19	3		22	10	40	22	5	4
40	40	18	3	22	3		23	11	42	25	6	5
45	50	20	4	30	4		31	14	55	37	7	9
50	52	23	6	37	9		33	27	56	44	8	11
55	56	27	21	45	14		36	48	56	47	11	13
60	64	29	22	47	15		37	53	58	50	12	14
65	67	33	26	53	17		41	56	59	54	14	16
70	69	36	33	57	21		42	63	59	59	15	17
75	73	41	39	63	24		43	66	60	62	17	18
80	76	48	42	70	29		47	74	62	67	21	23
85	79	52	46	77	35		50	77	63	71	24	28
90	84	56	68	84	43		56	85	65	79	31	35
95	89	64	77	93	52		62	92	73	86	40	43
100	100	100	100	100	100		100	100	100	100	100	100

OECD = Organization for Economic Cooperation and Development; ASEAN = Association of Southeast Asian Nations

Note: Calculated using US trade data at the Harmonized System 6-digit level (1988/92 revision). ASEAN 4 consists of Indonesia, Malaysia, the Philippines, and Thailand. The OECD category includes all OECD members prior to 2009 excluding Mexico, Poland, Slovakia, and Turkey.

Source: Authors' calculations based on US trade data obtained from Feenstra, Romalis, and Schott (2002).

nese exports to the United States in 2006 and then sorted the other countries' trade data by these rankings. We then cumulate the shares of foreign exports according to each percentile of Chinese rankings. Table 4.2 compares China's manufacturing exports to the United States with those of other countries according to these cumulative shares.

The data reveal the weak overlap in the export bundles of developing countries with the United States and other developed countries. Products that accounted for 50 percent of US imports from China in 2006 made up just 8 percent of US imports from high-income OECD countries and 11 percent of US exports. In contrast, these products accounted for 52 percent of US imports from the ASEAN 4 (Indonesia, Malaysia, the Philippines, and Thailand), 37 percent from Vietnam, but less than 10 percent from India and the category for other developing countries. Interestingly, these products made up 27 percent (Hong Kong) to 56 percent (Singapore) of US imports from selected high-income Asian economies, suggesting that the head-to-head competition is taking place between China and other countries within the Asian region rather than with other high-income economies, including the United States.

A similar story is evident if we look at products accounting for 80 percent of Chinese imports. These constituted just 21 percent of US imports from high-income OECD countries and 23 percent of US exports in 2006, but up to 76 percent of US imports from the ASEAN 4 and over 47 percent from the selected high-income Asian economies. It is clear that by and large the goods the United States imports from China are very different from those that it exports or that are exported to the United States by high-income countries outside of Asia. Most Chinese exports are not competing with the bulk of US or other developed-country exports, but they are competing with the rest of Asia. Support for this view is provided by Barry Eichengreen, Yeongseop Rhee, and Hui Tong (2007), who find that Chinese exports displaced those from less developed Asian economies in consumer goods (see also Blecker and Razmi 2009).

Unit Values

There has been some convergence in the composition of developed- and developing-country exports, but are the developing countries producing the same products in the categories in which exports overlap? To answer that question we turn to unit value data, which are obtained by dividing trade values in a particular category by a measure of quantity such as dozens or kilograms.[9] If

---

9. There are a number of data quality issues that arise in using this data. Errors in measurement can result in highly volatile unit value measures. The units of measurement are also not applied consistently over all periods and across countries. In what follows, we deal with outliers in unit values by eliminating the top and bottom 1 percent of data ranked according to price level. In constructing relative unit values, we also ensure that we only compare products measured using the same units.

US exports or imports from developed countries are similar to exports from developing countries in quality, composition, and price we would expect them to have similar unit values. But as we show, the unit values of US imports from developing countries are actually substantially lower than those of equivalent products imported from high-income OECD countries and products exported by the United States. Further, unlike the export similarity indices that indicate rising across-product similarity in developing-country exports with US exports, the unit value ratios reveal no such convergence. All told, these results suggest that although developing countries are increasingly exporting in categories in which developed countries also specialize, they are selling different and cheaper types of products.[10]

Our analysis is again based on annual data from 1990 to 2006. Unit values of imports from foreign countries are compared with import unit values from high-income OECD countries as well as unit values of aggregate US exports. In the comparison with the OECD countries, we first calculate the ratios of unit values using 10-digit data. We then weight the 10-digit unit value ratios by the annual share of each product in total US imports from high-income OECD countries.[11] For the comparison with US export unit values, only 6-digit HS data are available and we aggregate these using annual US export values as weights. The advantage of using OECD import unit values as the reference price is that we are able to present a much finer resolution of the relative price relationship.

Even at the 10-digit level, however, unit values are imprecise measures. In particular, relatively high values could indicate higher prices for similar products, higher quality, or within any product category a larger quantity of products with higher unit values. We try to condition for these effects later, but the simple relative unit value comparisons reported in table 4.3 are nonetheless quite remarkable and correlate very strongly with levels of development.

Our selected countries clearly group into two categories, particularly when import unit values are compared with US export unit values. The import unit values of high-income countries such as the United Kingdom, France, the category for other developed countries, Canada, Japan, and Germany on average equal or exceed US export unit values by up to 60 percent (figure 4.1). There is some movement in their relative price ratios over time, but in most cases the price relative to US exports is not too dissimilar in 2006 from 1990. US import unit values from Singapore are a striking excep-

---

10. A similar conclusion is reached by Fontagné, Gaulier, and Zignago (2008) in their cross-country comparison of unit values at the product level.

11. This measure therefore also captures the effect of changes in the US import bundle over time. The use of trade weights for a fixed period leads to the elimination of all products not exported in all years, but this does not alter the results much. The reason is that most of the growth in the value of imports from developing countries, including China, has been along the intensive margin since the early 1990s (Amiti and Freund 2010).

Table 4.3   Average unit values relative to OECD exports to the United States and aggregate US exports, ranked by price relative to the OECD countries in 2006

Country	Unit values relative to OECD exports			Unit values relative to US exports		
	1990	2000	2006	1990	2000	2006
United Kingdom	1.66	1.20	1.30	1.28	1.16	1.30
Singapore	1.04	0.96	1.19	0.64	0.93	1.19
Germany	1.38	1.02	1.07	1.20	0.97	1.06
Japan	1.13	1.11	1.05	1.02	1.06	1.08
Other developed	1.38	1.19	1.25	1.36	1.28	1.32
Other developing	0.74	0.89	1.00	0.97	0.95	1.08
Canada	1.06	0.94	0.84	0.94	0.99	1.00
France	1.50	1.03	0.83	1.53	1.19	1.29
ASEAN 4	0.53	0.63	0.65	0.44	0.42	0.40
Korea	0.59	0.62	0.59	0.46	0.52	0.61
Mexico	0.64	0.68	0.59	0.50	0.50	0.44
Taiwan	0.47	0.43	0.52	0.38	0.34	0.39
India	0.58	0.34	0.48	0.50	0.34	0.50
China	0.46	0.39	0.43	0.25	0.25	0.34
Vietnam	n.a.	0.17	0.37	n.a.	0.19	0.31
Hong Kong	0.65	0.41	0.32	0.46	0.42	0.35

n.a. = not available

OECD = Organization for Economic Cooperation and Development; ASEAN = Association of Southeast Asian Nations

Note: Unit values relative to OECD exports are based on Harmonized Tariff Schedule 10-digit-level data. Unit values relative to US exports are based on Harmonized System 6-digit-level data. The OECD category includes all OECD members prior to 2009 excluding Mexico, Poland, Slovakia, and Turkey. ASEAN 4 consists of Indonesia, Malaysia, the Philippines, and Thailand. The other developing countries category consists of the remaining low- and middle-income countries.

Source: Authors' calculations based on US trade data obtained from Feenstra, Romalis, and Schott (2002).

tion, rising from 64 percent of US export unit values in 1990 to 119 percent in 2006.

A second grouping covers the developing countries as well as some of the higher-income Asian economies such as Korea, Taiwan, and Hong Kong. Looking first at China, it is striking that Chinese import unit values at the product level have hardly changed relative to OECD imports and aggregate US exports over the entire period. On average, Chinese import unit values were 43 percent of OECD import values and 34 percent of US export unit values in 2006, insignificantly different from the relative unit values in the early 1990s.

Unit values of imports from India, Mexico, and the ASEAN 4 countries are also relatively low and stable, ranging from 40 to 60 percent of the price of US exports. The relative unit values of imports from Taiwan, Korea, and especially Hong Kong are surprisingly low, despite their relatively high per capita incomes. This has potentially important implications for the effect of

Figure 4.1 Weighted-average import unit values relative to US export unit values, 1990–2006

unit value (US = 1)

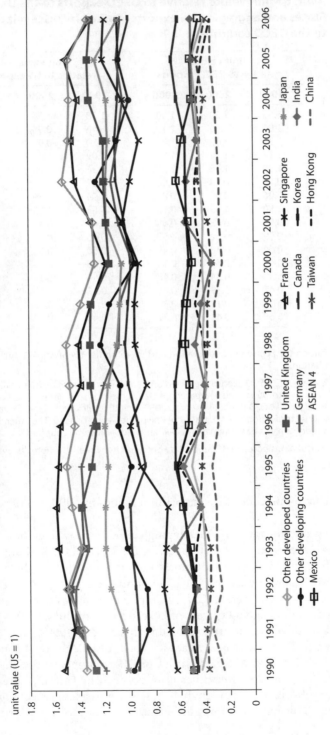

ASEAN = Association of Southeast Asian Nations

Notes: Calculated using 6-digit Harmonized System (1988/92 Revision) classification data and annual US exports as weights. ASEAN 4 consists of Indonesia, Malaysia, the Philippines, and Thailand. Foreign-country export unit values are calculated using US import data.

Source: Authors' calculations based on 6-digit Harmonized System classification data obtained from Feenstra, Romalis, and Schott (2002).

production fragmentation and outsourcing within the Asian region. According to our unit value data, widespread relocation of production from industrialized Europe or North America to Asia would be expected to raise within-product relative unit values in these countries. In contrast, production fragmentation driven by the relocation of production from newly industrialized Asian economies to their developing neighbors would have a much smaller impact on within-product unit values in the developing countries.

The one anomaly in these results is the category for other developing countries. These import unit values are very similar to US export unit values in all periods and show a slight increase relative to high-income OECD imports. This reflects a product composition effect: additional disaggregated analysis reveals that imports of nonpetroleum manufactures from other developing countries are concentrated in textiles and clothing (27 percent) and base metals (23 percent). As we show later in this chapter, these products show relatively small differences in prices across countries, including relative to US exports. The primary source of price differences across countries is in the machinery, transport, and specialized equipment sectors. Again, we explore this further in the disaggregated analysis presented later.

As reported in a working paper version of this chapter (Edwards and Lawrence 2010b), we have formally tested for the relationship between exporter income and within-product price variation using regression analysis. Our results confirm that relative unit values are explained well by per capita incomes.[12] However, we find that Chinese products trade at a substantial discount (29 log points) even after controlling for the country's GDP per capita, population, and other characteristics. This result is similar to that reported by Schott (2008), except that unlike his regressions, we find a significant discount even when population is included to capture greater production scale. Additional regressions also reveal no change in the Chinese discount over the period, a result that is consistent with the stable trends in unit values shown in figure 4.1. This suggests that Dani Rodrik's (2006) finding that Chinese exports are unusually sophisticated for their level of development needs to be qualified. The product categories in which Chinese exports fall may be unusually sophisticated, but judged by their unit values, the actual products they sell in these categories are not.

Technological Sophistication

The concern about emerging-market exports to the United States is not simply that they are becoming more similar to US exports in general but that the rising similarity has been driven by rapid increases in exports of "sophisticated" products from the United States. If production and export of sophisticated products stimulates an acceleration in overall growth of the economy and

---

12. See also Schott (2008) and Fontagné, Gaulier, and Zignago (2008).

supply of these very products, as is argued by Sanjaya Lall (2000) and Ricardo Hausmann, Jason Hwang, and Dani Rodrik (2007), then the sophistication of the current structure of exports is a foreshadow of competitiveness pressures that are to come.

What is meant by "sophistication" varies and can cover the use of sophisticated production processes to produce a standardized good or the export of goods that are themselves technologically advanced. Even the highly disaggregated product classification used by the US International Trade Commission cannot isolate the production process from product composition (Ferrantino et al. 2007). We are cognizant of this limitation. Nevertheless we use a product technology classification developed by Lall (2000) and refer the reader to the working paper version of this chapter (Edwards and Lawrence 2010b), where we find support for our argument using other product-level technology classifications: the advanced technology products classification developed by the US Census Bureau and an export measure developed by Hausmann and Rodrik (2003) that distinguishes products on the basis of the incomes of countries that export them.[13]

Lall (2000) classifies products at the 3-digit level of the SITC (Rev. 2) into primary products and resource-based, low-technology, medium-technology and high-technology manufactures.[14] Detailed descriptions and product examples for each of these categories are provided in table 4.4. In general, the skill requirements rise with the degree of technological complexity, although there are exceptions in all categories (e.g., among resource-based products, the synthesis of fuel from coal requires skill-intensive technologies).

Table 4.5 outlines the 1990 and 2006 share structure of US manufacturing imports for China, other developing countries, and high-income OECD countries according to Lall's (2000) technology classification. The table reveals the diverse patterns of specialization across regions as well as the remarkable shift in the composition of US imports from low- and middle-income countries toward medium- and high-technology products. High-income country exports to the United States are concentrated in medium- and high-technology manufactures and there has been little change in this structure over the full period.

Contrast this with Chinese exports to the United States. In 1990, 74 percent of US imports of manufactured goods from China were made up of low-technology products (mainly clothing) and only 7 percent of high-technology products. By 2006, high-technology products accounted for 35 percent of US imports of manufactured goods from China, with all of the increase attributable to electronics and electrical products. The share of high-technology

---

13. Sanjaya Lall, John Weiss, and Jinkang Zhang (2005) develop an alternative sophistication measure based on the income level of the exporting country. Conceptually, the approach is similar to that of Hausmann and Rodrik (2003) and therefore is not included in the analysis.

14. SITC is the Standard International Trade Classification.

Table 4.4 Lall (2000) technology classification of exports

Category	Product examples	Description
Primary products	Fresh fruit, meat, rice, cocoa, tea, coffee, wood, coal, crude petroleum, gas, and metals	Manufactures tend to be simple and labor intensive or intensive in use of natural resources.
Manufactured products		
Resource-based manufactures (RB)		
RB1: Agro/forest-based products	Prepared meats/fruits, beverages, wood products, and vegetable oils	
RB2: Minerals-based products	Ores and concentrates, petroleum/rubber products, cement, cut gems, and glass	
Low-technology manufactures (LT)		Manufactures tend to be undifferentiated products that compete on price (hence labor costs are important) and are produced using stable, well-diffused technologies.
LT1: "Fashion cluster"	Textile fabrics, clothing, headgear, footwear, leather manufactures, and travel goods	
LT2: Other low technology	Pottery, simple metal parts/structures, furniture, jewelry, toys, and plastic products	
Medium-technology manufactures (MT)		Products comprise the bulk of skill- and scale-intensive technologies in capital goods and intermediate products and tend to have complex technologies, with moderately high levels of R&D, advanced skill needs, and lengthy learning periods.
MT1: Automotive products	Passenger vehicles and parts, commercial vehicles, motorcycles and parts	
MT2: Process industries	Synthetic fibers, chemicals and paints, fertilizers, plastics, iron, and pipes/tubes	
MT3: Engineering industries	Engines, motors, industrial machinery, pumps, switchgears, ships, and watches	
High-technology manufactures (HT)		Products have advanced and fast-changing technologies, with high R&D investments, and require sophisticated technology infrastructures and high levels of specialized technical skills.
HT1: Electronics and electrical products	Office/data processing/telecommunication equipment, TVs, transistors, turbines, and power-generating equipment	
HT2: Other high technology	Pharmaceuticals, aerospace, optical/measuring instruments, and cameras	
"Special" transactions	Electricity, cinema film, printed matter, art, coins, pets, and nonmonetary gold	

Source: Lall (2000).

Table 4.5 **Share structure of US manufacturing imports by technology classification, 1990 and 2006** (percent)

Category	1990			2006		
	China	Other developing countries	High-income OECD countries	China	Other developing countries	High-income OECD countries
Primary product manufactures	1	10	5	1	8	5
Resource-based manufactures (RB)	3	20	17	5	13	18
RB1: Agro/forest-based products	1	13	12	3	8	11
RB2: Other resource-based products	2	7	6	2	5	7
Low-technology manufactures (LT)	74	36	14	38	29	9
LT1: "Fashion cluster"	56	29	7	23	22	3
LT2: Other low technology	18	7	7	15	7	7
Medium-technology manufactures (MT)	17	26	53	22	33	56
MT1: Automotive products	0	7	30	2	14	34
MT2: Process industries	2	5	6	3	7	8
MT3: Engineering industries	14	13	17	17	13	15
High-technology manufactures (HT)	7	18	15	35	25	17
HT1: Electronics and electrical products	6	17	14	34	23	9
HT2: Other high technology	1	1	2	1	1	9
"Special" transactions	0	1	1	1	1	1

OECD = Organization for Economic Cooperation and Development

Note: Some products classified by Lall (2000) as primary products fall under North American Industry Classification System (NAICS) 331-333 and are hence included as primary product manufactures in the table. The OECD category includes all OECD members prior to 2009 excluding Mexico, Poland, Slovakia, and Turkey.

Source: Authors' calculations based on US trade data obtained from Feenstra, Romalis, and Schott (2002) and the technology classification developed by Lall (2000).

products in US imports from the category other low- and middle-income countries also rose, but at a slower pace, from 18 to 25 percent.[15]

---

15. A comparable picture emerges when analyzing the United States according to the alternative technology classifications. Rodrik (2006), for example, finds that China's export profile to the world in the early 1990s was associated with an income level more than six times higher than its per capita GDP at the time. When we replicate his study for manufacturing products (Edwards and Lawrence 2010b), we find that US imports from other developing countries including Thailand,

Figure 4.2   China's export unit values relative to US export unit values, 1990–2006

unit value (US = 1)

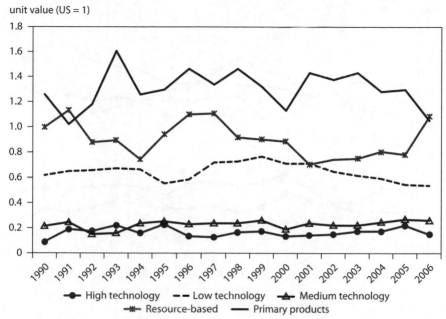

—●— High technology   — — Low technology   —▲— Medium technology
—✳— Resource-based   —— Primary products

Note: For each country, relative unit values are aggregated up using annual US exports are weights. The group "Primary products" reflects manufactures (North American Industry Classification System [NAICS] 331–333) classified as primary products by Lall (2000).

Source: Authors' calculations based on 6-digit Harmonized System classification data obtained from Feenstra, Romalis, and Schott (2002).

Again the rising technology intensity of developing-country exports (especially China) to the United States appears to confirm concerns about head-to-head competition with the United States in those products where America has a comparative advantage. However, as discussed earlier, import values obscure a high degree of within-product specialization. We therefore reevaluate the apparent rise in sophistication of developing-country exports to the United States using unit value data.

Figures 4.2 to 4.4 present the weighted-average unit value of US imports relative to US exports of manufactured goods for the period from 1990 to 2006. Figure 4.2 focuses on US imports from China, figure 4.3 focuses on import unit values from developing countries as a group, and figure 4.4 looks at import unit values from high-income OECD countries. In all cases, relative prices are first calculated at the 6-digit HS level and then aggregated up using annual US ex-

Mexico, Malaysia, Korea, India, and Indonesia are also more sophisticated than what is predicted on the basis of their per capita incomes.

Figure 4.3 Developing-country export unit values relative to US export unit values, 1990–2006

unit value (US = 1)

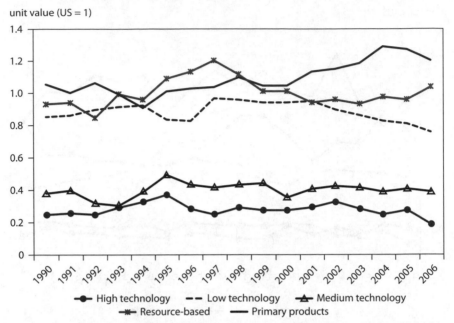

Note: For each country, relative unit values are aggregated up using annual US exports as weights. Weighted averages for regions are calculated by aggregating the country-level average using total bilateral import values as weights. The group "Primary products" reflects manufactures (North American Industry Classification System [NAICS] 331–333) classified as primary products by Lall (2000).

Source: Authors' calculations based on 6-digit Harmonized System classification data obtained from Feenstra, Romalis, and Schott (2002).

port values as weights. We are therefore comparing average within-product price differences assuming that the structure of trade reflects that of US exports.[16]

We first look at unit values of US imports from China and other developing countries relative to the price of US exports. The relative price measures group neatly into two categories. The relative prices of resource-based, low-technology, and primary manufactures range between 0.5 and 1.4 for China and 0.8 and 1.3 for all developing economies. This is to be expected, as these products, particularly resource-based ones, tend to be relatively undifferentiated.

Medium- and high-technology products are different. The unit values of US imports from China of these products lie between 15 and 30 percent of the equivalent products exported by the United States. Further, remarkably, there has been no significant movement in these relative prices over the en-

---

16. Note that the relative unit-value measures do not account for across-product specialization that was captured in our similarity index measures and therefore underrepresent the overall degree of specialization.

Figure 4.4 High-income OECD export unit values relative to US export unit values, 1990–2006

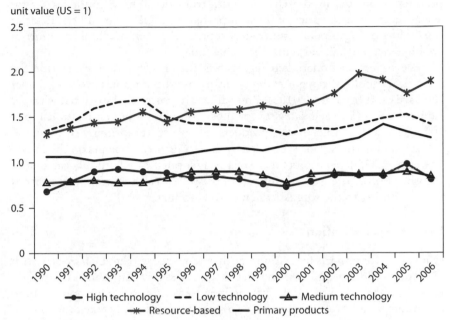

unit value (US = 1)

- ● High technology
- -- Low technology
- △ Medium technology
- ✳ Resource-based
- — Primary products

OECD = Organization for Economic Cooperation and Development

Note: For each country, relative unit values are aggregated up using annual US exports as weights. Weighted averages for regions are calculated by aggregating the country-level average using total bilateral import values as weights. The group "Primary products" reflects manufactures (North American Industry Classification System [NAICS] 331–333) classified as primary products by Lall (2000).

Source: Authors' calculations based on 10-digit Harmonized Tariff Schedule classification data obtained from Feenstra, Romalis, and Schott (2002).

tire 16 years covered in the sample. Looking at the average for all developing countries, the level of relative prices is slightly higher than for China alone, but there is also no change in the trend over time.

Contrast these figures with figure 4.4 comparing the unit values of US imports from high-income OECD countries with aggregate US exports. US imports of medium- and high-technology manufactures from high-income OECD countries are on average 80 percent of the unit value of the equivalent product exported by the United States. Import unit values of resource-based, low-technology, and primary manufactures are 30 to 90 percent higher (and increasing over time for resource-based products) than the equivalent aggregate US export price.

We have undertaken numerous exercises to confirm that these findings are not a particular outcome of our choice of technology classification, reference price, or weights. For example, we replicate these findings if we focus on China's top 30 export industries (box 4.1) and if we use import unit values from high-income OECD countries at the 10-digit level as the reference price and log mean shares as weights (table 4.6).[17] We see that high-technology products imported by the United States from developing countries are on average a third of the price of those imported from OECD members. Relative unit values of imports of resource-based products from developing countries are higher at 0.6–0.7, but remain less than one.[18]

We have also undertaken regressions that explain unit values for the various technology categories reported in our background working paper (Edwards and Lawrence 2010b). Unit values are positively associated with per capita incomes in each category for most countries, but the relationship is stronger for the sophisticated products relative to the primary-commodity-based manufactures. This is revealed by the stronger coefficients on the square of the log of GDP per capita for the relatively sophisticated product categories. In other words, the gap in unit values between wealthy and poor countries rises according to the sophistication of the product.[19]

Vertical Specialization

Our results for imports from China, both with respect to the small overlap with US exports and especially with respect to the low relative unit values of its high-tech products, are particularly striking because vertical specialization has been so prominent a feature of its trade.[20] This has predominantly taken the form of processing trade, where Chinese firms process or assemble imported intermedi-

---

17. We calculate the geometric average price inclusive of transport costs and tariffs relative to high-income OECD countries, where the OECD price is an import-weighted average price of OECD countries and weights on the relative price, wj_{ki}, are the logarithmic means of the import shares, normalized to sum to unity. Following Feenstra, Yang, and Hamilton (1999) the formula for the weights is:

$$w_{jki}(I_i) = \left(\frac{s_{ji}(I_i) - s_{ki}(I_i)}{\ln s_{ji}(I_i) - \ln s_{ki}(I_i)} \right) / \sum_{k \in I_j} \left(\frac{s_{ji}(I_i) - s_{ki}(I_i)}{\ln s_{ji}(I_i) - \ln s_{ki}(I_i)} \right),$$

where $s_{ji}(I_i)$ is the import share of product i in total US imports from country j or the OECD.

18. Classifying products according to the sophistication measure of Hausmann and Rodrik (2003) and the advanced technology products classification developed by the US Census Bureau leads to the same conclusion (Edwards and Lawrence 2010b): The more sophisticated the product is, the more the unit values of imports from developing countries decline relative to developed countries. We also independently replicate these findings using 6-digit HS level export data obtained from the UN Comtrade database. For example, we find that over the period 1996–2011, the unit values of Chinese exports were on average 90 percent of the unit values of US exports in primary products, 81 percent in resource-based products, 40 percent in low-technology products, 36 percent in medium-technology products, and 18 percent in high-technology products.

19. There is no significant price discount on imports of primary-product-based manufactures from China, but imports of high- and medium-technology products from China sell at 33 and 36 percent of the expected price, respectively.

20. Vertical specialization refers to the use of imported intermediate parts to create goods that are later exported. International trade arising from vertical specialization has become an increasingly important source of the growth in world exports since the 1970s (Hummels, Ishii, and Yi 2001).

Box 4.1 The United States and China: A disaggregated analysis

It is illuminating to take a closer look at the US-China data and see what they reveal about particular products. Table B4.1.1 presents a comparison of unit values, relative unit values, and cumulative trade shares for China's top 30 exports to the United States at the 6-digit level of the North American Industry Classification System (NAICS) in 2006. These products accounted for about 49 percent of all US manufactured imports from China.

Four of the top five Chinese industries and nine of the top 30 industries come from NAICS category 334, which covers computer and electronic products.[1] Apparel, textiles, and footwear products are also important, accounting for nine of the top 30 industries and 11 percent of the value of Chinese exports to the United States in 2006. The remaining categories are diverse. Computer and electronic products (334) constitute a sizable share of total US manufacturing exports (16.5 percent in 2006). Yet few of the large US export industries in the electronics sector are also prominent export industries for China. The strongest US performance in electronics was in semiconductors (334413), which constituted 4.3 percent of US exports in 2006, but only 0.6 percent of Chinese exports to the United States in 2007. Altogether, these top 30 Chinese export industries, which accounted for half of Chinese exports, accounted for only 13.6 percent of US manufac-

Table B4.1.1 Prices, relative prices, and cumulative trade shares of top 30 Chinese export industries in 2006

| NAICS code | Description | Units | Price per unit (US dollars) | | | Cumulative export share (percent) | | |
			China	High-income OECD	US exports	China	High-income OECD	US exports
334310	Audio and video equipment	Number	89	424	198	7	1	0
334111	Electronic computers	Number	652	1,901	2,490	13	1	1
334119	Other computer peripheral equipment	Number	113	508	907	18	2	2
334220	Radio, TV broadcasting and wireless equipment	Number	96	164	493	22	3	3
316214	Women's footwear (except athletic)	Pairs	8	52	19	24	3	3
333313	Office machinery	Number	84	1,939	757	26	3	3
335211	Electric housewares and household fans	Number	12	86	77	28	4	3
315239	Women's & girls' cut and sew outerwear	Dozen	82	247	73	30	4	3
316219	Other footwear	Pairs	8	37	15	31	4	3
331111	Iron and steel mills	Kilograms	1	1	2	32	6	4
315232	Women's & girls' cut and sew blouses and shirts	Dozen	84	143	29	33	6	4

(box continues next page)

Box 4.1 The United States and China: A disaggregated analysis
(continued)

Table B4.1.1 Prices, relative prices, and cumulative trade shares of top 30 Chinese export industries in 2006 *(continued)*

NAICS code	Description	Units	Price per unit (US dollars)			Cumulative export share (percent)		
			China	High-income OECD	US exports	China	High-income OECD	US exports
314129	Other household textile product mills	Number	5	11	7	34	6	4
316991	Luggage	Number	3	53	8	36	6	4
316213	Men's footwear (except athletic)	Pairs	14	53	35	37	6	4
334112	Computer storage devices	Number	35	211	1,495	38	6	5
332999	Other miscellaneous fabricated metal products	Kilograms	3	8	7	39	7	5
337127	Institutional furniture	Number	37	105	103	40	7	5
315234	Women's and girls' cut and sew suits, coats, skirts	Dozen	100	804	95	40	7	5
334418	Printed circuit assembly (electronic)	Number	30	58	28	41	7	5
335129	Other lighting equipment	Number	3	76	36	42	8	5
334419	Other electronic components	Number	9	52	126	43	8	6
336399	All other motor vehicle parts	Number	12	7	49	44	10	6
335121	Residential electric lighting fixtures	Number	10	100	46	44	10	6
326211	Tires (except retreading)	Number	39	78	89	45	10	6
335221	Household cooking appliances	Number	73	293	344	46	10	6
334210	Telephone apparatus	Number	39	365	963	46	10	6
325199	All other basic organic chemicals	Kilograms	7	31	4	47	12	9
334413	Semiconductor and related devices	Number	2	4	3	47	14	14
337121	Upholstered household furniture	Number	85	206	114	48	14	14
316992	Women's handbags and purses	Number	7	145	24	49	14	14

NAICS = North American Industry Classification System; OECD = Organization for Economic Cooperation and Development

Note: Products are classified according to multiple units, even within the NAICS 6-digit classification. The values in the table correspond to the unit associated with the largest Chinese trade flow within each product category. Price levels at the 6-digit NAICS level are constructed by weighting up unit values at the 10-digit HTS level (OECD and China) and 6-digit HTS level (United States) using trade values as weights.

Source: Authors' calculations based on 10-digit US Harmonized Tariff Schedule classification data obtained from Feenstra, Romalis, and Schott (2002).

(box continues next page)

turing exports in 2006 and 13.8 percent of exports from high-income countries of the Organization for Economic Cooperation and Development (OECD) to the United States.

Further, where there is an overlap, the unit values of the Chinese products are considerably lower than the equivalent US or OECD exports. For example, the average price per unit of audio and video equipment (334310), the top import industry from China in 2006, was $89. The comparable price of US exports in this industry was $198 and $424 for high-income OECD imports. There are very few instances (five) where the Chinese price exceeds that of the United States or the OECD (one). If we weight up the relative price data using Chinese import values as weights, all of these top products are on average 32 percent of the price of equivalent high-income OECD imports and 44 percent of the price of equivalent US exports.

1. They include audio and video equipment (334310), 6.6 percent of 2006 exports; electronic computers (334111), 6 percent; other computer equipment (334119), 5.1 percent; and wireless communications equipment (334220), 4.4 percent.

ate inputs and then export the finished product to the international market. Processing exports have accounted for more than 50 percent of Chinese exports since at least 1996 (Koopman, Wang, and Wei 2008) and have been an important driver of export growth over the past decade (Wang and Wei 2010).

Vertical specialization has important implications for our analysis of head-to-head competition between developed and developing countries in international trade. The production of exports involves multiple stages located in multiple countries. The source country is not necessarily the country where most of the value is added. For example, in the Chinese processing trade close to 60 percent of the inputs are sourced from other Asian economies, including Japan, Hong Kong, Taiwan, Korea, and Singapore (Dean, Fung, and Wang 2007). These economies form an "Asian supply network for China's global production sharing" (Dean, Fung, and Wang 2007, 10). The United States is also an important input supplier, including the supply of innovation, product design, software development, and many other inputs.

Take, for example, the iPod that Taiwanese firms located in China assemble for export to the United States. In a detailed breakdown of production costs, Greg Linden, Kenneth Kraemer, and Jason Dedrick (2009) find that the value added attributable to producers in China of the 30GB video model in 2005 was just under $4 of the $150 factory cost. The remaining factory costs are made up of the various intermediate inputs that are sourced from Japan, Taiwan, Korea, and the United States. In terms of value capture, the United States dominates, capturing $87 (or $162 if the product is sold in the

Table 4.6 Comparison of average relative import unit values by technology classification using log mean share weights, 1990–2006 (US = 1)

Country/grouping	High technology		Medium technology		Low technology		Resource-based		Primary products	
	1990–95	2001–06	1990–95	2001–06	1990–95	2001–06	1990–95	2001–06	1990–95	2001–06
Price relative to the United States										
China	0.101	0.155	0.149	0.152	0.633	0.572	0.682	0.582	0.885	1.063
Low- and middle-income countries	0.287	0.261	0.382	0.366	0.836	0.794	0.959	0.964	1.005	1.207
High-income countries	0.672	0.853	0.787	0.85	1.259	1.301	1.506	1.897	1.074	1.301
Price relative to OECD countries										
China	0.184	0.192	0.247	0.24	0.374	0.351	0.574	0.414	0.659	0.769
Low- and middle-income countries	0.317	0.292	0.517	0.526	0.428	0.392	0.702	0.597	0.789	0.842

Notes: The average is calculated as the exponent of the average log relative price. Country- level averages are constructed using log mean share weights. The averages for low- and middle-income countries are the import-weighted average of the country values.

Source: Authors' calculations based on US trade data obtained from Feenstra, Romalis, and Schott (2002) and the technology classification developed by Lall (2000).

United States) of the $190 gross profit associated with the sale of the iPod. The retail price of the iPod was $299.

In high-technology products, vertical specialization is especially prominent (Amador and Cabral 2009; Dean, Fung, and Wang 2007).[21] For example, processing exports make up 90 percent of Chinese exports of advanced technology products to the United States, with almost all of this produced by foreign-invested enterprises (Ferrantino et al. 2007). Indeed, the share of domestic value added in Chinese exports declines the more sophisticated the product becomes.[22] At the extreme are Chinese exports of computers and accessories, where the domestic value added is only 4.6 percent, but domestic value added is also low in other high-tech products including telecommunications equipment (14.9 percent); cultural, office, and other computer peripheral equipment (19.1 to 19.7 percent); electronic elements and devices (22.2 percent); and radio, television, and communications equipment (35.5 percent).

It is the Chinese exports of these products to the United States that have increased rapidly and raised concerns about head-to-head competition. Yet our price analysis indicates that despite the fact that these products contain a high share of value added that comes from more developed countries, they have much lower prices than products in the same categories that are imported from developed countries.

Price Dispersion by Technology Classification

High-tech products are those evolving the most rapidly, and we might expect a systematic relationship between the scope for product differentiation and the technological intensity of the product. To explore this further, we compare the cross-country dispersion of US import unit values across Lall's technological categories. Using 2006 US import data for manufactured goods at the 10-digit HTS level, we first divide US import unit values of each product from each country by the mean US import unit value of that product from all countries. We then take the natural logarithm of these demeaned import unit values such that, within each 10-digit product, average priced imports have a value of zero, more expensive imported products have a positive value, and lower-priced imports have a negative value.[23] The data are then used to construct the box plot diagrams presented in figure 4.5.

---

21. One reason for the dramatic increase in processing trade in high-tech products is the multilateral reduction in tariffs on information technology products from 1997 to 2000 as a result of the Information Technology Agreement enforced by the WTO. This led to an increase in varieties of information technology products imported (sourced from new countries) as well as a magnified reduction in prices (Feenstra, Yang, and Hamilton 2009).

22. Robert Koopman, Zhi Wang, and Shang-Jin Wei (2008) estimate that the foreign content of China's total exports is about 50 percent, but is 80 percent or more for sophisticated products where processing trade is high.

23. Relative unit values (RUV) are calculated as $RUV_{i,c,t} = \ln(UV_{i,c,t} / \frac{1}{N}\sum_{c=1}^{N} UV_{i,c,t})$, where i denotes HTS 10-digit product, c denotes country, and t denotes time.

Figure 4.5 Cross-country dispersion of US import unit values by technology classification, 2006

ln unit values (mean unit value = 0)

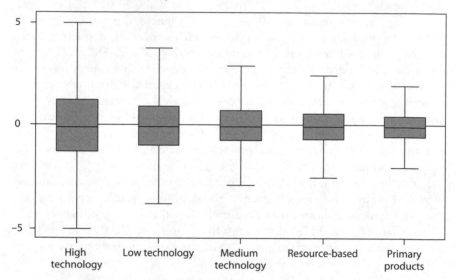

Note: The box plot is based on 2006 US import data with relative unit values calculated at the 10-digit level of the Harmonized Tariff Schedule. The box is bounded by the first and third quartile value. The upper adjacent limit is the largest data value that is less than or equal to the third quartile plus 1.5 x the interquartile range. The lower adjacent limit is the smallest data value that is greater than or equal to the first quartile minus 1.5 x the interquartile range. The adjacent limits are denoted by the horizontal bars at the top and bottom of each plot.

Source: Authors' calculations based on 10-digit Harmonized Tariff Schedule classification data obtained from Feenstra, Romalis, and Schott (2002).

These box plot diagrams conveniently illustrate the relationship between import price dispersion and the technology intensity of the product. The shaded box in each box plot depicts the interquartile range between the 25th and 75th percentiles of the demeaned import unit values. Also shown are the upper and lower adjacent limits denoted by the horizontal bars at the top and bottom of each plot. The upper adjacent limit is the largest data value that is less than or equal to the third quartile plus 1.5 times the interquartile range. The lower adjacent limit is the smallest data value that is greater than or equal to the first quartile minus 1.5 times the interquartile range. The box plots therefore reveal the extent to which unit values of US imports at the 10-digit level are dispersed across countries.

What is immediately evident is that the cross-country dispersion of US import unit values rises according to the technological intensity of the product. Focusing on the shaded box in each diagram, there is a decline in the interquartile range as one moves from the high-technology category to the primary-product-classified manufactures. This is also true of the range between the upper and lower adjacent limits. As shown in Edwards and Lawrence (2010b), equivalent relationships are found when using alternative technology classifications, including the advanced technology product classifications of the US Census Bureau and a NAICS 6-digit industry-level classification based on the share of nonproduction workers. Sophisticated products in all cases are characterized by a greater scope for price differentiation.

Although we do not measure characteristics of products directly, the price variation suggests that imports from different countries differ enormously in terms of their characteristics, and that the scope to differentiate a product increases the more sophisticated the product.[24] Take, for example, motor vehicles that differ vastly according to characteristics such as motor size, number of doors, type of gearbox, styling, quality of components, etc. Contrast this with resource-based products such as steel bars where the scope to differentiate the product is more restrictive.

This association provides additional insights into the nature of the apparent head-to-head competition between developed and developing countries. The restructuring of developing-country imports that has raised concerns about increased competition with US exports has been concentrated in those sophisticated product categories where the scope to differentiate products according to price is higher. US firms are more able to insulate themselves from this competition if they can differentiate their products.

To conclude, there are vast and sustained differences in unit values between developed- and developing-country exports. This is suggestive of a high degree of within-product specialization with China and other developing countries producing relatively low-priced products and varieties. Changes in the composition of trade flows give the impression of rising head-to-head competition with the United States in high-technology sectors, but this is not corroborated by an increased similarity in prices. The difference in unit values between US exports and developing-country imports actually rises the more

---

24. The figures are consistent with an alternative explanation, namely that the classification systems are not sufficiently refined to distinguish between different products. This is likely to be particularly pronounced for high-technology products where rapid innovation leads to repeated introductions of new and different products. There is some evidence from the trade data to support this. Lall's high-technology category covered 1,302 HTS 10-digit product lines with an average of $247 million of imports per product line in 2006. In contrast, the low-technology category covered 5,202 product lines with an average of $41 million of imports per product. Low-technology products are therefore more precisely defined, which may explain their relatively low degree of price dispersion at the product level across countries. In effect, the relationship between the scope for product differentiation and technological sophistication that we identify may merely be a product of the classification system. Simple regressions, however, suggest that this is not entirely the case. In regressions explaining the standard deviation of relative import unit values, the coefficient on the skill intensity of industries remains significant and positive (i.e., the variation of relative import unit values rises according to the skill intensity of the industry) even after controlling for the number of HTS 10-digit product lines and the average value of imports by product line within each industry. Similar results are found when using an HS 6-digit version of the Hausmann and Rodrik (2003) export productivity measure.

sophisticated the product. What sustains this is a systematic relationship between the scope for price differentiation and the sophistication of the product. Developing countries are able to enter into the export market for technology-intensive products, but do so at the lower end of the price spectrum.

Intermediate Inputs versus Finished Products

Our analysis thus far rests on the assumption that prices are a good proxy for differences in product quality and characteristics and that the large price differences we find reflect specialization in distinct products.[25] Yet there are objections that we need to consider. The first is that the data are not sufficiently disaggregated and are biased because the price differences we find reflect the effects of vertical specialization.

Growth in world trade over the past few decades has far exceeded growth in global production. One reason is the rapid growth of trade in intermediate inputs driven by multinational firms as they outsource input processing to their foreign affiliates (Hanson, Mataloni, and Slaughter 2005). An outcome is global production networks in which the various stages of the production process are located in different countries across the globe.

This has implications for how we measure and compare unit values of products. Unit values reflect the price of the traded good and hence the various components and value-added services embodied in the product. Intermediate inputs will therefore have a lower price per unit than the price of the product that embodies these inputs. It may well be that the vast price differences we find between developed and developing countries simply reflect specialization by developing countries in the intermediate input stage of the vertical supply chain.

Our earlier analysis draws on highly disaggregated 10-digit HTS level trade data, and we are careful to ensure that we only compare unit values across countries of the same 10-digit product. Nevertheless, even these highly disaggregated categories may include both intermediate and final goods. For example, say that developed and developing countries produce identical rotors and motors that are classified as "parts for washing machines." Since rotors are used in making motors, we would expect them to be cheaper. But if the developing countries make more rotors and the developed countries make more motors, their average import unit values would be different only because of mix effects. Unfortunately, we are unable to disaggregate the 10-digit data any further and hence cannot isolate this bias from our analysis.

However, we can compare relative prices of intermediate and final goods within our technology categories. Our technology categories aggregate the 10-digit relative unit values *across* intermediate and final goods and this may also distort the extent to which prices differ. To account for this concern, we separate out intermediate inputs from final goods (capital goods and consumer

25. See also Schott (2004, 2008) and Fontagné, Gaulier, and Zignago (2008).

Table 4.7 Weighted-average unit values of developing-country exports relative to OECD exports, 1990–2006

Category	Capital goods	Consumption goods	Intermediate goods	Passenger vehicles	Total
High technology	0.29	0.25	0.36		0.30
Medium technology	0.37	0.32	0.60	0.81	0.51
Low technology	0.35	0.38	0.55		0.40
Resource-based		0.65	0.66		0.65
Primary products		0.73	0.82		0.80
Total	0.31	0.38	0.58	0.81	0.44

Notes: The data are aggregated up to the end-use groups using a Harmonized System (HS) 6-digit map obtained from the United Nations Statistical Division (2007). Relative prices for each end-use group within the Lall (2000) categories are calculated for each country using relative prices at the HS 10-digit level and log mean expenditure shares as weights. The average relative prices for all developing countries presented in the table are calculated using country-level import values as weights. Cells are left blank when the end-use and technology categories do not overlap (e.g., capital goods include no resource-based products).

Source: Authors' calculations based on US trade data obtained from Feenstra, Romalis, and Schott (2002), Lall's (2000) technology classification, and end-use categories obtained from United Nations Statistical Division (2007).

goods) within each of the Lall technology categories and explore whether the differences are still present when looking only at finished goods.[26] Passenger vehicles are presented separately as they are both a capital and consumer good.

Table 4.7 presents the weighted-average unit values of US imports from developing countries relative to US imports from high-income OECD countries for each of the end-use groups within the Lall technology categories. The data cover the period 1990–2006. We compare unit values against OECD countries because we want to use the most disaggregated trade data possible, i.e., the 10-digit HTS level data. Comparisons of import unit values against US export unit values yield comparable results.

In general, the unit values of developing-country and OECD imports are indeed more similar for intermediate goods than for capital or consumer goods, but the gap still remains considerable, particularly in high-technology products. Imports of all high-technology capital goods from developing countries are on average 29 percent of the price of the good imported from the OECD countries. For high-technology intermediate inputs, the relative price ranges from 30 to 45 percent. Other than high-technology consumer goods

---

26. The classification of final and intermediate goods is based on the United Nations Classification by Broad Economic Categories (BEC), which closely resembles the US International Trade Commission's End-Use Classification. The various subcategories are aggregated into categories that approximate the three classes of goods in the System of National Accounts: capital goods, intermediate goods, and consumer goods (United Nations Statistical Division 2007).

that make up less than 10 percent of high-technology imports, there is also no sustained trend in relative prices over time.

These results are broadly replicated for medium- and low-technology products. The largest differences in unit values between developing-country and OECD-country imports are in final consumer and capital goods and, in contrast to high-tech products, the price gap appears to be rising. As found earlier, the price difference is smaller the less sophisticated the product: import unit values of final and intermediate goods are more similar for resource-based and primary-product manufactures (0.6–0.9) than for high- and medium-technology products (0.2–0.6).

Our conclusion of substantial price differences between developed- and developing-country exports that rise according to the sophistication of the product is therefore robust to the further subdivision of these products into final and intermediate goods. Nevertheless, it may still be the case that the trade data are too aggregated to adequately separate out intermediate from final goods within each product line. However, further disaggregation is unlikely to alter our conclusion that developed and developing countries have specialized in different products. Further disaggregation may reveal evidence of greater similarity of import unit values for particular products, but at the same time, it will most likely reveal evidence of greater across-product specialization. As we saw earlier, the overlap between the top Chinese imports and OECD or US exports at the 6-digit to 10-digit level is already low. Further disaggregation would reduce the overlap even more.

The Question of Quality

Thus far we have used product-level price differences to identify whether imports from developing countries are distinct from those from developed countries. This approach implicitly assumes that if products are equivalent, arbitrage would ensure that their prices would converge. When products are homogeneous this seems reasonable. However, if products are differentiated and consumers value variety, market equilibrium can sustain price differences for different varieties of the same product. The implication for our price analysis is that the cross-country differences in product prices we find could reflect differences in production costs of very similar products and not necessarily differences in the type or quality of the product (Hallak and Schott 2008, Khandelwal 2010, Mandel 2010).[27] Chinese goods might not actually be less sophisticated or different but simply cheaper versions of very similar products.

The association between relative market shares and relative prices can help us sort out whether price differences actually reflect products that differ in quality or just in price. We would expect that if higher prices reflect more costly

---

27. Benjamin Mandel (2010) uses transaction-level data and finds that the high unit values in wealthier countries belie specialization in low-priced varieties in less-quality-differentiated sectors and specialization in high-price varieties in more quality-differentiated sectors.

Figure 4.6   Identifying relative quality from relative prices and relative quantity, data processing machines, 2006

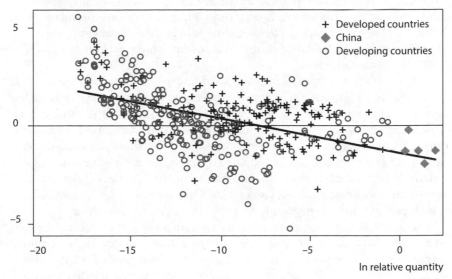

In relative price

In relative quantity

Source: Authors' calculations based on 10-digit Harmonized Tariff Schedule classification data obtained from Feenstra, Romalis, and Schott (2002).

products of a similar quality, market shares would fall, but where higher prices reflect higher quality, market shares should rise. Our approach to identifying whether price differences reflect quality differences or cheaper products, therefore, is to consider the market shares that are associated with given prices.

Our identification of quality is depicted in figure 4.6, a cross-country scatter plot of the (log) relative quantity and (log) relative price for data processing machines in 2006 (made up of HS 847120 and the subdivisions of HS 847190). There is clearly a negative relationship between relative price and relative quantity, the slope of which we can interpret as reflecting the price elasticity of substitution across the varieties in our sample. But the price-relative quantity combinations do not all fall on the regression line, and it is this variation—i.e., the deviations from the line—that we attribute to quality differences. For example, relatively high-quality varieties are situated to the right of (and above) the regression line, as the relative volume of imports exceeds what we would predict on the basis of relative price. Note also that in this example, it is the varieties from developed countries (indicated by +) that are mostly found in the high-quality domain. The Chinese products in the sample are cheap and have large market shares, but their close location to the line does not suggest that given their prices, their quality is unusual.

Based on this insight, as reported in greater detail in appendix 4A, we run regressions that detect unusual quality taking account of relative product prices, market shares, and a proxy for the number of varieties. This allows us to estimate where developing countries are located in the quality spectrum and whether this has changed over time. Figure 4.7 plots the unweighted mean (log) relative quality of (low- and middle-income) developing countries and (high-income) developed countries according to the various categories of Lall's classification system.

The average quality of all imports (solid line) from developed countries exceeds that of all imports (including developed and developing) by around 6 log points, and the premium has not changed significantly over the entire period. In contrast, the mean quality discount of imports from developing countries is around 11 log points, and apart from 1991 and 1992, there is also no discernible trend in the ratio. Thus developing countries, on average, not only export relatively low-priced varieties, but the quality of the varieties is relatively low, controlling for these relatively low prices.[28] This reinforces the conclusion that developed and developing countries specialize in different products.

There is also substantial quality heterogeneity across measures of product sophistication. In general, the relative quality of developing-country exports is lower in more sophisticated products. This holds for Lall's classification (resource-based products are an exception) as well as other measures of product-sophistication-based classifications presented in Edwards and Lawrence (2010b).

Conclusions

Using highly disaggregated trade data, we find that aside from natural-resource-intensive products such as steel, manufactured goods produced and exported by the United States and other developed countries are very different from those exported by developing countries in general and China in particular. Our analysis of unit values and relative quality reveals that even when they share similar product categories, these goods have a high degree of within-product specialization. Specialization is particularly high in sophisticated products in which developing countries have experienced considerable growth in exports. These exports are low-priced and low-quality varieties that differ

---

28. The degree of product specialization across developed and developing countries is actually greater than is implied by the relative quality results. The denominator in each relative quality observation covers all other countries, developed and developing. Similar quality levels among developing countries will therefore bias the log relative quality estimates toward zero. Further, the indicators only measure quality differences along the intensive margin (i.e., for products that overlap). The specialization by developed and developing countries in different products shown earlier is therefore not taken into account. Nevertheless, what is remarkable about the relative quality trend is that it has remained stable despite the increase in the range of products imported from developing countries over this period. The implication is that when developing countries export new products, they enter the market at the lower end of the quality spectrum.

Figure 4.7 Average relative product quality by technology classification for developed and developing countries, 1991–2006

a. Mean relative quality: Developed countries

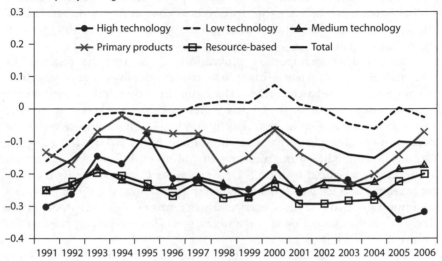

In relative quality (average = 0)

b. Mean relative quality: Developing countries

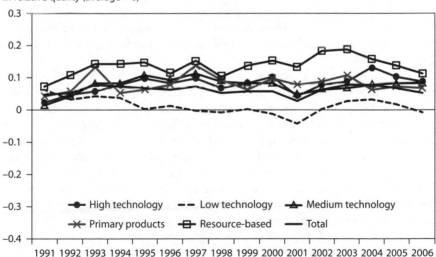

In relative quality (average = 0)

Note: Values reflect the cross-country simple average relative quality measure obtained from the 10-digit level of the Harmonized Tariff Schedule estimates for each of the Lall (2000) technology categories. A positive value indicates above-average levels of quality.

Source: Authors' calculations based on residuals from relative quality regression estimates.

substantially from those exported by high-income OECD countries and the United States. The scope for quality differentiation within these products is also higher than in less sophisticated products, but we find no evidence of within-product quality upgrading by developing countries on average in these technology-intensive products. Growth in exports from developing countries to the United States appears, therefore, to have come through increases in the supply of existing or very similar varieties, rather than through within-product upgrading of quality.

Our findings have important implications for the work that follows. The concerns raised by Paul Samuelson (2004) that developing-country growth reduces US welfare are based partly on the assumption that these countries have become competitors with the United States in export markets. But we have shown here that developing countries by and large do not compete with their developed-country counterparts in the same export markets. Indeed, great caution is required in using measures of "advanced technology" trade that are routinely produced by the US Department of Commerce in its monthly trade release to track performance. When imports from developing countries are important, trade balances, particularly in terms of high-tech products, are likely to involve comparing apples and oranges. This is especially the case for information technology products.

We point out in later chapters that the theory motivating Paul Krugman's[29] concern that trade with developing countries hurts unskilled workers assumes they export products that are perfect substitutes for those made in the United States. Empirical tests of the theory use US industry data to classify the skill intensity of US imports from developing countries. But the evidence we have produced indicates that developing-country exports are quite different products, and the products imported into industries that are classified as high-tech or skill-intensive may actually be quite standardized and unskilled-labor-intensive.

In concluding, we should acknowledge that while the evidence here casts doubt on the conventional (Stolper-Samuelson) theory that assumes domestic and imported products are perfect substitutes, it does not rule out the possibility that trade could cause wage inequality through other mechanisms. For example, this evidence *is* compatible with theories we discuss later (in chapter 8) that use the framework developed by Rudiger Dornbusch, Stanley Fischer, and Paul Samuelson (1980) to consider how factor returns are affected when specialization changes in countries that are fully specialized (Feenstra and Hanson 1996, Zhu and Trefler 2005).[30] This evidence is also compatible with forces that operate by influencing demand (Whalley and Abrego 2000).

---

29. Paul R. Krugman, "The Trouble with Trade; Keep Our Markets Open but Protect Those Who Get Hurt," *Pittsburgh Post-Gazette*, December 29, 2007, B-7.

30. Typically in these theories, two sets of countries are assumed: the North and the South. Initially, there is a cutoff point such that the more skilled-labor-intensive products are produced in the North and the more unskilled-labor-intensive in the South. They then consider a shock

Appendix 4A
Quality Measurement

Our approach to detecting quality considers the market shares that are associated with given prices. Where higher prices reflect more costly products of a similar quality, market shares should fall, but where higher prices reflect higher quality, market shares should rise. Based on this insight, our measure of relative quality is captured by the following relationship representing the consumption of goods (in category i) by US consumers from country j relative to any other country k:[31]

$$\ln(N_j x_j / N_k x_k) = -\sigma \ln(p_j / p_k) + \ln(N_j / N_k) + \sigma \ln(Q_j / Q_k),$$

where $N_j x_j / N_k x_k$ is the quantity of imports from country j relative to country k and is made up of symmetric varieties relative to k (N_j / N_k) (think different brands of similar products from each country relative to each other), and relative quantities of each variety (x_j / x_k). The variable p_j / p_k denotes relative prices, Q_j / Q_k denotes relative quality, and σ is the elasticity of substitution.

This relationship neatly captures three distinctive drivers of market share—price, variety, and quality—and demonstrates the problem of assuming that relative prices indicate relative quality. Price plays a role and consumers adjust to changes in the relative price of imports of equivalent quality by altering their relative consumption according to the elasticity of substitution (σ). Relative consumption differences could therefore sustain differences in prices, even though the quality of the products is equivalent. In addition, the number of varieties will also drive market share. And finally, consumer demand will be affected by relative quality.[32] Improvements in the relative quality of country j would raise demand for its products, even if prices and the number of varieties do not change. Quality in this model acts as a demand shifter.

The relationship also gives us insight into how firms may respond to competitive pressures. We do not develop the firm supply relationship (Hum-

---

(increased productivity in the South or capital inflows) such that the cutoff shifts, and production of the most unskilled-labor-intensive goods in the North shifts to the South, where they become the most skilled-labor-intensive products the South produces. Consequently, the relative demand for skilled labor goes up in both sets of countries.

31. This relationship is drawn from Hummels and Klenow (2005). Consumers maximize a Dixit-Stiglitz utility function:

$$U_m = \left[\sum_{j=1}^{J} \sum_{i=1}^{I} Q_{jmi} N_{jmi} x_{jmi}^{1-1/\sigma} \right]^{\sigma/(\sigma-1)} \quad \text{subject to } \sum_{j=1}^{J} \sum_{i=1}^{I} N_{jmi} p_{jmi} x_{jmi} \le Y_m,$$

where N_{jmi} is the number of symmetric varieties exported by country j to country m within category I, x_{jmi} is the quantity of each variety exported, Q_{jmi} is the quality of varieties exported, Y_m is country m's income, and p_{jmi} is the price of each unit. The first-order conditions give the optimal consumption relationship.

32. Note that relative demand is negatively related to quality-adjusted prices, $(p_j/Q_j)/(p_k/Q_k)$.

mels and Klenow 2005), but it is apparent from the relationship that there is a tradeoff between price and quality in supplying consumers with products. For example, firms in country j can offset a decline in relative demand associated with lower prices from country k by improving the quality of their products. The effect of import competition on output and employment of a firm is therefore influenced by the product market's scope for quality differentiation (Khandelwal 2010).

The consumer demand relationship forms the basis of our relative quality estimates using US import data. In the trade data, we observe total quantities Nx and prices, but not the number of varieties and quality. To identify relative quality, we use regression analysis. In particular, we estimate the following equation using data for the period 1990–2006:

$$\ln(RX_{jit}) = \beta_1 \ln(RP_{jit}) + \beta_2 \ln(rlabf_{jt}) + \beta_3 \ln(R\lambda_{jt}) + \mu_{it} + \varepsilon_{it},$$

where RP_{jit} is the geometric average of the cost, insurance, and freight (c.i.f.) price of product i (defined at the HTS 10-digit level) in country j relative to all other countries exporting that product to the United States.[33] RX_{jit} is the implicit relative quantity index calculated from the ratio of import values,[34] while $rlabf_{jt}$ is the geometric average of relative labor force which is used as a proxy for relative varieties.[35] The residual from the estimate, ε_{jit}, is interpreted as the measure of relative quality. In other words, we attribute relative import values in excess of what is predicted on the basis of prices and the labor force to the higher quality of the product.

The regression also includes a control for new product varieties, $R\lambda_{jt}$, defined at the 4-digit level of the SITC. Based on Feenstra, Yang, and Hamilton (1999) and Hummels and Klenow (2005), $R\lambda_{jt}$ measures the proportion of imports (at the SITC 4-digit level) from the rest of the world over which country

---

33. $RP_{ji} = \prod_{k \in K_{-j}} \left(\dfrac{p_{ji}}{p_{ki}} \right)^{w_{jki}},$

where K_{-j} is the set of all countries, excluding j, and the weights w_{jki} are the logarithmic means of the import shares, normalized to sum to unity. The formula for the weights is:

$$w_{jki}(I_i) = \left(\frac{s_{ji}(I_i) - s_{ki}(I_i)}{\ln s_{ji}(I_i) - \ln s_{ki}(I_i)} \right) \Big/ \sum_{k \in I_j} \left(\frac{s_{ji}(I_i) - s_{ki}(I_i)}{\ln s_{ji}(I_i) - \ln s_{ki}(I_i)} \right),$$

where $s_{ji}(I_i)$ is a constant fraction equal to one over the number of countries for which positive import data for product i are available ($s_{ji}(I_i) \equiv 1/N_{K_{-j}}$) and $s_{ki}(I_i)$ is the import share of product i from country k in total US imports from the sample of countries K_{-j} ($s_{ki}(I_i) \equiv p_{ki} N_k x_{ki} / \sum_{k \in I_i} p_{ki} N_k x_{ki}$).

34. $RIM_{ji} = RP_{ji} RX_{ji}$, where RIM_{ji} equals the value of US imports of product i from country j relative to its imports of i from all other countries.

35. This variable is suggested by a model in which each worker is a firm. Other studies such as Khandelwal (2010) and Hummels and Klenow (2005) use population as their proxy for variety. However, the relative labor force is a closer indicator of employment levels in each country. In practice, relative labor force and relative population are highly correlated.

j has an overlap.[36] This ratio rises with the importation of new products from country j (i.e., growth along the extensive margin). Intuitively, the introduction of new varieties by a country can be thought of as a reduction in the average price of imports from that country and hence is expected to have a positive impact on US demand for its products (Feenstra 1994).

Finally, 10-digit HTS product-by-year fixed effects, μ_{it}, are included to account for product-by-year specific trends in quality common to all countries. The inclusion of the fixed effect means that the regression explains within-product differences in relative output across countries.[37]

The regression equation is estimated for 648 categories of products defined at the 4-digit level of the SITC (Rev. 2). We use lagged relative prices as instruments for relative prices. This is necessary as optimizing firms simultaneously choose prices and quality (Hummels and Klenow 2005), implying a correlation between relative prices and the residual (relative quality). An alternative instrument is unit transport costs, but as argued by Armen Alchian and William Allen (1964) and estimated by David Hummels and Alexandre Skiba (2004), these are likely to be correlated with quality in our estimates, rendering them inappropriate for use as an instrument in our estimates.[38]

Summary statistics of the quality regressions are presented in table 4A.1. Overall the estimates are reasonably good. The average R-squared is 0.42 with a maximum of 0.9, and the first-stage F-statistic p-value is on average very low, indicating a generally significant association between the instrument (lagged relative price) and the relative price. The mean estimated elasticity of substitution is –1.75 and ranges from 3.58 to –16.39.[39] The relationships for the other variables are also consistent with expectations: relative import quantities from each country are positively associated with its relative labor force and increases in the range of products imported.

---

36. To be explicit, $R\lambda_{jt} = \lambda_{kt}/\lambda_{jt}$, where k denotes the rest of the world and, ignoring the number of symmetric varieties, $N\lambda_{kt} = \sum_{i \in I}p_{ki}x_{ki} / \sum_{i \in I_k}p_{ki}x_{ki}$ and $\lambda_{jt} = \sum_{i \in I}p_{jt}x_{ji} / \sum_{i \in I_j}p_{jt}x_{ji}$. The variable I is the set of products exported by both country j and k, while I_j and I_k are the set of products imported by the United States from country j and the rest of the world, respectively. In almost all cases, I_j is a subset of I_k with the result that $\lambda_{jt} = 1$.

37. The elasticity of substitution, β_1, is often interpreted as an indicator of horizontal differentiation (Broda and Weinstein 2006). In our estimates, we use the residual as an indicator of vertical differentiation across the quality spectrum.

38. Amit Khandelwal (2010) uses unit transportation costs, but exploits the within-product time variation of the variable, which he argues is less problematic than in estimates, such as ours, that exploit the cross-country variation within each product. An alternative instrument, ad valorem tariff rates, is also inappropriate as tariff levels interact with unit transportation costs to influence relative demand for high-quality goods (Hummels and Skiba 2004, Krishna 1987).

39. As in Khandelwal (2010), the (relative) quality of a country's exports is positively correlated with its GDP per capita. We find that the relationship with GDP per capita is stronger for high-technology products whether classified according to Lall (2000) or the US Census Bureau's advanced technology product classification. Unlike Khandelwal (2010), the estimated elasticities of substitution are significantly correlated with those estimated by Christian Broda and David Weinstein (2006), although the correlation coefficient is low.

Table 4A.1   Summary statistics of relative quality regression estimated at the SITC 4-digit level

	Mean value	Median value	1st quartile value	3rd quartile value	Maximum value	Minimum value
Relative *P* coefficient	−1.75	−1.70	−2.09	−1.26	3.58	−16.39
Relative *L* force coefficient	0.10	0.09	0.01	0.19	1.74	−1.68
Lambda ratio coefficient	2.52	2.17	0.71	3.76	85.07	−45.38
1st stage *F*-statistic *p*-value	0.01	0	0	0	0.98	0
Adjusted *R*-squared	0.42	0.44	0.32	0.54	0.90	−0.01
Observations per estimation	2,870	1,385	412	3,270	58,848	21
Fraction of estimations with statistical significance relative *P* coefficients	0.91	1	1	1		
Total estimations	647					
Total observations	2,602,020					

Notes: Summary statistics based on estimates using lagged relative price as instrument for current relative price.

Source: Authors' calculations based on relative quality regression estimated at the Standard International Trade Classification (SITC) 4-digit level.

We can also use our estimates to provide insight into product markets' scope for quality differentiation—or "quality ladders"—and hence the ability of US firms to respond to international competition by shifting into a differentiated product. Amit Khandelwal (2010), for example, finds that the decline in employment and output in US industries resulting from low-wage competition is substantially lower in industries characterized by long quality ladders.

Table 4A.2 presents various indicators of the scope for product differentiation according to technology classification. These indicators include the difference between the maximum and minimum relative quality, the 10th–90th percentile range of relative quality, and the standard deviations of relative quality and log unit values across countries, each calculated at the HTS 10-digit level. The table presents the mean of these product-level indicators across all countries and all periods.

We find that the scope for quality differentiation is greater in high-technology product categories, but only marginally more so than in the other technology categories that do not differ substantially from one another. For example, the mean ladder length of relative quality for high-technology products using the 10th–90th percentile range is 568 log points versus 494 to 519 log points for the other categories. The mean standard deviations in relative quality also do not differ widely across technology categories, although the deviation in relative quality is highest for high-technology products.

Contrast this with the much stronger positive relationship between price variation and sophistication shown in chapter 4 and in the mean standard deviations of relative unit values presented in the final column of table 4A.2.

**Table 4A.2   Indicators of quality differentiation by technology
classification, manufacturing sectors only**

Technology classification	Mean log ladder length	Mean log ladder length (10th to 90th percentile range)	Mean standard deviation relative quality	Mean standard deviation ln(unit value)
High-technology	7.24	5.68	2.35	1.76
Medium-technology	6.08	5.10	2.26	1.32
Low-technology	6.74	5.19	2.20	1.06
Resource-based	5.98	5.15	2.30	1.16
Primary product manufactures	5.66	4.94	2.29	0.97

Source: Authors' calculations based on residuals from relative quality regression estimates.

The relationship between the scope to differentiate products of equivalent quality horizontally and product sophistication is therefore stronger than the relationship between the scope for quality differentiation (vertical differentiation) and product sophistication.

Further, note that the variation in relative quality of US imports across countries far exceeds the variation in relative unit values. What this indicates is that the scope for quality differentiation far exceeds the scope to differentiate the product horizontally.

We are also interested in where individual countries are located in the quality spectrum and whether their position has changed over time.

The indicators of average quality in figure 4.7 mask large trends in relative quality at the country level. These trends are evident in figure 4A.1, which presents the average relative quality of all products for selected countries over the full period. The trends for sophisticated products are very similar (they are slightly more pronounced) (Edwards and Lawrence 2010b), so we focus on the average for all products.

What is noticeable is that there are contrary trends in relative quality across the sample of countries. Most obvious is the rapid increase in relative quality from China, followed by Mexico. Over the period 1991–2006, the estimated quality of Chinese imports rose by an astounding 124 log points and imports from Mexico by 47 log points. In contrast, estimates of relative quality declined for many of the Asian economies including Japan, Taiwan, the ASEAN 4, Korea, Singapore, and Hong Kong.

These dramatic changes in relative quality reflect far greater changes in relative import quantities than could be predicted from changes in relative prices. This is very apparent for imports of technology-intensive products from China. For example, consistent with our earlier analysis, the simple average price of high-technology products imported from China is 16 to 19 percent of other countries, and the average did not change much between

Figure 4A.1 Average product-level relative quality for selected countries, 1991–2006

In relative quality (average = 0)

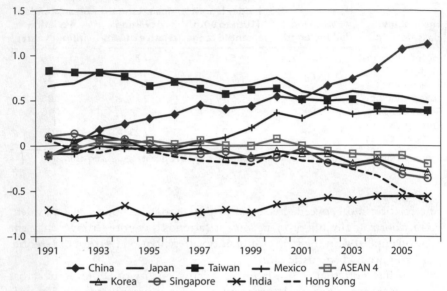

ASEAN = Association of Southeast Asian Nations

Notes: Values reflect the simple averages of the 10-digit Harmonized Tariff Schedule–level estimates of relative quality. All products are included. ASEAN 4 consists of Indonesia, Malaysia, the Philippines, and Thailand.

Source: Authors' calculations based on residuals from relative quality regression estimates.

1990 and 2006. The average quantity of imports at the HTS 10-digit level, however, increased dramatically from 7 times the quantity of imports from other countries in 1991 to 126 times the amount in 2006. The implication is that our estimates predict an exceptionally strong rise in the relative quality of the goods imported from China. This outcome is not unique to our estimates. Mary Amiti and Amit Khandelwal (2009) find that China was the quality leader in 44 percent of the total number of products it exported to the United States in 2005.

We identify two possible explanations for these trends, both of which suggest that caution should be exercised when analyzing relative quality at the country level using residual-based approaches such as ours and that of Khandelwal (2010).[40] The first explanation is that the constant elasticity of

40. Another problem is that the model imposes a constant elasticity of substitution over the entire period and assumes that the income and other price elasticities of demand for the products are equal. Reestimating the equations over shorter periods and at the HTS 10-digit level in an attempt to deal with these concerns does not alter our finding.

substitution function requires that products be sufficiently similar such that the reaction to demand for each product to other economic variables is identical, but also dissimilar enough for consumers to purchase both (Leamer and Stern 1970, 58). The degree of within-product variation of prices (and estimated quality) suggests that this assumption may not hold. In effect, the results may be picking up evidence of specialization by countries in different products, even within the narrowly defined HS 10-digit product categories.

A second and more plausible explanation is that these estimates of relative quality are distorted by processing trade.[41] The fragmentation of the production process leads to a change in the geographical sourcing of imports without commensurate changes in relative prices. Treating the residual in the estimates as a measure of quality therefore erroneously attributes these changes to changes in relative quality. This is particularly problematic if we are interested in analyzing changes in relative quality on a country-by-country basis. However, looking at the average effect for the full sample of countries is less problematic, as the outsourcing effects on relative quality offset each other. For example, we would measure a decline in Taiwan's relative quality and a rise in China's relative quality as Taiwan shifts production to the mainland. The average relative quality of both countries pooled together, however, should not change.

---

41. Processing trade also distorts the measure of quality upgrading developed by Randi Boorstein and Robert Feenstra (1991). In this approach, shifts in imports toward more expensive goods within a product category, as measured by an increase in the unit value index relative to the exact price index, are interpreted as quality upgrading. For example, final goods should be more expensive per unit than the price per unit of the components used in the production process. Hence, outsourcing of the assembly stage of the production of final goods from developed to developing countries will raise the average unit value relative to the exact price index and erroneously be interpreted as quality upgrading. This would also explain the relatively high unit values of China's processing trade found by Zhi Wang and Shang-Jin Wei (2010).

TRADE AND WELFARE: EXPLORING THE ECONOMISTS' CONCERNS

In a widely cited article, "Where Ricardo and Mill Rebut and Confirm Arguments of Mainstream Economists Supporting Globalization," Paul Samuelson (2004) castigated many in the economics profession for arguing that trade inevitably boosts national income in leading economies such as the United States and ignoring the long-recognized possibility that these gains could shrink.

"Economic history is replete with such examples," wrote Samuelson. "Even where the leaders continued to progress in absolute growth, their rate of growth tended often to be attenuated by an adverse headwind generated from low-wage competitors and technical imitators" (Samuelson 2004, 142).

International trade is beneficial because it allows countries to exchange domestically produced products for those produced abroad on better terms than would be obtained if a country were self-sufficient. And everything else being equal, the gains from exporting a given quantity of goods and services will be larger the better the terms of trade—the ratio of export to import prices. These prices will in turn reflect demand and supply conditions both at home and abroad. And since foreign growth could in principle affect prices in either direction, it is quite possible that in response to foreign growth, the gains from trade could increase or decrease.

Samuelson is surely correct in principle. While India was a major exporter of garments in the late 18th century, its domestic industry was destroyed when Britain emerged in the 19th century as the world's leading producer of garments. Similarly Britain in the late 19th and 20th centuries lost its dominance as the factory of the world when the United States and European nations narrowed and eventually eliminated many of Britain's technological advantages. But for our purposes, the key question is whether Samuelson's concern applies to the current experience of the United States in its trade with emerging-market economies.

To answer this question, in chapter 5 we outline Samuelson's theoretical reasoning, noting, as he recognizes, that it is simply an example of a large number of theories in which the gains from trade operate through changing relative prices. In all these theories the key issue is whether foreign growth is biased toward supplying more US imports at lower prices and raising demand for US exports or whether such growth raises US import prices and competes with US exports.

A summary measure of these forces is given by America's terms of trade. Since other sources of gains from trade come through exploiting scale economies and increased variety and productivity, the terms of trade are not a comprehensive measure. Nonetheless, they are an appropriate focus as they speak directly to Samuelson's concern. Accordingly, we initially explore the evidence based on the US terms of trade. We find compelling evidence that aside from oil, his concern is not borne out in the data—on the contrary, since the mid-1990s, the United States has experienced a strong improvement in its terms of trade with developing countries. We also provide more comprehensive estimates of trade gains that take account of benefits that operate through improving productivity and increasing product choice.

Applying a fair test of Samuelson's concerns also requires taking account of the fact that these improved nonoil terms of trade have been associated with larger trade deficits. Using a variety of methodologies in chapter 6, we show that the gains would remain even if the United States were to restore its trade balance to 1990 levels. In chapter 7 we appraise concerns about oil prices.

5

Developing-Country Growth and US Welfare

In this chapter we describe the theories that link trade in emerging-market economies to US welfare and then present evidence that indicates that the impact has been positive. We first discuss the models presented by Paul Samuelson (2004) and other eminent economists that challenge the idea that foreign growth is always good for the United States. These models, which assume products are standardized, focus on the impact of foreign growth on the US terms of trade as the key link between trade and welfare. They suggest the effects could be positive or negative and indicate that if foreign growth is biased toward increasing the relative supply of the goods the United States exports, and reducing the supply of US imports, US incomes could be reduced.

We then note a priori considerations suggesting that the adverse outcome is unlikely. John Hicks (1953), for example, conjectured that in early stages of development, countries are most likely to experience rapid productivity growth in the industries in which they have a comparative advantage, and thus their growth is initially likely to be export-biased and especially favorable to developed countries. We also note that standard trade theories suggest that countries are unlikely to compete head to head in export markets with countries that are at very different stages of development, and since the most important emerging-market economies currently have per capita incomes that are a fifth or less that the United States, such competition is unlikely.

The chapter then explores the behavior of the US terms of trade since 1950 and finds support for these considerations. Between 1950 and 1970, the US terms of trade initially improved as today's developed countries advanced toward US income levels. America's terms of trade declined, however, after 1970, once Europe and Japan reached around 70 percent of US per capita income levels. Since the early 1990s, as trade with emerging-market economies has increased, the nonoil terms of trade have again had a strong upward trend. Thus, the expected association between the (nonoil) US terms of trade and the income levels of its major trading competitors is again confirmed in the data from 1990 through 2010. This suggests that while today's emerging-market economies could eventually challenge the United States in its export markets, for some time to come developing-country growth is likely to be complementary rather than competitive with the United States.

Looking at the data, the fact that (nonoil) US terms of trade have improved is suggestive. But to attribute causation to growth in emerging-market economies, we need to control for other influences. We therefore report on the simulation study by Chang-Tai Hsieh and Ralph Ossa (2011), which finds a positive impact on the United States of Chinese productivity growth. Finally, we estimate the effects on US incomes of manufactured trade with emerging-market economies. Using the methods for estimating trade gains developed by Costas Arkolakis, Arnaud Costinot, and Andrés Rodríguez-Clare (2010) that take account of the gains from trade that come from specialization through comparative advantage, as well as increased product variety and enhanced firm efficiency, we find these to be significant. Using 2008 data suggests that US incomes would be reduced by 1.3 percent of GDP, i.e., about $500 per person, if imports from emerging-market economies were to be eliminated, with imports from China accounting for about half these effects.

Theory, Foreign Growth, and Welfare

Paul Samuelson's argument rests on the impact that foreign growth could have on America's welfare when comparative advantage changes. He analyzes the question with a classical Ricardian model in which patterns of comparative advantage reflect differences in industry labor productivity.[1] In Ricardo's original example, Portugal was the more developed country and could produce both cloth and wine more efficiently than England. But since England had a comparative advantage in cloth, Portugal and England both gained if England specialized in cloth and Portugal in wine. In Samuelson's model the United States plays the role of Portugal, the more productive economy, and China the role of England. He assumes an initial position in which the two countries are trading with each other, with each country specializing fully in the production of one good. In an economy with just one factor, labor, this implies that wages in each country are fixed in terms of the export good.

Samuelson then considers the impact on the United States of increased Chinese growth due to labor productivity improvements. One case is an improvement in productivity in the good that China exports—"export-biased" growth. This is clearly very good for the United States, since it reduces the relative price of the Chinese good and thus raises the buying power of American

---

1. Demand is assumed away by having similar spending patterns at home and abroad.

exports.[2] Therefore, Americans now get more imports for each unit of exports. This terms of trade shift in favor of United States implies that China confers some of the benefits of its increased productivity to the United States.[3]

In a second case where uniform productivity improvements occur in both the Chinese export industry and its import-competing industry, Americans also benefit from the increased relative world supply of Chinese exports, since China's comparative advantage does not change. But it is a third case—"import-biased growth"—that captures Samuelson's concerns.[4] This takes place when productivity improvements occur in China's import-competing industry, i.e., the industry in which the United States specializes. This is problematic for the United States because the US comparative advantage in its export industry is reduced and its terms of trade decline.[5] In the extreme example that Samuelson uses to make his point, Chinese productivity growth improves so much in its import-competing industry that the United States no longer gains anything from trade. Even though the United States is absolutely more productive than China in both industries, the improvement in productivity growth in the import-competing industry in China is sufficient to make the US absolute advantage in both industries the same. This means that neither country has a comparative advantage in either good. Trade between them ceases and both countries produce both products. The buying power of American wages declines and America loses all its gains from trade.[6]

Samuelson's central message that foreign growth could reduce American welfare is not dependent on the particular Ricardian model he uses. As he makes clear in both the title and arguments in his paper, he follows a long line of economists who have framed the issue in these terms (Johnson and Stafford 1993). Similar conclusions follow when comparative advantage is driven by relative factor endowments (the Heckscher-Ohlin model), or by demand patterns (the Linder model). They are also found in the framework developed by

---

2. Since the US economy is fully specialized, and there is just one factor of production, the purchasing power of US wages in terms of home-produced goods remains constant. But real wages in terms of foreign-produced goods rise. The extent to which real incomes rise at home will depend on the terms of trade and the share of income spent on imported goods.

3. In fact, this effect could be so large that such growth could actually make China worse off by flooding the world market with its exports—a phenomenon that Jagdish Bhagwati, who first pointed out this possibility, memorably described as "immiserizing growth" (Bhagwati 1958).

4. The distinction between export- and import-biased growth was introduced by Harry Johnson (1955a).

5. As Krugman (1994) points out in an explication of a similar model, the home country (the United States in our example) is hurt because wages rise in the foreign country, which makes its exports more expensive.

6. In fact, Samuelson's treatment is incomplete because there is a fourth possibility he does not mention. The shifts causing adverse terms of trade changes could be so large as to actually change comparative advantage. In this case, the home country could again gain because import-biased growth becomes export-biased growth and the terms of trade improve again, as the home country specializes in the product it formerly imported and the foreign country becomes an exporter of the goods in which its productivity growth is improving.

Ralph Gomory and William Baumol (2000) in which firms are competitive but there are external economies of scale at the industry level that can be reaped once foreign economies are large enough.[7] The general point in all these models is that the home country benefits from increases in net export supplies in the foreign country, whereas it loses if foreign growth is biased toward reducing foreign net demand for imports.

We should note that there are other models in which the view Samuelson attributes to many prominent economists doesn't apply, i.e., in which foreign growth necessarily improves home-country terms of trade. Generally, these are models with complete specialization, in which products have distinctive national characteristics (the Armington assumption) and countries all have similar demand behavior. In these models, growth raises relative supplies of foreign products and thus improves the terms of trade of their trading partners (Acemoglu and Ventura 2002).[8] However, as long as the foreign and the home country actually (or potentially) are able to produce similar products, the result that foreign growth could damage the home country could be possible.[9]

Knowing the impact of foreign growth on the terms of trade generally gives an idea of the direction in which welfare will change, but it does not indicate its magnitude. The magnitude of the welfare effect is dependent on the responsiveness in the home country in terms of both consumption and production to the change in terms of trade, as well as the importance of imports as a source of consumption. Given any improvement in the terms of trade, the larger the share of imports in consumption and the greater the change in production, the larger the impact on domestic incomes.

We should also emphasize that there are other sources of gains from trade besides comparative advantage that could influence the outcome. As the model pioneered by Krugman (1980) has demonstrated, there are additional gains from trade (and foreign growth) when, in the presence of scale economies, trade increases the variety of available products.[10] In the Krugman

---

7. In this model, foreigners are originally less productive in the industry producing US exports. But as they grow, they realize scale economies that allow them to compete in the US export sector, thereby reducing America's gains from trade. The Gomory and Baumol (2000) model is actually a generalization of the conventional textbook model of the case for infant industry protection. See, for example, Krugman (1987, 131–44). For an excellent review of these models and an argument that the outcomes they predict are sensitive to assumptions made, see Grossman and Rossi-Hansberg (2009).

8. Indeed, this argument is made by Daron Acemoglu and Jaume Ventura (2002) to explain why national income levels tend to stick together. This implies that the home country benefits from foreign growth through both more choice and improved terms of trade.

9. Krugman (1985) develops a one-factor model of technological diffusion in which the South catches up to the North and worsens the North's terms of trade. However, Susan Zhu (2007) considers a two-factor model in which the opposite result holds. The North's terms of trade improve, and although wage inequality rises, unskilled workers in the North can also gain.

10. Joseph Gagnon (2007), for example, develops a model based on Krugman's (1980) model of imperfect competition and product differentiation and shows how the negative terms of trade effect from export-biased growth may be offset by an increase in foreign demand for the varieties.

model, foreign growth benefits the home country by increasing the variety of the products it can buy. Indeed, Christian Broda and David Weinstein (2006) have found the welfare effects for the United States of increased import varieties to be substantial—2.6 percent of GDP from 1972 to 2001. Thus, even in cases where import-biased growth abroad might depress the home country's terms of trade, this growth might also increase the product choices available to the home country to a degree that more than offsets this effect. Another channel for trade gains could come through improving resource allocation at home by concentrating production in more productive firms. This source of gains is captured in the class of models with heterogeneous firms developed by Marc Melitz (2003). In more complex models (and in reality), therefore, changes in short-run domestic welfare from foreign growth will not be fully revealed by the changes in the terms of trade. Nonetheless, looking at the behavior of the terms of trade is a useful place to start.[11]

Hicks' Conjecture

Given the theoretical ambiguity of foreign growth on domestic welfare, as demonstrated in Samuelson's paper, ultimately the issue can only be settled by empirical investigation. But a priori considerations can provide a guide. The claims made by Samuelson actually echo those of John Hicks in his 1953 inaugural lecture on the dollar shortage. Like Samuelson, Hicks used the Ricardian model to consider the effects of foreign growth on domestic welfare, in his case, the effects of American growth—America was the developing country—on Great Britain—the developed country. Hicks argued that in the 19th century, Great Britain benefited immensely from US productivity improvements in agriculture—America's export-biased growth. But Britain's benefits were reduced later as these improvements slowed and the United States became more competitive in the manufacturing products that Britain exported. Hicks thus joined Samuelson in the view that this process of shifting from export- to import-biased growth could hurt the home country. Nonetheless, in the early stages of foreign development, Hicks made a persuasive argument that foreign growth will generally benefit the home country.

> We should . . . expect to find that the improvements which *start* a process of development will be export-biased. This is little more than a deduction from the general principle of the division of labour. Countries, like people, are most likely to make their improvements in those sorts of production which they already do relatively well than in those they do relatively badly. . . . Since it is the things which they make relatively

---

11. Under some circumstances, however, taking account of these additional potential sources of gain might not affect the outcome. Costas Arkolakis et al. (2008) demonstrated that changes in the gains from trade that operate through comparative advantage, variety, and firm heterogeneity can all be inferred from observed changes in openness provided certain conditions are met. (These include constant elasticity of substitution preferences, a single factor of production, linear cost functions, complete specialization, and iceberg trade costs.)

well which they will be exporting, or on the point of exporting, improvements in these industries will be export-biased. (Hicks 1953, 129)

In later phases of development, however, Hicks noted that patterns of growth could change:

> It has to be expected that some of the countries which were formerly customers [of the old centers], but which possess the right natural resources for home production of the things they used to import, when production is organized according to the new methods, will in time acquire the skills which will enable them to compete. . . . Thus when our analysis is put into an historical dress, it suggests as a normal sequence the succession of an export-biased by an import-biased phase. (Hicks 1953, 129–30)

While Hicks gives an intuitive explanation for his conjecture, it is actually implied by many of the theories that explain international patterns of specialization. Since incomes are determined by combining factor supplies and technology, countries with higher per capita incomes are likely to (1) be more intensively endowed with human, physical, and institutional capital and (2) have superior technologies. If tastes are associated with incomes, they also are likely have distinctive demand patterns that could yield scale economies from producing goods demanded at particular income levels. Thus there is likely to be a strong association between (1) per capita incomes and relative factor endowments such as human and physical capital—the Heckscher-Ohlin theory; (2) per capita incomes and technological capabilities—the Ricardian theory; and (3) per capita incomes and demand patterns—the Linder theory.[12] It would therefore not be surprising if per capita incomes serve as a powerful predictor of patterns of specialization.

Indeed, the strength of the association between specialization patterns and income levels is confirmed by the work of Ricardo Hausmann, Jason Hwang, and Dani Rodrik (2007), who find a very strong correlation between the goods a country exports and the goods exported by other countries with similar per capita incomes. This has also been revealed in the sequential patterns of specialization in the Asian economies as they have developed a phenomenon that has been dubbed "the flying geese."[13] Initially, Japan dominated exports of clothing and simple manufacturers, but as Japan developed it shifted toward more complex manufactured goods, ships and steel, while Hong Kong, Singapore, Taiwan, and Korea—the so-called newly industrialized economies (NIEs)—took over the export markets in products such as clothing and toys. Later Japan moved up the technological ladder into exporting autos and sophisticated capital goods, the NIEs moved into consumer electronics,

---

12. See Linder (1961). A more recent framework that emphasizes the role of demand patterns is Fajgelbaum, Grossman, and Helpman (2011).

13. The phrase "flying geese pattern of development" was coined by Kaname Akamatsu in articles in Japanese in the 1930s and used later by him in Akamatsu (1961, 1962). See also Kojima (2000) and Lin (2011).

Table 5.1   Purchasing-power-parity-converted GDP per capita relative to the United States at current prices, 1950–2009
(percent, United States = 100)

Country	1950	1960	1970	1980	1990	2000	2009
Developed countries	56	65	76	83	83	78	78
Canada	83	81	84	95	86	83	88
France	54	66	76	83	80	75	75
Germany	n.a.	n.a.	77	83	83	79	79
Japan	24	40	73	81	92	80	77
Italy	41	57	70	77	80	73	68
United Kingdom	76	81	76	76	76	77	81
Developing countries	n.a.	n.a.	n.a.	n.a.	n.a.	n.a.	n.a.
Brazil	15	19	22	32	23	20	23
China	n.a.	5	4	5	6	9	19
Hong Kong	n.a.	20	33	56	76	76	85
India	5	5	4	4	4	5	8
Korea	n.a.	11	14	21	39	50	58
Malaysia	n.a.	10	9	17	18	23	28
Mexico	26	29	30	39	28	27	28
Singapore	n.a.	28	33	58	74	99	112
Taiwan	n.a.	12	18	30	46	62	68
Thailand	8	7	9	11	15	15	19

n.a. = not available

Note: The Penn World Tables provide two series for China. The values presented here are those adjusted for the urban character of its International Comparison Program 2005 prices (China 2).

Source: Heston, Summers, and Aten (2011).

ships and steel, and countries such as Malaysia, the Philippines, Indonesia, and ultimately China took over clothing and consumer electronics.[14]

Evidence

If Hicks' conjectures are correct, the crucial issue vis-à-vis developing countries today is where they stand in the development process. The more similar these countries are to the United States in terms of per capita incomes, the more likely they are to become competitors for its exports.

Table 5.1 shows estimates of per capita incomes relative to those in the United States over time. In the 1950s, US imports were dominated by today's developed countries. As reported, per capita incomes in Europe and Japan in 1950 were one-half and one-fifth of US levels, respectively. Over the subsequent two decades, these developed countries were able to converge rapidly toward US levels and by the 1970s were at levels of about 70 percent of the

---

14. It should be noted that this pattern of specialization does not appear to be uniquely Asian, as might be implied from the metaphor. This is established by Marcus Noland (1997).

Figure 5.1   US terms of trade (goods and services), 1950–2010

index (2006 = 100)

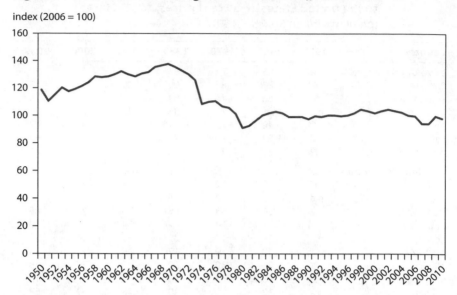

Source: Bureau of Economic Analysis, National Income Accounts data, www.bea.gov/national/index.htm (accessed on November 1, 2012).

United States. We see as well that while China and India have indeed grown rapidly over the past decade, their per capita incomes by 2009 remained just one-fifth and one-tenth of US levels, respectively. Korea (58 percent of the United States), Taiwan (68 percent), and Hong Kong (85 percent) are much closer, and Singapore has actually overtaken the US level, but as of 2009 the levels of major developing-country exporters of manufactured goods such as Mexico, Brazil, and most other developing countries still remained far below those of the United States. Developing countries therefore remain at the early stages of development relative to the United States, and their growth according to Hicks' conjecture is more likely to be export-biased.

The terms of trade provide an additional perspective. Figure 5.1 reports the chain-weighted US terms of trade for goods and services from 1950 to 2009.[15] Three phases are clear in the picture: an improving trend from the early 1950s through the late 1960s, a declining trend from 1970 through 1980, and then relative stability for the rest of period.[16]

---

15. We use the ratios of the implicit price deflator for exports of goods and services and income receipts to the corresponding implicit price deflator for imports divided by 100.

16. The US terms of trade declined between 1944 and 1950.

First Two Phases: 1950–80

The first two phases can be related to the relative per capita income levels of the United States and its developed trading partners. As is expected if foreign growth is export-biased, the US terms of trade improved steadily until the late 1960s. By the early 1970s, however, the major European economies and Japan had closed much of their productivity gap with the United States. Their per capita incomes were between 67 and 78 percent of US levels, respectively. Moreover, with lower labor participation their relative per-worker productivity levels were even closer to US levels. In response, their exports increasingly competed with those of the United States.

In 1971, the United States sustained its first merchandise trade deficit of the postwar era. The dollar had also become overvalued. As reflected in figure 5.1, in response there was a substantial decline in the US terms of trade over the 1970s as the Bretton Woods monetary system collapsed in the face of dollar devaluations in 1971 and 1973. A second factor was the interaction of increased oil imports and higher oil prices. Thus, the terms of trade declines were due both to oil and nonoil trade. By 1980, Europe and Japan had emerged as major competitors for US exports, and "competitiveness" had become a key issue in US policy discussions. In addition to these developments, two major oil shocks contributed to the fall in US terms of trade during the decade.

1980–2009: Manufactured Goods

Between 1980 and 2000, the United States actually grew slightly more rapidly than the rest of the world, and the major developed countries failed to close the remaining gap in per capita incomes (table 5.1). A key feature of US trade was the growth in US manufactured goods imports from developing countries. Figure 5.2 shows US imports from industrial and non-OPEC developing countries measured as a share of GDP between 1978 and 2008. Import penetration by developing countries rose in the 1980s and accelerated after 1993, when the United States signed the North American Free Trade Agreement with Mexico, and China emerged as a major exporter. By 2006, the value of non-OPEC developing-country goods imports was similar to the value of imports from industrialized countries.

This rapid growth in US imports came from countries whose levels of development were far lower than those of the United States. In 2009, for example, per capita GDP in China and Mexico were just 19 and 28 percent, respectively, of those in the United States, and even Taiwan (68 percent) and Korea (58 percent) had incomes relative to the United States that were only similar to those of Europe relative to the United States in the 1950s. If the Hicks conjecture is a guide, these countries should have sustained export-led growth that would improve the manufacturing terms of trade of the United States (and other developed countries). In fact, this is what has happened.

Figure 5.2   US merchandise imports, 1978–2008

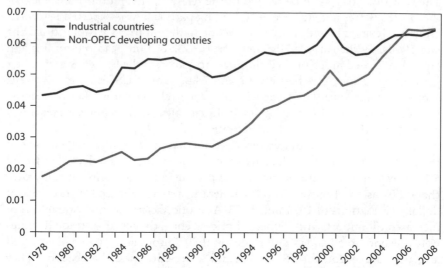

ratio to GDP (current dollars)

OPEC = Organization of Petroleum Exporting Countries
Source: Bureau of Economic Analysis.

The Bureau of Labor Statistics (BLS) computes separate import price series for US manufactured imports from industrialized and developing countries. This allows us to report series for the terms of trade distinguishing manufactured imports by origin. Figure 5.3 shows the ratios of the price indices of US nonagricultural exports to the manufactured import price indices from industrial and nonindustrial countries. They are distinctly different. The prices of US manufactured imports from developed countries (PMDC) have kept fairly closely in line with the prices of US nonagricultural merchandise exports (PXNAG). Basically there are relatively small changes in these terms of trade with developed countries. By contrast, the prices of US manufactured imports from developing countries (PMLDC) have fallen precipitously relative to the series for US nonagricultural exports, and as a result the US terms of trade with developing countries have a very strong upward trend. The overall US terms of trade in manufactured goods have therefore improved since the mid-1990s because of the improvement in the terms of trade with developing countries.

We show later that one very important driver of the declining relative prices of imports from developing countries has been the prices of computers and other electronics products. However, relative declines in other goods prices have also played a role. Since 2001, the BLS has calculated end-use price series for exports of all commodities excluding computers and semiconductors and imports of all commodities excluding computers, semiconductors,

Figure 5.3 Ratios of US nonagricultural export prices to prices of manufactured goods imports from developed and developing countries, 1990–2008

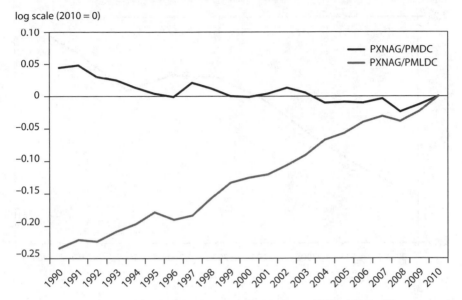

PXNAG = prices of US nonagricultural merchandise exports; PMDC = prices of US manufactured imports from developed countries; PMLDC = prices of US manufactured imports from developing countries

Source: Bureau of Labor Statistics.

and petroleum. This terms of trade series also shows a strong improvement between 2001 and 2008.

Chinese import prices clearly play an important role in this story. The BLS has produced indices for US imports from China only since 2003, but as shown in figure 5.4, using the overall nonagricultural price index for US exports, the US terms of trade with China have improved steadily since then. Indeed, in the eight years for which there are data they have improved by 24.8 percent

Assuming the mix and prices of goods exported by developed and developing countries to the United States are similar to those of goods exported to the rest of the world, these US manufacturing price data suggest that other developed countries should have experienced improvements in their manufactured goods terms of trade. Indeed, if the Hicks conjecture is correct, that is precisely what we would expect. This is confirmed by the data for Japan and Germany. As shown in figure 5.5, between 1996 and 2006, both countries showed trend improvements in their manufactured goods terms of trade similar to that of the United States. While there was some reversal after 2006 in the case of Japan, the German and US terms of trade continued to improve.

Figure 5.4   US nonagricultural export prices relative to Chinese manufactured import prices, 2003–11

ratio (2003 = 1)

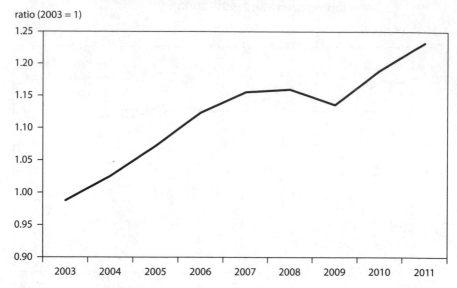

Source: Bureau of Labor Statistics.

Figure 5.5   Manufacturing terms of trade, 1996–2009

log scale (2006 = 0)

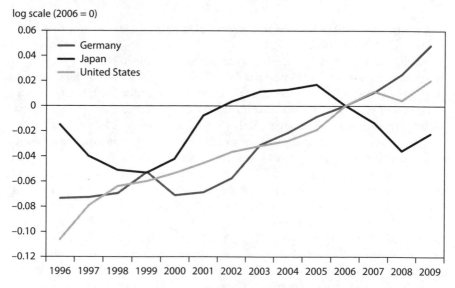

Source: Organization for Economic Cooperation and Development.

Figure 5.6   US terms of trade, 1980–2010

log scale (2005 = 0)

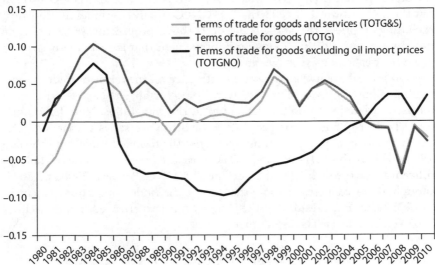

Source: Bureau of Economic Analysis.

In sum, while the concern raised by Samuelson and others is certainly a theoretical possibility, thus far the Hicks conjecture is a better prediction of US terms of trade trends in manufactured goods.

1980–2009: Other Goods and Services

Up until this point we have considered only the behavior of the import prices of manufactured goods. The US terms of trade are of course dependent on the movement of other prices as well. Figure 5.6 shows three different measures, all using the chain-weighted price indices that are developed for the national income accounts. These are the terms of trade for goods and services (TOTG&S), goods (TOTG), and goods excluding oil import prices (TOTGNO). These variables are all measured in logarithms and thus the y axis indicates percentage changes from the base year, which is 2005. What is striking is that all the measured variables remain within a fairly narrow bound of around 15 percent.

Between 1980 and 2008, the most comprehensive series for the terms of trade (TOTG&S) was basically unchanged. The TOTG was below its 1980 level, reflecting high oil prices, but the TOTGNO was actually higher than it had been in 1980, though not at its 1984 peak. Over the period, all the series generally mirror exchange rate changes but are far less volatile. They show substantial improvements and then declines in the 1980s. They also all follow the dollar when it strengthens after 1995. While TOTG&S and TOTG also follow the dollar down after 2002, the TOTGNO actually continues to rise. Thus, excluding oil prices, the TOTGNO reflects the improvement we have already noted for manufacturing goods, an improvement that is particularly striking given the weakening exchange rate.

Oil prices have had an important influence on the terms of trade. In particular, falling oil prices after 1987 were an important offset to the declining terms associated with dollar weakening in the mid-1980s. Note how much more TOTGNO falls as compared with the other two series at that time. Declining relative oil prices continued to boost the terms of trade until the late 1990s, so that the TOTG&S and TOTG measures, which include oil, fall significantly less through 1995 than do the TOTGNO. Between 2000 and 2008, though, oil price increases more than offset the underlying improvement in TOTGNO, with the result that the United States experienced similar declines in TOTG&S and TOTG during that period.

Identifying Developing-Country Impact

While suggestive, the prices of traded goods and services, as revealed in the terms of trade, are determined by a host of influences and not only by growth in developing countries—put technically, these prices are an endogenous variable. Thus, simply looking at prices ex post, we cannot be sure that the improvement in the US terms of trade is actually due to growth in emerging-market economies and not to some other source. It could be the case that developing-country growth had an adverse impact on the terms of trade that was offset by other factors. Indeed, without developing-country growth, perhaps the US terms of trade would have been even higher. To answer this question, it is necessary to have a methodology that isolates the impact of growth in developing countries from other causes of changes in the terms of trade and other sources of benefits from that trade.

One study that deals with these issues is by Hsieh and Ossa (2011) for Chinese growth. These authors build a multi-industry, multicountry general equilibrium model that integrates the models of comparative advantage (à la Ricardo), intraindustry trade (Krugman 1980), and firm heterogeneity (Melitz 2003). Hsieh and Ossa then estimate how total factor productivity growth in 2-digit Chinese industries between 1992 and 2007 affected real incomes in China and the rest of the world. Their estimates suggest that over this period, the cumulative impact was an increase of 0.48 percent in the average income in the rest of the world, and a 0.33 percent total increase in US income. Their estimates for the United States reflect an income gain of 0.76 percent in the US terms of trade that is partially offset by a –0.43 impact from production relocation. All in all, they find that about 2.2 percent of the improvements in Chinese industrial total factor productivity were transferred to the rest of the world.

Welfare

What impact have the changes in the terms of trade had on US welfare? Using the standard price series from the GNP accounts we found that there was a steady increase in the nonoil terms of trade of 14 log points between 1994 and 2008. Given that these imports have a share of about 5 percent on US spending, this would indicate an impact of about 0.7 percent on incomes overall.

However, there are reasons to believe this could understate the benefits. In particular, the BLS uses a Laspeyres index, which uses fixed base weights as the components of the end-use indices that are then used by the BEA to compute the deflators. A superior index is the Törnqvist index. According to Robert Feenstra, Marshall Reinsdorf, and Matthew Slaughter (2009), this leads to an additional 2.3 percent improvement in the terms of trade from 1994 to 2006. The BLS index also does not take account of increased varieties. These have been much greater in imports than exports. The estimates by Feenstra, Reinsdorf, and Slaughter suggest that the inclusion of varieties leads to much larger positive welfare effects—on the order of an additional 10 percentage point increase in the terms of trade over this period. A more accurate measure of the improvement in welfare could be on the order of 1.4 percent of US income.[17]

Gains from US Trade with Emerging-Market Economies

The numbers we have just cited use ex post terms of trade data, and as we have noted, these could be the result of many other influences, such as growth in the developed countries. While it is difficult to isolate changes in the overall terms of trade that are attributable to developing-country growth, and not other causes, we can estimate relatively easily the impact of cutting off trade with developing countries and replacing it with domestic production.

Arkolakis et al. (2008) develop a common estimator of the gains from trade that holds under a variety of trade models. Their basic estimator that measures the percentage change in real income necessary to compensate a representative consumer for going to autarky is given as $\delta^{1/\varepsilon} - 1$, where δ is the

---

17. In an alternative study, Marshall Reinsdorf (2010) uses Fisher indices to estimate the impact of the terms of trade on real US gross domestic income (GDI). He finds that trading gains have a median absolute effect on US real GDI of 0.2 percentage points in annual data over the period from 1973 to 2008. He decomposes the gains from trade into a terms of trade effect and a relative price of tradables effect. Rises in the terms of trade increase the growth rate of real GDI. Decreases in the price of tradables relative to gross domestic final expenditure raise real GDI if the economy has a trade deficit.

share of expenditure on domestic goods and ε is the elasticity of imports with respect to variable trade costs.

The one problem in calculating this value is that the import data do not distinguish between goods for final consumption and goods used as intermediate inputs in production. Consequently, studies by both Arkolakis, Costinot, and Rodríguez-Clare (2010) and David Autor, David Dorn, and Gordon Hanson (2012) use the ratio of imports to gross output (gross total expenditure) as a proxy for δ. Arkolakis, Costinot, and Rodríguez-Clare, however, present two additional variants of the basic gains from trade indicators that are more suitable for our analysis. In a world of tradable intermediate inputs, the estimator of the gains from trade becomes $\delta^{1/\beta\varepsilon} - 1$, where β is the share of nontradable inputs (e.g., factors) in the production of goods. Arkolakis, Costinot, and Rodríguez-Clare (2010) argue that β is on average equal to one-half. A further extension includes tariff revenue, in which case the estimator becomes $\delta^{1/\beta\varepsilon}(1 + T) - 1$, where T is the share of tariff revenues in the initial equilibrium.

In what follows, therefore, we use this version of the estimator to decompose the overall US gains from manufacturing trade into country components. The implicit assumption is that reductions in each country's share of US expenditure are fully offset by an increase in domestic production (and not by imports from other countries). Table 5.2 presents the estimates using the trade cost elasticity of –5. The final rows present the total welfare gains under different assumptions, including higher elasticities (leads to lower effects) and the inclusion or exclusion of intermediates and tariff revenues.

The table depicts some interesting trends. The overall gains from trade in manufactures according to this measure range from 1.2 to 2.6 percent of real income, depending on the assumptions regarding elasticity of imports with respect to trade costs and whether or not intermediate inputs are accounted for. Over the period from 1998 to 2008, the gains from trade rose from 2.3 to 2.6 percent, but then fell to 2.2 percent during the recession as import values fell. Using the higher trade cost elasticity of –10, the gains from trade are lower, but also rose from 1.2 to 1.4 percent over the same period.

There are some important variations at the country level that reflect the changing geographical composition of US imports. The gains from trade with emerging-market and developing countries rose steadily throughout the period and are larger than the gains from trade with advanced economies. In fact, the gains from trade in manufactured goods with advanced countries fell over the period.

The dominant source of these trends is China. Imports of manufactured goods from China raised real incomes by 0.2 percent in 1998, but by 2008 this had more than doubled to 0.6 percent or 25 percent of the overall gains from trade in manufactured goods. Given US national income in 2008 of $12.609 trillion, overall gains from manufactured goods trade would be $337.8 billion, or about $1,000 per person in the United States. The gains from Chinese im-

Table 5.2 Gains from trade in manufactured goods, 1998–2009 (log change in income x 100)

Economy	1998	1999	2000	2001	2002	2003	2004	2005	2006	2007	2008	2009
Major advanced economies	**1.030**	**1.056**	**1.071**	**0.969**	**0.939**	**0.916**	**0.951**	**0.940**	**0.931**	**0.903**	**0.856**	**0.663**
Canada	0.368	0.390	0.395	0.355	0.344	0.335	0.357	0.353	0.343	0.330	0.300	0.231
Japan	0.330	0.330	0.342	0.290	0.276	0.256	0.262	0.255	0.258	0.238	0.224	0.163
Germany	0.132	0.137	0.133	0.131	0.133	0.139	0.146	0.149	0.146	0.149	0.147	0.114
United Kingdom	0.081	0.081	0.080	0.076	0.072	0.072	0.072	0.071	0.072	0.071	0.071	0.062
France	0.057	0.056	0.059	0.059	0.056	0.055	0.056	0.054	0.055	0.058	0.058	0.049
Italy	0.062	0.061	0.062	0.058	0.058	0.058	0.059	0.058	0.057	0.058	0.056	0.044
Newly industrialized Asian economies	**0.245**	**0.251**	**0.269**	**0.222**	**0.215**	**0.205**	**0.215**	**0.191**	**0.187**	**0.175**	**0.162**	**0.140**
Singapore	0.045	0.041	0.040	0.030	0.029	0.027	0.026	0.024	0.027	0.027	0.021	0.023
Hong Kong	0.036	0.033	0.033	0.028	0.026	0.024	0.023	0.020	0.017	0.013	0.011	0.005
Taiwan	0.095	0.094	0.099	0.080	0.075	0.071	0.072	0.066	0.067	0.062	0.058	0.048
Korea	0.069	0.083	0.097	0.084	0.084	0.083	0.093	0.080	0.076	0.072	0.072	0.064
Other advanced economies	**0.182**	**0.187**	**0.206**	**0.204**	**0.212**	**0.223**	**0.235**	**0.232**	**0.238**	**0.237**	**0.239**	**0.208**
Emerging-market and developing economies	**0.775**	**0.822**	**0.912**	**0.869**	**0.923**	**0.967**	**1.076**	**1.145**	**1.237**	**1.252**	**1.255**	**1.108**
China	0.219	0.238	0.266	0.267	0.317	0.364	0.435	0.500	0.555	0.591	0.598	0.557
Mexico	0.208	0.229	0.254	0.246	0.244	0.230	0.238	0.233	0.253	0.255	0.243	0.225
India	0.024	0.025	0.027	0.024	0.028	0.029	0.033	0.036	0.040	0.041	0.043	0.038
ASEAN 4	0.145	0.148	0.157	0.138	0.138	0.131	0.132	0.138	0.141	0.129	0.122	0.103
Brazil	0.025	0.026	0.028	0.029	0.032	0.032	0.038	0.039	0.039	0.034	0.033	0.020
Other emerging-market economies	0.153	0.156	0.179	0.165	0.164	0.180	0.199	0.199	0.210	0.202	0.216	0.165
Total (ε = –5, including intermediates and tariff revenue)	2.305	2.395	2.548	2.341	2.367	2.391	2.558	2.603	2.693	2.665	2.606	2.185
Excluding intermediates	2.097	2.198	2.348	2.160	2.188	2.213	2.387	2.418	2.504	2.478	2.425	2.034
Excluding intermediates and tariff revenue	1.043	1.093	1.167	1.074	1.088	1.100	1.187	1.202	1.244	1.231	1.205	1.012
Total (ε = –10, including intermediates and tariff revenue)	1.249	1.288	1.364	1.253	1.266	1.277	1.365	1.385	1.431	1.417	1.384	1.161

ASEAN = Association for Southeast Asian Nations

Note: Trade data are obtained from US International Trade Commission. The data cover manufactured goods excluding petroleum and coal products manufacturing (NAICS 324). ASEAN 4 consists of Indonesia, Malaysia, the Philippines, and Thailand.

Source: Authors' calculations based on US trade data obtained from the US International Trade Commission.

ports would be $75.6 billion. Given the US population of 304.8 million, this works out to $249 per person. The gains from trade with emerging-market economies overall would be twice that.

In sum, not only do the raw data for the nonoil terms of trade show that these have improved due to US trade with developing countries, estimates of trade gains also indicate a positive impact on US living standards. In the frameworks we have used, however, it is assumed that trade is balanced, but in the US case, these terms of trade improvements have been associated with larger trade deficits. This has important implications for our story, as we elaborate in the next chapter.

6

US Welfare and the Trade Balance

The association between US welfare and the terms of trade drawn in chapter 5 rests heavily on the assumption that trade is balanced. This assumption also applies in the context of Paul Samuelson's (2004) Ricardian-based analysis of the possible effect of developing-country growth on US gains from trade. However, in our analysis of emerging-market-economy growth and US welfare, we need to take account of the fact that the United States has been running large trade deficits. This is necessary because the trade balance is likely to have an independent and systematic influence on the terms of trade. As we discuss in this chapter, larger trade deficits can induce higher terms of trade. Reducing the US current account to levels sustained in the early 1990s, for example, which requires a reduction in US spending relative to income, is likely to be associated with lower terms of trade. Consequently, a fair test of Samuelson's concerns needs to adjust for the effect of the trade deficit itself in boosting the terms of trade since the early 1990s.

This chapter isolates the contribution of the trade deficit to changes in the US terms of trade to allow for a more thorough evaluation of the effect of emerging-market economies on US welfare. The chapter first briefly describes the behavior of the current account from the early 1980s. We then explicate the theory of how changes in net foreign borrowing or lending (i.e., the current account) might affect the terms of trade. Finally, we draw on simulation models and econometric estimates of trade equations to isolate the net change in the terms of trade since 1990 after accounting for the effect of the trade balance.

The theory we will present suggests that because of a bias in preferences for home goods and/or the existence of nontraded goods, the impact of changes in the trade balance on the terms of trade can be captured in a transfer schedule that should have a negative slope. In other words, larger deficits are associated with higher terms of trade. This theoretical expectation is confirmed in simple plots of the association between the US terms of trade and the trade balance in goods and services. We find that, as expected, there is a negative association between the variables. Between 1990 and 2002, in fact, the plots are almost aligned in the line we would expect if we had identified the transfer schedule. From 2003 onward, however, there is a clear downward shift in the relationship, and lower terms of trade are consistent with any given trade balance. However, this decline is entirely due to oil. Once oil is excluded, we find again that the implied schedule has two distinct phases. There is a stable negative relationship during the 1990s, but from 2004 onward, in contrast to the downward shift in the transfer schedule when oil is included, the nonoil schedule actually shifted upward. As a share of GDP, for example, the nonoil trade deficit in goods and services in 2009 was the same in 1998, yet the nonoil terms of trade were 7 percent higher. This recent upward shift in the relationship is contrary to what we would expect if Samuelson's concerns about import-biased growth in developing countries were increasingly relevant. Instead, the data suggest recent strong export-biased growth in emerging-market countries.

While these plots using after-the-fact data are suggestive, their implications need to be confirmed using structural models in which the impact of particular causes can be isolated. We therefore corroborate this implication using two methodologies. First, we draw on Maurice Obstfeld and Kenneth Rogoff (2004), who use a general equilibrium simulation model to estimate the terms of trade effects of eliminating the US current account deficit. Second, we use our own structural model that we have estimated using a conventional trade equation framework. Both approaches indicate that even if the US current account deficit were eliminated, the United States would have nonoil terms of trade that are better than it had in the early 1990s. In addition, our trade equations model reveals that even faster growth in developing countries would benefit the United States, both by increasing the demand for US exports, and thus reducing the decline in the terms of trade associated with eliminating the trade deficit, and by increasing the variety of products available to Americans.

The Trade Deficit

As can be seen in figure 6.1, the US trade deficit in goods and services increased from 1.3 percent of GDP in 1990 to a peak of 5.7 percent of GDP in 2006. The deficit subsequently declined, initially in response to the weaker dollar and then in response to the sharp contraction of imports during the recession of 2008–09. Nevertheless, by 2010, when the economy had started to recover, the deficit at 3.9 percent of GDP still exceeded the high deficits recorded during the mid-1980s and was considerably larger than in the mid-1990s. Let us briefly review this development in greater detail and then consider its implications.

Figure 6.1   US nominal trade balance as a share of GDP, 1980–2010

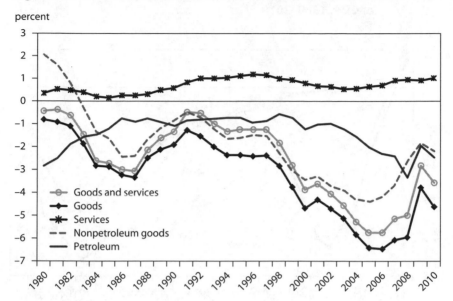

percent

Sources: Bureau of Economic Analysis.

The aggregate balance for goods and services hides an interesting com-positional story, which is that a third to half of the decline in the nominal trade balance can be attributed to petroleum products, a major US import. Oil imports rose from 1 percent of GDP in 2002 to 3.1 percent in 2008, substan-tially offsetting the improvement in the nonoil trade balance that took place after 2005–06. Oil import volumes represented a fairly constant share of real US GDP throughout the period, and the increased deficit associated with oil imports was the result of the rise in world prices from $27 a barrel in 2000 to a peak of almost $150 and an average of $95 in 2008.

Higher oil prices, however, are not the full story behind the growth in the trade deficit since the early 1990s. The oil price increase is concentrated in the post-2000 period, whereas the widening of the trade deficit commenced much earlier. The nominal trade deficit in nonpetroleum goods, for example, began to rise as a share of GDP after 1991, reaching a peak of 4.4 percent in 2005. This decline in the nonoil balance as a share of GDP was far greater than the decline attributable to oil in the post-2000 period.

The nonpetroleum trade deficit then narrowed from 2005 as US export volumes increased rapidly—averaging 7.9 percent per year—while nonoil im-port growth was slow. By the time of the financial crisis, the nominal trade deficit in the nonoil balance in goods and services, at 1.5 percent of GDP, was smaller than its 2000 ratio (a deficit of 2.6 percent of GDP), but it was still 1.9 percent larger than its peak in 1991, when it was in surplus. In other words,

Figure 6.2 US nominal bilateral merchandise trade balance as a share of GDP, 1980–2010

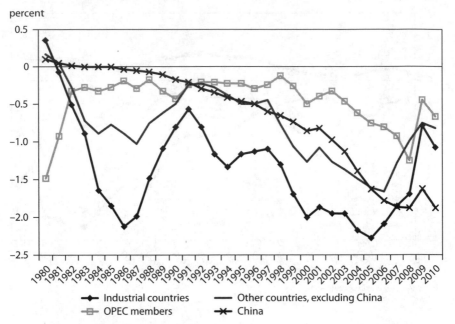

percent

OPEC = Organization of Petroleum Exporting Countries

Source: Bureau of Economic Analysis.

while a substantial portion of the nonoil trade deficit had been eliminated, it nevertheless remained high relative to the early 1980s and 1990s.

In the 1980s, the United States had also experienced large changes and deficits in the trade balance. What makes the post-1990s period distinctive is the magnitude of the deficit relative to GDP in 2005 as well as the geographical and commodity composition of the deficit. The geographical relationship is clearly revealed in figure 6.2, which presents trends in bilateral merchandise trade balances relative to US GDP for other industrialized countries, China, members of the Organization of Petroleum Exporting Countries (OPEC), and other countries.

The figure suggests why there are concerns regarding the competitiveness of the United States vis-à-vis developing countries. In contrast to the 1980s, when the emergence of the deficit was driven most strongly by trade with industrial countries, nonindustrialized countries and China were prominent in the recent period. Most noticeable is the emergence of a trade deficit with China, which rose from balanced trade in the mid-1980s to a deficit of close to 2 percent of US GDP in 2008. By 2008, the US trade deficit with China exceeded that of all other industrialized countries combined. Further, in comparison to other countries, the trade deficit with China remained relatively resilient throughout the period of the financial crisis. The overall trade deficit is therefore even more skewed toward China than prior to the crisis.

Similar trends are evident at the sector level, where the trade balance declined for all sectors except services, where it remained stable. There are nevertheless important variations. Two sectors—consumer goods, and computers, peripherals, and parts—require particular attention. The nominal trade balance in consumer goods declined from a surplus of 1.1 percent of GDP in 1990 to a deficit of 2.4 percent in 2005. The trade balance in computer products declined from a surplus of 0.05 percent of GDP in 1990 to a deficit of 0.38 percent in 2005. Moreover, unlike the other sectors, the trade balance in computer goods did not rise in response to the depreciation in 2002.

The trade balance in both these sectors is closely associated with trade with China.[1] In 1990, less than 1 percent of computer imports and 11 percent of consumer goods imports were sourced from China.[2] By 2006, the share of computer imports and consumer goods imports sourced from China had reached 46 and 35 percent, respectively. These trends, particularly for computer products, reflect a dramatic change in the geographical composition of US imports.

In sum, the nonpetroleum trade deficit widened for much of the post-1990 period. What differentiates this period from the early 1980s is the relative contribution of nonindustrialized countries and China in particular and the decline in the trade balances in consumer and capital goods—especially computers. These trends in the relative contribution of the deficit mimic changes in the debate on US competitiveness. Whereas in the early 1980s the fear was about the ability of the United States to compete against industrial countries like Japan and Germany, in the post-1990 period the debate is about competition from nonindustrialized countries in capital goods, especially electronics.

Correcting for the Trade Deficit

In Samuelson's paper and the other models we have discussed so far, it is assumed that trade is balanced. In reality, however, we have seen that over the period we are considering the United States experienced a substantial decline in its current account. As we have noted, this is a problem because theory suggests that there is likely to be a systematic relationship between the trade balance and the terms of trade. All else being equal, we would expect net capital inflows (as reflected in larger current account deficits) to induce higher terms

---

1. Consumer goods and computers together make up over 70 percent (76 percent in 1990 and 71 percent in 2006) of all merchandise imports from China.

2. Calculated using disaggregated trade data from the Center for International Data at the University of California, Davis, www.internationaldata.org (accessed on November 1, 2012). See Feenstra, Romalis, and Schott (2002) for details on the construction of the database. If trade with Hong Kong is included with that of China, the shares rise from just under 3 percent in 1990 to 38.5 percent in 2006.

of trade. Thus the effect of the trade deficit itself in boosting the terms of trade needs to be accounted for to provide a fair test of Samuelson's concern. In the US case, the relevant question is what would be the US terms of trade if the United States changed its spending patterns and thus restored the current account to its earlier levels.

The relationship between the current account (net borrowing) and the terms of trade in the face of spending changes is modeled in the theory known as the transfer problem.[3] The name comes from the recognition that in the short run international capital flows (or international grants) entail net transfers of goods and services from lenders to borrowers. The current account is by definition equal to the difference between national income and national spending. If international lending increases, the lenders must be reducing their spending relative to their incomes, while the borrowers must be increasing their spending relative to their incomes. Thus, globally, more spending will be undertaken by the borrowers and less by the lenders.

If, at the margin, borrowers and lenders spend their money on the same goods and services, relative prices in the world need not change. If Americans and Chinese spend their money equally between US and Chinese goods, for example, there would be no impact on the relative demand for US and Chinese goods if the Chinese save more and reduce their spending by a dollar and then lend it to the Americans, who reduce their saving and increase their spending by a dollar. Americans will simply buy the goods that the Chinese formerly bought. But if national spending patterns differ, relative prices may have to change in order to balance supply and demand in the product markets. If countries all have a higher propensity to buy their own goods and services, for example, we would expect that stronger terms of trade would be associated with larger trade deficits. If Americans and Chinese each allocate three-quarters of their money to their home goods, reducing spending by a dollar in China will reduce demand for Chinese goods by 75 cents, and increasing it in the United States by a dollar will increase the demand for Chinese goods by just 25 cents. Thus, home-biased spending implies that US borrowing will reduce the relative price of Chinese goods and services (and thus increase the relative price of American goods and services).

This relationship is incorporated in a number of simple theory-based models. Obstfeld and Rogoff (2004) constructed a two-country, three-good general equilibrium model to explore the implications for the US terms of trade as well as the US real exchange rate—the prices of goods and services in the United States relative to those in the rest of the world—of eliminating

---

3. There is a vast literature on the transfer problem, as indicated in the famous debate between John Maynard Keynes and Bertil Ohlin over the German transfer problem. A transfer could in principle move the terms of trade in either direction, depending on the relative marginal propensities to consume. The standard presumption, however, is that an inflow of capital (a transfer into a given country) will increase its terms of trade—the schedule slopes down to the right. Classic articles include Samuelson (1952, 1954), Johnson (1955b), Jones (1970), and Bhagwati, Brecher, and Hatta (1983).

the US current account imbalance.[4] Their model simply takes the spending changes necessary to eliminate the current account as given and does not capture the intertemporal and other considerations that might induce these.

The United States is assumed to be endowed with a fixed quantity of a tradable and nontradable good and, in addition, it imports a third good from abroad. A key assumption is that countries seek to consume more of their home products at given prices (home bias). If the US current account deficit is eliminated, the shift from US to foreign spending reduces the price of the US export good relative to the imported good. Within the United States, the price of the nontradable good relative to the tradable good also falls in response to the decline in domestic demand for US nontradables. The lower relative price of nontradables induces American consumers to shift their spending away from tradable toward nontradable goods, but encourages American producers to shift productive resources into the traded goods sector. Abroad, the price movements are in the opposite direction. All told, eliminating the US trade deficit worsens the US terms of trade and weakens the real US exchange rate. Prices in both US nontraded and export sectors decline. Thus, we are led to expect a downwardly sloped (negative) relationship between the terms of trade and the current account balance. Smaller deficits will be associated with worse terms of trade (and a weaker real exchange rate).

We should note that home bias is not required for this outcome. In theory, even if preferences are similar, the presence of trade transaction costs could also produce a negatively sloped function because the transaction costs make some goods and services nontradable—i.e., too expensive to trade. Again, Obstfeld and Rogoff (1996) develop a two-country, multigood Ricardian model with this property.[5]

Robert Dekle, Jonathan Eaton, and Samuel Kortum (2007) undertake a similar analysis in a multiproduct, multicountry Ricardian model. In the Ricardian framework, given relative productivity at home and abroad, relative wages will determine patterns of specialization. In a two-country framework, if the home country has wages that are twice as high as the foreign country, it will only be able to produce those goods in which it is at least twice as productive.[6] When there are nontraded goods and services, a reduction in domestic spending relative to incomes (i.e., net foreign lending) reduces the demand for nontradables. This leads to a reduction in relative nontraded prices and wages

---

4. A simple model of this process with two goods (one traded and one nontraded) can also be found in Krugman and Obstfeld (2003, 104–09).

5. In this model countries produce all goods for which their relative labor productivity exceeds their relative wages. See Dornbusch, Fischer, and Samuelson (1977).

6. In a multigood Ricardian framework, a uniform improvement in foreign productivity increases the range of industries in which it can compete. The home relative wage falls, and some industries migrate from the home country to the foreign country. However, the home country gains because its real wages rise. The relative price of the goods that the home country continues to produce rises. This case in discussed in Obstfeld and Rogoff (1996, 240–43), Dornbusch, Fischer, and Samuelson (1980), and Zhu (2007).

at home compared with those abroad. With given patterns of comparative advantage, lower relative wages at home increase the range of tradable products in which the lending (home) country is competitive and conversely reduce the range of goods in which the foreign country is competitive. Thus, production of some tradables shifts to the lending country and the terms of trade of the lending country decline. Large trade surpluses are therefore associated with lower US wages relative to the rest of the world and worse US terms of trade associated with lower real wages.[7]

Assessing Trade Performance

On the basis of this discussion we would expect that if the only change were in international lending and borrowing, there would be a negatively sloped relationship or schedule tracking the relation between the terms of trade and the trade balance. All else being equal, we would expect to find stronger US terms of trade associated with a larger US trade deficit.[8]

This is the schedule TT we have depicted in figure 6.3 as a downward-sloping schedule that relates the terms of trade to the trade balance. A pure transfer to the United States would move the economy from A to B, increasing the trade deficit (from C to D) but also increasing the terms of trade. Conversely, if the United States reduced its spending relative to income, i.e., borrowed less while the rest of the world did the opposite, i.e., lent less, the equilibrium would move from B to A and its terms of trade would decline as global spending on US products declined.

On the other hand, if there were a decline in US trade performance, (competitiveness) as captured in Samuelson's model because of import-biased growth abroad, the entire schedule would move downward (from TT to T^1T^1 in figure 6.3). With no additional capital, international borrowing, or lending, import-biased growth abroad would lower the terms of trade associated with any given trade balance, moving the economy to E, the point at which the trade balance is unchanged. In contrast, uniform technological change or export-biased growth abroad would shift the TT schedule upward for any given trade balance.

If we were to assume that the shocks that shift the transfer schedule up and down are separable from those that move the economy along the schedule, we could distinguish the effects of changes in the underlying determinants of the relative prices of international goods and services (tastes, incomes, factor endowments, technologies, microeconomic policies, etc.) from a movement along a given TT schedule that is due to changes in international borrowing and lending, i.e., expenditure changes. For example, although Samuelson's

---

7. This model is developed in Obstfeld and Rogoff (1996, 235–43). They present evidence of a positive slope in the relationship between changes in net foreign assets (i.e., current account surpluses) and real exchange rates.

8. For applications of this approach, see Baily and Lawrence (2006a, 2006b).

Figure 6.3 How shifts in the transfer schedule provide a measure of trade performance

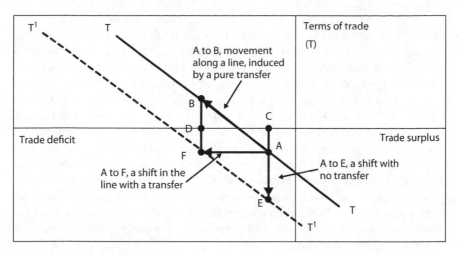

Source: Authors' illustration.

example related to a foreign shock that reduced the US terms of trade with balanced trade, we can equate his concern in the context of unbalanced trade as a downward shift in the entire TT schedule.

We do need to be cautious in making such an assumption because the current account will be driven by intertemporal considerations. In a frictionless, multigood Ricardian model, unanticipated permanent changes might not change the balance between present and future spending and thus have no current account effects, so our separation would be valid and permanent shocks would shift the transfer schedule up and down. However, an unexpected temporary shock could affect the real interest rate and thus induce current account changes as well as terms of trade changes, and thus the separation assumption need not always be valid.[9] Temporary shocks could also lead to permanent changes in wealth that would not be taken into account when computing the welfare implications of such changes. Thus, the full effects on welfare are not fully captured by the terms of trade at a particular point in time. In addition, the intertemporal considerations need to be weighed.[10]

---

9. This example is discussed in Obstfeld and Rogoff (1996, 244–48).

10. A country might well be better off by borrowing at one point in time and repaying its debts later, even if ultimately it has worse terms of trade than if it had not borrowed. Consider a decline in the real interest rate that induces borrowing $1 today and paying back $2 tomorrow. The terms of trade improvement in the first period might be less than the decline in the second. Nonetheless, welfare might still be improved. Conversely, even if the United States does close its current account, it will still be left with the change in its international indebtedness, and this could imply lower living standards in the future.

Our interest in this study is the impact of foreign economic growth, but after the fact, many shocks both at home and abroad could affect the outcome. This implies that we need to be cautious about attributing shifts in the TT curve purely to foreign growth. Domestic policies and performance could be responsible. Import tariffs influence not only trade flows but also the terms of trade. By restricting imports through tariff protection, large countries such as the United States are able to drive down the price of their imports and hence raise their terms of trade. Reductions in US tariffs, or alternatively increases in foreign tariffs imposed on US exports, would therefore also shift the TT schedule downward. Population growth and demand shifts are other factors. In a simple, multigood Ricardian model, relatively strong population growth abroad places downward pressure on foreign wages but stimulates home wages and therefore the home country's terms of trade through increases in demand for home exports. Similarly, shifts in global preferences toward US goods are expected to raise the US terms of trade (Dornbusch, Fischer, and Samuelson 1977). All told, therefore, while the schedule we have illustrated is a useful heuristic, to apply it empirically, a means for sorting out these various shocks should be provided.

Graphical Analysis of the Relationship between Terms of Trade and Trade Balance

The transfer theory leads us to expect that the terms of trade will improve when countries run larger trade deficits. The simplest empirical approach is to plot the association between the trade balance and the terms of trade relationship. Bearing in mind the qualifications discussed above, this association should not be interpreted as causal. The plots capture the ex post relationship between two highly endogenous variables, and as we have noted, in theory, depending on what kinds of shocks are hitting the economies, the relationship between them could take many forms. Nevertheless, such diagrams are useful in evaluating whether shifts in the relationship between the trade balance and the terms of trade are consistent with the concerns raised by Samuelson. Figure 6.4 therefore plots the association between the trade balance in goods and services and the terms of trade for the years from 1990 to 2009.

Variable Construction

Various rigidities in adjusting prices, contracts, and production processes imply that the terms of trade and the trade balance do not immediately and simultaneously equilibrate in response to exogenous shocks, including, among others, consumer preferences, future expectations, tariff changes, and government expenditure. The trade balance in goods and services in figure 6.4 is therefore calculated as the three-year moving average ratio of the nominal trade balance in goods and services to GDP multiplied by 100. For our price

Figure 6.4 Nominal trade balance in goods and services and lagged terms of trade, 1990–2009

terms of trade

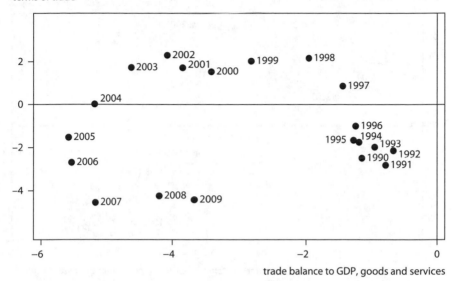

trade balance to GDP, goods and services

Note: The trade balance in goods and services is calculated as the three-year moving average ratio of the nominal trade balance in goods and services to GDP multiplied by 100. For our price variable we use the three-year moving average of the US terms of trade indices (in logs multiplied by 100).

Source: Authors' calculations using data obtained from the Bureau of Economic Analysis.

variable we use the three-year moving average of the US terms of trade indices (in logs multiplied by 100).[11]

During the 1990s, we find a negative, although variable, association between the trade balance and the terms of trade that is broadly consistent with our theoretical expectations—a rise in terms of trade is associated with a larger US trade deficit. However, looking at the more recent observations in the plot, there is a noticeable shift downward of the relationship. In 2000 and 2009, for example, the trade balance as a share of GDP was similar, but the terms of trade had fallen by around 6 percent.

The key factor explaining the decline after 2003 is oil. The increase in oil prices contributed substantially toward the widening of the trade deficit after 2000. This is made clear when we exclude oil imports (and oil import prices) from the estimates (figure 6.5). We now find that from the 1990s through 2004 the relationship traces out what appears to be a remarkably stable negatively sloped schedule that conforms to our expectations using the transfer

---

11. The relevant data are obtained from the Bureau of Economic Analysis.

Figure 6.5 Nominal nonpetroleum trade balance and lagged terms of trade, 1990–2009

nonpetroleum terms of trade

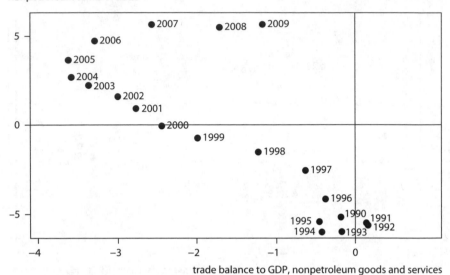

trade balance to GDP, nonpetroleum goods and services

Source: Authors' calculations using data obtained from the Bureau of Economic Analysis.

framework. As of 2004 we actually see a dramatic improvement in the nonoil terms of trade for any given trade balance (figure 6.5). By 2009, the nonpetroleum terms of trade were 7 log points greater than in 1998, despite similar ratios of the nonpetroleum trade balance to GDP. Further, if we project the slope of the nonoil transfer schedule from 1990 to 2003 to simulate a return of the three-year average trade-balance-to-GDP ratio from 2009 to 1990 levels, we find that the adjusted (nonoil) terms of trade in 2009 were 8.5 log points greater than in 1990.[12]

The US nonoil terms of trade were therefore higher in 2009 than in 1990, even after accounting for the increase in the trade deficit over this period. This shift is contrary to what we would expect if Samuelson's concerns about import-biased growth in developing countries were valid and were the dominant reason for the shift in the transfer schedule. Rather, the data are more consistent with strong nonoil export-biased growth in foreign countries that would have enhanced US welfare.

---

12. The slope of the schedule from 1990 to 2003 is –2.35. To return the three-year average nonoil trade-balance-to-GDP ratio in 2009 to the 1990 average level would require a reduction in the deficit of 1 percentage point and a decline in in the terms of trade from 5.66 to 3.32 (i.e., 2.3 log points). These adjusted terms of trade are 8.49 log points greater than the three-year moving average terms of trade in 1990 (–5.17).

In sum, the United States experienced dramatic increases in the trade deficit from the early 1990s, as trade with developing countries rose sharply. Increases in the oil price played a considerable role in increasing the deficit, and our diagrammatic analysis suggests that this reduced US living standards after 2002. During the 1990s and early 2000s, however, we find no support for Samuelson's concerns that developing-country growth is adversely affecting US living standards through the nonoil terms of trade. On the contrary, we find that the nonoil terms of trade associated with a given trade balance actually improved after 2004, leaving the US economy with a higher nonoil terms of trade in 2009 than in 1990, even after adjusting for the increase in the trade deficit. Outside of its impact on oil, the US terms of trade improvement therefore appears to have been beneficial to US welfare.

Welfare

Simulation Models

The figures presented are not structural models of the complex relationships underpinning shifts in both the trade balance and the terms of trade. The relationships depicted are nevertheless corroborated by theory-based structural models.

Obstfeld and Rogoff (2004), for example, use their two-country, three-good general equilibrium model to simulate the implications for the US terms of trade and the real exchange rate if the United States closed the current account deficit from 5 percent of GDP to full balance. They model spending behavior as reflecting choices between tradable and nontradable goods and services as well as between importables and exportables. This allows them to estimate changes in both the real exchange rate and the terms of trade associated with current account adjustment. They then assume that the deficit is closed through spending shifts—i.e., reductions in US aggregate demand and increases in foreign aggregate demand—while holding output at home and abroad constant.

They simulate achieving balance using a variety of calibration parameters and adjustment processes. They find that, depending on their assumptions about the responses of demand to relative prices, the real exchange rate depreciation required to facilitate balance varies between 33.6 and 14.7 percent. The terms of trade changes that are associated with these real exchange rate changes are, however, much smaller. Such changes require terms of trade declines of 7.1 and 3.4 percent, when the required real exchange change is 33.7 and 14.7 percent, respectively. Thus, each 1 percent decline in the real exchange rate results in changes in the terms of trade of between 0.21 percent (i.e., 7.1/33.7) and 0.23 percent (3.4/14.7).

The associated change in the terms of trade derived by Obstfeld and Rogoff is actually remarkably close to what would be predicted by a linear estimate of a transfer schedule over the period 1980–2003. When we ran a regression line that relates the terms of trade to the current account balance (inclusive of oil) as a share of GDP over 1980–2003, we estimated a slope coefficient of –1.56 (the slope equals –1.41 over the shorter 1990–2003 period). According to this regression coefficient, the closing of a 5 percent of GDP deficit would historically be associated with a 7.805 percent decline in the terms of trade—a result that is very similar to the upper estimate of Obstfeld and Rogoff.

These simulations suggest that the nonoil terms of trade gains in recent years are unlikely to be fully offset, even if the United States were to close the current account. Using 2010 data, the trade balance would need to rise by 3.6 percent of GDP to eliminate the entire deficit. According to the Obstfeld-Rogoff simulations, this would reduce the US terms of trade by between 2.5 and 5.1 percent. Most of this adjustment in the current account is likely to come about through changes in the nonoil trade balance. Oil imports made up 15 percent of total imports of goods and services in 2010. Hence, the decline in the nonoil terms of trade if the entire adjustment were to come about through changes in the nonoil trade balance would be around 15 percent larger than the aggregate terms of trade, i.e., a decline of between 3 and 6 percent. These values are still smaller than the 7 to 8.5 percent upward shift of the nonoil terms of trade that we find in figure 6.5. This implies that even with Obstfeld and Rogoff's most adverse estimates of the terms of trade, a modest improvement in the nonoil terms of trade would remain if the United States were to restore balance, even taking into account the increased costs of imported oil.

These simulations suggest that the closing of a large US current account deficit could require fairly large movements in the real US exchange rate and quite substantial reductions in dollar wages in the United States compared with those in the rest of the world. However, the models also suggest that the changes relevant for living standards, such as the reductions in the terms of trade and the fall in real wages, are much smaller.[13]

This limited impact of real exchange rate adjustment on the US terms of trade and thus real US incomes reflects two key features of the US economy: first, a large share of the economy produces nontradables, and second, a large share of tradables production is consumed at home. A considerable part of the adjustment in the US current account requires shifting US spending away from tradable goods and services and US production toward these goods and services. But this occurs by changing the relative price of tradables to nontradables. While changes in the prices of nontradables will affect the real exchange rate and relative wages in the United States compared to the rest of the world, internal relative price changes do not affect aggregate US welfare or real wages in terms of nontraded goods. Whatever some Americans lose from these inter-

---

13. Simulations using the Dekle, Eaton, and Kortum (2007) model, for example, calculate that eliminating the 2004 US current account deficit would reduce wages in the United States relative to those abroad by 7 percent but that real wages in the United States would only fall by less than 1 percent.

nal shifts, other Americans will gain. Thus, the net real income and aggregate welfare effects operate only via trade, and given the small share of trade in the economy, the real income effects are quite modest. In addition, the more substitutable that foreign and domestic tradables are, the smaller the terms of trade shifts required to achieve any given trade balance.[14]

Trade Models

As described more fully in our background paper for this study (Edwards and Lawrence 2012), we have explained the evolution of the US nonoil trade balance by decomposing changes in the nominal trade balance into its structural determinants using standard trade equations. Our aim is to isolate how developing countries have influenced US trade flows and to explore the implications of developing-country growth on the US terms of trade in this framework. The analysis obtains on average a historical relationship between the real exchange rate and the terms of trade (the pass-through relationship) that resembles the relationship implied by Obstfeld and Rogoff. Indeed, we find that the pass-through may have recently declined. This lends support to the conclusion that even with balanced trade the United States would have experienced some improvement in its nonoil terms of trade.

As described more fully in the background paper, we have estimated trade prices and trade volumes separately. First we specify and estimate various equations for export prices, import prices, and the terms of trade following the standard approaches surveyed by Pinelopi Goldberg and Michael Knetter (1997).[15] We then estimate equations for import and export volumes, relating these to relative price and activity variables.

Our results have important implications for this discussion. First, there is a noteworthy decline in recent pass-through of exchange rates into prices that is evident in the data and confirmed by our regressions. In most periods up to 2002, there is a reasonably close association between the real exchange rate and the terms of trade. The terms of trade improved for most end-use categories during periods of dollar appreciation (1980–85 and 1995–2002) and worsened during periods of dollar depreciation (1985–90). This close association also explains the similar trends in the nonoil terms of trade and real exchange rate relative to the trade balance during these periods.

After 2002, however, the relationship between the terms of trade and real exchange rate reverses for many sectors. The dollar depreciated by 17 percent from 2002 to 2007, but the nonoil terms of trade actually improved. This is

14. Obstfeld and Rogoff (2004) show that higher elasticity of substitution between traded and nontraded goods (= 2) and between imported and exported goods (= 3) reduces the required depreciation (from 33.6 to 14.7 percent) and the decline in the terms of trade (3.9 percent).

15. We regress the growth in US export and import prices on domestic or foreign marginal production costs, the nominal effective dollar to foreign currency exchange rate, the price of foreign or US substitutes, the price of commodities, and the lagged dependent variable.

reflected in our regression coefficients. We find that the long-run exchange rate pass-through to the terms of trade of each 1 percent change in the dollar fluctuated between 0.3 and 0.4 percent up to the beginning of the 1990s, but then declined secularly, reaching less than 0.1 percent for the 15-year period ending in 2007. If shorter periods are selected, the pass-through coefficient actually becomes negative as the sample enters the post-2000 period. This suggests that the relationship between the terms of trade and the real exchange rate (the pass-through coefficient) derived by Obstfeld and Rogoff of around 0.22 percent is very reasonable.

The literature indicates that one source of the decline in pass-through to import prices is China. Mario Marazzi et al. (2005) find that the pass-through has declined most steeply in those product categories in which China expanded its import market share most rapidly. The effect is closely related to China's peg to the dollar over much of the post-2000 period. Paul Bergin and Robert Feenstra (2009) show theoretically that the rising import shares of countries with fixed exchange rates lead to a disproportionate reduction in the pass-through of exchange rates to US import prices. They estimate that the rising share of trade from China, or from all countries with fixed exchange rates, explains a decline in pass-through by about one-fifth of its size over the period 1993–2006.

In effect, by pegging its currency to the dollar, China (and other pegging countries) disciplines pricing behavior of other exporters. When currencies appreciate in other countries relative to the dollar, the presence of China seems to have restrained these countries' ability to pass on their higher dollar costs. The result is that the impact of China on the US terms of trade is actually greater than its share in US trade flows.

An important consequence is that the price effects of a Chinese appreciation in reducing this discipline could be considerable. An appreciation of the renminbi could lead to a more sizable decline in the US terms of trade as other developing countries raise their own export prices.

Changes in the composition of US imports have also contributed to a decline in the pass-through. Imports have shifted toward finished-goods imports (consumer goods, capital, and automotive products) where the pass-through is relatively low, and the decline is away from material-intensive goods (food and beverages, nonoil industrial supplies) where the pass-through is higher (Marazzi et al. 2005, Campa and Goldberg 2005).[16] The change in composition also explains the association between China's share and the decline in the pass-through, as it is in the finished products that China's import shares increased the most.

We have also estimated trade volume regressions and explored their stability. We find that for each 1 percent increase in US growth, imports rise by 1.6

---

16. However, Gita Gopinath and Roberto Rigobon (2008) find that within-product changes in the frequency of price adjustments are the main determinant of a decline in the average price stickiness of US imports.

percent. While 1 percent growth in foreign income raises US export volumes by 2.1 percent in the long run, it also raises US import demand in the form of new varieties by 0.78 percent.[17] All told, therefore, equal growth rates in the United States and the rest of the world will lead to larger trade deficits for the United States, but faster growth in the rest of the world increases US exports by more than US imports. Thus, had developing countries grown even faster, the variety of imports available to Americans would have been even greater and the terms of trade associated with any given trade balance even higher.

Finally, we use the structural trade volume and price equations to simulate the impact of a restoration of the US nonoil trade balance from 2007 to 1990 levels. According to our estimates, this would require a depreciation of 15 percent in the real dollar exchange rate. Using the average pass-through coefficient of 0.25, the required depreciation would be associated with a 3.75 percent reduction in the nonoil terms of trade. Yet the actual nonoil US terms of trade, after taking into account exchange rate and commodity price trends, improved by 8.8 log points from 1990 to 2007.

According to our estimates, therefore, a restoration of the US nonoil trade balance from 2007 to 1990 levels would still leave the United States with a 5 log-point improvement in the nonoil terms of trade. In addition, the country would enjoy an increase in the varieties of imports. We conclude, therefore, that foreign growth unambiguously improved aggregate US welfare over the period from 1990 to 2007 even when the trade deficit is taken into account.

In sum, our graphical analysis, the simulations based on Obstfeld and Rogoff, and our regression estimates all suggest that even taking into account the impact of larger trade deficits on the terms of trade, growth in developing countries has been good for the United States. Contrary to the concerns raised by Samuelson, the US nonoil terms of trade have increased from the early 1990s, even after accounting for the increase in the trade deficit. These trends are consistent with export-biased growth in developing countries, which has enhanced US gains from trade through improvements in the US nonoil terms of trade and increased the variety of products available to Americans.

---

17. This estimate is similar to those of the IMF (2007), Peter Hooper, Karen Johnson, and Jaime Marquez (2000), Paul Krugman and Richard Baldwin (1987), and Peter Hooper and Catherine Mann (1987) but exceeds those of Hendrik S. Houthakker and Stephen Magee (1969), who estimate a long-run foreign income elasticity close to 1. We are nevertheless concerned that the high-income elasticity arises from the use of hedonic price indices in the capital goods sector. Rapid improvements in the quality and characteristics of computer products increase the measured quantity of these goods, even if there is no change in the number of items produced. This effect is equivalent to an increase in varieties, which biases the estimated income elasticities upward. For a similar reason, computer products were excluded from the estimates in Lawrence (1990).

7

Oil

We have seen in the earlier chapters that oil price fluctuations have had a profound impact on the US current account, terms of trade, and welfare. This has been most noticeable since 2003, when dramatic increases in the price of oil more than offset improvements in the nonoil terms of trade. The earlier chapters attributed much of the improved nonoil terms of trade to export-biased growth in developing countries. But Lawrence Summers has emphasized that oil prices are not independent of developing-country growth.[1] Indeed, since oil is scarce (and especially limited in supply in the short run), increased global demand arising from developing-country growth drives up its price. As a large net importer of oil, the United States is adversely affected by this scenario.

If valid, the possibility arises that the gains to US consumers from cheaper nonoil merchandise imports associated with developing-country growth may have been more than offset by rising oil prices. This chapter therefore unpacks the determinants of the oil price increases since 2000 using an elementary demand-supply framework that allows us to estimate the separate effects of changes in demand and supply conditions in developed and developing countries.

This exercise suggests that the shortfall in the supply of oil by advanced countries is the predominant source of the overall world demand-supply gap that drove increases in oil prices after 2000. Chinese demand for oil was indeed a significant contributor to price pressures after 2000 and especially after

---

1. Lawrence Summers, "America Needs to Make a New Case for Trade," *Financial Times*, April 27, 2008.

2008, but much of its impact was offset by increases in the net supply of oil by OPEC and other emerging-market economies, such as those in the former Soviet Union. In contrast, declines in the supply of oil by advanced countries (particularly North Sea oil), combined with income growth (albeit modest), led to large increases in the net demand for oil by these countries. All told, we find that the net pressures on global demand attributable to advanced economies caused about 80 percent of the oil price increases between 2000 and 2008. After 2008, the relative contribution of the advanced economies declined, but they still accounted for about two-thirds of the rise between 2000 and 2011. Thus, while the US terms of trade have declined due to oil, the role of emerging-market economies in this decline is far less than many believe.

The chapter also looks at the future scenarios for global demand and supply of oil developed by the US Energy Information Administration (EIA 2011, 2012). These projections show how relatively small supply and demand imbalances can result in world crude oil prices in 2035 (in 2010 dollars) ranging from $50 to $200 per barrel. For a large net importer of oil like the United States, price increases toward the upper-bound estimate will have additional adverse effects on welfare. Further, tightness in the world oil markets, combined with shocks from political and other sources, also exposes the United States to considerable fluctuations in its terms of trade and macroeconomic balances. On the other hand, relatively small improvements in conservation and production could lead to considerably lower prices globally, and increases in US production and conservation could reduce US vulnerabilities to such disturbances. However, over time this concern is likely to diminish. Indeed, according to the International Energy Agency (IEA 2012) by 2030 the United States could become a net oil exporter so that higher oil prices will become a source of improved US welfare rather than a reason for concern.

This chapter first looks at the dependence of the United States on oil imports and its vulnerability to oil price shocks. The next section explains the recent oil price boom, attributing oil price changes to the supply and demand conditions in OECD and non-OECD countries. The chapter ends by looking to the future and presents various scenarios for the global energy economy.

Oil Price Fluctuations and the US Economy

As noted earlier, oil price fluctuations have had a profound impact on the US economy. This is clearly revealed by the dramatic changes since 1970 in the cost of US petroleum imports as a share of GDP (figure 7.1). The first major price increase in late 1973 came at a time when US oil import volumes were rising, and although import growth had begun to wane by the time of the second shock in 1979, the cost of oil imports increased from just 0.25 percent of GDP in 1971 to 3.2 percent in the first quarter of 1980. Thereafter real oil prices declined steadily, and although import volumes increased after 1986, the cost of oil imports had shrunk back to just half a percent of GDP by 1999.

Figure 7.1   US petroleum imports as share of GDP, 1969–2011

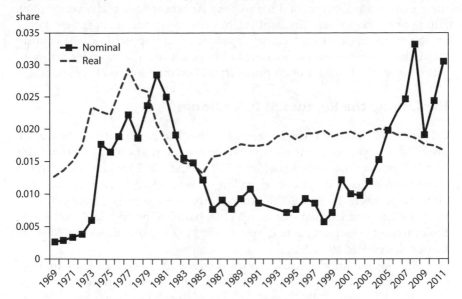

Source: Bureau of Economic Analysis, National Income Accounts data, www.bea.gov/national/index.htm (accessed on November 1, 2012).

Import volumes actually remained a constant share of real GDP until the global financial crisis, but after the 2001 recession prices rose steadily as the market tightened. Import costs doubled to reach 1 percent of GDP in 2002 and by 2006 had doubled again. In the second quarter of 2008 they peaked at record levels—3.5 percent of GDP.[2] Prices plummeted in the face of the crisis and by the first quarter of 2009 oil import costs had fallen to just 1.5 percent of GDP. Thereafter, however, as the world economy began to recover, oil prices began to increase again, and although by 2011 US import volumes of petroleum products were 12.3 percent below their 2005 levels, the 3.1 percent nominal share of these imports was almost back to the 3.3 percent recorded in 2008.[3]

The effect of oil price changes on the US economy is thus mixed: sometimes oil price declines have helped stabilize the economy but at other times their effects have been extremely damaging. For example, in 1974, 1980, 1990,

---

2. We should note that the United States also has substantial volumes of oil exports, so the net welfare exposure of the economy is overestimated by considering only imports. For example, the trade balance in petroleum products on an end-use basis was equivalent to 1.8 and 2.2 percent of GDP in 2010 and 2011, respectively.

3. Crude oil prices averaged $74.60 and $99.82 a barrel, respectively. Bureau of Economic Analysis, US International Trade in Goods and Services, Tables 8 and 10, www.bea.gov/international/index.htm (accessed on November 1, 2012).

and 2007–08 the price increases diminished purchasing power at times when the economy was slowing for other reasons. At other times, such as early 2009, falling prices helped stabilize demand, but thereafter rising prices were a drag on the recovery. Given US levels of dependence on imported oil, the country clearly has a strong interest not only in low prices but also in stable prices. In this context, the behavior of oil prices after 2000 merits closer examination.

Explaining the Recent Oil Price Boom

Oil prices in 2003 were at the same levels as they had been in 2000. The average prices of two types of crude oil reported by the International Monetary Fund (*World Economic Outlook* database) were $28.32 and $28.78, while in the United States average gasoline prices per gallon were $2.03 and $2.01 in 2000 and 2007, respectively. By July 2008, however, the average price of imported petroleum fuel products had soared to $124 a barrel. Spot oil prices on the New York mercantile exchange actually peaked at $147, and on average in 2008 the United States paid $95 a barrel.

The reasons for the soaring price increase have been a major topic of debate. Fingers have been pointed at both the Organization of Petroleum Exporting Countries (OPEC) and "oil speculators," but many have claimed that the rapid growth in emerging-market economies such as China was the most important reason. According to oil expert James L. Smith (2009, 155), for example, "Surely one of the biggest shocks that started the run-up in oil prices in the early 2000s was the sharp rise in demand for oil from China and other developing nations."

Indeed, Chinese demand growth was extraordinarily strong between 2000 and 2008. Oil consumption increased by 49 percent, from 4.8 to 7.85 million barrels a day (mbd) over the full period and by an astounding 25 percent just between 2002 and 2004. Since Chinese oil production rose over the same period by just 17 percent to 3.97 mbd in 2008, the rapid growth in net demand from Chinese imports was an important reason for the price pressures. But developments in other emerging-market economies actually offset some of the Chinese impact, so that overall, the increases in net demand from the advanced (Organization for Economic Cooperation and Development) countries were larger than that of the emerging-market economies taken together.

The impact of supply shortfalls and demand growth can be estimated with a simple demand and supply framework. This is necessary because the (ex post) data on actual consumption already reflect the influence of high prices. To capture the demand pressures generated by growth, therefore, it is necessary to estimate the (ex ante) demand that would have existed had prices not increased.[4]

---

4. In order to identify the demand curve, we assume that at each point in time, oil supplies are given.

Table 7.1 Sources of oil market supply and demand pressure

Indicator		World	Advanced economies	Emerging-market economies	United States	China
GDP growth, 1995–2000 (log points)	(1)	0.18	0.16	0.22	0.20	0.41
Oil consumption growth, 1995–2000 (log points)	(2)	0.10	0.06	0.17	0.11	0.36
Income elasticity, 1995–2000 (log points)	(3) = (2)/(1)		0.39	0.76	0.53	0.86
GDP growth, 2000–2008 (log points)	(4)		0.17	0.50	0.17	0.78
Ex ante demand, 2000–2008 (log points)	(5) = (4) × (3)		0.07	0.38	0.09	0.67
Ex ante demand growth, 2000–2008 (million barrels a day)	(6)	14.26	3.07	11.19	1.70	3.02
Production growth, 2000–2008 (million barrels a day)	(7)	7.62	–2.32	9.93	–0.55	0.59
Shortfall, 2000–2008 (million barrels a day)	(8) = (6) – (7)	6.64	5.39	1.26	2.25	2.43
Shortfall share, 2000–2008 (percent)		100.00	81.00	19.00	34.00	37.00
Shortfall, 2000–2011 (million barrels a day)		8.92	5.93	2.99	1.42	3.62
Shortfall share, 2000–2011 (percent)		100.00	66.50	33.50	15.93	40.55

Sources: International Monetary Fund, *World Economic Outlook* database; International Energy Agency.

The steps we take to do this are traced out in table 7.1. We use data from a more normal period (1995 to 2000) when the annual price of crude was fairly stable, averaging around $19 a barrel. While prices were as low as $13 a barrel in 1998 and as high as $28 in 2000, in the other years they were very close to the period average of $19.[5] Since oil consumption is generally relatively unresponsive to relative prices in the short run, we ignore the responses to price changes and assume all changes during that period were due to income growth. This allows us to estimate the responsiveness of oil demand to income growth in advanced and emerging-market economies (i.e., the income elasticity of demand). We then use that elasticity to project what oil demand would have been given income growth had prices remained constant, which we call ex ante demand. Since supply did not keep up with demand, after-the-fact higher prices forced reductions in actual consumption, but we take the difference

---

5. The price is the simple average of three average petroleum spot prices (APSP): Dated Brent, West Texas Intermediate, and the Dubai Fateh, taken from the IMF's *World Economic Outlook* database.

between ex ante demand and actual supply as an indication of the pressures exerted on world prices by different countries and parts of the world.

We start by reporting the logarithmic (basically percentage) changes in GDP growth (row 1) and oil consumption (row 2) from 1995 through 2000, assuming the data for OECD consumption growth represent oil consumption growth in the advanced countries and the data for non-OECD countries represent consumption growth in emerging-market countries.[6] As reported in row 3, taking the consumption-to-GDP-growth ratios of the variables, we obtain estimates of 0.39 and 0.76 for income demand elasticities for advanced and emerging-market economies, respectively (and 0.86 and 0.53 for China and the United States, respectively).

As shown in row 4, between 2000 and 2008, real GDP in the advanced and emerging-market economies increased by 17 and 50 log points, respectively. The elasticity estimates imply that at constant prices, this would have raised oil demand by 7 and 38 log points in advanced and emerging-market economies, respectively (row 5). Applying these growth rate estimates to OECD and non-OECD oil consumption in 2000, we conclude that ex ante world oil demand increased by 17.1 points or 14.3 mbd—with 3.1 mbd attributable to income growth in developed countries and 11.2 mbd to income growth in developing countries (row 6).

Given this growth in demand, had world oil production increased by 17.1 log points or 14.3 mbd, real oil prices would not have changed. In fact, world production increased by just 10.7 log points, i.e., by just 7.62 mbd (row 7). This implied a shortfall of 6.64 mbd in world production that had to be rationed through higher prices (row 8). If the demand elasticity for oil is 0.05 (one-twentieth), prices would have had to rise by 184 percent to clear the market.[7] Prices of $28 a barrel in 2000 would increase to $80 in 2000 dollars by 2008. The US consumer price index increased by 25 percent between 2000 and 2008. Thus, the $80 prices would translate to $100 in 2008 prices. In fact, the IMF measure of oil prices in 2008 averaged $97 a barrel. These are very much back-of-the-envelope calculations, but they do show how the supply and demand fundamentals could have resulted in oil prices at the average levels of 2008.

But how much of this increase in price can be attributed to demand and supply conditions in developed and emerging-market economies? Remarkably, between 2000 and 2008, as a group, countries that were not members of the OECD increased their oil production by 9.93 mbd or 16.7 log points. This was just 0.4 log points less than the pace that would have been required

---

6. There is a (small) mismatch and upward bias in the income-demand elasticity, since the oil consumption data for the OECD include growth in the oil consumption of economies such as Turkey, Mexico, and Korea that are included in the emerging-market-economy GDP aggregate.

7. John Cooper (2003) finds short- and long-run elasticities for the United States of 0.06 and –0.46, which is reached after seven years. Salman Ghouri (2001) actually estimates long-run price elasticities of –0.045, –0.06, and –0.13 for the United States, Canada, and Mexico, respectively. According to Smith (2009), estimates of –0.05 and –0.30 are typical short- and long-run elasticities.

Table 7.2   International crude oil and liquid fuel supply, 2000 and 2008
(million barrels a day, except OECD commercial stocks)

Region/country	2000	2008	Change, 2000–08 (log points)
OECD	23.2	20.9	−0.105
United States (50 states)	9.1	8.5	−0.063
Canada	2.8	3.4	0.197
Mexico	3.5	3.2	−0.081
North Sea	6.2	4.3	−0.363
Other OECD	1.8	1.6	−0.131
Non-OECD	54.5	64.5	0.167
OPEC	31.2	35.7	0.135
Crude oil portion	28.2	31.3	0.104
Other liquids	3.0	4.5	0.393
Former Soviet Union	8.2	12.5	0.424
China	3.4	4.0	0.161
Other non-OECD	11.8	12.2	0.040
Total world production	77.8	85.4	0.093
Non-OPEC production	46.6	49.7	0.065

OECD = Organization for Economic Cooperation and Development; OPEC = Organization of Petroleum Exporting Countries

Source: US Energy Information Administration.

to maintain global price stability had their share in production remained constant, and only 1.26 mbd short of the 11.2 mbd required to meet the growth in emerging-market-economy demand alone. As shown in table 7.2, OPEC production expanded somewhat more slowly than this required pace—by 13.5 log points—but this was offset by the rapid growth in supply coming from the former Soviet Union. Thus, while developing-country growth drove the global demand for oil, these countries taken as a whole almost offset this demand through increased supply growth.

The same cannot be said of the OECD. Between 2000 and 2008, OECD production, which constituted 30 percent of world production in 2000, declined by almost 10 percent or 2.3 mbd. The largest factor was the drop of 1.9 mbd from North Sea oil production. There were also declines in production in the 50 US states (by 0.54 mbd or 6 percent) and Mexico (0.27 mbd or 7.8 percent). Smith (2009) ascribes this to the increased cost of oil production. Ex ante, the shortfall in the OECD from 3.07 mbd in demand growth plus the 2.32 mbd in supply totaled 5.39 mbd. This represented 81 percent of the overall world demand-supply gap.

Chinese demand was indeed a significant contributor to price pressures during the period. Taken alone, excess ex ante net demand from China contributed 37 percent of the pressures (row 9 of table 7.1). But strikingly, even though the US growth rate was slower and income elasticity lower than China's, because of the scale of America's oil use and the decline in its oil production, the contribution of the 50 US states was of a similar order of magnitude, 34 percent (row 9).

This is a very rough calculation and the numbers should be taken with a large grain of salt. First, we have assumed that the income-demand elasticities we found between 1995 and 2000 did not change over the next decade. In addition, we have implicitly assumed similar price-demand elasticities in developed and developing countries and similar pass-through of crude oil prices into final demand. In fact, neither of these assumptions is warranted and they go in opposite directions. On the one hand, it is likely that consumer demand in developing countries is more responsive to price changes. The responses could also be smaller in rich countries with high oil taxes. This would mean that the contributions of the rich countries were actually larger. On the other hand, governments in developing countries have raised subsidies and not passed higher oil prices through to final consumers. This could lead to smaller responses and larger contributions to higher prices than we have imputed. In addition, over time there has been massive structural change in countries such as China and this is likely to have increased its oil income-demand elasticity.

Nonetheless, we have been able to provide a coherent account of the annual behavior of oil prices using simple supply and demand analysis. We stress "annual." Our job has been made easier because oil prices fell so dramatically in response to the global financial crisis. While we were able to track the annual average in 2008, we have not attempted to explain the short-run spike that drove prices as high as $147 a barrel in July of that year. Undoubtedly, as James Hamilton (2009) explains well, in the short run other factors enter. Some reflect developments in the oil market itself. For example, inventory levels, mismatches in the delivery of particular grades with refinery capacity, and the behavior of hedge funds and other speculators. But it is certainly not necessary to resort to cataclysmic explanations such as "peak oil"—the imminent running out of reserves. Global oil demand is extremely unresponsive to price changes, so relatively small supply shortfalls can lead to very high prices.

Our calculations also imply that the decline in US welfare from oil price shocks cannot be attributed to developing-country growth alone. Indeed, most of it reflects behavior in the advanced economies. Adverse oil supply shocks in OECD countries that led to major demand-supply shortfalls in these countries was the predominant source of oil price pressures from 2000 to 2008.

Since 2008, the picture has changed somewhat, primarily as a result of the recessions in the OECD and continued growth in developing economies. In addition, US production has increased while consumption has declined. As reported in the final row of table 7.1, we have carried out a similar analysis for the full period from 2000 to 2011. Over that period growth in advanced and emerging-market economies increased by 67 and 17.6 long points, respectively. Their production shortfalls relative to projected ex ante demands were 5.9 and 3.0 mbd, respectively. Thus we still find that over the entire period the overwhelming contribution to higher prices—66.5 percent—can be ascribed to the advanced economies, while the estimated increase in China's contribution has increased to 41 percent and the US impact has fallen to 16 percent. In recent years, therefore, the emerging-market economies and especially China are clearly having a greater impact.

The Future

Annual income twenty pounds, annual expenditure nineteen six, result happiness. Annual income twenty pounds, annual expenditure twenty pound ought and six, result misery.

—Mr. Micawber, in Charles Dickens' *David Copperfield*

The EIA (2011) presents three scenarios for the global energy economy from 2008 to 2035 in which the outcomes differ because of differences in supply growth. The scenarios are summarized in table 7.3.[8] All three scenarios are predicated on the same global GDP growth, so they allow us to see the responsiveness of prices to changes in supply.[9] Like Mr. Micawber in the quotation above, the projections show how relatively small supply-demand imbalances can radically change outcomes—from happiness to misery (for oil consumers). If global supplies of liquid fuels grow at 1.6 percent per annum between 2008 and 2035, the result is world crude oil prices (low-sulfur light crude) in 2035 of $50 a barrel (in 2009 dollars). If world production grows at 1 percent per annum, however, prices rise to $125. And if the production growth rate is just 0.8 percent annually, prices reach $200. The bottom line is that all it takes to shift from the high-price scenario to the low-price scenario in which real oil prices grow 5.3 percent more slowly is for supplies to increase 0.8 percent a year faster. The shift from the reference case to the low-price scenario takes growth of just 0.6 percent per year.[10]

While the low-price scenario developed by the EIA is driven by increased production, it suggests another way to achieve low prices: technological and other improvements that reduce oil consumption and increase the production of oil and oil substitutes outside OPEC. If these could achieve overall reductions in net demand for oil of 20 percent relative to the current reference case, the price outlook could be dramatically altered. Acting alone, the OECD could achieve this by reducing its oil consumption by 40 percent or by 1.5 percent annually relative to the reference case. The conservation would have to come

---

8. The EIA refers to these as "traditional" scenarios, since until recently its approach was to hold GDP constant and only change supply to generate different price paths. However, more recently the EIA has allowed both demand and supply to shift when generating the scenarios.

9. Between 2008 and 2035, GDP growth measured at purchasing power parity is assumed to average 2.5, 3.4, and 4.6 percent annually for the United States, the world, and the non-OECD countries, respectively.

10. This results from the fact that oil demand is very inelastic—indeed, the price differences between the low- and high-price scenarios imply a demand elasticity of –0.15.

Table 7.3   Energy Information Administration scenario projections for liquid fuels

Indicator	2008	2035 Low	2035 Reference	2035 High
Oil price in 2009 dollars (per barrel)		50.0	125.0	200.0
World production/consumption (million barrels a day)	85.7	131.5	112.2	107.4
Annual growth rate (percent)		1.6	1.0	0.8
OECD consumption (million barrels a day)	48.0	56.0	50.0	48.0
OPEC production (million barrels a day)	35.6	68.0	46.9	34.1
Annual growth rate (percent)		2.4	1.0	−0.2
Non-OPEC production (million barrels a day)	50.0	63.5	65.3	73.3
Annual growth rate (percent)		0.9	1.0	1.4
Annual world GDP growth (percent)		3.4	3.4	3.4

OECD = Organization for Economic Cooperation and Development; OPEC = Organization of Petroleum Exporting Countries

Source: US Energy Information Administration, September 2011.

in the transportation sector, which accounts for the largest increment in total liquids demand, at nearly 80 percent of the total world increase.

Faster Growth in Emerging-Market Economies

The EIA has another set of simulations in which it explores the implications of different GDP growth rates. For our purposes a particularly interesting scenario compares prices in the base case, in which the non-OECD economies grow at an annual rate of 4.6 percent per year, with a scenario in which the growth in these countries averages one percentage point lower, i.e., 3.6 percent. This slower growth suffices to change the reference case (with $125 a barrel in 2009 prices) into the low-price scenario with prices of $50 a barrel in 2035. In other words, a 1 percent slower growth rate in emerging-market economies has the same impact on global prices as faster global production of 0.6 percent per year.[11] Comparing these scenarios indicates that allowing for supply responses due to price changes, each 1 percent slower growth in emerging-market countries reduces the annual growth rate in prices by 3.6 percent. In 2011, when crude oil averaged $100 a barrel, US net imports of petroleum and products were equivalent to 2.2 percent of US GDP. Thus each 1 percent of long-run growth in emerging markets would increase US costs

---

11. In both the reference and slow-growth scenarios, the advanced economies (the OECD countries) grow at the same 2.1 percent annual rate, and in both scenarios global oil production is similar. In 2035, it averages 113 mbd in the low-price, slow-growth scenario versus 112 mbd in the reference case.

by eight-tenths of a percent of GDP (0.022 × 0.036), i.e., eight-hundredths of a percent per year. In 2011, for example, net imports of petroleum products were $326 billion. Thus the added net import costs of 1 percent faster growth in emerging-market economies would have been $11.7 billion.

We should emphasize that these are long-run scenarios and thus both supply and demand are more responsive to shocks than they would be if the growth rate change were very sudden. Nonetheless, the implication is that while the welfare effects of faster growth in emerging-market economies is negative, the impact would be relatively modest and offset by the impact of this growth in boosting the demand for US exports and the increased variety of products available to Americans.

Energy "Independence"?

It is noteworthy that in all three scenarios produced by the EIA on the basis of its share of GDP, the US economy's dependence on net imported oil is reduced but it is never "energy independent." (Energy independence is sometimes defined with respect to US dependence on oil imports outside North America, so that imports from Canada and Mexico are considered domestic.) From an economic (as opposed to a strategic) standpoint, however, what matters is the share of expenditures on net imports in US GDP (or spending). Net imports are the relevant variable, since the United States is also a significant exporter of refined petroleum products such as kerosene, jet fuel, gasoline, and ethanol.[12] This dependence will change to reflect three factors. The first factor is changes in the quantity of net imports. Because of increased domestic production and conservation, this is expected to decline. In 2010, for example, the share of net imports in US liquid fuels consumption was 49.6 percent. In 2035, that share of net imports is projected at 41.7 percent in the reference case and 56 and 23.7 percent in the low- and high-price scenarios, respectively. The second factor is changes in real oil prices. The increase in real oil prices between 2010 and 2035 from $100 to $125 a barrel (in 2010 dollars), for example, will offset declines in import volumes. The third factor is the growth in GDP, which raises the denominator of the ratio. With 2.5 percent annual growth in the economy between 2009 and 2035, as projected by the EIA, for example, GDP in 2035 will be 87 percent larger than in 2010.

Taking these three factors together indicates that in the reference case, as a share of GDP, expenditures on net imports of petroleum products will be 86 percent of their 2010 levels. (They will amount to 1.43 percent of GDP versus the 1.8 percent and 2.2 percent shares recorded in 2010 and 2011, respectively.) By 2035, with lower oil prices (i.e., $50 a barrel in 2010 dollars) the share is

---

12. For example, in 2011, the value of US petroleum product exports ($113.2 billion) was equal to 0.25 of US imports of these products ($439.3 billion), according to the Bureau of Economic Analysis, International Trade in Goods and Services, Annual Revision for 2011, Table 8, www.bea.gov/international (accessed on November 1, 2012).

just 0.8 percent of GDP. In the high-price scenario of $200 a barrel, the share is just 1.3 percent, since domestic supply is considerably greater. Thus in all these scenarios, the sensitivity of US welfare to changes in emerging-market-economy growth is expected to decline over time, and in the low-price scenario to be only about a third (0.8 versus 2.2) of what it was in 2011. This would reduce the costs of additional growth in emerging-market economies relative to GDP to about three-one-hundredths of a percent for each percent of growth.

It should be emphasized that while a huge amount of work and detail goes into these scenarios, they are subject to very high degrees of uncertainty. The reference scenario, for example, foresees considerable growth in unconventional supplies of liquid fuels from Brazil, Canada, and the United States as well as significant growth in natural gas production.[13] On the other hand, the US and global supply situations have been changing quite dramatically in recent years and the projections could be underestimating the enhanced potential for increased supplies of oil and natural gas. In particular, improvements in oil extraction techniques provide opportunities for enhanced recovery from old US oil wells where some 60 to 70 percent of the oil remains.[14] In addition, new discoveries and production techniques have dramatically increased the estimates of technically recoverable US natural gas reserves. Exploiting these does present major challenges relating to production costs, uncertain depletion rates, infrastructure, and environmental concerns, but a concerted policy strategy to deal with these could further reduce US oil import volumes. Between 2010 and 2020, for example, the EIA scenarios used here project US petroleum liquids production to grow by 1.8 mbd by 2020 from 2011 levels of 9 mbd. But the National Petroleum Council projects 2.3 mbd, while Citibank has an even bolder projection of 6.6 mbd.[15] A crucial assumption behind these projections, however, is that oil prices remain around at least $70 a barrel through 2020. A significant decline in oil prices could dramatically alter the medium-term production prospects by reducing incentives to develop alternative fuels.

The abundance of US natural gas raises the potential for its use in vehicles to replace petroleum either as compressed natural gas or converted into methanol. Since this presents challenges in developing fueling stations, use in large trucks and fleets is seen as offering the greatest opportunities. In addition, there is the possibility of using gas to generate power for electric vehicles. Government policies encouraging these developments could further reduce

---

13. A more recent simulation undertaken by the EIA reaches similar conclusions (EIA 2012). In its 2012 scenarios, which start in 2010, its base case for oil prices in 2035 is $132.96 in 2010 dollars for a barrel of imported crude oil. The prices are $53.10 and $187 a barrel in the low- and high-price scenarios, respectively.

14. These include improvements in hydraulic fracturing (fracking) techniques and horizontal drilling.

15. Citibank's forecast includes an additional 2.5 mbd from deepwater sources and 2.3 mbd from shale liquids. See Baily and Lee (2012).

America's net oil imports. Indeed, in November 2012 the IEA produced a projection that suggests that by 2030, the United States could actually become a net oil exporter.

Conclusions

Three conclusions emerge from this analysis. First, as in the past, the price that the United States will pay for its oil imports in the future rests on a knife edge. It is quite possible to accommodate emerging-market-economy growth without higher real oil prices through relatively small changes in the production and conservation of liquid fuels. Especially in transportation, advances in energy sources that are alternatives to oil and are widely diffused internationally could be particularly beneficial.

Second, Lawrence Summers' concern about the adverse impact of faster growth in emerging-market economies on the costs of US imports of petroleum is warranted but its importance is likely to diminish over time. EIA simulations suggest that keeping supplies constant, a one percentage point faster annual growth rate trend in emerging-market economies would raise world oil prices by 3.6 percent per year. Given US net oil dependence in 2011 of 2.2 percent of GDP, this is equivalent to $11.7 billion or eight-one-hundredths of a percent of US GDP.

And third, while the scenarios produced by the EIA as of 2012 still suggest that the United States is unlikely to eliminate its net dependence on imported oil, under all its scenarios its dependence as a share of GDP is expected to decline. Thus, the adverse impact of faster trend growth in emerging-market economies that operates through higher oil prices is likely to diminish over time, and recent projections by the IEA (2012) actually suggest that by 2030, the United States could become a net oil exporter.

IV

TRADE AND WAGE INEQUALITY: EXPLORING THE ECONOMISTS' CONCERNS

The US terms of trade have been boosted since the mid-1990s by the declining relative prices of manufactured goods imported from developing countries. This should give comfort to economists like Paul Samuelson who have expressed concerns about their decline. But it also raises alarms for those who worry about wage inequality. If imports from developing countries are intensive in their use of unskilled labor and if unskilled-labor-intensive products are falling in relative price, theory implies that this could have an especially adverse impact on the wages of unskilled US workers. This is not a new concern and was the subject of intensive investigation in the 1980s. Surprisingly, however, given the large rise in US manufactured imports from developing countries since the mid-1990s, relatively few studies have examined the more recent data. In the next two chapters we explore these concerns. In chapter 8 we outline the theoretical frameworks economists have developed to explain the connection between trade and wage inequality. In chapter 9 we summarize current empirical research on the question and present evidence of our own.

8

Developing-Country Trade and US Wages: Theoretical Perspectives

In a column written in 2007, Paul Krugman argued that "growing US trade with third world countries reduces the real wages of many and perhaps most workers in this country."[1] If Krugman is correct and most American workers are actually hurt, the rationale for free US trade could indeed be undermined.[2] This brief review of Krugman's theory argues that his case is based on a framework that requires extremely strong assumptions about US patterns of trade specialization and how the US labor market works. While more realistic alternative frameworks also demonstrate that trade could affect wages, their implications for economywide relative wage inequality and the real wages of unskilled workers are nowhere near as sweeping.

To make his case, Krugman implicitly invokes the model of trade introduced by Eli Heckscher and Bertil Ohlin, which emphasizes the role of factor endowments in determining trade specialization.[3] The model predicts that countries will specialize in products that are intensive in their relatively abundant factors of production. Assuming two factors of production, skilled and unskilled labor, the model implies that developing countries with relatively abundant supplies of unskilled labor will export unskilled-labor-intensive

---

1. Paul R. Krugman, "The Trouble with Trade; Keep Our Markets Open but Protect Those Who Get Hurt," *Pittsburgh Post-Gazette*, December 29, 2007, B-7.

2. Dani Rodrik (2011, 60) writes, "A deserving argument against free trade must overcome at least one of two hurdles. . . . [T]he economic gains from freer trade must remain small compared to the distributional costs; and trade must entail practices that violate prevailing norms and social contracts at home."

3. See Krugman and Obstfeld (2003, chapter 4) for a discussion of the Heckscher-Ohlin model.

products (e.g., clothing). Developed countries, on the other hand, with relatively abundant supplies of skilled labor, will export products that are skilled-labor-intensive (e.g., aircraft). If developing countries liberalize, they will increase their imports of skill-intensive products. To pay for these products they will have to export additional quantities of unskilled-labor-intensive products. This will reduce the world relative price of these products. Conversely, import liberalization in developed countries would reduce the domestic relative price of unskilled-labor-intensive products. In both cases, therefore, as trade barriers are reduced we would expect unskilled-labor-intensive products to become cheaper in developed countries.[4]

A related theory, developed by Wolfgang Stolper and Paul Samuelson (1941), provides a link between product prices and the returns to factors of production. It shows in the case of two goods and two factors that a decline in the relative price of a product will reduce both the relative and absolute earnings of the factor used relatively intensively in its production.[5] Thus, by helping skilled workers and hurting the unskilled, a reduction in the relative price of unskilled-labor-intensive products will increase wage inequality. A key insight in the Stolper-Samuelson theory is the "magnification effect." Under conditions of nonspecialization—i.e., the country continues to product both products—the returns to the factor used relatively intensively in the import industry—i.e., wages of unskilled workers in developed countries—will fall by more than import prices. This means that the price changes due to removing trade barriers will not only increase wage inequality but also make unskilled workers absolutely worse off.[6]

This then is the basis for Krugman's statement. If trade with developing countries reduces the real wages of unskilled workers, and all US workers without college degrees are defined as "unskilled," then a large majority—about 70 percent—of the US labor force could be hurt by trade.[7]

The Stolper-Samuelson result does not pertain only to price changes caused by trade—product price changes from any source will mandate these changes in factor prices—but if a country is a price taker and traded goods

---

4. In developing countries, on the other hand, the relative price of unskilled-labor-intensive products will increase.

5. Factor intensity is defined by the factor shares in total costs. If there are two factors, skilled (s) and unskilled labor (u), and two goods, a skilled-labor-intensive good x and an unskilled-labor-intensive good y, there is a one-to-one relationship between the relative prices of the goods and the relative wages of skilled workers, Ws, and unskilled workers, Wu. Using an * to indicate proportional rates of change, and Sx and Sy as the shares of skilled labor in the production cost of x and y, respectively, then: $Px^* - Py^* = (Sx - Sy)(Ws^* - Wu^*)$.

6. If there are more than two factors, as Ronald Jones and José Scheinkman (1977) show, at least one factor will be made worse off by any relative price decline and at least one factor will be made better off. Thus, every good, according to their terminology, is a friend to some factor and an enemy to some other factor.

7. Using the alternative classification of workers as production and nonproduction workers leads to a similar conclusion, since almost 70 percent of workers meet this definition as well.

prices are determined in international markets, the Heckscher-Ohlin and Stolper-Samuelson theories can be merged to connect increased trade with developing countries and factor incomes in a causal relationship we refer to as HOSS (borrowing the first letter of the last names of the four authors). Taken together these theories imply that trade liberalization (or anything else that increases the world relative supply of unskilled-labor-intensive products) increases wage inequality in developed countries and causes real wage reductions for unskilled workers.

Since Stolper-Samuelson assumes that factors are homogeneous, factor markets competitive, and skilled and unskilled labor fully mobile throughout the economy, its predictions are extremely powerful. The potential for mobility implies that all workers with similar skill levels receive the same wages no matter where they work. Workers in each skill category are perfect substitutes. We produced evidence in chapter 3 that only a relatively small share of the US workforce is employed in industries that produce tradable goods and services. But in the Stolper-Samuelson model this does not matter. The forces that affect the workers who produce tradable goods and services have similar effects on workers who produce nontraded goods and services. If the wages of unskilled workers producing clothing fall, for example, workers with similar skill levels in nontraded activities such as food servers in restaurants experience similar wage declines. Richard Freeman (1995) memorably captured the power of this process in the title of his survey paper on the links between trade and wages when he asked "Are Your Wages Set in Beijing?"

Moreover, if specialization is incomplete, and technologies are unchanged, internationally traded goods prices are the only determinant of domestic factor prices.[8] This means that the demand for these factors is perfectly elastic (horizontal) and changes in relative factor supplies at home affect factor prices only if they alter global prices.[9] In the case of countries too small to affect world prices, changes in domestic factor supplies simply shift the composition of output. If a country experiences an increase in the supply of unskilled labor, for example, these workers are absorbed into the labor force not by a change in wages but by an increase in the output of the unskilled-labor-intensive industry and a reduction of output in the skill-intensive sector.[10]

The Stolper-Samuelson framework can also explain the impact of productivity changes on factor prices. In a small economy in which the prices of traded goods are determined on world markets, an increase in productivity in an industry acts just like a price increase. It raises the real return to the factor used relatively intensively in the industry experiencing productivity growth

---

8. Trade economists refer to the insensitivity of factor prices to factor supplies as the factor price equalization theorem.

9. For a figure illustrating demand when there is complete and incomplete specialization, see Wood (1995, 60). For the case with more goods than factors, see Haskel and Slaughter (2001).

10. This is known as the Rybczynski effect.

and lowers the real return to the other factor.[11] A similar response occurs if the prices of imported inputs used by the industry change. As shown by Gene Grossman and Esteban Rossi-Hansberg (2008), cheaper imported inputs—due to offshoring, for example—operate exactly like sector-biased productivity growth. They raise the return to the factor used relatively intensively in the production of the industry that uses the inputs and reduce the return to the other factor.[12]

The Heckscher-Ohlin theory is alluring because of its simplicity as a teaching tool and these strong implications. The assumption of costless mobility provides it breathtaking explanatory power because, assuming given technology, it can account for economywide developments in factor returns by looking only at trade. The framework also allows for an exploration of the relative roles of trade, offshoring, and sector-biased technological change as sources of relative wage changes. It is no surprise that it has been the centerpiece of many empirical studies on the impact of trade on income inequality—some of which we review in the next chapter—as well as studies explaining class-related political positions on open trade.[13]

Restrictive Assumptions: Nonspecialization and Perfect Labor Mobility

Although appealing in their simplicity and ease of application, the assumptions required for the HOSS theory are extremely restrictive.[14] Indeed, they are so severe that the original Stolper-Samuelson paper was first rejected for publication as a theory by the editors of the *American Economic Review*. They acknowledged that it was a "beautiful theoretical performance" but felt that it "does not have anything to say about any real life situations with which the theory of international trade has to concern itself" (Cline 1997, 43). Given the profound influence of the theory, this appraisal has often been used to show

---

11. As Edward Leamer (1994, 1998) has emphasized, given product prices, it is the sectoral location of technological improvement rather than whether the improvement is neutral or biased toward a particular factor that matters. However, this strong result is dependent on the assumption that prices are unchanged. If prices fall, they offset this effect. As Krugman (2000) shows, sector bias might not matter at all if the technological change is global and the technological improvement is passed through into product prices. For a discussion of this issue, see Robert C. Feenstra, Offshoring in the Global Economy: Lecture 1: Microeconomic Structure; Lecture 2: Macroeconomic Implications, Ohlin Lecture presented at the Stockholm School of Economics, September 17–18, 2008.

12. Thus, paradoxically, given final product prices, as Grossman and Rossi-Hansberg (2008) show, offshoring some of the assembly operations of an unskilled-labor-intensive industry would actually raise the economywide relative wages of unskilled workers.

13. For an application of Stolper-Samuelson to international public opinion, see Mayda and Rodrik (2002). For a description of its use in the politics of trade, see Alt and Gilligan (1999).

14. See Davis and Mishra (2007) for a trenchant analysis of the HOSS theory.

how out of touch such editors may have been, but in fact, there may well have been some merit in their reactions.

One important assumption is incomplete specialization. Domestic factor prices will depend only on the prices of goods and services that are actually produced domestically, and if an imported product is not produced locally, its price will not directly affect factor prices. Thus the key to tightly connecting all traded goods prices and domestic factor prices is the assumption that specialization is incomplete and similar versions of the goods and services that are imported are all produced at home.

As we have noted, the Stolper-Samuelson theorem shows that the scarce-factor group—consider this group to be unskilled labor in developed countries, for example—must lose from trade because its wages will fall by more than the decline in price of the importable good they produce. But if there is specialization, the strong relationship between import prices and real factor returns breaks down. If the imported product is not produced at home and its price falls, all domestic producers could gain. In this case, therefore, Krugman's claim that a majority of workers would be hurt by trade would not hold.

Noncompeting Goods

Complete specialization can occur if all products are homogeneous but some imported products are not produced domestically, and/or if imports and domestic goods are imperfect substitutes. In conventional Heckscher-Ohlin models, products are assumed to be homogeneous and goods produced at home are identical to imports. But specialization can arise when countries have very different factor endowments (Dornbusch, Fischer, and Samuelson 1980) and move out of what is called the "cone of diversification." This is not simply a theoretical possibility. Peter Schott (2003) has emphasized the empirical problems of applying the "single cone" version of Heckscher-Ohlin theory, which requires that all countries produce all types of goods. On the other hand, he finds empirical support for a "multicone" equilibrium in which countries specialize in the subset of goods that are most suited to their endowments.[15]

Imperfect Substitutes

If imports and the goods produced at home are imperfect substitutes, as is the case with differentiated products, import prices will affect domestic product and factor prices only indirectly—if they change the prices of domestic goods via substitution effects on demand.[16] John Whalley and Lisandro Abrego

---

15. Peter Debaere and Ufuk Demiroglu (2003) similarly find that while OECD countries have sufficiently similar factor endowments to produce the same set of goods, this is not the case for countries generally.

16. More generally, domestic factor supplies matter for factor prices, if there are more factors than goods.

(2000) show that if, rather than infinite (i.e., perfect substitutes), the elasticity of substitution between imports and domestic products is unity, so that consumers, for example, allocate constant shares of their spending to imported and domestic varieties, changes in import prices will not influence domestic product or factor prices at all.[17] Again the possibility that products differ systematically because of their production location is not simply a theoretical possibility. Many trade models adopt the so-called Armington assumption that products have distinctive national attributes.

Changes in Specialization[18]

For a given array of imported products, specialization might limit the effects of trade on domestic factor prices, but under some circumstances changes in specialization might still have effects. One example is where countries move from incomplete to complete specialization; a second is where countries are initially fully specialized, but patterns of specialization change and goods that were originally produced at home are later produced abroad.

In the debate in the 1990s, Adrian Wood (1994) was a noteworthy dissenter from the view that trade with developing countries had not been a serious source of wage inequality. He argued that the developed countries had made a transition from incomplete to complete specialization. At first, as trade with developing countries was initiated, it had adverse effects on the wages of unskilled workers in the United States and other developed countries via traditional Stolper-Samuelson effects, since imports were becoming cheaper and imports and domestic products were close substitutes. Over time, however, imports drove out domestic production and the economy thus became fully specialized. Technically, the economy moved out of the cone of diversification, in which labor demand was flat and dependent only on traded prices, to specialization, in which domestic factors such as relative supplies also affected wages.

Imagine, for example, two types of TVs, black and white and color, which are imperfect substitutes. Originally, the United States produces both using skilled and unskilled labor. But over time, production of the most unskilled-labor-intensive products—black and white TVs—moves abroad, and the US economy becomes fully specialized in color TVs. The producers of black and white TVs are displaced and need to be reemployed. In this case, there is now just one US product, color TVs, and two factors of production, skilled and

---

17. If the elasticity of substitution is less than unity, the sign of the effect actually changes: Lower import prices of unskilled-labor-intensive products would increase domestic prices of domestic substitutes. The effects *would* be present with the expected signs if the elasticity were greater than unity, but would be far more muted than assumed in the case of perfect substitutes.

18. In small countries, as long as the number of traded products produced domestically exceeds the number of factors, replacing some domestic production with imports will not change relative factor prices. But if there are more factors than produced goods, changes in domestic factor supplies affect factor prices.

unskilled labor. This means relative factor supplies do affect factor prices and there could be a one-time adjustment in which the relative wages of unskilled workers decline to induce other employers to hire them.[19] Estimating the impact of that adjustment requires knowing the factor content of black and white TVs. We should obviously not use the skill intensity of employment in color TVs to estimate this relative wage impact. Wood complained, however, that most studies used developed-country input-output coefficients to estimate the net factor content of trade. This biased the studies to severely underestimate the relative wage impact of the displaced unskilled worker.

Once specialization is complete, however, the strong link between the prices of black and white TVs and US factor prices is broken. If there are additional declines in the prices of black and white TVs, but no impact on the prices of color and high-definition TVs, US consumers gain, but US relative factor prices are unaffected. Indeed, the same reasoning that led Wood (1995) to argue that the initial effects of trade had been underestimated also led him to reject the forecasts of those who argued that the impact of trade on the relative wages of unskilled workers in developed countries would become increasingly pronounced over time (e.g., Sachs and Shatz 1994).[20] Instead, Wood argued—presciently, we believe—that these pressures would diminish because additional downward movements in the prices of most unskilled-labor-intensive products would not put pressures on the wages of unskilled workers in developed countries once they no longer produced such goods.

If there are many products, even if countries are fully specialized, technically they occupy different cones of diversification—changes in specialization could impact relative wages. Assume, for example, that there are two countries, North and South, and many products that can be arranged in descending order according to their skill intensity, as in Dornbusch, Fischer, and Samuelson (1980). Initially there is a particular cutoff point such that the more skill-intensive products are produced in the North and the more unskilled-labor-intensive in the South. Then assume there is a shock such that the cutoff shifts and the production of what were previously the most unskilled-labor-intensive goods in the North shifts to the South.[21] In this case, production in both the North and the South becomes more skill-intensive.[22] Relatively more unskilled workers will be displaced compared with the overall

---

19. A similar process is modeled by Feenstra and Hanson (1996). See also Feenstra (2004, 106–18).

20. Wood (1995, 77) wrote, "I do not expect unskilled workers in developed countries to be much hurt by even major new entry into the world market for low-skill-intensive manufacturers, simply because these goods are no longer produced in developed countries. The entry of China and India, pushing down the world prices of these goods, will benefit developed-country workers, skilled and unskilled alike."

21. Such a shock might be increased productivity in the South, as in Zhu and Trefler (2005), or capital inflows into the South, as in Feenstra and Hanson (1996).

22. There is an old joke told differently by members of Harvard and MIT that from a Harvard perspective states, "When the worst Harvard professor moves to MIT it raises the average caliber of professors in both places."

share of unskilled workers in the Northern economy. As a result, in order to reemploy these workers, the relative wages of unskilled workers would have to fall in the North. In the South, the introduction of the most skill-intensive industry will raise the relative demand for skilled workers. Thus the relative wages of skilled workers increase in both the North and the South. It should be noted, however, that in this framework, while such changes in specialization do increase wage inequality, unlike the typical Stolper-Samuelson case they do not necessarily reduce the absolute wages of unskilled workers in each country.

Intermediate Inputs

Declines in the prices of noncompeting goods might raise the real incomes of all who consume them, but some noncompeting goods could also be used as intermediate inputs to produce domestic products. In this case, again, these price changes could affect domestic factor prices not through the conventional demand channel but by changing the profitability of the assembly operations in which they are used. Cheaper imported auto parts, for example, could increase the profitability of auto assembly. This might increase the returns to the factor used intensively in assembly. Given final goods prices, this effect operates exactly like sector-biased productivity growth and raises the return to the factor used relatively intensively in assembly.[23]

Grossman and Rossi-Hansberg (2008) provide a comprehensive treatment of the effects of offshoring intermediate inputs and identify this "productivity effect" as one of three channels through which imported intermediate inputs could affect domestic factor prices.[24] In a price-taking nonspecialized economy with fixed prices for final goods, this effect will dominate. Thus, cheaper inputs in unskilled-labor-intensive industries due to offshoring will raise relative wages of unskilled workers. However, this productivity effect could be offset partially or more than completely by two other impacts if prices change. These are already familiar. The first is the relative price or Stolper-Samuelson effect. If the country is large enough to influence prices, and its output expands because of outsourcing, world prices of the unskilled-labor-intensive product could fall and thus reduce the returns to the factor used intensively in the outsourcing industry. The second, which Stolper and Samuelson call the labor supply effect, is the case even in a small economy in which relative factor supplies can affect relative factor prices. This occurs if there are more factors of production than products, or if countries are fully specialized and

---

23. This effect has also been recognized by Robert Feenstra and Gordon Hanson (1999), who note that offshoring will show up in the industry aggregate production function as a change in total factor productivity.

24. See also Robert C. Feenstra, Offshoring in the Global Economy: Lecture 1: Microeconomic Structure; Lecture 2: Macroeconomic Implications, Ohlin Lecture presented at the Stockholm School of Economics, September 17–18, 2008.

specialization patterns change.[25] Under conditions where relative factor supplies matter for factor prices, if unskilled-labor-intensive tasks were once undertaken at home and these move offshore, the unskilled-labor factors previously engaged need to be reemployed. This could lead to an expansion in unskilled-labor activities, resulting in reduced unskilled-labor-intensive product and factor prices.

Acknowledging specialization and the presence of noncompeting goods therefore presents challenges for applying the HOSS theory empirically. Simulation models that assume that all imported products are still produced domestically and ignore the possibility of specialization could give inaccurate results. Price studies should only include changes in the prices of tradable products that are actually produced domestically, and while these prices might be influenced by trade, the effects need to be explicitly modeled. In addition, as Wood (1994) pointed out, if there is specialization the net factor content approach cannot be applied in a straightforward manner using domestic input coefficients.[26] Instead the factor contents of the products that are no longer produced in the country need to be taken into account. Moreover, the propositions based on Stolper-Samuelson that one factor will necessarily lose as a result of trade are not necessarily true.

Other Theories

In addition to nonspecialization, applying the HOSS theory also requires assuming that factor markets are competitive and factors homogeneous and mobile. For competitive labor markets, for example, workers with particular skill levels—for example, college education—all need to earn the same wage regardless of where they work. In reality, however, many labor markets are imperfect, and the same worker could be paid differently in different jobs. Unions, for example, can obtain premiums for workers who would earn lower wages in other activities. Also, in reality, some factors might be immobile. In the short run, there are costs to renegotiating wages and changing jobs, and thus similar workers could earn different wages. But even in the long run, while some worker attributes such as the ability to read and calculate may be mobile and useful in many jobs, other attributes might be highly specific to a particular occupation or job and thus immobile. For example, occupational skills (such as those of plumbers versus carpenters) are highly specific and not necessarily interchangeable. Similarly, some attributes may only be valuable in

25. In the case they consider, the country produces only one product with two factors of production, and some unskilled-labor-intensive tasks are offshored. This creates an excess supply of unskilled workers and thus reduces their relative wages. In this case, as with the full specialization we discussed above, however, while wage inequality might rise, real wages of skilled workers could still improve.

26. Alan Deardorff (1997) points out that if there are noncompeting imports, the effect of trade is the same as a Hicks-neutral increase in productivity growth that would allow the noncompeting imports to be produced in the home country.

one job or task. For example, a nurse might be highly paid because of relationships with patients in a particular doctor's office that were built up over many years, but far less valuable if she were able to find another nursing job.

Specific Factors

Since trade changes product prices, it can affect the returns-to-worker attributes that are specific. If factors are immobile, for example, theory indicates that opening up to trade raises the returns to specific factors in export industries (since trade raises export prices and lowers them in import-competing industries) (Jones 1971, Mussa 1974, Neary 1978). In this way, trade could induce greater inequality, but these specific effects would be confined to just a few industries. These specific effects can be combined with those operating through mobile factors. If a mobile factor is introduced into a model with two immobile factors, the theory suggests that the impact of trade on the mobile factor is ambiguous. If labor markets are imperfect, trade can also impact industry-specific factor rents such as union wage premiums. As emphasized by Rodrik (1997), unions could be forced to accept lower wages if trade makes the derived demand for their services more elastic.[27]

Wages could also be firm-specific when firms are heterogeneous, as in Melitz (2003). In the Melitz model, lower trade costs boost profitability in the most productive (exporting) firms. However, profits are squeezed in less-productive firms. Thus, within industries, profit inequality increases in the short run. In his original version, Melitz assumes that workers all earn similar wages, but by linking firm wages to firm profitability theorists have found new channels by which trade affects firm wages when there are labor market imperfections that allow similar workers to earn different wages depending on which firms they work for. These include "notions of fairness" (Egger and Krieckemeier 2009), rent sharing between owners and workers (Amiti and Davis 2008), changes to incentives to search for good workers (Helpman, Itskhoki, and Redding 2010), reduced worker shirking (Davis and Harrigan 2007), implicit contracts between firms and workers (Bertrand 2004), and upgraded skills (Verhoogen 2008).

Heterogeneous Workers

The HOSS framework generally assumes a limited number of factors, such as skilled and unskilled labor. But new theories also consider implications if workers are more heterogeneous in their skills (Yeaple 2005). The virtue of such frameworks is that they can produce more complex outcomes in the wage distribution. In these models, opening to trade can affect the process by which workers sort into firms and, through this, earnings related to skill. Arnaud

---

27. For an argument that international competition could raise wages in a union setting, see Lawrence and Lawrence (1985).

Costinot and Jonathan Vogel (2010) explore a framework in which workers have different skills and can be arrayed along a continuous distribution. They show that if comparative advantage is driven by differences in endowments of skilled workers, and developed countries have more skilled workers at every rank in their distribution, opening up North-South trade could lead to increased wage inequality that resembles the Stolper-Samuelson effect in the two-factor setting. However, they also show that if developed countries have technologies that are biased toward using more skilled workers, opening up to trade could lead to more equal wages in the developed countries. Thus if both effects are operating, increased North-South trade need not cause more inequality. Matching models can also produce more complex outcomes in which trade results in wages of medium-skilled workers lagging behind those at the top and bottom of the distribution (Costinot and Vogel 2010, Blanchard and Willmann 2008). They could also explain how trade could especially raise wages at the very highest (superstar) levels (Manasse and Turrini 2001).

These alternative perspectives change how we think about the links between trade and wage inequality and are more likely to account for the wide variety of relative wage outcomes that have occurred in developing countries that have undergone trade liberalization.[28] They allow explanations of inequality that reflect more than the returns to broad skill categories and yield more complex predictions about the effects on the wage distribution. In some cases, the theories imply that the effects of trade on wages will not be economywide. In some specific-factor models, only the workers directly involved in trade, or who work in particular firms, have their wages affected. In these cases, trade can increase wage inequality, but it is quite limited in scope. In other theories, there are both specific and general equilibrium effects, but the general equilibrium effects could be more attenuated than assumed in Stolper-Samuelson, since factors are not all affected in the same way.[29]

In sum, the HOSS framework is powerful and offers a straightforward way to test the effects of trade on relative wages throughout the economy. But it rests on extremely strong assumptions—in particular, that the economy is nonspecialized, factors are homogeneous, factor markets competitive, and factors fully mobile. If these assumptions are not valid, the implications of increased trade with developing countries for wage inequality may be very dif-

---

28. See the excellent survey by Pinelopi Goldberg and Nina Pavcnik (2007).

29. The approaches that emphasize worker heterogeneity can be blended with Stolper-Samuelson theory to capture more complex and more realistic outcomes. For example, Jonathan Haskel, Robert Lawrence, Edward Leamer, and Matthew Slaughter (2012) develop a model in which some workers' skills are complementary with capital, while others' skills are not. In this case, the unskilled workers earn the same wage no matter where they work, but the skilled workers earn more in capital-intensive industries. The authors show how a rise in the price of capital-intensive goods can increase profits and the premiums earned by highly skilled workers while lowering the return to unskilled labor. They also show how some types of human capital, e.g., movie making or investment banking, could have their returns raised by increased globalization or technologies such as the internet. For a discussion of globalization and the returns to superstars, see Lawrence (2008).

ferent, and other frameworks and empirical methods must be used for testing them. The HOSS framework is also relatively limited, since it is concerned only with the dimension of wage inequality that is associated with returns to homogeneous and mobile factors. Recognizing that factors are immobile leads to consideration of returns that reflect industry- and region-specific factors. Recognizing that firms are heterogeneous leads to consideration of returns to firm-specific wages. Recognizing that wages may also reflect returns to skills that are heterogeneous leads even to the consideration of the effects on individual wages.

Stolper-Samuelson is a general equilibrium theory. Remarkably, and not always appreciated, it implies there will be no relationship between the wages of a worker and the trade (or lack of trade) in the industry where the worker is employed. In a two-factor model, for example, what matters only is how trade affects the relative price of the traded industry that uses the worker's services relatively intensively. By contrast, the specific-factors theories can be tested by linking wages to particular firm, industry, and regional characteristics.[30]

We have already described in chapter 2 the empirical studies on the United States that explore the effects of imports from and offshoring to developing countries such as Mexico, China, and India on the wages of workers in particular industries, occupations, and regions, as well as on the earnings of workers who have been displaced and forced to find new jobs, sometimes in sectors that are different from those in which they were originally employed. For the most part, these studies can be considered applications of the specific-factors models that we have just described. While their findings are not always consistent, these studies do suggest that trade with developing countries has caused displacement and depressed wages in some industries, locations, and occupations. The effects on displaced workers who experience loss in specific human capital when forced to take jobs at lower wages are also clear. Stolper-Samuelson, however, is about the returns to factors throughout the economy, and in the next chapter, we explore how well it explains recent US outcomes.

---

30. An early version of this approach was Revenga (1992).

9

Trade and the US Skill Premium

When the facts are simple, simple explanatory theories seem adequate. In the 1980s, wage inequality was a major contributor to increased income inequality in the United States. The earnings of workers with high skill levels by all measures (education, occupation, experience) outpaced those with less skill. Inequality was evident whether the data were for women or men, and whether the focus was on the lower or the upper half of the wage distribution.

It was not surprising, therefore, that the debates over wage inequality were joined using simple models that assumed there were just two mobile and homogeneous factors—skilled and unskilled labor. On the one hand, some labor economists assumed a closed economy and used a simple model in which technological change was sufficiently biased towards increasing the use of skilled labor to generate increasing skill premiums (Katz and Murphy 1992). On the other hand, since this inequality occurred at the same time that the US economy was becoming more open, especially with respect to trade with developing countries, it was quite natural that other researchers considered whether the HOSS could provide the explanation.[1]

Given the power of the theory and the tools available to apply it, there was a slew of studies by the mid-1990s by economists estimating the impact of trade on relative wages in the United States. These studies had little to say about the increase in the inequality of earnings of workers with similar observable skill levels (for these an approach exploring more specific returns would

---

1. HOSS, which is based on the names of Heckscher-Ohlin and Stolper-Samuelson (1941), refers to a merging of the two theories to connect increased trade with developing countries and factor incomes in a causal relationship; see chapter 8.

have been better), but the appeal of the HOSS framework was that it could provide estimates of the impact of changes operating through trade on the observable skill premium, which was a substantial source of increased income inequality over the period.

Four methods were applied to test the Stolper-Samuelson theory. One approach estimated changes in factor prices due to trade by calculating the net factor content of trade using US input-output coefficients. This reflects the insight that in the conventional framework, trade and factor movements are substitutes. Trade is considered equivalent to adding to the economy the factors contained in imports and subtracting the factors contained in exports (Borjas, Freeman, and Katz 1997).[2] The challenge in these studies was to precisely identify the skill content of traded goods. Most studies used US input coefficients. Adrian Wood (1994), however, developed a more complex procedure to support his view that many imported products were no longer made in the United States.

A second approach built small general-equilibrium simulation models of relative wage determination (Krugman 1995, Cline 1997) in two-sector, two-factor models. These models were used to estimate the likely factor-price impact of exogenous shocks such as trade liberalization and/or growth abroad that influence relative wages by affecting trade flows. The challenge in using these models was calibration with appropriate parameters for factor-income shares and elasticities of substitution.[3]

A third approach considered the implications of changes in traded goods prices for changes in factor prices.[4] The most straightforward application was simply to assume the United States is a price taker and to identify the impact of trade with changes in the prices of tradable goods. The question was whether prices (or prices taking account of productivity—effective prices) had moved in a way that would favor skilled or unskilled workers (Lawrence and Slaughter 1993).

But prices of traded goods are themselves endogenous variables (Deardorff and Hakura 1994). And if a country is not a price taker, traded goods

---

2. Alan Deardorff and Robert Staiger (1988) provided a theoretical justification for this application under certain conditions. They demonstrated that using a net-factor content approach to estimate changes in factor prices could be interpreted as implicitly comparing the factor-price changes between two equilibria under conditions of self-sufficiency. This is an appealing property, but it should be noted that the technology and demand assumptions required for endowment changes and trade to produce equivalent effects on factor prices are very restrictive. In their original paper, for example, to establish their strongest propositions, Deardorff and Staiger needed to assume Cobb-Douglas preferences and technologies. Deardorff (1997) extends the analysis for constant elasticity of substitution production functions and elaborates on the fairly restrictive assumptions required to use this approach. See also Leamer (1996).

3. Ceteris paribus, the more different the factor intensities and the lower the elasticity of substitution between factors, the larger the relative factor-price changes associated with a given volume of trade.

4. For a review of these studies, see Slaughter (2000).

prices cannot be taken as exogenous. The challenge was how to distinguish between the price effects of exogenous variables that can be considered as due to "trade" (e.g., domestic and/or foreign tariff changes, changes in foreign tastes, technologies, and endowments) and other potential sources of price change (e.g., domestic technological change or factor supplies).

Robert Feenstra and Gordon Hanson (1999) pioneered a fourth approach to deal with the endogeneity issue with a two-stage procedure. First they estimated the impact of exogenous variables that were associated with trade (such as imported inputs) and technology (such as computer use) on domestic industry prices. Then, in a second stage, they estimated the factor-price changes that would be mandated by these price effects. Thus, instead of simply assuming all changes in domestic prices were due to trade or technology, they could more credibly argue that they had isolated the price changes due to these factors separately, and then estimated their separate effects on factor prices.

The results of the studies undertaken in the 1990s using these methodologies were fairly mixed, with many studies finding effects that were significant but not large. While there were noteworthy outliers on both the high sides (Wood 1994, Cline 1997) and low sides (Bhagwati 1991, Lawrence and Slaughter 1993), William Cline (1997, 144) argued in his comprehensive survey that "a reasonable estimate based on the literature would be that international influences contributed about *20 percent* [italics added] of the rising wage inequality in the 1980s."[5]

What accounted for the rest? While causes such as immigration (Borjas, Freeman, and Katz 1997), declining union power (Card 2001), falling minimum wages (Card 1999), and a change in wage norms (Levy and Temin 2007) were all considered as other reasons, the most powerful source of the rise in the skill premium was attributed to skill-biased technological change, which many associated with the introduction of new information technology (Berman, Bound, and Machin 1998; Autor, Katz, and Krueger 1998; Goldin and Katz 2007, 2008).[6]

Income inequality had also increased in the 1980s and 1990s in many developing countries. This development, as emphasized early by Steven Davis (1992), seemed at odds with the conventional HOSS view of the world, in which liberalization in developing countries with an abundance of unskilled labor should have generated greater income and wage equality.[7] It gave rise to

---

5. Two of the three papers in a symposium sponsored by the *Journal of Economic Perspectives* in 1995 reached similar conclusions. Richard Freeman (1995, 25) concluded "standard factor content analysis studies indicate that trade can account for 10 to 20 percent of the overall fall in demand for unskilled-labor needed to explain rising wage differentials." David Richardson (1995, 51) opined, "trade is a moderate contributing source of income inequality trends; it may not overshadow other sources, but it cannot be shrugged away."

6. There are skeptics about the role of technological change in US wage inequality. See, for example, Lemieux (2006) and Mishel and Bernstein (1998). See also Autor, Katz, and Kearney (2005).

7. In a two-country model with a developed and developing country, the HOSS view would indeed predict that liberalization would lead to more wage equality in the developing country. But if there were several developing countries and only one liberalized, while its wages would become

an extensive literature that has been well surveyed by Pinelopi Goldberg and Nina Pavcnik (2007) (see also Harrison 2007). They conclude that the (developing-country) experience "provides little support for conventional wisdom that trade openness in developing countries would favor the less fortunate (at least in relative terms)" (Goldberg and Pavcnik 2007, 77).[8] But they also emphasize that the mechanisms causing inequality in particular countries are likely to be "country, time and case specific" (p. 78).

Recent Developments

With the signing of the North American Free Trade Agreement (NAFTA) and the emergence of China in the mid-1990s, the pace of US trade with developing countries accelerated. This was true not only for goods but, after 2000, also services. As the internet became widespread and global telecommunications costs plunged, US firms turned increasingly to India and other low-wage countries for business process outsourcing (e.g., data entry and call centers) and software services (Amiti and Wei 2005).

Paul Krugman (1995) had originally argued that trade with developing countries was too small to have much of an impact on wage inequality in the United States. But he had also been vocal in making the point that the volume of trade was an important clue to the size of its potential effects on relative wages (Krugman 2000). In 2008, Krugman noted that after a decade of very rapid growth, the value of US manufactured imports from developing countries as a whole exceeded that of similar imports from developed countries. He also pointed out that very low-wage countries such as China made up a greater share of these imports. He argued that the debate needed to be revisited, since the effects were likely to have grown.

Support for his view also seems to come from the import price data. As shown in figure 9.1, the import prices of manufactured imports from developing countries have declined precipitously since 1990 relative to import prices of manufactured goods from developed countries. Viewed through the HOSS prism in which developing countries are expected to specialize in unskilled-labor-intensive products while developed countries specialize in skilled-labor-intensive products, this relative price could be seen as a proxy for the ratio of unskilled-labor-intensive to skilled-labor-intensive products. This price evidence suggested that trade could be causing additional wage inequality.

---

more equal, a lower world price for unskilled-labor-intensive products could lead to increased wage inequality not only in the developed country but also in the other developing countries.

8. Among the plausible explanations they discuss for this failure to confirm the Stolper-Samuelson view are skill-biased technological change, the effects of increased openness in raising the demand for higher-quality products that require more skilled workers, the fact that the tariff and other barriers that were reduced most actually protected least skilled workers, and the possibility that in a multicone world relatively more advanced developing countries were becoming more specialized in skill-intensive products (Feenstra and Hanson 1996). As the title of their paper indicates, Donald Davis and Prachi Mishra (2007) similarly make the case that "Stolper-Samuelson is dead."

Figure 9.1 Ratio of import prices of manufactured goods from developing countries to import prices of manufactured goods from developed countries, 1990–2008

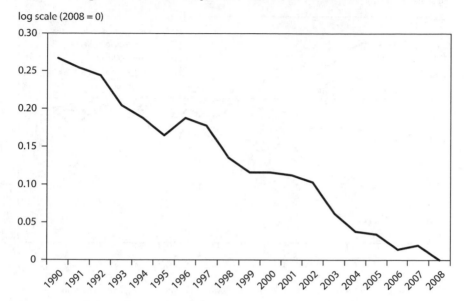

log scale (2008 = 0)

Source: Bureau of Labor Statistics, Import Price data.

We show in what follows, however, that despite the plausibility of these views, none of the four approaches indicates that there have been large impacts on relative wages that have operated through Stolper-Samuelson effects.

Wage Behavior

Before we proceed to explore these approaches, we should note two striking features of the recent data that create problems for applying the methodologies. First, the division of workers into two neat categories—skilled and unskilled—does not capture what has happened to wages in recent years. The evidence of increased wage inequality along the lines of observable returns to skill is far more mixed than it was earlier.[9] Figure 9.2 plots the ratios of annual full-time earnings of high school dropouts, workers with some college, and those with college and advanced degrees relative to workers with a high school education for the period 1975–2008. As depicted by the fan produced

---

9. Paul Krugman (2008) and one of us (Lawrence 2008) also have a difference of opinion on whether in fact wage inequality actually did increase in the United States, particularly after 2000. Unlike the 1980s, when almost every possible classification of wages by skill (occupation, education, experience, 10th, 50th, and 90th percentiles) shows a rise in inequality, the picture is at best very mixed after 2000.

Figure 9.2 Full-time wages relative to high-school graduates, 1975–2008

log scale (2000 = 0)

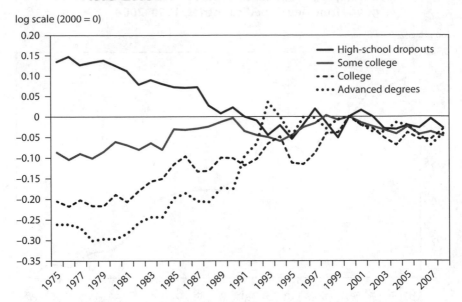

Source: Bureau of Labor Statistics and US Census Bureau, Current Population Survey, www.census.gov/cps (accessed on November 1, 2012).

by these data, the rise in inequality in the 1980s is very striking. The earnings of workers with less than a high school education fell steadily relative to high school graduates, while the earnings of workers with college and advanced degrees rose, with the rise in the latter clearly the largest. But in the mid-1990s the patterns clearly changed. The lines are much closer together, indicating much smaller and basically trendless changes. After 2000, for example, these data appear to show that high school graduates actually saw small improvements in their earnings relative to those with college and advanced degrees.[10,11]

The Economic Policy Institute has used data from the Current Population Survey to estimate the college premium in a regression controlling for a

---

10. In the 1980s, there had also been a strong declining trend in the employment ratio of production to nonproduction workers. This had been interpreted by some as evidence of skill-biased technological change (Berman, Bound, and Griliches 1994; Berman, Bound, and Machin 1998) and as evidence of the offshoring of unskilled-labor activities (Feenstra and Hanson 1996). But the declining trends reversed in the early 1990s, and the employment ratio of production to nonproduction workers was no different in 2006 than in 1996.

11. Using only data on wages of production and nonproduction workers as an indicator of occupational wage inequality could be too crude to capture wage inequality along occupational lines. It is noteworthy, therefore, that Avraham Ebenstein at al. (2009, 31) report that interoccupational wage differentials actually narrowed strongly between 1984–85 and 2001–02.

variety of worker attributes (age, experience, race, region, and marital status). It finds there was almost no change in the college premium for women after 1995 (46.6 percent).[12] The premium for men increased from 1995 to 2000 from 37.2 to 42 percent, but in the following nine years rose by just 2.6 percent. While relative production-worker wages declined through 2000, the trend then changed and the relative wages of production workers in 2008 were the same as in 1997.[13]

The story is murkier, however, when other indicators of inequality are used. One commonly used metric does not distinguish workers by education or skill but simply ranks them by their wages and then explores how well workers at different positions in the rankings have fared over time. This indicates that wages at both the 90th and the 10th percentiles rose relative to those at the 50th percentile between 1988 and 2002. Between 2002 and 2009, however, both the 50:10 and especially the 90:10 ratios actually increased.[14] Moreover, the striking and sustained increases in relative wages in the 90th and 95th percentiles continued between 2000 and 2009.[15] Thus these data do suggest increased wage inequality.[16]

It is, however, always possible that, but for the effect of trade, US wages along the lines of skill might have become more equal. So these ex post wage data do not necessarily settle the debate on the marginal effects of developing-country trade.

Industry Skill Intensities

A second problem confronting those seeking to apply the conventional HOSS method is the skill-intensity measures of US industries. Applications of the HOSS framework assume that industries are homogeneous entities that produce distinctive, undifferentiated products with production processes that can be characterized by their factor intensities. This leads to the presumption that US imports from developing countries occur in relatively unskilled-labor-intensive US industries, while US exports are concentrated in more skill-intensive industries. It turns out, however, that the relationships between

12. Sponsored jointly by the US Census Bureau and the US Bureau of Labor Statistics, the Current Population Survey is the primary source of labor force statistics for the population of the United States, www.census.gov/cps (accessed on November 1, 2012).

13. See Economic Policy Institute, State of Working America, http://stateofworkingamerica.org (accessed on November 1, 2012).

14. Ibid., footnote 13.

15. In addition, since 2000, inequality has taken the form of a shift in income from wages to profits rather than changes in relative wages along the lines of skill. Indeed, had the share of compensation in corporate value added in 2009 been the same as in 2000, wages would have been 8 percent higher. And in this context, the two-factor version of Stolper-Samuelson that might fit would be one with capital and labor, rather than skilled and unskilled labor.

16. For a comprehensive analysis, see Acemoglu and Autor (2010).

US industry skill intensities and the origins of US manufactured imports are much weaker than might be presumed. Indeed, at the most disaggregated level for which matched skill and product data can be obtained there is no relationship at all.

Since they are available at a disaggregated level, we have used data on the employment share of production workers as an indicator of unskilled-labor intensity (box 9.1). However, we have confirmed these results with education level (college and high school) as a proxy for skills at more aggregated levels. We have ranked the 372 US 6-digit manufacturing industries for which we have both trade and industry data by skill intensity (we use the average share of nonproduction workers in employment in 1997, 2002, and 2007). These account for about 80 percent of US manufacturing employment. We then calculate the share of total US manufactured imports from developing countries that occurred in each industry and plot these in figure 9.3. If the conventional view is correct we might expect that most US imports from developing countries would be found in the lowest-skill industries in the left part of figure 9.3. But we see that substantial shares have also occurred in many of the most skill-intensive US industries.

We also use these import shares to calculate the weighted average nonproduction worker ratios of imports from developed and developing countries. On average, as reported in appendix 9A, nonproduction (skilled) workers accounted for 29 percent of employment in all US manufacturing industries in 1997, 2002, and 2007.[17] Using manufactured imports from developing countries in these years to weight the 6-digit US industry employment ratios indicates a typical nonproduction worker ratio of 36 percent, and using manufactured imports from developed countries as weights indicates a ratio of 35 percent. Thus, imports from both developing and developed countries tend to be concentrated in more skill-intensive US industries, and using US skill measures, their average skill ratios are virtually identical. Indeed, as shown in appendix 9A, using data at both the 4- and 6-digit levels, dropping industries from the computer and electronics category from the sample, and using payroll shares rather than employment ratios as our indicator of skill intensity does not change the results. When US input ratios are used, overall imports from developing countries appear as skill-intensive as imports from developed countries and, as we also show, as skill-intensive as US manufacturing in general and US exports in particular.

The lack of association at a highly disaggregated level between imports from developing countries and skill intensity is consistent with at least four different explanations. First, the Heckscher-Ohlin theory is wrong, and developing countries have not actually specialized in goods that are unskilled-labor-intensive. Second, there are "factor intensity" reversals, and the goods imported from developing countries are produced using unskilled-labor-

---

17. A more extensive discussion is provided in a background working paper (Edwards and Lawrence 2010a).

Box 9.1 Defining skilled and unskilled labor

This study uses the classification of US workers into production and nonproduction workers as our proxy for "skilled" and "unskilled" workers. However, as reported in appendix 9A, we have also done some of the calculations using data on education (college and noncollege graduates) at the most disaggregated levels available.

There are two ways factor intensity can be measured. The first is to use employment shares (e.g., the ratio of skilled to unskilled workers) and the second is to use cost shares (e.g., the ratio of the payroll shares received by skilled and unskilled workers). If factors of a particular type all receive the same wage, it will make no difference which measure is used. However, if there are wage differences among industries—for example, because of specific skills—industry rankings could be different. Cost rather than employment shares are the relevant variable for relating factor prices to goods prices.

Input-Output Tables prepared by the Bureau of Economic Analysis match trade and employment data for 86 different manufacturing industries at the 4-digit level of the North American Industry Classification System (NAICS).[1] This is the most disaggregated level for which data on worker educational levels are available. More disaggregated census data are available for manufacturing at the 6-digit level, which reports on about 470 different industries. However, employment at this level is only categorized according to production and nonproduction workers.

These measures are not ideal proxies for skill, as nonproduction workers, for example, include some relatively poorly paid white-collar office workers. They do, however, have the virtue of being available at the 6-digit (and 4-digit) NAICS level. This is a high level of disaggregation allowing for a more refined analysis of the trade-wage relationship.[2] The measures also allow for an exact matching of product prices and cost shares at the industry level.

Moreover, distinguishing between production and nonproduction workers segments the manufacturing labor force into groups with shares and wages that are not very different from a classification system based on education.[3] For example, in 2005 production-worker wages in manufacturing were on average 65 percent of the wages of nonproduction workers. In the same year, the weekly wages of full-time male and female workers with a high school degree were 60 and 62 percent, respectively, of the wages of male and female workers with college degrees. Similarly, the percentage of manufacturing employment with a college degree is quite similar to the percentage of employment of nonproduction workers. This is borne out by the similar results we obtain in appendix 9A.

Workers earning the average wage of nonproduction workers of $65,000 in 2007 would fall between the 80th and 90th percentiles. Workers earning $37,000, the nonproduction average, would fall just below the 60th percentile.

---

1. Bureau of Economic Analysis, Input-Output Tables, www.bea.gov/industry/index.htm (accessed on November 1, 2012).

2. On average in 1997, 2002, and 2007, the typical 6-digit industry had 31,000 employees.

3. In 2007, production workers accounted for 71 percent of manufacturing employment. On average, production-worker wages at $37,512 were 57.6 percent of the $65,083 earned by nonproduction workers.

Figure 9.3 Share of US manufactured imports from developing countries in 6-digit NAICS industries ranked by skill intensity, 1997–2007

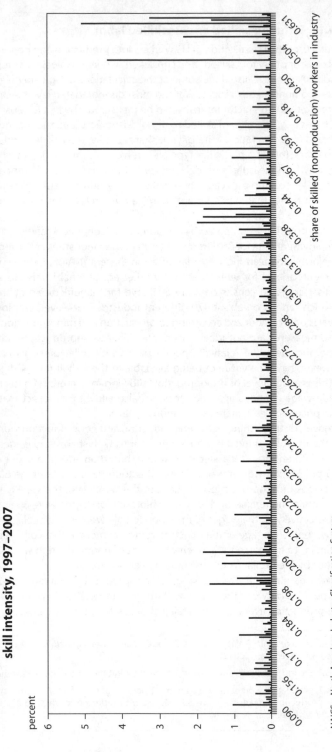

NAICS = North American Industry Classification System

Source: US International Trade Commission Trade Data and Census Data from Annual Survey of Manufacturers.

intensive methods in developing countries but using skill-intensive methods in the United States. Third, much of the value added in the goods ascribed to developing countries has actually been added in developed countries (e.g., iPod, which is stamped "made in China" but actually has a substantial amount of value added in the United States), so these are actually skill-intensive goods. And fourth, developed and developing countries are basically producing different goods or adding value to different parts of the supply chain.

The first hypothesis is implausible, since there is considerable empirical support, albeit with qualifications for Heckscher-Ohlin (Helpman 1999, Romalis 2004). If factor-intensity reversals or supply chains are the full explanation, the goods produced by developed and developing countries should nonetheless still be similar. However, 10-digit unit value data we presented in chapter 4 support the interpretation that these are different goods rather than simply different parts of the supply chain. We found marked differences in the unit values of goods exported by developing countries and those exported to the United States by developing countries, as well as those exported by the United States. We also found that these differences were evident even in categories for final goods.

If the goods ascribed to developing countries as imports actually had large amounts of value added in developed countries, then they might actually be skill-intensive and their declining prices would not indicate that wage inequality would occur if their prices fell. But again, we have found that even in high-technology products, their relative unit values are low. It is therefore quite likely that the goods imported by the United States from developing countries are far less skill-intensive than implied by the US input coefficient data.

Indeed, we encountered a similar paradox in our investigation in chapter 4 of whether developed and developing countries compete head to head. In the raw data, we reported that several developing countries such as China have large trade surpluses in "high-tech" products. However, in that analysis we found that, especially when it came to products that are classified as high-tech or skill-intensive, there were substantial differences in the quality and the 10-digit unit values of US imports from developing countries and the exports of the United States and other developed countries. By differentiating between finished products and intermediate inputs, we were also able to exclude the explanation that the imports from developing countries were simply less finished products.

Thus, given these findings, the obvious explanation is that imports from developing countries and domestically produced products are fundamentally different, and therefore the skill intensity of domestic products is not a good measure of the skill intensity of these imports. And the implication is that the US economy is in many cases specialized and no longer produces many of the products it imports. This suggests that in some cases the methodologies we now describe are mistaken when they make the assumption that US and imported products in the same industry are identical, and their findings may have to be questioned (or reinterpreted).

Studies of Recent Data

Factor Content

Given the results we have just presented, it is no surprise that using US input coefficients to estimate the recent net factor content of US trade does not suggest that recent trade has had large effects on relative US wages. Lawrence Mishel, Jared Bernstein, and Heidi Shierholz (2009) report on an input-output analysis that estimates the net factor content of US trade, dividing workers into those with less than a bachelor's degree and those with a bachelor's degree or more. They estimate that over the period from 1979 to 2005, overall trade displaced 4.2 percent of jobs for workers in the United States with less than a bachelor's degree and 2.9 percent of jobs for workers with a bachelor's degree or more. This trade shock therefore increased the relative supply of noncollege-educated workers by 1.3 percent. Most of this change—one percentage point—took place in the 1980s, while the change between 2000 and 2005 was just 0.4 percent. Over the entire period, therefore, if the elasticity of substitution between these types of workers was unity, a 1.3 percent decline in the relative wage of workers without a bachelor's degree would have been required to reequilibrate the labor market. Thus, the net factor approach using US input coefficients suggests that trade has not had a major impact on US wage inequality since 1980.

When Krugman (2008) tried to prove his conjectures about the large recent impact of developing trade on US wage inequality, he confronted these factor-content numbers and threw up his hands, arguing that the industry data were too aggregated to find the effects that were occurring within industries. He speculated, but did not attempt to show, that imports from developing countries were competing in less-skill-intensive niches that are embedded in more skilled US industries. For example, assume that the US computer industry as a whole is skilled-labor-intensive, but the laptop assembly industry in the United States is unskilled-labor-intensive. If the trade data classify laptop imports from developing countries as imports of computers and we use the skill measures for the entire US computer industry as our measure of the skill intensity of these imports, we would erroneously conclude that US imports of computers from developing countries are skill-intensive.

Simulation

Josh Bivens (2007), however, used a simulation model—ironically one developed by Krugman (1995)—that simply assumes that *all* imports from developing countries are unskilled-labor-intensive and uses assumed and fairly extreme coefficients for skilled-labor and unskilled-labor intensities. Krugman develops a two-good model in which skilled wages are initially twice those of unskilled wages, and in which skilled workers are initially assumed to account for 50 and 20 percent of employment in aircraft and apparel, respectively. This approach is thus not subject to the problem of aggregation bias and can be interpreted as capturing the shifts in tasks rather than products.

Applying this model, Bivens found that increased US trade with developing countries between 1995 and 2006 from 3.5 to 4.9 percent of GNP raised the US wage-skill premium by just 2.1 percent. Lawrence Katz (2008) has pointed out that (since there were already some less-developed-country imports in 1980) using this methodology implies that about 15 to 19 percent of the increase in the 26 percent log-point increase in the college wage premium from 1980 to 2006 can be ascribed to trade. Apparently adding in data from the recent experience using this methodology does not materially affect the results obtained in the earlier studies: trade is a factor, but not a large one when it comes to economywide wage inequality.

While quite small, Bivens' estimate is interesting because it can be viewed as an upper-bound estimate of the effects, since it likely overstates the impact of developing-country trade on wage inequality even under the assumption of perfect labor mobility.[18] First, it is likely to overestimate the unskilled-labor intensity of imports from developing countries by not taking account of the intermediate inputs of skilled-labor-intensive products these imports might contain. Think of assembly in China using inputs from Japan or the United States such as in the iPod (Linden, Kraemer, and Dedrick 2009). Second, it ignores the possibility that US firms might have adopted more skill-intensive technologies in their efforts to compete with developing-country products (so-called factor-intensity reversals). If US goods that compete with developing-country imports are actually skill-intensive rather than, as assumed, unskilled-labor-intensive, declining import prices from developing countries would actually reduce rather than increase wage inequality. Third, it ignores the possibility that some US imports from developing countries may not have been produced in the United States at the start of the period. And finally, the model's parameters may overstate the skill differences in industries that are actually involved in US trade both by ascribing all production to value added in either the skilled-labor-intensive or unskilled-labor-intensive sector and by ignoring the inputs from other factors of production and sectors—such as services—that are more likely to be more similar in skill intensity. Indeed, value added in manufacturing typically accounts for only half of the value of manufactured goods in final sales.[19]

---

18. It should be noted, however, that the results are sensitive to the parameter that is assumed for the elasticity of substitution between skilled and unskilled labor. In the Krugman (1995) model this is set at unity. As Cline (1997, 161–63) notes, there is a large range of estimates in the literature, and parameters less than one would indicate larger wage effects.

19. The assumed coefficients probably overestimate the share of skilled workers. Bivens (2007) follows Krugman (1995) and assumes that in the United States, export-industry skilled workers are half the workforce and earn two-thirds of the wage income. In fact, using census data for 1997, 2002, and 2007 for 473 6-digit industries, we find that the average payroll share of skilled (nonproduction) workers is two-thirds or higher for US industries that account for only 6 percent of overall employment.

With minor tweaks, the Krugman framework can also be used to simulate and calibrate the relative wage effects in a model when specialization patterns change and the economy becomes fully specialized, as modeled by Wood (1994).[20] In other words, we are simulating what might have happened if imports from emerging-market economies displaced the entire US production of unskilled-labor-intensive products. In autarky, the economy is assumed to produce two products, but with trade the less-skilled-labor-intensive product is no longer produced and imports rise by 5 percent of GDP to replace products formerly produced at home All displaced workers must therefore be employed in the other industry. This gives rise to the same relative wage adjustments as in the Bivens simulation for an increase in less-developed-country imports of 5 percent of GDP and suggests an impact on the order of 2 percent between 1995 and 2006. As with the Bivens simulation, however, this is likely to be an upper bound because of the qualifications already noted.

In sum, an upper-bound estimate of the effects of the growth of imports from developing countries between 1995 and 2006 is 2.1 percent.[21] This would be the case either if the economy remained incompletely specialized or if the least skilled production were eliminated in an economy that then became fully specialized.

Analysis of Prices

We are still left, however, with the price evidence that is captured in figure 9.1. Taken at face value, relative import prices appear to confirm the HOSS story. As shown in figure 9.1, between 1990 and 2008, the prices of manufactured imports from developing countries fell dramatically relative to the prices of imports from developed countries.[22] However, recall that in theory wages reflect the marginal revenue product of labor, i.e., the marginal product of labor multiplied by the product price. Thus, what matters for US wages are domestic prices that are adjusted for productivity, and accordingly we consider the behavior of domestic value-added prices and multifactor productivity.

---

20. We assume an initial ratio of skilled to unskilled wages of 2, and the share of skilled labor in employment of Industry 1 of 0.5 and Industry 2 of 0.2. The share of Good 1 in spending is 95 percent, and skilled workers account for 48 percent of the labor force. Initially, six workers are employed in Industry 2 (4.8 unskilled and 1.2 skilled) and 95 workers in Industry 1. When Industry 2 is forced to shut down, the ratio of skilled to unskilled workers employed in Industry 1 must fall by 7 percent. With a substitution elasticity of 1, this gives rise to a 7 percent decline in relative wages of unskilled workers. This is basically the same result as obtained by Bivens for an increase of around 5 percent in the share of less-developed-country imports in spending.

21. Between 2006 and 2011, the ratio of US manufactured imports from non-OECD countries increased from 4.97 to 5.66 percent. Thus, the model would provide estimates of the rise in the skill premium for the full period from 1995 to 2011 of about 3 percent.

22. As shown in chapter 2, there were similar declines in import prices from developing countries relative to US nonagricultural export prices.

We have productivity and value-added data from 1987 to 2006 for all the 4-digit North American Industry Classification System (NAICS) industries that constitute the US manufacturing sector. While these data are again more aggregated than we would like, they have three virtues: (1) they provide comprehensive coverage of the manufacturing sector; (2) they are measures of value-added deflators rather than final output and by excluding input costs capture precisely the variable that is directly related to industry wages and profits; and (3) they can be matched with estimates of multifactor productivity growth that have been calculated by the Bureau of Labor Statistics (BLS) and skills as indicated by employment shares of production and nonproduction workers.

Import-Share-Weighted Prices

Using manufacturing import trade data at the 4-digit NAICS level for all industries except refined petroleum, we aggregate the value-added price deflators, weighting them by the average share of each industry in US manufactured imports from developing and industrial countries between 1997 and 2006.[23] The relative domestic prices in industries with high shares of developing-country imports appear to mirror those of import prices. Between 1987 and 2006, the developing-country import-weighted price series declined by 45 log points relative to the developed-country import-weighted series. While not strictly comparable because of weighting differences, the decline in this relative domestic price measure between 1990 and 2006 of 41 log points is even greater than the 25.3 log-point drop in the relative price of developing-country imports shown in figure 9.1.[24]

Factor prices such as real product wages will, however, reflect not only product prices but also productivity. In addition to product prices, therefore, productivity changes should be accounted for. Accordingly, we use the matched BLS data on multifactor productivity growth to estimate changes in "effective prices," i.e., price changes plus productivity changes.[25] As reported

---

23. NAICS trade data are available only after 1997.

24. Robert Lawrence and Matthew Slaughter (1993) did not find that in the 1980s the relative price of unskilled-labor-intensive products had declined in terms of domestic prices. However, Robert Feenstra (2004, 105) argued that this domestic price evidence could be misleading if there were declines in the prices of intermediate inputs. Indeed, he pointed out that in several countries domestic prices had risen more rapidly than import prices, and he suggested the reason was declining intermediate input prices. However, what we find here is that compositional differences are important. Imports in general, and imports from developing countries in particular, are especially concentrated in electronics products, the prices of which have fallen rapidly. When domestic prices are reweighted giving these industries a greater weight than they have in domestic output, they also rise more slowly.

25. Robert Feenstra, Marshall Reinsdorf, and Matthew Slaughter (2009) are also critical of the way in which the BLS calculates trade-price indices and hence the GDP deflators. In particular, the BLS excludes increases in varieties of imports coming from new supplying countries and measures import prices free of tariffs. This tends to bias deflators downward and productivity estimates upward. The bias is particularly acute in information technology products. As we sum changes

Table 9.1 Weighted relative effective prices, 4-digit NAICS industries, 1987–2006 (log scale, 2006 = 0)

Prices	1987	1990	1995	2000	2005	2006
Developing-/developed-country import weights						
1 Deflators	0.45	0.41	0.28	0.12	0.02	0
2 Multifactor productivity (inverse)	0.39	0.36	0.24	0.09	0.02	0
3 Effective prices (1)–(2)	0.06	0.05	0.04	0.03	0	0
Production/nonproduction employment weights						
4 Deflators	−0.13	−0.12	−0.09	−0.04	−0.01	0
5 Multifactor productivity (inverse)	−0.11	−0.10	−0.07	−0.04	−0.01	0
6 Effective prices (4)–(5)	−0.02	−0.02	−0.02	0	0	0

NAICS = North American Industry Classification System

Note: Developing-country import weights = average share of industry in US manufactured imports from developing countries, 1997 to 2006; developed-country import weights = average share of industry in US manufactured imports from developing countries, 1997 to 2006; production employment weights = average share of industry in US manufacturing employment of production workers, 1997, 2002, and 2007; nonproduction employment weights = average share of industry in US manufacturing employment of nonproduction workers, 1997, 2002, and 2007.

Sources: Bureau of Labor Statistics Multifactor Productivity Data, www.bls.gov/mfp/home.htm (accessed on November 1, 2012); US International Trade Commission Interactive Tariff and Trade DataWeb, http://dataweb.usitc.gov (accessed on November 1, 2012).

in row 3 of table 9.1, we subtract the inverse of the log of relative productivity growth from the relative price changes to estimate changes in relative effective prices. Productivity growth was especially high in the sectors with declining relative prices, and as a result effective prices suggest wage pressures that are far more muted than if the relative prices were assumed to be the only determinant of wages. The relative developing-to-industrial-country import-weighted measure of effective domestic prices still has a downward trend, but the decline over the 30-year period from 1987 to 2006 is just 6 log points (compared with 45 log points for prices alone). In our description in the previous chapter of how Stolper-Samuelson effects operate, we emphasized the symmetrical influences of prices and productivity changes. Thus, even though prices fell especially rapidly in sectors with large shares of imports from developing countries, the pressures on wages in these industries were strongly dampened because of faster productivity growth.

Skill-Share-Weighted Prices

But do these price changes translate into declining prices of relatively unskilled-labor-intensive products? To answer this question we weight both the industry price and productivity measures by industry employment of production and

---

in the deflator with productivity growth, the biases offset each other and so are less likely to be a problem for our analysis.

Figure 9.4 Domestic effective prices weighted by import shares and production and nonproduction employment, 1987–2006

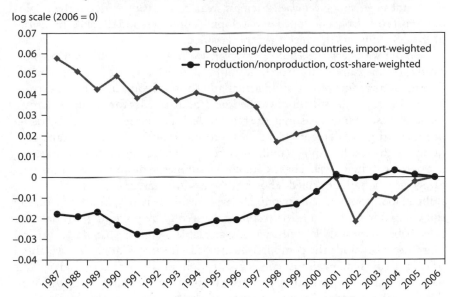

log scale (2006 = 0)

Source: Authors' calculations using data from the Bureau of Economic Analysis and Bureau of Labor Statistics.

nonproduction workers. We use Census data and average industry employment shares for 1997, 2002, and 2007. This produces surprising results (rows 4 to 6 of table 9.1). Between 1987 and 2006, this price measure increases by 13 log points more when weighted by industry-production-worker employment than it does when weighted by industry-nonproduction-worker employment. In contrast to the impression left by the import-share-weighted prices, therefore, using domestic employment weights, this result appears to imply pressures for greater wage equality with production-worker employment being associated with increasing relative prices.

Again, these pressures are muted when productivity changes are accounted for. Weighted by production-worker employment, effective prices rise by just 2 percent more than when weighted by nonproduction workers. Thus, there appear to be very modest price pressures for increased wage equality—although the Stolper-Samuelson theory does indicate a "magnification effect" depending on relative factor shares that could be quite large if these shares are relatively close.[26] The contrasting trends in the import-weighted and skill-weighted US industry price series is vividly captured in figure 9.4. All told, therefore, we see

26. Using an * to indicate proportional rates of change, and Sx and Sy as the shares of skilled labor in the production cost of x and y, respectively, the theory indicates that $Px^* - Py^* = (Sx - Sy)$ $(Ws^* - Wu^*)$. This implies larger changes in wages for any given relative price changes when $Sx - Sy$ is small, so long as both products continue to be produced.

that changes in developed- and developing-country import-weighted prices and effective prices do not translate into changes in skill-weighted prices. This is actually not surprising given the extremely weak relationship between the origins of imports (i.e., from developed or developing countries) and the skill intensities of the US industries in which they are classified.

Before we reject the HOSS, however, we need to consider two possible sources of measurement error that could affect this result. First, when the BLS measures some prices, and particularly those of computers and electronics products, it makes distinctive "hedonic" adjustments for quality improvement. If these are mismeasured, the rapidly declining prices (and rapidly rising productivity growth) recorded for these products could be inaccurate and contaminate the results. And second, there could be aggregation bias from using data at the 4-digit level. These data could submerge more refined industrial categories that are unskilled-labor-intensive within larger categories in which skilled labor dominates. Appendix 9B explores these issues, first by excluding the computer sector from the results, and second by providing estimates of price behavior and skill intensity using available 6-digit NAICS data. We find that once we exclude the computer industries, effective relative skill-weighted prices actually remain almost constant throughout the period. Indeed, what is so striking about these results, particularly for the period after 1995 for which the weights are more relevant, is how small the changes in both relative prices and relative effective prices are. All told, therefore, if the computer sectors are excluded from the data, the overall price changes still do not mandate changes in the relative wages of skilled workers.

Mandated Wage Changes

The (effective) price evidence we have produced is an ex post outcome and reflects all the determinants of industry prices rather than only those due to trade. Prices and productivity in a large country such as the United States are outcomes of a range of domestic forces (research and development, tastes, imperfect competition) as well as international forces (tariffs, foreign prices, commodity cycles, international transport costs). It is possible, therefore, that price pressures from developing countries have been a force for wage inequality, but these pressures have been offset by changes in other variables that influence US value-added prices and productivity. There is always the possibility that "but for trade" US wage inequality might have fallen. We can answer this "but for" question using a fourth empirical approach that takes greater care about causation.

In a two-stage process, the approach first estimates the effects of trade and other variables on domestic prices. It then uses these estimates to determine the relative wage changes mandated by the price changes due to those variables. This approach comes from Robert Feenstra and Gordon Hanson (1999), who developed measures of outsourcing and the adoption of computers and used the approach to estimate the effects on relative wages between 1979 and

1990.[27] Depending on their estimates, they find that outsourcing accounts for 10 to 25 percent of the rise in wage inequality, while the adoption of computers explains 25 to 100 percent of the increase. More recently, Nino Sitchinava (2008) refined and updated the methodology used by Feenstra and Hanson to measure outsourcing more accurately. She also finds a role for both outsourcing and the adoption of computers on the skilled-unskilled wage gap between 1989 and 1996. However, she concludes that neither of these factors affects wages between 1997 and 2004.

To isolate the contribution of developing-country trade to changes in US wages, we also apply this two-stage procedure, as reported in appendix 9C and in a background working paper (Edwards and Lawrence 2010a). The first stage estimates the effect of developing-country trade on US effective prices. A key innovation in our analysis compared to existing literature (Leamer 1998, Feenstra and Hanson 1999, Haskel and Slaughter 2003) is that we use import unit values rather than quantitative measures of import intensity or technology (Feenstra and Hanson 1999) as our indicator of international competition.[28] The mandated wage results we obtain indicate that trade-induced domestic price changes have not caused rising wage inequality along skill lines in recent years. We do, however, find that the impact of developing-country trade on US wage inequality is not equal across all countries. For example, our estimates indicate that Chinese import prices mandated a rise in the total return to labor and a slight increase in wage inequality, but these effects were offset by price movements from other developing countries.

Wages in the Middle

We noted that one of the challenges facing recent studies is that wage outcomes have become more complex. In particular, over some periods the weakest wage growth has been for workers in the middle of the range. To explain more complex outcomes in the wage distribution, theories need more than two types of workers. In response to these new developments, labor economists Frank Levy and Richard Murnane (2006) and David Autor, Lawrence Katz, and Melissa Kearney (2005, 2006) posit a new theory of skill-biased technological change in which computers complement nonroutine cognitive tasks and substitute for routine tasks, but have little effect on manual tasks found at the bottom. The result is downward pressure on wages and employment opportunities on workers in the middle and upward pressures at the top.

---

27. Feenstra and Hanson justify their model theoretically in the context of a fully specialized economy in which the relative wage effects operate through changing imported input prices.

28. An exception is the study of Jonathan Haskel and Matthew Slaughter (2001), who include import prices for the OECD, newly industrialized economies (NICs), and the non-OECD rest of the world in their wage regressions for the United Kingdom. Their international price variables are unable to explain any of the rise in UK wage inequality experienced during the 1980s. Haskel and Slaughter (2003) also include tariff and transport costs in their study of the United States.

Claudia Goldin and Lawrence Katz (2007) and Janet Yellen[29] suggest that the globalization of production has similar properties in inducing polarization of wage distribution. They argue that suppliers of personal services at the low end escape downward pressures from trade because these services must be provided locally. But those at the top are rewarded by trade, while those in the middle are hurt by offshoring. In the previous section, we discussed that some new trade theories in which workers are heterogeneous could also potentially account for such an outcome (Blanchard and Willmann 2008, Costinot and Vogel 2010).

Guy Michaels, Ashwini Natraj, and John Van Reenen (2010) have tested the wage polarization hypothesis in a sample of 11 countries using 25 years of data. They find statistically significant support for the technological change polarization explanation but not the explanation based on trade. This accords with Lawrence (2008), in which one of us finds a tendency for trade displacement to occur disproportionately among workers earning close to the median wage but estimates that the effects are too small to have affected aggregate wage trends in a major way.[30]

Conclusions

We have offered several methods of analysis and all suggest that the fears of large effects leading to rising skill-related US wage inequality from developing-country imports in recent years are unwarranted. While conventional trade theory makes such expectations plausible, our investigations reveal that they are far off the mark. After summarizing briefly the results of studies through the mid-1990s, we reported that since the late 1990s the rise in wage inequality has been less pervasive than earlier. In addition, we noted that at the most disaggregated level for which comprehensive wage and employment data related to skill level are available, we find that the US industries competing with developing-country imports are not particularly intensive in unskilled labor. This paradoxical result reinforces our earlier conclusion that developing countries have become specialized in many products that are no longer produced in the United States.

Factor content of trade simulations that use US input coefficients suggests the effects on wage inequality are extremely small. Even though they exaggerate the unskilled-labor content of US imports and ignore the possibility that many imported products are no longer produced in the United States, simulation models suggest that trade with developing countries has

---

29. Janet L. Yellen, Economic Inequality in the United States, speech to the Center for the Study of Democracy, University of California, Irvine, November 6, 2006.

30. In the period from 2000 to 2005, one of us (Lawrence 2008) estimates using the BLS Input-Output Tables that 1.3 million job opportunities in US manufacturing were lost due to trade. This compares with a labor force of over 140 million (or 70 million between the 25th and 75th percentiles). Even if most of the displaced workers earned above the median wage in the economy, this impact is unlikely to have affected employment composition or wages in a major way.

warranted only small changes in the US skills premium. We have noted that these simulations can also be interpreted as estimates of wage changes stemming from changes in US patterns of specialization when the economy is fully specialized. We have explored the effective price evidence and found that these have not mandated changes in relative wages over the past decade. We have also used mandated wage regressions and found no effects on inequality that can be explicitly ascribed to the import prices of developing countries. These results all suggest that the HOSS approach to US wage inequality has had little to offer in recent years; nor do other methods indicate large effects.

If Krugman's concerns were valid and the HOSS story were an accurate depiction of the effects of US trade with developing countries, the implications of that trade for all unskilled US workers could be grave. Not only would their wages fall behind in relative terms, but they could be absolutely worse off. Fortunately, however, our evidence suggests that while there are workers who lose from such trade, they are most likely to be those who are dislocated and compete directly with imports rather than all workers with similar skills throughout the economy. Indeed, when imports are no longer produced domestically, most workers in the United States will benefit as consumers, while a relatively small share actually compete head to head. We should emphasize, however, that while this chapter has focused on the HOSS story, its negative findings do not imply that trade with developing countries has no impact on wages through other mechanisms. Indeed, as described in chapter 2, there are effects that are evident in specific industries, regions, and occupations, rather than economywide inequality along the lines of skill.

Appendix 9A
Are Developing-Country Manufactured Imports Intensive in Unskilled Labor?

The conventional HOSS framework assumes that industries are homogeneous entities that produce distinctive undifferentiated products with production processes that can be characterized by their factor intensities. This leads to the presumption that US imports from developing countries occur mostly in relatively unskilled-labor-intensive industries—an assumption that is important in building simulation models. It turns out, however, that the relationships between industry skill intensities and the origins of US manufactured imports are extremely weak.

This result is very surprising because the literature provides evidence that imports from developing countries have higher shares in less-skilled-labor-intensive US industries.[31] Indeed, our data also yield this result when equal weight is assigned to each 6-digit industry. But for the purposes of estimating the impact on relative wages, the size of the imports from developed and developing countries in each industry should also be taken into account. In the net factor content approach, for example, the impact of trade will depend on the total value of skilled and unskilled labor involved in trade.[32] Similarly, industry size will affect how price changes due to trade translate into mandated wage changes.

Despite their dominance in individual unskilled-labor-intensive industries, most of the imports from developing countries are in fact not concentrated in unskilled-labor-intensive US industries. To explore this, we rank 372 6-digit industries by skill intensity (we use the average share of nonproduction workers in employment in 1997, 2002, and 2007). We divide these industries into deciles with roughly equal shares in manufacturing employment. We then calculate the share of overall US manufactured im-

---

31. John Romalis (2004) and Andrew Bernard, Stephen Redding, and Peter Schott (2007) find that imports from developing countries have higher shares in less-skill-intensive industries. Edward Leamer and James Levinsohn (1995) criticize cross-commodity studies of export performance on the grounds that they have unclear theoretical foundations. If factor prices are lower in developing countries and technologies are similar, how can developed countries compete at all in any particular industry? Either the products must be imperfect substitutes or there must be some aggregation of products. To place his analysis on firmer grounds, Romalis therefore incorporates both transportation costs and monopolistic competition into a Heckscher-Ohlin model.

32. In our 6-digit data using 372 industries we find that developing countries obtain an additional 0.84 percent market share for each percentage point increase in the employment share of (unskilled) production workers in industry employment. The regression is: $Lshldci$ = 0.84 $Lprodempi$ (t = 3.2) − 0.75 (7.7), R^2 = .027. This is very similar to Romalis (2004, 83), who finds an elasticity of 0.93 when relating developed-country shares in imports to industry skill intensity. Running the same regression using average industry imports from developing countries between 1997 and 2007 to weight the observations, however, we find no relationship at all. The estimated elasticity falls to −.12 and is not significant.

Table 9A.1 Composition of US manufacturing imports from developed and developing countries by industries ranked by employment skill intensity, 1997–2007 (percent)

Decile	Average skill/ employment[a]	Share of overall manufactured imports from developed countries[b]	Share of overall manufactured imports from developing countries[c]	Developing-country market share in imports[d]
1	0.17	5	6	57
2	0.20	6	9	63
3	0.22	12	7	42
4	0.24	6	5	48
5	0.26	5	6	58
1–5		34	33	53
6	0.30	7	8	54
7	0.35	11	18	65
8	0.42	15	14	53
9	0.50	21	9	33
10	0.67	12	18	63
6–10		66	67	54
Total		100	100	54

a. Percent of nonproduction workers in total employment share (average of 1997, 2002, and 2007).
b. Share of decile in overall US manufactured imports from developed countries (1997–2007).
c. Share of decile in overall US manufactured imports from developing countries (1997–2007).
d. Average share of imports from developing countries in decile imports.

Source: US Census Bureau data.

ports from developed and developing countries that fall into each of these deciles. The results are presented in table 9A.1. If the conventional view is correct, we might expect that most US imports from developing countries would be found in the lowest-skill deciles and by contrast most imports from developed countries in the top deciles. In addition, we might expect to find the market share of imports from developing countries to be highest in the lowest-decile industries and to decline as we consider higher-skill deciles.

What is striking, however, is that imports from both developing and developed countries are relatively concentrated in more skill-intensive US industries, with a remarkably similar two-thirds of the imports from both developed and developing countries coming in the US industries in the five highest skill deciles. Even more remarkably, 18 percent of imports from developing countries fall in the very top decile in skill intensity, compared with only 11 percent of the imports from developed countries. We might also have expected that the developing-country market share in each industry's total imports would fall as the deciles become more skill-intensive. But as shown in column 5 of table 9A.1, developing countries accounted for 53 percent of all imports in the five least-skill-intensive deciles and 54 percent of all manufactured imports in industries in the top five deciles. Moreover, developing countries accounted for 63 percent of the imports in the most skill-intensive deciles. In addition,

Table 9A.2 Manufacturing payroll and employment shares using nonproduction worker and college education measures to define skilled workers (average for 1997, 2002, and 2007)

Classification	Developing-country imports	Developed-country imports	Ratio of developing/ developed countries
Production/nonproduction worker			
Payroll shares of manufacturing nonproduction workers weighted by:			
4-digit (59 industries)	0.475	0.430	1.11
4-digit without NAICS 334 (computers and electronics)	0.379	0.374	1.01
Employment shares of manufacturing nonproduction workers weighted by:			
4-digit (59 industries)	0.348	0.336	1.03
4-digit without NAICS 334 (computers and electronics)	0.262	0.292	0.90
Educational attainment			
Payroll share			
4-digit (59 industries)	0.434	0.371	1.17
4-digit without NAICS 334 (computers and electronics)	0.320	0.314	1.02
Skilled worker payroll share			
4-digit (59 industries)	0.275	0.243	1.13
4-digit without NAICS 334 (computers and electronics)	0.180	0.203	0.89

NAICS = North American Industry Classification System

Source: Bureau of Economic Analysis, Annual Census of Manufacturing and Current Population Surveys.

we do not find that over time—i.e., between 1997 and 2007—imports from developing countries became more concentrated in unskilled-labor-intensive industries. In fact, we find no correlation between changes in less-developed-country import shares and skill intensity between these years.

Factor intensity can be measured as we have done by physical inputs—i.e., the number of skilled and unskilled workers—but it can also be measured by factor shares in value added. Indeed, it is this latter measure that is required for the Stolper-Samuelson framework when linking product prices and factor rewards. This approach also suggests that imports from developing countries are not especially unskilled-labor-intensive.

Table 9A.2 reports estimates of the average payroll share of nonproduction workers as our measure of skill intensity. Again we average the data for 1997, 2002, and 2007. To obtain an estimate of the representative skill intensity of imports from developing countries, we weight the 4-digit NAICS individual industry payroll shares of nonproduction workers by the share of each industry in US imports of manufactured goods from developing countries.[33] We obtain a weighted-average, nonproduction-worker payroll share of 48 percent. We then weight the same industry-nonproduction-worker payroll shares by industry import shares from developed countries and obtain a weighted-average, nonproduction-worker payroll share of 43 percent. In other words, developed-country imports appear to be slightly less skilled-labor-intensive than developing-country imports.[34] Additional disaggregation using 6-digit levels does not change the qualitative nature of these results, and similar results are obtained if we use employment shares rather than payroll shares to measure skill intensity.[35] All told, therefore, the US industries accounting for most of the imports from developing countries do not use unskilled labor relatively intensively. Not reported in the table, in a similar calculation at the 4-digit level using US manufactured exports as weights, we find that the weighted payroll share of skilled labor for exports of 39 percent is almost the same as that for imports from developing countries (38 percent).

These results are important for our analysis. They suggest that even at the most disaggregated level feasible, net factor content of trade analysis using recent data will not indicate that trade induced large increases in relative wage inequality. Indeed, since we have considered only the direct factor inputs, input-output analysis (which takes account of inputs from other industries embodied in exports and importables) is likely to show even smaller differences in factor intensity.

As shown in table 9A.2, using education as a measure of skill rather than the production/nonproduction worker classification, we have relied upon yields showing conclusions very similar to the relative skill intensity of US imports from developed and developing countries. We have used 4-digit data for 2002 to make our comparison, and overall we find that using US employment measures as well as payroll shares, imports from developing countries are more concentrated in industries that are college-education-intensive than

---

33. We use average payroll shares for 1997, 2002 and 2007, and average import shares from 1997 to 2007. Let $Snpi$ denote the payroll share of nonproduction workers in industry i, $MLDCi$ the value of imports from developing countries in industry i, and $MLDC$ the total value of imports from developing countries. We use $MLDCi/MLDC$ for weighting the individual payroll shares ($Snpi$) to obtain a representative skill-intensity measure for imports from developing countries. We then use the shares of imports to each industry, t, from developed countries ($MDCi/MDC$) as weights for each $Snpi$ to obtain a representative skill-intensity measure for imports from developed countries.

34. Dropping the 4-digit industries that constitute the computers and electronics sectors (NAIC 334) indicates that these imports play an important role in the results. Without these industries the average skill intensity of imports declines, but the average skilled-labor intensity of imports from developed countries (36 percent) still remains lower than imports from developing countries (38 percent).

35. At the 6-digit level we have data on 372 industries for which we can match trade and employment. These industries account for almost 80 percent of US manufacturing employment.

imports from developed countries.[36] Excluding NAICS category 334 (computers and electronics) eliminates the differences when payroll shares are used as skill measures, and with employment shares both the occupation and education measures give similar results. All told, this exercise suggests that the production/nonproduction worker classification, the only measure available at a highly disaggregated level, is a useful proxy, and in addition, that our paradoxical results remain even when education is used as the measure of skill.

---

36. We have used Integrated Public Use Microdata Series–Current Population Survey (IPUMS-CPS) data for March 2002. Skilled workers were defined as workers who have obtained a bachelor's degree, while unskilled workers were defined as those with any lower educational attainment. The IPUMS manufacturing sector data were assigned NAICS numbers corresponding to the definition of the manufacturing sector defined by that number. Since there are more NAICS 4-digit categories than IPUMS industries, it was necessary in some cases to aggregate several 4-digit NAICS industries to obtain an exact correspondence.

Appendix 9B
Measurement Error in the Price Data

Two possible sources of measurement error could affect our finding that changes in developed- and developing-country import-weighted prices and effective prices do not translate into changes in skill-weighted prices. First, when the BLS measures certain prices, and particularly those of computers and electronics products, it makes distinctive "hedonic" adjustments for quality improvement. If these are mismeasured, the rapidly declining prices (and rapidly rising productivity growth) recorded for these products could be inaccurate and contaminate the results. And second, there could be aggregation bias from using data at the 4-digit level.[37] These data could submerge more refined industrial categories that are unskilled-labor-intensive within larger categories in which skilled labor dominates.

In what follows we explore these issues, first by excluding the computer sector from the results, and second by providing estimates of price behavior and skill intensity using available 6-digit NAICS data.

Computers and Electronics

We can get a sense of the role of computer prices by looking at manufactured goods import prices. The BLS does not publish the disaggregated component price indices for manufactured prices of imports from industrialized and developing countries. However, it does publish commodity import price indices at the 4-digit HTS level. Accordingly we have constructed a new "non-computer" manufactured import price series by assuming that imports from developing and developed countries have similar price behavior. We use three electronics import price series: automatic data processing (ADP) machines (HTS 8471), parts for ADP machines (HTS 8473), and electronic integrated circuits (HTS 8542). Using their average trade shares between 1997 and 2008 as weights, we extract these three series and reweight the residual.

Between 1997 and 2008, the complete measure of manufactured imports from developing countries falls by 18 log points compared with the price index of imports from developed countries. However, once the three electronics series are excluded, the price index of other manufactured imports from developing countries actually increases by 5.5 percent (log points) relative to the price index of manufactured imports from developed countries. Under the classical HOSS assumptions, these trends in relative prices would reduce wage inequality in the United States.

If electronics prices of imports from developed and developing countries have actually been different, and if the weights the BLS uses are different from those we have used, this procedure introduces measurement error, and the estimates should be taken with a grain of salt. Nonetheless, the measure-

---

37. For evidence on aggregation bias, see Feenstra and Hanson (2000).

ments demonstrate the degree to which these three prices are likely to have influenced the results.

Value-Added Prices

We can, however, be more precise about the role of these products in the domestic price and productivity outcomes. The price declines have been quite astonishing. In 1987, for example, the respective prices of computers (NAICS 3341) and semiconductors (NAICS 3344) were 2,446 and 650 percent higher than in 2006. Prices for communications (NAICS 3342), audio (NAICS 3343), and optical equipment (NAICS 3346) also show strong downward trends. At the same time, multifactor productivity growth has been very rapid. Productivity in 2006 was 20.5 and 12.5 times higher in computers and semiconductors, respectively, than it was in 1987.

Dropping the measures of the six 4-digit NAICS 334 (electronics) sectors from our sample produces some interesting changes and reveals again the large role that these observations play in the results. The effects can be seen in table 9B.1. Excluding these variables leaves us with very small effects. Instead of a 45 log-point decline between 1987 and 2006, the decline in the relative import-weighted domestic price series is now only 4 log points for the period as a whole—all of which is completed by 1995. The decline in effective prices is just 3 percent, and again the measure is unchanged between 1995 and 2006. Similarly, instead of a 13 percent rise in relative production-worker-weighted prices, these prices fall, but by just 1 percent over the entire period. Effective relative skill-weighted prices remain almost constant throughout the period. Indeed, what is so striking about these results particularly for the period after 1995, for which the weights are more relevant, is how small the changes in both relative prices and relative effective prices are. All told, therefore, if the computer sectors are excluded from the data, the overall price changes still do not mandate changes in the relative wages of skilled workers.

Should the computer industry be included in data? In an earlier debate, Jeffrey Sachs and Howard Shatz (1994) were critical of Robert Lawrence and Matthew Slaughter (1993) for including it. They argued that measurement error was so rife in the prices of these products—they are measured using hedonic price regressions—and their behavior such an outlier that they should not be included.[38] If we follow this advice and exclude computers and electronics, there is little to suggest that recent domestic price movements have mandated lower wages for unskilled workers.

On the other hand, by excluding computers and electronics we could be overlooking an important source of wage pressures. The sector does after all

---

38. It is certainly well recognized that because prices are changing so rapidly, fixed-weight indices give results that are very sensitive to the base year that is used. For this reason, chain-weighted indices are now used in the US national income accounts. See also Feenstra, Reinsdorf, and Slaughter (2009).

Table 9B.1 Weighted relative effective domestic prices without computers, 4-digit NAICS industries excluding NAICS 334, 1987–2006 (log scale, 2006 = 0)

Measure	1987	1990	1995	2000	2006
Deflators					
Developing/developed countries	0.04	0.03	0.00	0.01	0.00
Production/nonproduction	0.01	0.01	0.01	0.00	0.00
Effective prices					
Developing/developed countries	0.03	0.02	0.01	0.00	0.00
Production/nonproduction	0.01	0.01	0.01	0.01	0.00

NAICS = North American Industry Classification System

Note: Developing-country = average share of industry in US manufactured imports from developing countries, 1997 to 2006; developed-country = average share of industry in US manufactured imports from developing countries, 1997 to 2006; production = average share of industry in US manufacturing employment of production workers, 1997, 2002, and 2007; nonproduction = average share of industry in US manufacturing employment of nonproduction workers, 1997, 2002, and 2007. The following 4-digit NAICS industries are excluded: NAICS 3341, 3342, 3343, 3344, 3345, and 3346.

Sources: Bureau of Labor Statistics, Multifactor Productivity Data, www.bls.gov/mfp/home.htm (accessed on November 1, 2012); US International Trade Commission Interactive Tariff and Trade DataWeb, http://dataweb.usitc.gov (accessed on November 1, 2012).

account for a third of all manufactured imports from developing countries and a high share of US manufacturing productivity growth. Including the data for computers and electronics indicates that the relative prices of skill-intensive industries have fallen—which, ceteris paribus, would be good for unskilled wages—but that these price pressures have been offset by rapid productivity growth. Both with and without computers, therefore, the implication, consistent with actual wage behavior, is that in recent years trade is not a major source of increasing US wage inequality.

Aggregation

There are data available at the 6-digit NAICS level for producer prices and production- and nonproduction-worker employment. This is a high level of disaggregation, with average employment in each 6-digit industry of about 30,000 workers. But the data are not ideal—first because producer prices include the cost of inputs not produced in each industry, and second because price measures should be adjusted for productivity growth and these are not available.

Currently, 456 producer price indices are available at the 6-digit NAICS level. Unfortunately, some of these have only been introduced recently (after 2003). We were, however, able to obtain continuous measures for about 280 price indices, excluding refined petroleum, that are available back to 1994. These accounted for about 70 percent of all US manufactured imports in 2000. We weight these prices by the average shares of developing- and developed-country imports between 1997 and 2006.

As was shown in figure 9.4, we obtain results that are qualitatively similar but more extreme than those at the 4-digit level, suggesting that aggregation does dampen some of the differences. When the computer and electronics industries are included in the data, the downward trend in the relative developing-country import-weighted producer prices is even stronger than the decline in similarly trade-weighted 4-digit deflators. Between 1994 and 2006, the years for which we have overlapping data, the relative import-weighted producer prices decline by 44 log points compared with the 32 log-point decline in the correspondingly weighted 4-digit price deflator measure. Prices weighted by production-worker employment shares increase by 15 log points relative to prices weighted by nonproduction worker shares. This is also more than the 11 log-point increase over the same period with similarly weighted 4-digit deflators.

While larger price pressures are uncovered by disaggregation, therefore, again the price pressures from developing-country imports do not translate into price pressures in sectors with high shares of production workers. Thus, further disaggregation of the data does not provide evidence for the substantial wage effects expected by Krugman (2008).

Computer prices influence this result too. Excluding the 29 6-digit NAICS 334 industries, the decline in the developing-/developed-country import-weighted producer price is 9 log points rather than 44 log points. This compares with the drop of just 1 percent for the similarly weighted 4-digit deflators when computers are excluded. After dropping the NAICS 334 industries, the relative production-worker prices no longer rise but instead now decline over the period (i.e., by 3 log points between 1994 and 2008). Thus, when computers and electronics are excluded, the downward import-weighted producer price pressures do translate into some increased inequality along the lines of skills, but only by 3 log points over the 14-year period.

Appendix 9C
Isolating the Role of Trade with Mandated Wage Regressions

This appendix seeks explicitly to control for the role of force operating through trade in US wage behavior. It isolates the contribution of developing-country trade to changes in wages using US import unit values and tariffs. The analysis follows Feenstra and Hanson (1999) and is conducted in two stages. The first stage isolates the impact of imports on US effective prices (value added plus productivity) using 4-digit NAICS level data. This is done by regressing effective prices on unit value indices of goods imported by the United States from other developed countries, China, Mexico, an Asian group, and a group combining the other developing countries. Other structural determinants such as average tariff rates, investment in information capital stock, capital intensity, and skill intensity are also included in the specification.[39]

The second stage uses these estimated price changes to determine the relative wage changes mandated by these import price changes. This is done by regressing the predicted change in effective price associated with import unit values on factor cost shares (three factors are used: production workers, nonproduction workers, and capital).[40] The estimated coefficients can be interpreted as the change in the return to labor and capital mandated by changes in the price of competing imports. We also estimate the changes in factor returns mandated by changes in US tariff rates imposed on developing and developed countries.

The mandated wage approach has been widely used to isolate the effect of developing-country trade on US wages (Leamer 1998, Feenstra and Hanson 1999, Haskel and Slaughter 2003). Where our study differs from these is that we use direct measures of import competition, namely import unit values, as our explanatory variables. Other studies have used quantitative measures of import intensity or technology (Feenstra and Hanson 1999) or measures

---

39. The equation we estimate is specified as $\Delta \log P_{jt} + \Delta \log TFP_{jt} = \sum Z_{kjt} \delta_k + \upsilon_{jt}$, where P denotes value-added price, TFP denotes total factor productivity, υ_{jt} is the random error, and the estimated coefficients δ_k capture the contribution of the structural variables Z_k to changes in effective prices. In effect, this equation is the reduced form of separate price and total factor productivity equations. Feenstra and Hanson (1999) use a variable termed "effective TFP" in their effective price measure. This is calculated as the primal measure of TFP plus the average deviation of industry-specific, factor-price changes from their mean levels. We do not have wage data by production and nonproduction worker for the entire period and therefore use only the primal measure of TFP.

40. The second-stage regression is specified as $\hat{\delta}_k Z_{kjt} = \sum_{k \in I} \theta_{ijt} \beta_{ki} + \varepsilon_{kjt}$, where θ_{ijt} is the share of factor i (production worker, nonproduction worker, capital) in the average cost of producing one unit of value added of product j. The coefficient β_{ki} is interpreted as the change in price of primary factor i that can be attributed to the structural variable Z_k. The mandated wage analysis is strictly imbedded in the Stolper-Samuelson theoretical framework where factors are mobile across sectors such that the zero profit condition is maintained in each sector. Our focus is therefore on identifying the long-run effect on wages from changes in prices of competing imports.

of tariff and transport costs (Haskel and Slaughter 2003) to explain wage inequality.[41]

Results

The mandated wage regressions corroborate the earlier analysis that finds a minor impact of developing-country trade on US wage inequality. The first-stage price regressions reveal that US effective prices are responsive to changes in the border price of imports, whether originating from changes in the foreign selling price of competing goods or from changes in US tariff rates. A small but statistically significant positive association is found between US effective prices and unit values of US imports from developed countries, China and other developing countries, but no relationship is found for imports from Mexico and the Asian group.[42] In addition we find that tariff protection raises US effective prices—a 10 percent rise in aggregate import prices is associated with a 1.8 percent rise in US effective prices—but, interestingly, this association is driven by tariff barriers on trade from developing countries.

These price equations establish a mechanism through which international competition influences the effective return to US producers.[43] In the second stage of the analysis, we use these results to establish whether changes in foreign prices gave rise to economically significant changes in US wages and wage inequality, measured as the ratio of wages of nonproduction to production workers.

The results of the mandated wage regressions reveal a fair amount of variation across countries. The sector bias of developed-country price changes from 1993 to 2006 mandated a 4.6 percent rise in the nominal wage of nonproduction workers and a 5.7 percent rise in the return to capital. No change in the wage of production workers is mandated.

---

41. An exception is the study by Haskel and Slaughter (2001), who include import prices for the OECD, newly industrialized countries, and the non-OECD rest of the world in their wage regressions for the United Kingdom. Their international price variables are unable to explain any of the rise in UK wage inequality during the 1980s.

42. We construct Törnqvist indices at the 4-digit NAICS level for the period 1993–2006 using highly disaggregated (10-digit HTS level) US import unit values. The data are obtained from Feenstra, Romalis, and Schott (2002). New products are included in the Törnqvist index, but we do not adjust for the biases that the entry of new products and exit of old products have on the index (Feenstra 1994, Broda and Weinstein 2006). One limitation of our measure of import-price competition is that unit values are not true price indices in that changes in the composition and quality of imports affect the calculated unit value even if product prices are unchanged. We attempt to limit these biases by using highly disaggregated trade data, but as shown in chapter 4 and by Peter Schott (2004) heterogeneity in prices across countries and measurement errors are evident even at this level of disaggregation.

43. Strictly speaking, we have identified the association between US effective prices and international prices. It remains possible that an unobserved third factor may be driving the association. We are therefore circumspect about attributing causality to the relationship.

For developing countries, we find contrasting and offsetting effects on wages from import prices. Chinese import unit values from 1993 to 2006 raised wage inequality (by 2.15 percent), but this is more than offset by the inequality-reducing impact of imports from other developing economies (4.27 percent) and the decline in mandated wages of nonproduction workers from tariff liberalization. Similarly, prices of Chinese imports into the United States mandated a statistically significant rise in the return to labor relative to capital, but this was also offset by sectoral trends in US import prices from other developing economies.

Taken together, US imports from developing countries mandated no change in US wage inequality from 1993 to 2006.[44]

An implication drawn from the results is that developing countries do not all have equivalent effects on wage inequality in the United States. But overall, the regression analysis suggests that trade-induced domestic price changes due to developing economies are not a cause of rising wage inequality in recent years. Further discussion is provided in our background paper (Edwards and Lawrence 2010a).

---

44. Similarly, estimates based on aggregate US import unit values calculated using all countries reveal no significant change in relative wages, but do reveal a significant rise in the return to capital relative to labor.

10

Conclusions and Policy Implications

This study has examined concerns about the effect of growth in emerging-market economies on the US economy and particularly American workers. We have found evidence that imports from emerging-market economies have resulted in dislocation and wage loss for some American workers. However, the contribution of trade with these countries to the trends and fluctuations in US employment is far less important than the public believes. Rather, the trends and fluctuations overwhelmingly reflect domestic economic developments. The declining share of manufacturing employment in the United States, in particular, is long-lived and results primarily from combining rapid productivity growth and demand that is insufficiently responsive to the falling prices that this productivity engenders. The periods in the United States with high unemployment are not those with rapid import growth. On the contrary, the recessions that began in 2001 and 2008 and produced high unemployment resulted from shocks in US financial markets (the dot.com bubble and financial crisis) that had local origins and were actually mitigated by the drop in imports associated with the shock. More generally, worker dislocation due to import competition and offshoring constitutes only a very small share of the workers who are involuntarily displaced annually—our estimate suggests on the order of 2 percent.

If the fears expressed by some economists were warranted, emerging-market-economy growth could actually further contribute to reductions in US living standards and downward pressures on wages. Fortunately, in our view, other than in oil, where we did find modest negative effects, we believe this view is mistaken. Indeed, the central implication of this study is that for the most part growth in emerging-market economies is part of the solution to

America's current adjustment challenges rather than part of the problem. All else being equal, such growth is likely to stimulate demand for US exports and improve America's terms of trade. This suggests that policies that promote foreign economic development and growth remain in America's economic interest.

The United States has benefited from the acceleration of developing-country growth since the mid-1990s and would continue to benefit if that growth were sustained or to accelerate in the immediate future. As might be expected, given their income levels, developing countries have been pursuing a strategy of export-led growth that has resulted in declining relative prices of their manufactured goods exports. For the most part the United States does not compete head to head with emerging-market economies in its export markets. Since the mid-1990s, therefore, coincident with increased growth in US imports from developing countries, America's manufacturing terms of trade have trended upward. Simulations using theory-based structural models and econometric estimates of trade equations both indicate that this improvement has been such that assuming it altered its spending patterns, the United States could return to the trade balance it had in 1990 and still have better nonoil terms of trade than it had at that time. In addition to the improvements in the terms of trade, developing-country growth has provided US producers with growing markets and access to a greater variety of inputs and services, and US consumers with a greater variety of finished products. We have estimated that overall the gains from manufacturing trade with emerging-market economies average about $500 per person per year.

Some dispute the proposition that developing countries are not competing directly with the United States in export markets by pointing to the large trade deficits the United States has sustained in high-technology products. They claim that its policies have already allowed China to surge ahead technologically and thereby pose a major threat to US commercial and security interests (Preeg 2004, McMillon 2007). But we have found that the trade data, especially when the data relate to so-called high-technology products, need to be interpreted with great caution. The alarms raised about Chinese technological prowess as a grave threat to the United States should not be heeded. There are certainly areas where there is intense competition (solar energy) or where the Chinese are ahead (high-speed rail), but there is overwhelming evidence that in general developed and developing countries are exporting products with very different levels of sophistication. Moreover, given the large role for processing trade, Chinese data in particular need to be handled with great care. While China has rapidly increased the value of its exports in "high-tech" categories, the relative prices (unit values) of its products have remained low. The apparent improvement in the product quality of Chinese exports is strongly influenced by the relocation of production from other Asian economies.

Those concerned about America's ability to innovate may also take some comfort from a comprehensive analysis undertaken by the Rand Corporation on US competitiveness in science and technology (Galama and Hosek 2008, xvi):

The United States accounts for 40 percent of total world R&D spending and 38 percent of patented new technology inventions by the industrialized nations of the Organisation for Economic Cooperation and Development (OECD), employs 37 percent (1.3 million) of OECD researchers (FTE), produces 35 percent, 49 percent, and 63 percent, respectively, of total world publications, citations, and highly cited publications, employs 70 percent of the world's Nobel Prize winners and 66 percent of its most-cited individuals, and is the home to 75 percent of both the world's top 20 and top 40 universities and 58 percent of the top 100.

In addition, they observe that while "China, India, and South Korea are starting to account for a significant portion of the world's S&T [science and technology] inputs and activities (R&D funding in dollars at purchasing power parity, research jobs, S&T education) and are showing rapid growth in outputs and outcomes, they account for a very small share of patents, S&T publications, and citations" (Galama and Hosek 2008, xvi).

It is possible that the favorable terms of trade trend could change in the future.[1] It is also likely that as they grow, developing countries will move into the production of more sophisticated products, and that as wages rise in China, the country's most labor-intensive manufactured exports will become more expensive. But given the fact that per capita incomes of China and India are still far less than those of the United States, these developments are likely to reach significant magnitudes only several decades from now. If we assume, for example, that the United States grows at 2.7 percent per year between 2010 and 2030, while China and India average growth of 6.7 and 7.4 percent, respectively, then China and India will respectively reach 59.7 and 26 percent of US per capita incomes on a purchasing power parity basis only by 2030 (Lawrence 2012).

As large developing countries converge more closely to developed-country per capita income levels, the mix of goods and services they export could shift to resemble more closely the exports of today's industrialized countries in both composition and sophistication. While some changes of this nature are already apparent, especially in leading emerging-market economies such

---

1. If the conventional framework based on incomplete specialization provides a more accurate depiction of global trade patterns and the entire world falls within a single integrated equilibrium, the future could be quite different and more threatening. For example, Hans Fehr, Sabine Jokisch, and Laurence Kotlikoff (2008) build a simulation model assuming mobility and an integrated equilibrium. They find that a worldwide increase in the relative (effective) supply of unskilled labor due to Chinese and Indian productivity improvements could lead to a doubling in the ratio of high- to low-skilled wages over the next century. They also find, however, that this increase in unskilled labor raises overall incomes in developed countries, as well as the returns to skilled workers. This tendency could be mitigated by improvements in education levels in India and China, but nonetheless the simulation is a counterweight to the more optimistic arguments we have presented that are based on a model with greater specialization. However, refusing to engage in such trade does not seem to be the answer either. Fehr, Jokisch, and Kotlikoff run another interesting simulation in which they exclude China and India from the model and find that by the end of the century, the effect is to reduce US and developed-country GDP by 14 and 17 percent, respectively. In other words, despite trade contributing to wage inequality, under the model presented by these authors, trade with these developing countries is very beneficial to the United States in the aggregate.

as Korea and Taiwan, if the experience is similar to the earlier convergence of Europe and Japan to US per capita income levels, the challenges are only likely to occur on a sizable scale quite far out in the future. Moreover, this convergence in income levels will give rise to two countervailing forces. On the one hand, it could, as Paul Samuelson (2004) has argued, reduce America's gains from trade by raising import costs and providing more competition for US exporters. On the other hand, convergence could also lead to more intraindustry trade of the kind that is typical between countries at similar income levels. This would generate more gains from trade for the United States by increasing product variety through more opportunities to exploit economies of scale. The net impact of these two effects could in principle go in either direction.

The same holds true for the offshoring of services. Generally, in the medium term, as Bradford Jensen (2011) has argued, this development will benefit the United States as a major net exporter of high-end services. Even if all the jobs estimated by Alan Blinder in Bhagwati and Blinder (2009) as "potentially" offshorable were in fact to be offshored, the adjustment is likely to take place over several decades and represent something on the order of 1 percent of employment per year. All job loss is not created equal, and the adjustment could be particularly painful if offshoring requires people to change occupations rather than just change jobs. But even an upper estimate of the required adjustment seems within the scope of the US economy, provided that it occurs relatively slowly.[2]

What Do These Findings Imply for Policy?

This section briefly outlines the adjustment challenges that America faces and considers policies to meet them. These challenges are coming at a bad time. Between 2000 and 2011, Americans experienced increases in real wages and family incomes that were modest at best. Additional pressures are likely to be exerted by the retirement of the baby-boomer generation (increased social security payments) and rapidly increasing health costs. Paychecks have also been squeezed by high oil prices, and if policies to deal with climate change are to be effective the costs of fossil fuels should be raised even further. In addition to depressing income growth, the financial crisis has destroyed wealth, depressed the economy, and raised unemployment levels. Both low-interest rate monetary policies and expansionary fiscal policies were marshaled in efforts to stabilize the economy and engender recovery, but a result is a large budget deficit and a vastly expanded central bank balance sheet.

While the policies to address the crisis have achieved some success, eventually they will need to be reversed. The central task for US policy is to effect a transition to a self-sustaining economy that is less reliant on government

---

2. There are reasons to believe that it will be slow. The full effects of exchange rates on trade flows, for example, can take up to five years. Even when communication and transportation costs are zero, contrary to the title of Thomas Friedman's (2005) bestselling book, the world is not flat and a large number of obstacles to offshoring remain (Ghemawat 2007).

stimulus and foreign borrowing and more reliant on private activity financed by increased domestic saving. For several years, the US economy will still have to grow faster than its long-term potential in order to absorb the high levels of unemployment. Achieving this growth while simultaneously increasing national saving to replenish wealth will not be easy. This is especially the case because over the medium term the government fiscal position, thrown into deficit by the recession, will have to be restored to a more sustainable level with some combination of higher revenues and reduced spending.[3] While there is a legitimate debate over the pace at which the federal deficit should be reduced, and indeed legitimate fear of trying to make the adjustment too rapidly, there is no doubt that over the medium and long run a credible strategy for deficit reduction is required. The sooner a commitment to a long-term strategy is adopted, the better for the country, since confidence that deficits are under control in the future will be reflected in lower long-term interest rates and thus be more stimulatory in the present.

America has to finance more of its spending domestically and borrow less from the rest of world. This requires reducing expenditures relative to incomes. There is no free lunch. This adjustment necessarily involves some combination of increased national saving (either lower private and/or public consumption) and/or reduced domestic investment. Since increased public and private investment are required for growth, ideally the adjustment should take the form of increased national saving.

As Americans spend less of their incomes, more of the demand for their production will have to come from foreigners. There are at least five effective ways to increase the foreign demand for US goods and services: (1) faster foreign income growth; (2) increased foreign spending relative to incomes; (3) reductions in the relative prices of US products; (4) the production of more attractive and innovative US goods and services; and (5) more open foreign markets. In what follows we briefly discuss each, then turn to a discussion of policies relating to the issues of income inequality, dislocation, and oil.

Faster Foreign Growth

The emerging-market economies, in particular, can offer vibrant markets for US goods and services. Ranking countries by their per capita incomes in 2010, and averaging the forecasts of five research organizations, we find that countries with 50 percent or less of US GDP are expected to account for 80 percent of global growth on a purchasing power basis between 2010 and 2030. China alone will account for 35 percent of growth and India 17 percent (Lawrence 2011). It is fortunate, therefore, that the emerging-market economies have been able to recover relatively rapidly from the global slowdown and that as a result US exports, especially to Asia, have contributed to the recovery.[4] America's fate

---

3. For a review of the fiscal outlook, see Gagnon (2011) and CBO (2012).

4. See, for example, IMF (2012).

in the decades to come rests in part on its ability to sustain these countries' growth at a rapid pace and their willingness to open their markets to US goods and services. As we have discussed, foreign growth raises US exports and increases the variety of products available to Americans. Such growth, therefore, reduces the need for more costly adjustments that involve a weaker dollar, lower terms of trade, or investments to improve US innovation.

Increased Foreign Absorption

America's adjustment challenges will also be aided if emerging-market and advanced economies that have substantial current account surpluses (such as China and Germany) achieve more of their growth through increased domestic expenditures relative to their incomes. Indeed, the measures these countries need to take to reduce global imbalances are the opposite of those that should be made by the United States. For their growth, they need to rely less on exports and more on some combination of increased public and private expenditure. In these countries, stronger real exchange rates (and thus less reserve accumulation) should be part of the adjustment process. The objective of shifting the Chinese economy toward a more consumption-led growth path espoused in the Twelfth Five-Year Guideline approved by the National People's Congress in China in 2011 should contribute to this adjustment process.

Switching Expenditure toward US Products

The demand for US products will rise in the face of faster foreign growth and increased foreign absorption, but in addition, the US share in any given amount of foreign spending can be increased by reducing the prices of US goods and services relative to those of its competitors or by making these more attractive through innovation.

One important mechanism that encourages switches in spending is a weaker US real exchange rate. When the dollar falls, the prices of foreign goods and services measured in dollars rise and both Americans and foreigners switch their spending toward US products. On the import side, the effects of a weaker dollar on volumes and prices move in opposite directions and can partially or even fully offset each other. On the one hand, higher import prices raise the dollar value of imports and move the trade balance toward larger deficits. On the other hand, the response of domestic demand to higher prices leads to a reduction in the volume of imports that tends to reduce the value of imports and move the trade balance toward smaller deficits. In the case of exports, however, prices and quantities move in the same direction. Higher dollar prices and increased volumes both operate to reduce the deficit. Thus, most of the adjustment in the current account to exchange rate changes comes in US exports.[5]

---

5. Our regressions undertaken as background for this study suggest that a 10 percent weaker dollar raises US import prices by about 3 percent and reduces import volumes by around 5 percent.

The fact that exports are especially important for adjusting the current account is significant because our analysis in chapter 4 strongly suggests that developed and developing countries export different products. This implies that changes in developed-country exchange rates such as the euro, yen, and Canadian dollar are likely to be far more important drivers of US export performance than the exchange rates of developing countries. A stronger real renminbi, for example, would reduce Chinese exports to the United States, but these exports are more likely to be replaced with exports to the United States by other emerging-market countries whose products are closer substitutes for Chinese exports than goods still produced in the United States.

Nonetheless, even if a stronger renminbi does not directly have a major impact on the US current account, appreciation would affect the Chinese current account and thus spur Chinese policies to replace export-led growth with domestic-led spending, and this shift would in turn stimulate exports to China from the United States and other countries.

A weaker real exchange rate can facilitate the adjustment of US spending relative to income, but it is also costly. In particular, as we have explored in this study, US welfare could be reduced if the terms of trade fall, and the evidence indicates that depreciation is generally associated with such a decline. The terms of trade change is generally far less than the exchange rate change because a weaker dollar is not fully passed through into higher import prices, and export prices also rise. Our research for this study found that the terms of trade decline would be about a quarter of the exchange rate change, and we estimate that a decline of about 15 percent in the real exchange rate would be required to reduce the trade deficit in nonoil goods and services to its 1990 levels. Since imports of goods and services make up 15 percent of GDP, the impact of the depreciation on US welfare would amount to just over half a percent of GNP ($0.15 \times 0.25 \times 0.15 = 0.56$ percent). Other studies such as Obstfeld and Rogoff (2004) and Dekle, Eaton, and Kortum (2007) reach similar conclusions, as we noted in chapter 6.

Innovation

An alternative mechanism for generating increased demand for US products is to make them more attractive and innovative. By and large this rests in private hands, but such activity can be encouraged by government policy. The case for government programs that spur technological development is especially strong because in general the social benefits from innovation exceed those that can be captured by private innovators. The case is even stronger in relation to advances in the production and conservation of energy, since technological advances could bring additional strategic ("energy independence") and environmental benefits.

This means an overall reduction in import dollar values of just 2 percent. By contrast, a 10 percent weaker dollar would raise export volumes by 9 percent and values by 10 percent.

Policies to encourage innovation need to be multifaceted. Policies should address (1) the availability of skilled workers, scientists, and engineers by encouraging education and training; (2) the availability of ideas and knowledge through public incentives for research through direct grants and subsidies (e.g., from the National Science Foundation and National Institutes of Health), tax credits (e.g., the R&D tax credit), and intellectual property protection (patents); and (3) ensuring demand, especially when public purposes are to be served. The government can either itself serve as a customer or ensure private demand using taxes or subsidies.[6] The US government in particular has stimulated major inventions such as the jet aircraft, the semiconductor, and the internet in its role as a customer, and currently plays a vital role in driving innovation, especially in energy, environmental protection, and health. The motives for these policies for the most part are enhancing domestic welfare, but a byproduct—particularly when other countries have similar goals—is likely to be increased US exports.

However, innovation and broader industrial support policies need to be undertaken with great care. The government should generally be complementing the actions of the private sector and not substituting for actions that firms would undertake in any case.[7] Policies that seek simply to subsidize some kind of domestic production (e.g., manufacturing or high value-added activity) and do not explicitly aim at market failures are unlikely to satisfy this requirement.

Changes in the terms of trade (and the real exchange rate) and industrial policies are substitutes, and the focus of the discussion should be on whether industrial policies can do better than the automatic market adjustment. In principle, this should be possible, since markets are prone to failures. But the challenge is finding approaches that identify and rectify the cases where these failures are likely. In particular approaches should involve nurturing behavior

---

6. For an analysis of how not to promote technology using the example of biofuels, see Lawrence (2010).

7. An example of a poorly focused policy proposal is that of Ralph Gomory, who has advocated using the US tax code to "reward any corporation, large or small, that maintains high-value-add-per-US-employee." Ralph Gomory, "A Time for Action, Jobs, Prosperity and National Goals," *Huffington Post*, January 25, 2010, www.huffingtonpost.com/ralph-gomory/a-time-for-action-jobs-pr_b_434698.html (accessed on November 1, 2012). Value added per employee can be high for a variety of reasons, not all of which are socially desirable and several of which do not reflect market failure. For example, value added per worker could be high simply because capital-intensive production methods are used. Would we want to reward firms that replace their workers with machinery? Alternatively, value added per worker could be high because workers have higher levels of education. Education is of course beneficial, but why should the tax code promote the hiring of these workers over those with less education? Value added per worker could also be high not because firms become more productive, but because they outsource their most labor-intensive activities, and acquire more capital-intensive methods. Finally, value added per worker could be high because unions have strong bargaining power. Ironically, this could reflect a market failure and lead to less output than is optimal. Indeed, Lawrence Katz and Lawrence Summers (1989) have argued that these rents are very substantial. But achieving this would require a more focused policy than that recommended by Gomory.

where social benefits exceed private gains.[8] The United States should not rush into adopting industrial policies based on fears of emerging foreign competition (whether fair or unfair) or the size of the trade deficit. The benchmark against which new industrial policies should be judged is rather whether they are likely to achieve US adjustment at lower cost than the automatic adjustment that will occur through the market responses generated by exchange rate changes and lower prices of US goods, and not the false claims that the choice is between perpetual trade deficits or adopting interventionist industrial policies that pick winners and losers.

In an era of budgetary constraints, the United States can promote exports and encourage domestic investment and production by adopting smarter regulatory and tax policies. For example, the United States has a system of national security controls on exports. Making the system more rational could enhance export performance at relatively low cost (Richardson 1993). Similarly, educated foreigners have made important contributions to the US skill base. Yet even foreigners who have been educated in the United States at US expense are often prevented from seeking employment and remaining in the country. A more open immigration policy for skilled and educated workers would enhance the attractiveness of the United States as a location for production and innovation (Kirkegaard 2007).

Especially when it comes to high-technology sectors such as biotechnology, healthcare, energy, or finance, regulatory frameworks and the market need to be aligned. Instead of being viewed as incompatible, regulation and the market should be understood to be complementary. Absent public confidence in regulation, new products cannot be introduced. These frameworks require governments that continuously interact with the private sector in order to provide the appropriate regulatory frameworks. This requires finding mechanisms for joint collaboration and interaction, without being captured (Rodrik 2010).

The US corporate tax system should also be reformed.[9] The best way to do this is probably to broaden the corporate tax base by allowing far fewer deductions while reducing the corporate tax rate to levels typically found in other countries (Desai, Foley, and Hines 2009).[10] Given that only about a quarter of corporate profits are collected as taxes, whereas the corporate rate

---

8. Classic examples are the provision of public goods and the promotion of innovation when individual discoveries are copied by others, or the realization of so-called external scale economies in which all firms within an industry benefit from each other's actions. This can occur through cheaper access to materials because of industry scale and the ability to attract more customers because operating on a larger scale gives producers more prominence. An excellent empirical exploration of external scale economies can be found in Ellison, Glaeser, and Kerr (2010).

9. See Hufbauer and Moran (2010) and Hufbauer and Assa (2007) for a more complete discussion of this issue.

10. Mihir Desai, Fritz Foley, and James Hines (2009, abstract) find that "Estimates produced using this instrument indicate that 10% greater foreign investment is associated with 2.6% greater domestic investment, and 10% greater foreign employee compensation is associated with 3.7% greater domestic employee compensation."

is 35 percent for large companies (and almost 40 percent when state taxes are included), there seems to be considerable room to move in this direction.

Trade Policy

An active trade policy focused on the emerging-market economies has a vital role to play in helping America meet its adjustment challenges and promote its long-run economic interests. US exports can be boosted by a weaker dollar or increased investment in industrial policies that make US goods and services cheaper, more attractive, or more prominent. But these measures are costly. A weaker dollar raises the costs of buying foreign products, while innovation, investment, and trade promotion all require additional resources.

By contrast, policies that open foreign markets can boost the demand for US products without additional outlays by Americans. They provide US firms more opportunities to make sales of products they already produce without having to reduce their prices. They make the United States a more attractive location to source exports and thus also provide incentives for firms to invest more in the United States. Many of America's innovative achievements need to be protected with patents and copyrights, and thus improved enforcement of US intellectual property rights abroad can also raise US incomes and stimulate additional investment and innovation (USITC 2011).

An alternative US strategy for trade policy could be to raise domestic barriers to generate more demand for US production through import substitution. Instead of seeking to ensure that foreign countries play by the rules, the United States could break them on the grounds that others are cheating. But erecting higher barriers at home would be misguided, impractical, and unwise. Misguided because there are substantial gains from trade; impractical because the intertwining of domestic and foreign production in supply chain networks makes withdrawal difficult and costly; and unwise because it could set off foreign retaliatory responses that could endanger the recovery and make everyone worse off.

How then can the benefits from a trade policy that opens foreign markets be reaped? The United States cannot impose its will on others, but needs to act bilaterally and collectively to construct and maintain a trading order that supports its economic interests. This is increasingly challenging in a global system in which large emerging-market economies are becoming more influential over time.

Emblematic of the trade policy challenges for the United States to construct a new order are those associated with China's rise. In some respects, the Chinese market is fairly open. Chinese tariffs average 10 percent and China has generally been hospitable to foreign investment, especially firms producing for export. But to promote its development, China also has an extensive array of measures designed to encourage domestic innovation and production that are an increasing source of friction with its trading partners. These involve an undervalued currency, subsidies such as cheap energy, strategic use of state-owned enterprises, preferential government procurement to promote indigenous innovation, investment restrictions in certain sectors, technology transfer requirements, and measures to reserve key raw materials such as rare earths for domestic use. Copyright, trademark, and other intellectual property violations are also widespread.

Disciplining such policies requires leveraging China's need for global engagement. As with all great economic powers, China must create a political superstructure that supports its needs. China must therefore weigh whatever benefits these policies might provide domestic firms against the costs they impose on China's ability to engage globally. China needs open markets for its exports, abundant supplies of foreign raw materials and intermediate inputs that are not produced domestically, and opportunities for its firms to invest abroad. China has tried to meet these needs through diplomacy, aid, and numerous free trade agreements and cooperative arrangements with other countries, but the centerpiece of China's strategy has been its membership in the World Trade Organization (WTO). In 2001, the United States supported Chinese accession to the WTO, but only when the latter agreed to tough conditions for market opening. The United States used China's interest in WTO membership to induce it to adopt more open policies, and both China and the United States have benefited as a result. The United States needs to learn from this success and build on it.

We have used China as an example, but the United States faces similar challenges in other large emerging markets such as India and Brazil. The United States should not try to inhibit emerging-market growth, nor should it try to dictate the domestic policies of these countries, but US policies should create incentives for them to adopt policies that minimize discrimination against foreign products and firms and thus nudge them in the direction of other nations that have successfully achieved global leadership. These US policies should have multilateral, regional, and bilateral dimensions.

The WTO should be especially useful for this purpose. It is the major forum for relationships with America's largest trading partners such as the European Union, Japan, China, India, and Brazil, with which the United States has not signed free trade agreements. US engagement needs to be more active both in bringing cases to enforce its rights under existing agreements and in negotiating new rules that improve market access.

Disputes

The WTO dispute settlement system has been quite effective (Lawrence 2007). WTO rules constrain protectionist behavior, discipline the use of subsidies, prohibit the use of discriminatory regulations, and require enforcement of intellectual property protection. The system's multilateral nature helps secure its legitimacy and thereby reduces the political and diplomatic costs associated with bilateral disputes. It provides mechanisms not only for resolving disputes but also for retaliation within prescribed bounds when compliance cannot be achieved. Since large countries such as China, the United States, and the European Union have an interest in the system, their records in coming into compliance when found in violation have generally been quite good.

The United States needs to be active in using the system. The problems faced by US firms when they compete internationally are often similar to those faced by firms from other countries. Indeed the list of complaints voiced by Europe when it comes to China, for example, is virtually identical to that of the United States. The United States, European Union, Mexico, and other countries have joined in bringing a few cases, most notably on the recent issue of China's embargoes on exports of rare earths, but their efforts should be more concerted and coordinated.

There are legal tools for private firms to bring cases against unfair foreign practices that occur in US markets such as dumping, subsidies, and intellectual property violations. But abroad, the firms depend more heavily on the US government to promote their interests. Private firms and organizations do not have the right to bring cases at the WTO, so dispute settlement is an area in which the private sector has to work hand in hand with the government. Thus, the barriers in foreign markets and the practices confronting private firms have to be communicated to the US government so that it can seek their removal. US firms and business organizations should be more proactive in generating these cases.[11]

New Agreements

The WTO can be used to further reduce barriers and discriminatory treatment in trade. But the system is in trouble because the Doha Round is at an impasse. A revitalized US trade policy could help bring the Doha Round to a reasonably satisfactory conclusion.

The round has serious problems. Dubbed the Doha Development Agenda, it was meant to promote the interests of developing countries and was centered on agriculture. There are, however, many other issues on the table and all are part of a single undertaking in which "nothing is agreed until everything is agreed." Launched in 2001, the round was supposed to end in 2005. Given the number and diversity of the members, the practice of requiring consensus for all decisions, and the complexity of the package, it is no wonder that every deadline has been missed.

These delays have been costly because the world has changed. The prioritization of agriculture was questionable from the start (the payoffs in reducing industrial tariffs and liberalizing services are much larger) and has become increasingly problematic. In 2001, global food prices were low and the major issues were import barriers and subsidies for production in developed coun-

---

11. In conversation, Gary Hufbauer of the Peterson Institute for International Economics has advocated granting a private right of action for firms to bring cases similar to that provided in investment disputes. This is a proposal worthy of serious consideration.

tries. These problems remain, but in 2011, global food prices are high and volatile, and the key farm trade issue not covered by the talks is the export restraints imposed by many developing countries. In 2001, China was a newly acceding member that needed time to adjust, and many developing countries in Africa and Latin America had experienced two decades of slow growth. But as of 2011, China is the world's largest exporting nation, and many developing countries have enjoyed a decade of unprecedented growth. The US priority in the round—to obtain meaningful market-opening concessions from the large emerging-market economies—has been hard to achieve because developing countries have acted as a bloc to limit their concessions. From a US vantage point, the bargain currently on the table looks small and uncertain (Schwab 2011).

Increasingly there are calls for the members to terminate the negotiations by admitting failure or by harvesting the concessions that have already been made. But failure would damage the system, while harvesting gains is problematic, since offers were made on the assumption that additional concessions would be forthcoming.

One final effort should be made. But absent a meaningful agreement, the round should be ended, since its presence prevents dealing with new issues that merit attention. The concessions already agreed upon for the least developed countries should be granted and the agreements on trade facilitation that relate to transit trade, limiting border fees and formalities, and making trade policy information more transparent should be adopted.

Beyond Doha: A Variable Geometry

The challenge in the aftermath of Doha is how to revitalize the WTO. An alternative approach to multi-issue rounds is to proceed separately with specific issues, but not require all members to join. WTO members are diverse and one size does not fit all. Instead of a system in which all developed and developing members are required to adhere to all rules, a more attractive approach would entail a variable geometry with mandatory core commitments supplemented by plurilateral agreements to which only some members belong. These agreements could take a variety of forms. They could involve new rules, the full liberalization of sectors, and agreements on trade facilitation. Some could extend most favored nation treatment to all members, others only to those who sign up. Some could become binding on members only when a critical mass sign up (Lawrence 2007).

The approach would end the simplistic distinctions between developed and developing countries and allow members from both groups to adopt rules that meet their interests. Examples might include foreign investment, rules for state-owned enterprises, restrictions on export barriers, restrictions on energy subsidies, competition (antitrust) policies, regulatory practices, customs procedures, liberalization of key services sectors, additional intellectual property protection, and rules of origin in preferential trade arrangements. Willing countries might also deal with issues such as labor and environmental standards through this mechanism.

Free Trade Agreements

The WTO plays an essential role at the heart of the trading system. It is the only forum for effectively dealing with issues such as farm subsidies, which need to be negotiated multilaterally to avoid some countries free riding on the reductions of others. But the diversity of its membership—there are over 150 members at vastly different stages of development—makes it difficult and indeed inappropriate to reach agreements that apply equally to all. By contrast, free trade agreements between pairs or groups of trading partners offer opportunities for deeper integration between countries that may be better suited to their needs. They also offer opportunities to demonstrate the feasibility of new approaches to trade, and can effectively promote pressures for competitive liberalization.

The prototypical agreement signed by the United States has included the removal of almost all border barriers between the partners, full liberalization of services unless explicitly mentioned, strong intellectual property protection, liberalization of foreign direct investment, government procurement liberalization, enforcement of core labor rights and environmental standards, and numerous other regulatory provisions.

While the template has evolved over time—in particular, the provisions on labor rights have become more demanding—the United States has generally insisted on it partly because making concessions in one agreement could set a precedent for those that follow, and partly because the template has been crafted to maximize the chances of the necessary congressional ratification. These agreements have been successful in forging deeper links between the United States and compliant and—with the exception of Canada and Korea—generally small trading partners. However, the agreements have yet to prove their usefulness either for linking larger groups of countries together or for concluding bilateral agreements with large and more significant trading partners. Indeed, US efforts in the 1990s to conclude a single hemispheric agreement—the Free Trade Area of the Americas—ended in failure.

The Trans-Pacific Partnership negotiations offer an important opportunity to develop a model that can be effective both in dealing with deeper integration issues and in providing mechanisms that make it relatively easy for additional countries to join. In particular, the United States could lead in creating an effective and integrated environment for the operation of regional supply chains that could enhance the competitiveness of all participants and put pressure on other countries in the Pacific and elsewhere to offer similar opportunities. But it might take a willingness on the part of the United States to move away from the rigid approaches it has insisted upon in other agreements. One example relates to developing common and simple rules that would allow participants to cumulate value added in any country in the group to qualify for duty-free entry.

Major partners bring far more to the table, but are also likely to demand more flexibility on the part of the United States. A comprehensive deep integration agreement with the European Union that covered issues that are not dealt with in the WTO (such as investment, mutual recognition of regulations, and additional intellectual property rules) would be especially meaningful, but the European Union would resist including agriculture. India is involved in talks with the European Union and has an agreement with Japan. It would also be a very attractive partner for an agreement with the United States, but would strongly reject the inclusion of labor and environmental standards and demand liberalization for professional services providers. Deviating from the blueprint could involve political costs, but these need to be weighed against the potential strategic and economic advantages of agreements with these larger countries. Absent such concessions, the United States could find its exporters further disadvantaged.

Income Inequality

While trade policy can improve US welfare, it is inappropriate as a policy instrument for dealing with income inequality. Even assuming, contrary to our findings here, that Stolper-Samuelson effects are powerful, to make relative wages more equal using trade policies, protection would have to target unskilled-labor-intensive goods and services in an effort to increase their relative price. But as we have seen, because of the complexity of international specialization patterns, this would not be synonymous with imposing tariffs on all imports from developing countries or on all imports in particular industries. Thus, such policies might be not only very costly in terms of reducing the gains from trade but also very difficult to implement effectively. The more appropriate response would be to reap the gains from trade, and use tax and transfer programs as redistributive instruments. More progressive taxes and transfers are far preferable as an instrument to deal with income inequality. In any case, we have not found that trade with developing countries in goods and services has been a powerful recent driver of wage inequality, and in particular since 2000, wage inequality has not been a major reason for increased income equality. Other factors have led to concentrated income gains at the very top of the income distribution (Lawrence 2008).

Dislocation

Transfer programs should be supplemented with enhanced adjustment assistance. Even if trade with developing countries does not cause inequality, it does lead to job losses and displacement that are particularly painful for those affected. Trade has undoubtedly contributed to job losses, although other sources of change—such as technology and demand shifts—have probably generated even more displacement. Improved policies are thus urgently needed to help workers (Rosen 2008) and communities (Deep and Lawrence 2008) adjust to these shocks. Ideally, these policies would not be confined to workers displaced by trade, but would offer all displaced workers a combination of benefits. As Grant Aldonas, Robert Lawrence, and Matthew Slaughter (2007) describe in greater detail, these programs should include unemployment and healthcare benefits, training and reemployment assistance, and wage-loss insurance for workers who find new jobs at lower wages.

In sum, addressing the adjustment challenges currently facing the United States would be facilitated by faster growth in emerging-market economies and increased openness of their markets. In addition, the benefits of that growth that operate through improving America's terms of trade and providing increased variety should help offset some of the costs that are entailed by the need to improve the competitiveness of US goods and services either through a lower dollar or through new industrial and regulatory policies.

Oil

Emerging-market-economy growth can have an adverse impact on the United States by driving up oil prices. Trying to limit foreign growth through trade or other policies in order to reduce their oil demand (and greenhouse gas emissions) is unlikely to be an effective strategy. Indeed, it could be counterproductive, since developing countries would undoubtedly respond by refusing to cooperate on global environmental agreements. Instead, the United States should have a strategy that emphasizes the development of new energy-saving technologies that can be applied at home and abroad, as well as increased efforts to develop domestic and international energy production.

For a large net importer like the United States, tightness in world oil markets has major macroeconomic externalities. Higher oil prices induce stagflation, boosting the price level and reducing aggregate demand. The United States needs to lead in conserving oil and developing alternative fuels and energy, but price volatility and particularly the prospect of lower prices inhibit these developments. While current expectations as embodied in Energy Information Agency (EIA 2012) projections are for high future oil prices, the very thin margin between over- and under-supply could again lead to a period in which prices are depressed. Concerns about dependence on foreign oil and global warming, and wariness about future gas price hikes, may lead some Americans to voluntarily reduce their oil consumption, but most need stronger incentives. After previous oil price hikes, consumers did little to change their behavior and soon went back to their gas-guzzling ways. Incentives are also needed for firms developing alternative energy technologies. Government programs to develop new technologies will not work if there are market forces moving in an opposite direction.

One approach would be policies aimed at raising domestic oil prices in the medium run. The key to changing US consumer behavior and providing incentives for alternative fuels is a guarantee that in the not-too-distant future—say in five years' time, and for some time after that—gasoline in the United States will cost no less than something like $6 a gallon (in today's dollars). This would lead buyers of cars and trucks to make different choices.

It would also provide the incentives for firms to develop domestic energy supplies of both oil and its substitutes.

The US government may not control the world price of oil, but it can guarantee a minimum domestic price by imposing a variable import duty on oil imported at less than the target price. Increases that would gradually rise to achieve the desired price path over the medium run could be scheduled. Variable import duties are easy to administer and the United States has retained the flexibility to raise them under WTO rules.[12] They can be used to provide a floor on domestic prices as world prices fluctuate. They would simultaneously provide incentives for conservation and for domestic production of both oil and alternative energy, and are the right tool to deal with the security and strategic concerns that arise from dependence on imported oil. Alternative approaches would use variable domestic gas taxes or gasoline consumption permits, but these would be more complicated to administer when world oil prices fluctuate, and neither would encourage domestic oil production.

The greatest medium-term pressures on the global oil market will come from rapid Chinese growth, and the United States therefore has an immense interest in China's development and adoption of alternative sources of energy other than fossil fuels—oil because the United States is a net oil importer, and coal because Chinese use is such a potent source of greenhouse gas emissions. In this regard, it is especially unfortunate that the United States has chosen to view Chinese policies to develop solar energy technology as a competitiveness threat rather than a positive development. Indeed, rather than seeking to discourage these efforts the United States should be applauding them.

Conclusions

The United States faces daunting challenges: high unemployment, budget and current account deficits, income inequality, and issues involving the consumption of fossil fuels in general and imported oil in particular. Some would add to this list the problem of foreign economic growth, especially in emerging markets. In this study, however, we have explored their arguments and found them wanting. Instead, we have found considerable evidence that while adjusting to foreign economic growth does present America with challenges, growth in emerging-market economies is in America's economic interest. It is hard, of course, for Americans to become used to a world in which the preponderance of economic activity is located in Asia. But one of America's great strengths is its adaptability. And if it does adapt, the American economy can be buoyed by that rising tide.

---

12. The United States has not bound its oil tariffs at the WTO. They are, however, bound under the North American Free Trade Agreement, and the United States should ideally coordinate the action with Mexico and Canada to avoid leakage.

References

Acemoglu, Daron. 1998. Why Do New Technologies Complement Skills? Directed Technological Change and Wage Inequality. *Quarterly Journal of Economics* 113, no. 4: 1055–89.

Acemoglu, Daron. 2003. Patterns of Skill Premia. *Review of Economic Studies* 70, no. 2: 199–230.

Acemoglu, Daron, and David Autor. 2010. *Skills, Tasks and Technologies: Implications for Employment and Earnings*. NBER Working Paper 16082. Cambridge, MA: National Bureau of Economic Research.

Acemoglu, Daron, and Jaume Ventura. 2002. The World Income Distribution. *Quarterly Journal of Economics* 117, no. 2: 659–94.

Akamatsu, Kaname. 1961. A Theory of Unbalanced Growth in the World Economy. *Weltwirtschaftliches Archiv* 86: 196–217.

Akamatsu, Kaname. 1962. A Historical Pattern of Economic Growth in Developing Countries. *The Developing Economies* 1, no. S1: 3–25.

Alchian, Armen A., and William R. Allen. 1964. *University Economics*. Belmont, CA: Wadsworth.

Aldonas, Grant, Robert Z. Lawrence, and Matthew Slaughter. 2007. *Succeeding in the Global Economy: An Agenda for the American Worker*. Washington: Financial Services Forum.

Alt, James E., and Michael Gilligan. 1999. The Political Economy of Trading States: Factor Specificity, Collective Actions Problems and Domestic Political Institutions. In *International Political Economy: Perspectives on Global Power and Wealth*, ed. Jeffry Frieden and David A. Lake. Belmont, CA: Wadsworth.

Amador, Joao, and Sonia Cabral. 2009. Vertical Specialization Across the World: A Relative Measure. *North American Journal of Economics and Finance* 20, no. 3: 267–80.

Amiti, Mary, and Donald R. Davis. 2008. *Trade, Firms, and Wages: Theory and Evidence*. NBER Working Paper 14106. Cambridge, MA: National Bureau of Economic Research.

Amiti, Mary, and Caroline Freund. 2010. The Anatomy of China's Export Growth. In *China's Growing Role in World Trade*, ed. Robert C. Feenstra and Shang-Jin Wei. Chicago: University of Chicago Press.

Amiti, Mary, and Amit K. Khandelwal. 2009. *Competition and Quality Upgrading.* NBER Working Paper 15503. Cambridge, MA: National Bureau of Economic Research.

Amiti, Mary, and Shang-Jin Wei. 2005. Fear of Service Outsourcing: Is It Justified? *Economic Policy* 20, no. 42: 308–47.

Anderson, Richard G., and Charles S. Gascon. 2007. *The Perils of Globalization: Offshoring and Economic Insecurity of the American Worker.* Federal Reserve Bank of St Louis Working Paper 2007-004A. St. Louis: Federal Reserve Bank of St. Louis.

Arkolakis, Costas (Konstantinos), Arnaud Costinot, and Andrés Rodríguez-Clare. 2010. New Trade Models, Same Old Gains? *American Economic Review* 102, no. 1: 94–130.

Arkolakis, Costas (Konstantinos), Svetlana Demidova, Peter J. Klenow, and Andrés Rodríguez-Clare. 2008. Endogenous Variety and the Gains from Trade. *American Economic Review, Papers and Proceedings* 98, no. 4: 444–50.

Autor, David H., David Dorn, and Gordon H. Hanson. 2012. *The China Syndrome: Local Labor Market Effects of Import Competition in the United States.* NBER Working Paper 18054. Cambridge, MA: National Bureau of Economic Research.

Autor, David H., Lawrence F. Katz, and Melissa S. Kearney. 2005. *Trends in US Wage Inequality: Re-Assessing the Revisionists.* NBER Working Paper 11627. Cambridge, MA: National Bureau of Economic Research.

Autor, David H., Lawrence F. Katz, and Melissa S. Kearney. 2006. The Polarization of the US Labor Market. *American Economic Review* 96, no. 2: 189–94.

Autor, David H., Lawrence F. Katz, and Alan B. Krueger. 1998. Computing Inequality: Have Computers Changed the Labor Market? *Quarterly Journal of Economics* 113, no. 4: 1169–213.

Baily, Jonathan, and Henry Lee. 2012. North American Oil and Gas Reserves: Prospects and Policy. Belfer Center for Science and International Affairs, Harvard Kennedy School. Photocopy (July).

Baily, Martin Neil, and Robert Z. Lawrence. 2004. What Happened to the Great US Job Machine? The Role of Trade and Electronic Offshoring. *Brookings Papers on Economic Activity* 35, no. 2: 211–84.

Baily, Martin Neil, and Robert Z. Lawrence. 2006a. *Can America Still Compete or Does It Need a New Trade Paradigm?* Policy Briefs in International Economics 06-9. Washington: Peterson Institute for International Economics.

Baily, Martin Neil, and Robert Z. Lawrence. 2006b. Competitiveness and the Assessment of Trade Performance. In *C. Fred Bergsten and the World Economy,* ed. Michael Mussa. Washington: Peterson Institute for International Economics.

Baldwin, Robert E., John H. Mutti, and J. David Richardson. 1980. Welfare Effects on the United States of a Significant Multilateral Tariff Reduction. *Journal of International Economics* 10, no. 3: 405–23.

Barefoot, Kevin B., and Raymond Mataloni, Jr. 2011. Operations of U.S. Multinational Companies in the United States and Abroad: Preliminary Results from the 2009 Benchmark Survey. *Survey of Current Business* (November). Washington: US Bureau of Economic Analysis.

Baumol, William J., and William G. Bowen. 1965. On the Performing Arts: The Anatomy of Their Economic Problems. *American Economic Review* 55, no. 2: 495–502.

Bergin, Paul R., Robert C. Feenstra, and Gordon H. Hanson. 2007. *Outsourcing and Volatility.* NBER Working Paper 13144. Cambridge, MA: National Bureau of Economic Research.

Bergin, Paul R., and Robert C. Feenstra. 2009. Pass-Through of Exchange Rates and Competition between Floaters and Fixers. *Journal of Money, Credit and Banking* 41, no. S1: 35–70.

Berman E., J. Bound, and Z. Griliches. 1994. Changes in the Demand for Skilled Labor within U.S. Manufacturing Industries: Evidence from the Annual Survey of Manufacturing. *Quarterly Journal of Economics* 109, no. 2: 367–98.

Berman E., J. Bound, and S. Machin. 1998. Implications of Skill-biased Technological Change: International Evidence. *Quarterly Journal of Economics* 113, no. 4: 1245–280.

Bernard, Andrew, J. Bradford Jensen, and Peter K. Schott. 2006. Survival of the Best Fit: Competition from Low-Wage Countries and the (Uneven) Growth of U.S. Manufacturing Firms. *Journal of International Economics* 68, no. 1: 219–37.

Bernard, Andrew B., Stephen J. Redding, and Peter K. Schott. 2007. Comparative Advantage and Heterogeneous Firms. *Review of Economic Studies* 74, no. 1: 31–66.

Bertrand, Marianne. 2004. From the Invisible Handshake to the Invisible Hand? How Import Competition Changes the Employment Relationship. *Journal of Labor Economics* 22, no. 4: 723–65.

Bhagwati, Jagdish. 1958. Immiserizing Growth: A Geometrical Note. *Review of Economic Studies* 25, no. 3: 201–05.

Bhagwati, Jagdish. 1991. *Free Traders and Free Immigrationists: Strangers or Friends?* Russell Sage Foundation Working Paper. New York: Russell Sage Foundation.

Bhagwati, Jagdish. 2009. Don't Cry for Free Trade. In *Offshoring of American Jobs? What Response from U.S. Economic Policy?* by Jagdish Bhagwati and Alan Blinder. Cambridge, MA: MIT Press.

Bhagwati, Jagdish, and Alan Blinder. 2009. *Offshoring of American Jobs? What Response from U.S. Economic Policy?* Cambridge, MA: MIT Press.

Bhagwati, Jagdish, Richard A. Brecher, and Tatsuo Hatta. 1983. The Generalized Theory of Transfers and Welfare: Bilateral Transfers in a Multilateral World. *American Economic Review* 73, no. 4: 606–18.

Bivens, Josh. 2007. *Globalization, American Wages and Inequality, Past, Present and Future.* Working Paper 279. Washington: Economic Policy Institute.

Blanchard, E., and G. Willmann. 2008. Trade, Education, and the Shrinking Middle Class. University of Virginia. Photocopy.

Blecker, Robert A., and Arslan Razmi. 2009. Export-led Growth, Real Exchange Rates and the Fallacy of Composition. In *Handbook of Alternative Theories of Economic Growth*, ed. Mark Setterfield. Northampton, MA: Edward Elgar.

Blinder, Alan S. 2006. Offshoring: The Next Industrial Revolution? *Foreign Affairs* 85, no. 2: 113–28.

Blinder, Alan S., and Mark Zandi. 2010. Stimulus Worked. *Finance and Development* 47, no. 4: 14–17.

Boorstein, Randi, and Robert C. Feenstra. 1991. Quality Upgrading and Its Welfare Cost in U.S. Steel Imports, 1969-74. In *International Trade and Trade Policy,* ed. Elhanan Helpman and Assaf Razin. Cambridge, MA: MIT Press.

Borga, Maria. 2006. *Trends in Employment at US Multinational Companies: Evidence from Firm-Level Data.* Washington: Brookings Institution.

Borjas, George, Richard Freeman, and Lawrence Katz. 1997. How Much Do Immigration and Trade Affect Labor Market Outcomes? *Brookings Papers on Economic Activity* 1: 135–64.

Bosworth, Barry P., and Jack E. Triplett. 2003. Productivity Measurement Issues in Services Industries: Baumol's Disease Has Been Cured. *Economic Policy Review* 9, no. 3: 23–33.

Brainard, Lael, and David Riker. 1997. *US Multinationals and Competition from Low-Wage Countries.* NBER Working Paper 5959. Cambridge, MA: National Bureau of Economic Research.

Brambilla, Irene, Daniel Lederman, and Guido Porto. 2010. *Exports, Export Destinations, and Skills.* NBER Working Paper 15995. Cambridge, MA: National Bureau of Economic Research.

Broda, Christian, and David Weinstein. 2006. Globalization and the Gains from Variety. *Quarterly Journal of Economics* 121, no. 2: 541–85.

Brown, Sherrod. 2004. *Myths of Free Trade: Why American Trade Policy Has Failed.* New York: The New Press.

Burfisher, Mary E., Sherman Robinson, and Karen Thierfelder. 2001. The Impact of NAFTA on the United States. *Journal of Economic Perspectives* 15, no. 1: 125–44.

Bustos, Paula. 2007. *The Impact of Trade on Technology and Skill Upgrading: Evidence from Argentina.* CREI and Universitat Pompeu Fabra Working Paper (November). Department of Economics and Business, Universitat Pompeu Fabra.

Caliendo, Lorenzo, and Fernando Parro. 2009. *Estimates of the Trade and Welfare Effects of NAFTA.* University of Chicago Working Paper. Chicago: University of Chicago.

Campa, Jose, and Linda Goldberg. 2005. Exchange Rate Pass-Through into Import Prices. *Review of Economics and Statistics* 87, no. 4: 679–90.

Card, David. 1999. Wage Inequality in the United States during the 1980s: Rising Dispersion or Falling Minimum Wage? *Quarterly Journal of Economics* 114, no. 3: 977–1023.

Card, David. 2001. The Effect of Unions on Wage Inequality in the U.S. Labor Market. *Industrial and Labor Relations Review* 54, no. 2: 296–315.

CBO (Congressional Budget Office). 2012. *The Long-Term Budget Outlook.* Washington: Congress of the United States.

Choate, Pat. 2008. *Dangerous Business: The Risks of Globalization for America.* New York: Alfred A. Knopf.

Cline, William R. 1992. *The Economics of Global Warming.* Washington: Institute for International Economics.

Cline, William. 1997. *Trade and Income Distribution.* Washington: Institute for International Economics.

Cline, William R., and John Williamson. 2012. *Estimates of Fundamental Equilibrium Exchange Rates, May 2012.* Policy Briefs in International Economics 12-14. Washington: Peterson Institute for International Economics.

Cohen, Stephen S., and John Zysman. 1988. *Manufacturing Matters.* New York: Basic Books.

Cooper, John C. B. 2003. Price Elasticity of Demand for Crude Oil: Estimates for 23 Countries. *OPEC Review* 27, no. 1: 1–8.

Costinot, Arnaud, and Jonathan Vogel. 2010. Matching and Inequality in the World Economy. *Journal of Political Economy* 118, no 4: 747–86.

Crino, Rosario. 2010. Service Offshoring and White Collar Employment. *Review of Economic Studies* 77, no. 2: 595–632.

Davidson, Carl, and Steven J. Matusz. 2009. *International Trade with Equilibrium Unemployment.* Princeton, NJ: Princeton University Press.

Davis, Donald R., and Prachi Mishra. 2007. Stolper-Samuelson Is Dead: And Other Crimes of Both Theory and Data. In *Globalization and Poverty,* ed. Ann Harrison. Chicago: University of Chicago Press.

Davis, Donald R., and J. Harrigan. 2007. *Good Jobs, Bad Jobs, and Trade Liberalization.* NBER Working Paper 13139. Cambridge, MA: National Bureau of Economic Research.

Davis, Steven J. 1992. Cross-Country Patterns of Change in Relative Wages. In *NBER Macroeconomic Annual 1992,* Volume 7. Cambridge, MA: National Bureau of Economic Research.

Davis, Steven J., John C. Haltiwanger, and Scott Schuh. 1996. *Job Creation and Destruction.* Cambridge, MA: MIT Press.

Dean, Judith, K. C. Fung, and Zhi Wang. 2007. *Measuring the Vertical Specialization in Chinese Trade.* Office of Economics Working Paper 2007-01-A. Washington: US International Trade Commission.

Deardorff, Alan. 1997. *Factor Prices and the Factor Content of Trade Revisited: What's the Use?* Research Seminar in International Economics Discussion Paper 409. University of Michigan.

Deardorff, Alan V., and Dalia Hakura. 1994. Trade and Wages: What Are the Questions? In *Trade and Wages Leveling Down?* ed. Jagdish Bhagwati and Marvin Kosters. Washington: American Enterprise Institute.

Deardorff, Alan V., and Robert W. Staiger. 1988. An Interpretation of the Factor Content of Trade. *Journal of International Economics* 24, no. 1-2: 93–107.

Debaere, Peter, and Ufuk Demiroglu. 2003. On the Similarity of Country Endowments. *Journal of International Economics* 59: 101–36.

Deep, Akash, and Robert Z. Lawrence. 2008. *Stabilizing State and Local Budgets: A Proposal for Tax-Base Insurance.* The Hamilton Project Discussion Paper. Washington: Brookings Institution.

Dekle, Robert, Jonathan Eaton, and Samuel Kortum. 2007. *Unbalanced Trade.* NBER Working Paper 13035. Cambridge, MA: National Bureau of Economic Research.

DeLong, J. Bradford, and Lawrence H. Summers. 2012. Fiscal Policy in a Depressed Economy. Brookings Institution, Washington. Photocopy.

Desai, Mihir A., C. Fritz Foley, and James R. Hines, Jr. 2005. *Foreign Direct Investment and Domestic Economic Activity.* NBER Working Paper 11717. Cambridge, MA: National Bureau of Economic Research.

Desai, Mihir A., C. Fritz Foley, and James R. Hines, Jr. 2009. Domestic Effects of the Foreign Activities of U.S. Multinationals. *American Economic Journal* 1, no. 1: 181–203.

Dickens, William, and Stephen Rose. 2007. Blinder Baloney. *International Economy* (Fall): 18–83.

Dornbusch, Rudiger, Stanley Fischer, and Paul A. Samuelson. 1977. Comparative Advantage, Trade and Payments in a Ricardian Model with a Continuum of Goods. *American Economic Review* 67, no. 5: 823–39.

Dornbusch, Rudiger, Stanley Fischer, and Paul A. Samuelson. 1980. Heckscher-Ohlin Trade Theory with a Continuum of Goods. *Quarterly Journal of Economics* 93, no. 2: 203–24.

Ebenstein, Avraham, Ann Harrison, Margaret McMillan, and Shannon Phillips. 2009. *Estimating the Impact of Trade and Offshoring on American Workers Using the Current Population Surveys.* NBER Working Paper 15107. Cambridge, MA: National Bureau of Economic Research.

Edwards, Lawrence, and Robert Z. Lawrence. 2010a. *US Trade and Wages: The Misleading Implications of Conventional Trade Theory.* NBER Working Paper 16106. Cambridge, MA: National Bureau of Economic Research.

Edwards, Lawrence, and Robert Z. Lawrence. 2010b. *Do Developed and Developing Countries Compete Head to Head in High-tech?* NBER Working Paper 16105. Cambridge, MA: National Bureau of Economic Research.

Edwards, Lawrence, and Robert Z. Lawrence. 2012. A Structural Model of the US Trade Account. Photocopy.

Egger, Hartmut, and Udo Kreickemeier. 2009. Firm Heterogeneity and the Labor Market Effects of Trade Liberalization. *International Economic Review* 50, no. 1: 187–216.

EIA (Energy Information Administration). 2011. *Annual Energy Outlook 2009.* Washington: US Department of Energy.

EIA (Energy Information Administration). 2012. *Annual Energy Outlook 2012.* Washington: US Department of Energy.

Eichengreen, Barry, Yeongseop Rhee, and Hui Tong. 2007. China and the Exports of Other Asian Countries. *Review of World Economics* 143, no. 2: 201–26.

Ellison, Glenn, Edward L. Glaeser, and William R. Kerr. 2010. What Causes Industry Agglomeration? Evidence from Coagglomeration Patterns. *American Economic Review* 100, no. 3: 1195–213.

Fajgelbaum, Pablo D., Gene M. Grossman, and Elhanan Helpman. 2011. *Income Distribution, Product Quality and International Trade.* NBER Working Paper 15329. Cambridge, MA: National Bureau of Economic Research.

Fallows, James. 2010. How America Can Rise Again. *Atlantic Monthly* (January/February).

Falvey, R. E., and N. Gemmel. 1996. Are Services Income-Elastic? Some New Evidence. *Review of Income and Wealth* 42, no. 3: 257–69.

Farber, Henry S. 2005. *What Do We Know about Job Loss in the United States? Evidence from the Displaced Workers Survey, 1984–2004.* Princeton University Industrial Relations Section Working Paper 498. Princeton, NJ: Princeton University.

Farber, Henry S. 2009. *Job Loss and the Decline in Job Security in the United States.* Princeton University Industrial Relations Section Working Paper 520. Princeton, NJ: Princeton University.

Feenstra, Robert C. 1994. New Product Varieties and the Measurement of International Prices. *American Economic Review* 84, no. 1: 157–77.

Feenstra, Robert C. 2004. *Advanced International Trade: Theory and Evidence.* Princeton, NJ: Princeton University Press.

Feenstra, Robert C., and Gordon H. Hanson. 1996. Foreign Investment, Outsourcing and Relative Wages. In *The Political Economy on Trade Policy: Papers in Honor of Jagdish Bhagwati,* ed. Robert C. Feenstra, Gene M. Grossman, and Douglas Irwin. Cambridge, MA: MIT Press.

Feenstra, Robert C., and Gordon H. Hanson. 1999. The Impact of Outsourcing and High-Technology Capital on Wages: Estimates for the U.S., 1979–1990. *Quarterly Journal of Economics* 114, no. 3: 907–40.

Feenstra, Robert C., and Gordon H. Hanson. 2000. Aggregation Bias in the Factor Content of Trade: Evidence from U.S. Manufacturing. *American Economic Review* 90, no. 2: 155–60.

Feenstra, Robert C., Marshall B. Reinsdorf, and Matthew J. Slaughter. 2009. *Effects of Terms of Trade Gains and Tariff Changes on the Measurement of U.S. Productivity Growth.* NBER Working Paper 15592. Cambridge, MA: National Bureau of Economic Research.

Feenstra, Robert C., John Romalis, and Peter K. Schott. 2002. *US Imports, Exports, and Tariff Data, 1989–2001.* NBER Working Paper 9387. Cambridge, MA: National Bureau of Economic Research.

Feenstra, Robert C., Tzu-Han Yang, and Gary G. Hamilton. 1999. Business Groups and Product Variety in Trade: Evidence from South Korea, Taiwan, and Japan. *Journal of International Economics* 48, no. 1: 71–100.

Fehr, Hans, Sabine Jokisch, and Laurence J. Kotlikoff. 2008. *Dynamic Globalization and Its Potentially Alarming Prospects for Low-Wage Workers.* NBER Working Paper 14527. Cambridge, MA: National Bureau of Economic Research.

Ferrantino, Michael, Robert Koopman, Zhi Wang, Falan Yinug, Ling Chen, Fengjie Qu, and Haifeng Wang. 2007. *Classification and Statistical Reconciliation of Trade in Advanced Technology Products The Case of China and the United States.* Brookings-Tsinghua Center for Public Policy Working Paper 20070906EN. Brookings-Tsinghua Center for Public Policy.

Finger, J. Michael, and Mordechai E. Kreinin. 1979. A Measure of Export Similarity and Possible Uses. *Economic Journal* 89, no. 356: 905–12.

Fletcher, Ian. 2009. *Free Trade Doesn't Work: What Should Replace It and Why.* Washington: US Business and Industry Council.

Fontagné, Lionel, Guillaume Gaulier, and Soledad Zignago. 2008. Specialization across Varieties and North-South Competition. *Economic Policy* 23, no. 53: 51-91.

Frauenknecht, Andre. 2009. Is Chinese Export Growth Detrimental to U.S. Welfare? Master's Thesis. University of Cape Town.

Freeman, Richard B. 1995. Are Your Wages Set in Beijing? *Journal of Economic Perspectives* 9, no. 3: 15-32.

Friedman, Thomas L. 2005. *The World Is Flat: A Brief History of the Twenty-First Century*. New York: Farrar, Straus and Giroux.

Gagnon, Joseph E. 2007. Productive Capacity, Product Varieties, and the Elasticities Approach to the Trade Balance. *Review of International Economics* 15, no. 4: 639-59.

Gagnon, Joseph E., assisted by Marc Hinterschweiger. 2011. *The Global Outlook for Government Debt over the Next 25 Years: Implications for the Economy and Public Policy*. Policy Analyses in International Economics 94. Washington: Peterson Institute for International Economics.

Galama, Titus, and James Hosek. 2008. *U.S. Competitiveness in Science and Technology*. Santa Monica, CA: Rand Corporation.

Ghemawat, Pankaj. 2007. *Redefining Global Strategy: Crossing Borders in a World Where Differences Still Matter*. Cambridge, MA: Harvard Business School Press.

Ghouri, Salman Saif. 2001. Oil Demand in North America: 1980-2020. *OPEC Review: Energy Economics & Related Issues* 25, no. 4: 339-55.

Goldberg, Pinelopi Koujianou, and Michael M. Knetter. 1997. Goods Prices and Exchange Rates: What Have We Learned? *Journal of Economic Literature* 35, no. 3: 1243-72.

Goldberg, Pinelopi Koujianou, and Nina Pavcnik. 2007. Distributional Effects of Globalization in Developing Countries. *Journal of Economic Literature* 45, no. 1: 39-82.

Goldin, Claudia, and Lawrence F. Katz. 2007. Long-Run Changes in the Wage Structure: Narrowing, Widening, Polarizing. *Brookings Papers on Economic Activity* 2: 135-68.

Goldin, Claudia, and Lawrence F. Katz. 2008. *The Race between Education and Technology*. Cambridge, MA: Harvard University Press.

Golub, Stephen. 1998. Does Trade with Low-Wage Economies Hurt American Workers? *Federal Reserve Bank of Philadelphia Business Review* (March-April): 3-15.

Gomory, Ralph E., and William J. Baumol. 2000. *Global Trade and Conflicting National Interests*. Cambridge, MA: MIT Press.

Gopinath, Gita, and Roberto Rigobon. 2008. Sticky Borders. *Quarterly Journal of Economics* 123, no. 2: 531-75.

Gosselin, Peter. 2008. *High Wire: The Precarious Financial Lives of American Families*. New York: Basic Books.

Grossman, Gene, and Esteban Rossi-Hansberg. 2008. Trading Tasks: A Simple Theory of Offshoring. *American Economic Review* 98, no. 5: 1978-97.

Grossman, Gene, and Esteban Rossi-Hansberg. 2009. External Economies and International Trade Redux (July). Available at www.princeton.edu/~grossman/ExternalEconomies.pdf (accessed on November 1, 2012).

Hacker, Jacob S. 2006. *The Great Risk Shift: The New Economic Insecurity and the Decline of the American Dream*. Oxford: Oxford University Press.

Hallak, Juan Carlos, and Peter K. Schott. 2008. *Estimating Cross-Country Differences in Product Quality*. NBER Working Paper 13807. Cambridge, MA: National Bureau of Economic Research.

Hamilton, James D. 2009. Causes and Consequences of the Oil Shock of 2007-08. *Brookings Papers on Economic Activity* 40, no. 1: 215-83.

Hanson, Gordon H., Raymond J. Mataloni, Jr., and Matthew J. Slaughter. 2003. Expansion Abroad and the Domestic Operations of US Multinational Firms. Photocopy.

Hanson, Gordon H., Raymond J. Mataloni, Jr., and Matthew J. Slaughter. 2005. Vertical Production Networks in Multinational Firms. *Review of Economics and Statistics* 87, no. 4: 664–78.

Harrison, Anne E., ed. 2007. *Globalization and Poverty*. Chicago: University of Chicago Press.

Harrison, Anne E., and Margaret S. McMillan. 2006. *Outsourcing Jobs? Multinationals and U.S. Employment*. NBER Working Paper 12372. Cambridge, MA: National Bureau of Economic Research.

Harrison, Anne E., Margaret S. McMillan, and Clair Null. 2007. U.S. Multinational Activity Abroad and U.S. Jobs: Substitutes or Complement? *Industrial Relations* 46, no. 2: 347–65.

Harrison, Anne E., John McLaren, and Margaret S. McMillan. 2010. *Recent Findings on Trade and Inequality*. NBER Working Paper 16425. Cambridge, MA: National Bureau of Economic Research.

Haskel, Jonathan E., and Matthew J. Slaughter. 2001. Trade, Technology and U.K. Wage Inequality. *Economic Journal* 111, no. 468: 163–87.

Haskel, Jonathan E., and Matthew J. Slaughter. 2003. Have Falling Tariffs and Transportation Costs Raised U.S. Wage Inequality? *Review of International Economics* 11, no. 4: 630–50.

Haskel, Jonathan, Robert Z. Lawrence, Edward E. Leamer, and Matthew J. Slaughter. 2012. Globalization and U.S. Wages: Modifying Classic Theory to Explain Recent Facts. *Journal of Economic Perspectives* 26, no. 2: 119–40.

Hausmann, Ricardo, and Dani Rodrik. 2003. Economic Development as Self-Discovery. *Journal of Development Economics* 72, no. 2: 603–33.

Hausmann, Ricardo, Jason Hwang, and Dani Rodrik. 2007. What You Export Matters. *Journal of Economic Growth* 12, no. 1: 1–25.

Helpman, Elhanan. 1999. The Structure of Foreign Trade. *Journal of Economic Perspectives* 13, no. 2: 121–44.

Helpman, Elhanan, Oleg Itskhoki, and Stephen Redding. 2010. Inequality and Unemployment in a Global Economy. *Econometrica* 78, no. 4: 1239–83.

Herrendorf, Berthold, Richard Rogerson, and Akos Valentini. 2011. Growth and Structural Transformation. Photocopy.

Heston, Alan, Robert Summers, and Bettina Aten. 2011. Penn World Table Version 7.0. Center for International Comparisons of Production, Income and Prices, University of Pennsylvania.

Hicks, John R. 1953. An Inaugural Lecture. *Oxford Economic Papers* 5, no. 2: 117–35.

Hooper, Peter, and Catherine L. Mann. 1987. The U.S. External Deficit: Its Causes and Persistence. *Proceedings*: 3–127. Federal Reserve Bank of St. Louis.

Hooper, Peter, Karen Johnson, and Jaime Marquez. 2000. *Trade Elasticities for the G7 Countries*. Princeton Studies in International Economics 87. Princeton, NJ: Princeton University.

Houser, Trevor, Rob Bradley, Britt Childs, Jacob Werksman, and Robert Heilmayr. 2008. *Leveling the Carbon Playing Field: International Competition and US Climate Policy Design*. Washington: Peterson Institute for International Economics.

Houthakker, Hendrik S., and Stephen Magee. 1969. Income and Price Elasticities in World Trade. *Review of Economics and Statistics* 51, no. 2: 111–25.

Hsieh, Chang-Tai, and Ralph Ossa. 2011. *A Global View of Productivity Growth in China*. NBER Working Paper 16778. Cambridge, MA: National Bureau of Economic Research.

Hufbauer, Gary Clyde, and Ariel Assa. 2007. *US Taxation of Foreign Income*. Washington: Peterson Institute for International Economics.

Hufbauer, Gary Clyde, and Theodore H. Moran. 2010. *Higher Taxes on Multinationals Would Hurt US Workers and Exports*. Policy Briefs in International Economics 10-10. Washington: Peterson Institute for International Economics.

Hufbauer, Gary Clyde, and Jeffrey J. Schott. 2005. *NAFTA Revisited: Achievements and Challenges*. Washington: Institute for International Economics.

Hufbauer, Gary Clyde, Steve Charnovitz, and Jisun Kim. 2009. *Global Warming and the World Trading System*. Washington: Peterson Institute for International Economics.

Hufbauer, Gary Clyde, and Jeffrey J. Schott. 2012. *Will the World Trade Organization Enjoy a Bright Future?* Policy Briefs in International Economics 12-11. Washington: Peterson Institute for International Economics.

Hummels, David, and Peter J. Klenow. 2005. The Variety and Quality of a Nation's Exports. *American Economic Review* 95, no. 3: 704–23.

Hummels, David, and Alexandre Skiba. 2004. Shipping the Good Apples Out? An Empirical Confirmation of the Alchian-Allen Conjecture. *Journal of Political Economy* 112, no. 6: 1384–402.

Hummels, David, Jun Ishii, and Kei-Mu Yi. 2001. The Nature and Growth of Vertical Specialization in World Trade. *Journal of International Economics* 54, no 1: 75–96.

Hummels, David, Rasmus Jorgensen, Jakob Munch, and Chong Xiang. 2010. *The Wage and Employment Effects of Outsourcing: Evidence from Danish Matched Worker-Firm Data*. NBER Working Paper 17496. Cambridge, MA: National Bureau of Economic Research.

IEA (International Energy Agency). 2012. *World Energy Outlook* (November). Paris.

IMF (International Monetary Fund). 2007. *World Economic Outlook: Spillovers and Cycles in the Global Economy* (April). Washington.

IMF (International Monetary Fund). 2012. *World Economic Outlook: Growth Resuming, Dangers Remain* (April). Washington.

Jacobson, Louis S., Robert J. LaLonde, and Daniel G. Sullivan. 1993. Earnings Losses of Displaced Workers. *American Economic Review* 83, no. 4: 685–709.

Jensen, J. Bradford. 2011. *Global Trade in Services: Fear, Facts, and Offshoring*. Washington: Peterson Institute for International Economics.

Jensen, J. Bradford, and Lori G. Kletzer. 2005. Tradable Services: Understanding the Scope and Impact of Services Offshoring. In *Brookings Trade Forum 2005: Offshoring White-Collar Work*, ed. Susan M. Collins and Lael Brainard. Washington: Brookings Institution Press.

Johnson, George E., and Frank P. Stafford. 1993. International Competition and Real Wages. *American Economic Review* 83, no. 2: 127–30.

Johnson, Harry G. 1955a. Economic Expansion and International Trade. *Manchester School of Social and Economic Studies* 23: 95–112.

Johnson, Harry G. 1955b. The Transfer Problem: A Note on Criteria for Changes in the Terms of Trade. *Economica* 22, no. 86 (May): 113–21.

Jones, Ronald W. 1970. The Transfer Problem Revisited. *Economica* 37, no. 146: 178–84.

Jones, Ronald W. 1971. A Three-factor Model in Theory, Trade and History. *In Trade, Balance of Payments and Growth: Essays in Honor of C. P. Kindleberger*, ed. J. N. Bhagwati et al. Amsterdam: North-Holland.

Jones, Ronald W., and José Scheinkman. 1977. The Relevance of the Two-Sector Production Model in Trade. *Journal of Political Economy* 85, no. 5: 909–35.

Jorgenson, Dale W., Mun Ho, and Jon Samuels. 2010. New Data on U.S. Productivity Growth by Industry. Paper presented for the first World KLEMS conference, Harvard University, August 19–20. Available at www.worldklems.net/conferences/worldklems2010_jorgenson. pdf (accessed on November 1, 2012).

Kambourov Gueorgui, and Iourii Manovskii. 2009. Occupational Mobility and Wage Inequality. *Review of Economic Studies* 76, no. 2: 731–59.

Karabay, Bilgehan, and John McLaren. 2009. *Trade, Off-shoring and the Invisible Handshake.* NBER Working Paper 15048. Cambridge, MA: National Bureau of Economic Research.

Katz, Lawrence F. 2008. Comment on "Trade and Wages Reconsidered." *Brookings Papers on Economic Activity* (Spring): 143–49.

Katz, Lawrence F., and Kevin M. Murphy. 1992. Changes in Relative Wages, 1963–1987: Supply and Demand Factors. *Quarterly Journal of Economics* 107, no. 1: 35–78.

Katz, Lawrence F., and Lawrence Summers. 1989. Industry Rents: Evidence and Implications. *Brookings Papers on Economic Activity: Microeconomics:* 209–75.

Kennedy, John F. 1963. *Public Papers of the Presidents of the United States: John F. Kennedy, 1963.* Volume 3. Washington: US Government Printing Office.

Kennedy, Paul. 1989. *The Rise and Fall of the Great Powers: Economic Change and Military Conflict from 1500 to 2000.* New York: Vintage Books.

Khandelwal, Amit. 2010. The Long and Short (of) Quality Ladders. *Review of Economic Studies* 77, no. 4: 1450–76.

Kirkegaard, Jacob Funk. 2007. *The Accelerating Decline in America's High-Skilled Workforce: Implications for Immigration Policy.* Policy Analyses in International Economics 84. Washington: Peterson Institute for International Economics.

Kiyota, Kozo. 2008. *Are US Exports Different from China's Exports? Evidence from Japan's Imports.* University of Michigan Research Seminar in International Economics Discussion Paper 576 (April).

Kletzer, Lori. 2001. *Job Loss from Imports: Measuring the Costs.* Washington: Institute for International Economics.

Kletzer, Lori, and Robert E. Litan. 2001. *A Prescription to Relieve Worker Anxiety.* Policy Briefs in International Economics 01-2. Washington: Institute for International Economics.

Kojima, Kiyoshi. 2000. The "Flying Geese" Model of Asian Economic Development: Origin, Theoretical Extensions, and Regional Policy Implications. *Journal of Asian Economics* 11, no. 4: 375–401.

Koopman, Robert, Zhi Wang, and Shang-Jin Wei. 2008. *How Much of Chinese Exports Is Really Made in China? Assessing Domestic Value-Added When Processing Trade Is Pervasive.* NBER Working Paper 14109. Cambridge, MA: National Bureau of Economic Research.

Krishna, Kala. 1987. Tariffs versus Quotas with Endogenous Quality. *Journal of International Economics* 23, no. 1–2: 97–112.

Krugman, Paul R. 1980. Scale Economies, Product Differentiation, and the Pattern of Trade. *American Economic Review* 70, no. 5: 950–59.

Krugman, Paul R. 1985. A "Technology Gap" Model of International Trade. In *Structural Adjustment in Developed Open Economies,* ed. Karl Jungenfelt and Sir Douglas Hague. New York: St. Martin's Press.

Krugman, Paul R. 1987. Is Free Trade Passé? *Journal of Economic Perspectives* 1, no. 2: 131–44.

Krugman, Paul R. 1994. Does Third World Growth Hurt First World Prosperity? *Harvard Business Review* (July–August): 113–21.

Krugman, Paul R. 1995. Growing World Trade: Causes and Consequences. *Brookings Papers on Economic Activity* 26, no. 1: 327–77.

Krugman, Paul R. 2000. Technology, Trade and Factor Prices. *Journal of International Economics* 50, no. 1: 51–71.

Krugman, Paul R. 2008. Trade and Wages, Reconsidered. *Brookings Papers on Economic Activity* 1 (Spring): 103–37.

Krugman, Paul R., and Richard E. Baldwin. 1987. The Persistence of the U.S. Trade Deficit. *Brookings Papers on Economic Activity* 18, no. 1: 1–56.

Krugman, Paul R., and Maurice Obstfeld. 2003. *International Economics: Theory and Policy.* Boston: Addison-Wesley.

Lall, Sanjaya. 2000. *The Technological Structure and Performance of Developing Country Exports.* QEH Working Paper 44. Queen Elizabeth House, Oxford University.

Lall, Sanjaya, John Weiss, and Jinkang Zhang. 2005. *The 'Sophistication' of Exports: A New Measure of Product Characteristics.* QEH Working Paper 123. Queen Elizabeth House, Oxford University.

Lawrence, Colin, and Robert Z. Lawrence. 1985. Manufacturing Wage Dispersion: An End-Game Interpretation. *Brookings Papers on Economic Activity* 1.

Lawrence, Robert Z. 1984. *Can America Compete?* Washington: Brookings Institution.

Lawrence, Robert Z. 1990. US Current Account Adjustment: An Appraisal. *Brookings Papers on Economic Activity* 2: 343–82.

Lawrence, Robert Z. 2007. *The United States and the WTO Dispute Settlement System.* New York: Council on Foreign Relations.

Lawrence, Robert Z. 2008. *Blue-Collar Blues: Is Trade to Blame for Rising US Income Inequality?* Policy Analyses in International Economics 85. Washington: Peterson Institute for International Economics.

Lawrence, Robert Z. 2010. *How Good Politics Results in Bad Policy: The Case of BioFuels Mandates.* Working Paper for the Belfer Center for Science and International Affairs and Center for International Development, Harvard Kennedy School (September).

Lawrence, Robert Z. 2011. Manufacturing Globalization. *Foreign Affairs* (November/December).

Lawrence, Robert Z. 2012. *Growth in ASEAN, China and India: Implications for the Rest of the World.* Paper for an Asian Development Bank Study on the Role of Key Emerging Economies— ASEAN, PRC, and India—for a Balanced, Sustainable, and Resilient Asia. Photocopy.

Lawrence, Robert Z., and Matthew J. Slaughter. 1993. International Trade and American Wages in the 1980s: Giant Sucking Sounds or Small Hiccup? *Brookings Papers on Economics: Macroeconomics* 2: 161–226.

Leamer, Edward E. 1994. *Trade, Wages and Revolving Door Ideas.* NBER Working Paper 4716. Cambridge, MA: National Bureau of Economic Research.

Leamer, Edward E. 1996. *What's the Use of Factor Contents?* NBER Working Paper 5448. Cambridge, MA: National Bureau of Economic Research.

Leamer, Edward E. 1998. In Search of Stolper-Samuelson Effects on U.S. Wages. In *Imports, Exports and the American Worker,* ed. Susan Collins. Washington: Brookings Institution.

Leamer, Edward E., and James Levinsohn. 1995. International Trade Theory: The Evidence. In *Handbook of International Economics,* edition 1, ed. G. M. Grossman and K. Rogoff. Amsterdam: Elsevier.

Leamer, Edward, and Robert M. Stern. 1970. *Quantitative International Economics.* Allyn and Bacon International Series in Economics. Boston: Allyn and Bacon.

Lemieux, Thomas. 2006. Increasing Residual Wage Inequality: Composition Effects, Noisy Data, or Rising Demand for Skill? *American Economic Review* 96, no. 3: 461–98.

Levy, Frank, and Richard J. Murnane. 2006. For Now, Middle-Skilled Jobs Are the Most Vulnerable. *CESifo Forum* 7, no. 2.

Levy, Frank, and Peter Temin. 2007. *Inequality and Institutions in 20th Century America.* NBER Working Paper 13106. Cambridge, MA: National Bureau of Economic Research.

Lin, Justin Y. 2011. *From Flying Geese to Leading Dragons: New Opportunities and Strategies for Structural Transformation in Developing Countries.* World Bank Policy Research Working Paper 5702. Washington: World Bank.

Linden, Greg, Kenneth L. Kraemer, and Jason Dedrick. 2009. Who Captures Value in a Global Innovation Network? The Case of Apple's iPod. *Communications of the ACM* 52, no. 3: 140–44.

Linder, Staffan Burenstam. 1961. *An Essay on Trade and Transformation.* Stockholm: Almqvist & Wicksell.

Liu, Runjuan, and Daniel Trefler. 2008. *Much Ado About Nothing: American Jobs and the Rise of Service Outsourcing to China and India.* NBER Working Paper 14061. Cambridge, MA: National Bureau of Economic Research.

Liveris, Andrew N. 2010. *Make It in America: The Case for Reinventing the Economy.* New Jersey: John Wiley.

Longworth, Richard C. 2008. *Caught in the Middle: America's Heartland in the Age of Globalism.* New York: Bloomsbury.

Magee, Stephen P. 1972. The Welfare Effects of Restrictions on U.S. Trade. *Brookings Papers on Economic Activity* 3: 645–701.

Manasse, P., and A. Turrini. 2001. Trade, Wages and Superstars. *Journal of International Economics* 54, no. 1: 97–117.

Mandel, Benjamin R. 2010. *Heterogeneous Firms and Import Quality: Evidence from Transaction-level Prices.* International Finance Discussion Paper 991. Washington: Board of Governors of the Federal Reserve System.

Mankiw, N. Gregory. 2012. *Macroeconomics.* New York: Worth Publishers.

Marazzi, M., N. Sheets, R. Vigfusson, J. Faust, J. Gagnon, J. Marquez, R. Martin, T. Reeve, and J. Rogers. 2005. *Exchange Rate Pass-Through to U.S. Import Prices: Some New Evidence.* International Finance Discussion Paper 833. Washington: Board of Governors of the Federal Reserve System.

Mayda, Anna Maria, and Dani Rodrik. 2002. Why Are Some People (and Countries) More Protectionist than Others? *European Economic Review* 49, no. 6: 1393–691.

McAfee, Andrew, and Eric Brynjolfsson. 2011. *Race Against the Machine.* Lexington, MA: Lexington Frontier Press.

McLaren, John, and Shushanik Hakobyan. 2012 (revised). *Looking for Local Labor Market Effects of NAFTA.* NBER Working Paper 16535. Cambridge, MA: National Bureau of Economic Research.

McMillon, Charles W. 2007. China's Soaring Financial, Industrial and Technological Power. Washington: MBG Information Services (September). Available at www.uscc.gov/research papers/2008/07_09_prc_modernization.pdf (accessed on November 1, 2012).

Melitz, Marc. 2003. The Impact of Trade on Intra-Industry Reallocations and Aggregate Industry Productivity. *Econometrica* 71, no. 6: 1695–725.

Michaels, Guy, Ashwini Natraj, and John Van Reenen. 2010. *Has ICT Polarized Skill Demand? Evidence from Eleven Countries over 25 Years.* CEP Discussion Paper 987. London: Centre for Economic Performance.

Mishel, Lawrence, and Jared Bernstein. 1998. Technology and the Wage Structure: Has Technology's Impact Accelerated Since the 1970s? *Research in Labor Economics* 17.

Mishel, Lawrence, Jared Bernstein, and Heidi Shierholz. 2009. *The State of Working America 2008/2009.* Washington: Economic Policy Institute.

Moran, Theodore H. 2009. *American Multinationals and American Economic Interests: New Dimensions to an Old Debate.* Working Paper 09-3. Washington: Peterson Institute for International Economics.

Moran, Theodore H. 2010. Foreign Multinational Manufacturing Investors Are Transforming the Chinese Economy—Or Are They? Photocopy.

Moretti, Enrico. 2010. *Local Labor Markets*. NBER Working Paper 15947. Cambridge, MA: National Bureau of Economic Research.

Moretti, Enrico. 2012. *The New Geography of Jobs*. New York: Houghton Mifflin Harcourt.

Muendler, Marc-Andreas, and Sascha O. Becker. 2006. *Margins of Multinational Labor Substitution*. University of California at San Diego Working Paper (April 15). University of California at San Diego.

Mussa, Michael. 1974. Tariffs and the Distribution of Income: The Importance of Factor Specificity, Substitutability, and Intensity in the Short and Long Run. *Journal of Political Economy* 82, no. 1: 191–204.

NAM (National Association of Manufacturers). 2010. Export Expansion Estimates for Additional Trade Agreements. Available at www.nam.org/~/media/2A51F467160D4ABF84E9DF40A2AD6C44/Export_Expansion_Estimates_for_Additional_Trade_Agreements.pdf (accessed on November 1, 2010).

Neal, Derek. 1995. Industry-Specific Human Capital: Evidence from Displaced Workers. *Journal of Labor Economics* 13, no. 4: 653–77.

Neary, J. Peter. 1978. Short-Run Capital Specificity and the Pure Theory of International Trade. *Economic Journal* 88, no. 351: 488–510.

Noland, Marcus. 1997. Has Asian Export Performance Been Unique? *Journal of International Economics* 42, no. 1–2: 79–101.

Nordhaus, William. 2005. *The Sources of the Productivity Rebound and the Manufacturing Employment Puzzle*. NBER Working Paper 11354. Cambridge, MA: National Bureau of Economic Research.

Nordhaus, William. 2006. *Baumol's Cost Disease: A Macroeconomic Perspective*. NBER Working Paper 12218. Cambridge, MA: National Bureau of Economic Research.

NSF (National Science Foundation). 2010. Science and Engineering Indicators 2010. www.nsf.gov/statistics/scind10 (accessed on November 1, 2012).

Nye, Joseph. 1991. *Bound to Lead: The Changing Nature of American Power*. New York: Basic Books.

Obstfeld, Maurice, and Kenneth Rogoff. 1996. *Foundations of International Macroeconomics*. Cambridge, MA: MIT Press.

Obstfeld, Maurice, and Kenneth Rogoff. 2004. *The Unsustainable Current Account Position Revisited*. NBER Working Paper 10869. Cambridge, MA: National Bureau of Economic Research.

Pierce, Justin R., and Peter K. Schott. 2009. *Concording US Harmonized System Categories over Time*. Center for Economic Studies Working Paper 09-11. Washington: US Census Bureau.

Preeg, Ernest H. 2004. *The Threatened U.S. Competitive Lead in Advanced Technology Products (ATP)*. Washington: Manufactures Alliance/MAPI.

Prestowitz, Clyde. 2010. *The Betrayal of American Prosperity: Free Market Delusions, America's Decline, and How We Must Compete in the Post-Dollar Era*. New York: Free Press.

Revenga, Ana L. 1992. Exporting Jobs? The Impact of Import Competition on Employment and Wages in U.S. Manufacturing. *Quarterly Journal of Economics* 107, no. 1: 255–84.

Reinsdorf, Marshall B. 2010. Terms of Trade Effects: Theory and Measurement. *Review of Income and Wealth* 56, no. S1: S177–S205.

Richardson, J. David. 1993. *Sizing Up US Export Disincentives*. Washington: Institute for International Economics.

Richardson, J David. 1995. Income Inequality and Trade: How to Think, What to Conclude. *Journal of Economic Perspectives* 9, no. 3 (summer): 33-55.

Rodrik, Dani. 1997. *Has Globalization Gone Too Far?* Washington: Institute for International Economics.

Rodrik, Dani. 2006. What's So Special about China's Exports? *China & World Economy* 14, no. 5: 1-19.

Rodrik, Dani. 2010. The Return of Industrial Policy. Project Syndicate (April 12). Available at www.project-syndicate.org/commentary/rodrik42/English (accessed on November 1, 2012).

Rodrik, Dani. 2011. *The Globalization Paradox: Democracy and the Future of the World Economy.* New York: W. W. Norton and Company.

Romalis, John. 2004. Factor Proportions and the Structure of Commodity Trade. *American Economic Review* 94, no. 1: 67-97.

Romalis, John. 2007. NAFTA's and CUSFTA's Impact on International Trade. *Review of Economics and Statistics* 89, no. 3: 416-35.

Rosen, Howard. 2008. *Strengthening Trade Adjustment Assistance.* Policy Briefs in International Economics 08-2. Washington: Peterson Institute for International Economics.

Rowthorn, Robert, and Ramana Ramaswamy. 1997. *Deindustrialisation: Causes and Implications.* IMF Working Paper 97/42. Washington: International Monetary Fund.

Rowthorn, Robert, and John R. Wells. 1987. *Deindustrialization and Foreign Trade.* Cambridge: Cambridge University Press.

Sachs, Jeffrey D., and Howard J. Shatz. 1994. Trade and Jobs in U.S. Manufacturing. *Brookings Papers on Economic Activity* 1: 1-84.

Samuelson, Paul A. 1952, 1954. The Transfer Problem and Transport Costs. *Economic Journal* 62, no. 246 (1952): 278-304; *Economic Journal* 64, no. 254 (1954): 264-89.

Samuelson, Paul A. 2004. Where Ricardo and Mill Rebut and Confirm Arguments of Mainstream Economists Supporting Globalization. *Journal of Economic Perspectives* 18, no. 3: 135-46.

Scheve, Kenneth S., and Matthew J. Slaughter. 2004. Economic Insecurity and the Globalization of Production. *American Journal of Political Science* 48, no. 4: 662-74.

Schmidt, Stefanie R. 1999. Long-Run Trends in Workers' Beliefs about Their Own Job Security: Evidence from the General Social Survey. *Journal of Labor Economics* 17, no. 4: S127-S141.

Schott, Peter K. 2003. One Size Fits All? Heckscher-Ohlin Specialization in Global Production. *American Economic Review* 93, no. 3: 686-708.

Schott, Peter K. 2004. Across-product Versus Within-product Specialization in International Trade. *Quarterly Journal of Economics* 119, no. 2: 646-77.

Schott, Peter K. 2008. The Relative Sophistication of Chinese Exports. *Economic Policy* 23, no. 53: 5-49.

Schwab, Susan. 2011. After Doha: Why the Negotiations Are Doomed and What to Do About It. *Foreign Affairs* (May/June).

Scott, Robert E. 2011. *Heading South: Trade and Job Displacement after NAFTA.* Washington: Economic Policy Institute.

Scott, Robert E. 2010. *Rising China Trade Deficit Will Cost One-Half Million U.S. Jobs in 2010.* Issue Brief 283 (September). Washington: Economic Policy Institute.

Sethupathy, Guru. 2009. *Offshoring, Wages, and Employment: Theory and Evidence.* Johns Hopkins University Working Paper. Baltimore: Johns Hopkins University.

Sitchinava, Nino. 2008. Trade, Technology and Wage Inequality: Evidence from U.S. Manufacturing 1989-2004. University of Oregon. Photocopy.

Slaughter, Matthew J. 2000. What Are the Results of Product-Price Studies? In *The Impact of International Trade on Wages,* ed. Robert C. Feenstra. Chicago: University of Chicago Press.

Smith, James L. 2009. World Oil: Market or Mayhem? *Journal of Economic Perspectives* 23, no. 3: 145–64.

Spence, Michael. 2011. Globalization and Unemployment: The Downside of Integrating Markets. *Foreign Affairs* (July/August).

Spence, Michael, and Sandile Hlatshwayo. 2011. *The Evolving Structure of the American Economy and the Employment Challenge.* New York: Council on Foreign Relations.

Stolper, Wolfgang, and Paul Samuelson. 1941. Protection and Real Wages. *Review of Economic Studies* 9, no. 1: 58–73.

Subramanian, Arvind. 2011. *Eclipse: Living in the Shadow of China's Economic Dominance.* Washington: Peterson Institute for International Economics.

Sun, Guang-Zhen, and Yew-Kwang Ng. 2000. The Measurement of Structural Differences between Economies: An Axiomatic Characterization. *Economic Theory* 16, no. 2: 313–21.

United Nations Statistical Division. 2007. Future Revision of the Classification by Broad Economic Categories (BEC), ESA/STAT/AC.124/8. United Nations Department of Economic and Social Affairs Statistical Division.

USITC (United States International Trade Commission). 2011. *China: Effects of Intellectual Property Infringement and Indigenous Innovation Policies.* Investigation No. 332-519. USITC Publication 4226 (May). Washington.

Van Grasstek, Craig. 2011. Dereliction of Duties. Washington. Photocopy.

van Welsum, Desiree, and Xavier Reif. 2006. Potential Offshoring: Evidence from Selected OECD Countries. In *Offshoring White-Collar Work,* ed. Susan M. Collins and Lael Brainard. Washington: Brookings Institution Press.

Verhoogen, Eric. 2008. Trade, Quality Upgrading, and Wage Inequality in the Mexican Manufacturing Sector. *Quarterly Journal of Economics* 123, no. 2: 489–530.

Vernon, Raymond. 1966. International Investment and International Trade in the Product Cycle. *Quarterly Journal of Economics* 80, no. 2. 190–207.

Victor, David G. 2004. *Climate Change: Debating America's Options.* Washington: Council on Foreign Relations/Brookings Institution Press.

Wachter, Michael L., and Susan L. Wachter, eds. 1981. *Towards a New U.S. Industrial Policy?* Philadelphia: University of Pennsylvania Press.

Wang, Zhi, and Shang-Jin Wei. 2010. What Accounts for the Rising Sophistication of China's Exports? In *China's Growing Role in World Trade,* ed. Robert C. Feenstra and Shang-Jin Wei. Chicago: University of Chicago Press.

Whalley, John, and Lisandro Abrego. 2000. *Demand Side Considerations and the Trade and Wages Debate.* NBER Working Paper 7674. Cambridge, MA: National Bureau of Economic Research.

Wood, Adrian. 1994. *North-South Trade, Employment and Inequality: Changing Fortunes in a Skill-Driven World.* Oxford: Clarendon Press.

Wood, Adrian. 1995. How Trade Hurts Unskilled Workers. *Journal of Economic Perspectives* 9, no. 3: 57–80.

Yeaple, Stephen R. 2005. A Simple Model of Firm Heterogeneity, International Trade, and Wages. *Journal of International Economics* 65, no. 1: 1–20.

Zhou, Liu. 2006. The Economic Interdependence of China and the World. PhD dissertation. Harvard University.

Zhu, Susan Chu. 2005. Can Product Cycles Explain Skill Upgrading? *Journal of International Economics* 66, no. 1: 131–55.

Zhu, Susan Chu. 2007. On the Welfare Implications of Southern Catch Up. *Economic Letters* 94 (March): 378–82.

Zhu, Susan Chu, and Daniel Trefler. 2005. Trade and Inequality in Developing Countries: A General Equilibrium Analysis. *Journal of International Economics* 65, no. 1: 21–48.

Index

aggregate demand, 34–42
aggregate employment. *See* total jobs
aggregate welfare, 22–23
aggregation bias, 22
alternative energy products
    Chinese production of, 88, 236
    energy independence and, 181–83
    policy implications, 250–51
Armington assumption, 138
Asian economies, specialization patterns in, 140–41
autonomous demand, 34, 37, 39b, 41, 43

Buffett, Warren, 5
Bureau of Economic Analysis (BEA)
    government consumption tables, 75n
    Input-Output Tables, 45–46
        manufacturing jobs, 59b–60b, 80, 81f, 218n
        worker classification, 207b
    multinational employment data, 84
Bureau of Labor Statistics (BLS)
    Business Employment Dynamics Survey, 46–47
    Current Employment Statistics Survey, 64n
    Current Population Survey, 50–51, 65n, 204–205
    import price series, 144

Job Opening and Labor Turnover Survey, 47
Laspeyres index, 149
Mass Layoff Statistics, 48, 48n
measurement error, 216, 227–30
productivity growth estimates, 213, 213n
US imports from China indices, 145
Business Employment Dynamics Survey (BLS), 46 47

capital flows, 26–27
China
    alternative energy products, 88, 236
    exchange rates, 168, 241
    export industries, disaggregated analysis, 111b–113b
    export share, 98t, 99
    export unit values, 103, 107f, 107–10
    in global supply chains, 93
    head-to-head competition, 23, 26
    high-tech exports, 88, 104–107, 236
    import prices, 145, 146f, 217, 233
    most favored nation status, 4
    oil prices and, 10, 171–72, 174, 177–78, 251
    per capita income, 142, 237
    productivity growth, 136–37, 148–49, 237n
    product quality, 129–31, 131n

China—*continued*
    services trade, 51–52
    terms of trade, 145, 146*f*
    trade gains, 150–52
    US trade deficit with, 156–57
    US trade policy on, 244–45
    vertical specialization, 110–15
    within-product specialization, 117
    WTO accession, 42, 245
classical trade models, 6
    assumptions inherent in, 11–12, 62–63,
        87, 135, 153, 157, 187–88
    on trade deficits, 19
    on wage inequality, 21–22
    on welfare effects, 17, 136–39
Clinton, Hillary, 6, 6*n*
comparative advantage
    in high-tech products, 94
    trade gains from, 136–38
competitiveness. *See also* head-to-head
        competition
    overview of, 16–17, 87–89
    employment and, 31
    high-technology products, 16–17, 88,
        91–94
    innovation and, 24–25
    trade deficit and, 156–57
    wages and, 53, 54
computer products
    exclusion from data, 216, 225, 228–30,
        229*t*
    prices of, 227
    trade in, 83–84
cone of diversification, 191, 192–93
consumption
    manufacturing jobs and, 73–79, 76*f*, 85
    patterns of, 19
    share of imports in, 138
current account balance
    policy implications, 24, 31, 238, 241
    terms of trade and, 19–20, 158
Current Employment Statistics Survey
    (BLS), 64*n*
Current Population Survey (BLS), 50–51,
    65*n*, 204–205

deindustrialization, 15, 67–79
demand
    aggregate, 34–42
    autonomous, 34, 37, 39*b*, 41, 43
    comparative advantage and, 137–38
    employment growth and, 34–35, 37–42
    income elasticity of, 73

manufacturing jobs and, 11, 58, 67–79,
    76*f*, 85
    for oil, 174–79, 175*t*
    price effects, 72–73
    substitution effects on, 191–92
    for US products, 24–25, 240–41, 244
disaggregation, 229–30
dispute settlement system (WTO), 245–46
Dixit-Stiglitz utility function, 125*n*
Doha Development Agenda, 1, 246
Doha Round, 3, 25, 246
domestic spending
    employment growth and, 38, 42
    manufacturing jobs and, 73–79, 76*f*, 85
    policy implications, 239

economic conditions, manufacturing jobs
    and, 64–66
economic growth, developing-country
    benefits of, 9–10, 12, 23–25, 42, 133–34,
        236
    welfare effects, 135–52
economists' concerns
    overview of, 6–10, 87, 133–34, 235
    competition (*See* competitiveness)
    wages (*See* wage inequality)
    welfare (*See* welfare)
education, as skill measure, 223*t*, 224–25
elasticity of substitution, 130–31, 130*n*, 192,
    192*n*, 211*n*
electronic products
    exclusion from data, 216, 225, 228–30,
        229*t*
    prices of, 227
    trade in, 83–84
employment. *See also* labor market; worker(s)
    benefits of trade for, 11–12, 14, 42, 236
    import growth and, 11, 35–36, 36*f*, 43
    job loss (*See* lost jobs)
    labor market volatility, 14
    labor supply, 34, 194–95
    macroeconomic policy and, 31, 42–43
    in manufacturing (*See* manufacturing
        jobs)
    in nontradable sectors, 60
    public's concerns about, 2–6, 29–31,
        87, 235
    total, 13–14 (*See also* total jobs)
    sector share in, 60–61, 61*f*
energy independence, 181–83
Energy Information Administration (EIA),
    250
Engel's law, 73

environmental factors, 26
equipment spending, 77–79, 78f
European Union, 249
exchange rates
    policy implications, 24–25, 240–41, 244
    terms of trade and, 166–68
export(s). *See also* product(s)
    across-product specialization in, 91–92
    differentiation of (*See* head-to-head
        competition)
    overlap between, 94–103, 120
        cumulative shares, 97–99, 98t
        similarity indices, 95–97, 96t
        by unit values, 99–103, 101t–102t,
            107f–109f, 107 10
    policy implications, 243
    prices of (*See* prices)
    specific factors, 196–98
    technological sophistication (*See*
            high-technology products;
            technological sophistication)
    unit values of (*See* unit values)
export-biased growth, 136–37, 139, 142, 169

factor content, 210, 218–19
factor endowments
    comparative advantage and, 137–38
    specialization and, 187–88
factor intensity, 94, 188n, 223
factor prices
    determinants of, 189–90, 200–201,
        213–14
    effect of trade on, 62–63
    equalization theorem, 189n
factors of production
    assumptions about, in trade theories,
        62–63, 187–88
    prices and, 188 (*See also* Stolper-
        Samuelson theory)
finished goods, manufacturing trade in, 18,
    92–94, 118–20
fiscal policy
    employment and, 42–43
    study implications for, 24–25, 238
Fischer, Stanley, 124, 193
flying geese pattern of development, 140n,
    140–41
foreign growth
    benefits of, 9–10, 12, 23–25, 42, 133–34,
        236
    export-biased, 136–37, 139, 142, 169
    import-biased, 137, 139, 160
    oil prices and, 180–81

    pace of, 239–40
    welfare effects (*See* welfare)
foreign policy, 9
free trade agreements
    employment growth and, 14, 42
    job concerns and, 4
    during Obama administration, 3
    policy implications, 248–49
Free Trade Area of the Americas, 248

gains from trade. *See* trade gains
GDP per capita
    export similarity and, 92, 97, 97n
    product quality by, 127n
general equilibrium simulation models, 154,
    158–59, 200
general equilibrium theories, 197–98
geographical composition of US imports,
    150–52
global financial crisis
    effects of, 3–4, 29
    policy responses to, 9, 238–39
    recovery from
        employment and, 42–43
        role of trade in, 33–34, 41
    trade deficit after, 40–42
globalization
    firm stability and, 49n
    of labor market, 60
    policy implications, 240
    wage distribution and, 218
global supply chains, 93, 209

good jobs, 30–31. *See also* manufacturing
    jobs
Great Britain, 139, 217n

Harmonized Tariff Schedule (HTS)
    classification data, 89, 91, 95, 95n,
    118
Hausmann, Ricardo, 103, 104, 110n, 140
head-to-head competition, 16–17, 91–131.
    See also competitiveness
    conclusions, 122–24, 236
    export overlap, 94–103, 120
        cumulative shares, 97–99, 98t
        similarity indices, 95–97, 96t
        unit values, 99–103, 101t–102t,
            107f–109f, 107–10
    intermediate inputs versus finished
        products, 118–20
    policy implications, 23, 26
    quality issues (*See* product quality)

head-to-head competition—*continued*
    technological sophistication, 103–15
        price dispersion by, 115–18, 116f
        vertical specialization, 110–11, 118
    welfare effects, 135
Heckscher, Eli, 187
Heckscher-Ohlin theory, 187–88
    comparative advantage, 137
    Krugman's theory and, 87n
    labor mobility, 190
    skill premiums, 206–209
    specialization patterns, 94, 140, 191
    Stolper-Samuelson theory merged with,
        189
heterogeneous workers, 196–98, 221
Hicks, John, 18, 135
    on welfare effects, 139–49
high-speed railroads, 88, 88n, 236
high-technology products
    Chinese share in, 88, 104–107, 209
    classification of, 104–107, 105t–106t
    competitiveness concerns and, 16–17,
        88, 91–94
    GDP per capita and, 127n
    policy implications, 243
    price differentiation in, 92, 115–18, 116f,
        144–45
    product cycle, 93–94
    quality differentiation, 128, 129–31, 209
    US trade in, 88–89, 91, 94, 157, 236
    vertical specialization in, 115, 118
home bias, 159
HOSS theory, 189
    measurement error, 216, 227–30
    restrictive assumptions, 189–95
    skill premium, 199–200, 205–209, 212,
        219
    worker heterogeneity, 196–98, 221

immigration, 27
immiserizing growth, 137n
import(s)
    composition of, 22, 36–37, 103, 139
        exchange rates and, 168
        geographical, 150–52
    demand and, 33–34, 37–42
    employment content of, 11, 35–36, 36f,
        43
    prices of (See prices)
import-biased growth, 137, 139, 160
import-share-weighted prices, 213–14, 214t
import substitution
    close, 87, 89
    elasticity of, 131, 131n, 192, 192n, 211n

imperfect, 191–92
perfect, 124
policy implications, 244
price differences, 93
income elasticity, 73, 169n
    oil, 176–78
income inequality
    overview of, 87–89
    causes of, 199–202
    gains from trade and, 136
    policy implications, 25, 249
    policy response to, 10
India
    export similarity, 96t, 96–97
    garment industry, 133
    head-to-head competition, 23, 26
    offshoring to, 2, 15, 29, 42, 48, 51–52,
        202
    oil prices and, 10
    per capita income, 142, 237
    productivity growth, 237, 237n
    trade agreements, 249
induced demand, 34, 37, 39b, 40, 43
industrial policy, 5, 24–25, 242–44
Information Technology Agreement (WTO),
    115n
innovation, 24, 237, 241–44
Input-Output Tables (BEA), 45–46
    manufacturing jobs, 59b–60b, 80, 81f,
        218n
    worker classification, 207b
Integrated Public Use Microdata Series-
        Current Population Survey
        (IPUMS-CPS), 225n
intermediate goods
    manufacturing trade in, 18, 92–94,
        118–20
        skill intensity and, 211
        wage inequality and, 194–95
international capital flows, 26–27
international trade. See trade
investment expenditures, 77–79

Job Opening and Labor Turnover Survey
    (BLS), 47
jobs. See employment

Keynes, John Maynard, 34, 158n
Krugman, Paul
    competitiveness concerns, 16, 124
    on factor content, 210
    on income elasticity, 169n
    on sector bias, 190n
    skill intensity simulation, 210–12, 211n

on technological diffusion, 138*n*
on trade gains, 138–39
trade models used by, 11–12
wage inequality concerns, 7–8, 87–89,
137*n*, 187, 202, 203*n*, 219

labor market. *See also* employment; worker(s)
closing of, 60–63
imperfections, 195–96
surveys of, 46–52, 64*n*–65*n*
volatility of, 14
labor mobility, wages and, 53, 189–95
labor productivity. *See* productivity growth
labor supply, 34, 194–95
Laspeyres index (BLS), 149
Linder model, 137, 140
living standards
effects of trade on, 11, 152, 165
policy implications, 24
location. *See also* offshoring
of manufacturing jobs, 59*b*–60*b*, 84
tradable services and, 62
wages and, 53
lost jobs, 30, 45–52
causes of, 11, 14, 46
deindustrialization and, 67
empirical studies of, 50–51
policy implications, 25, 31, 55, 250–51
services, 51–52
survey evidence, 48–50

macroeconomic policy, 31, 42–43, 238
magnification effect, 188, 215
mandated wages, 216–17, 231–33
manufacturing
demand for goods, 11, 73–77, 76*f*, 85
policy implications, 240–41, 244
versus services, 75–76, 76*f*, 85
finished goods, 18, 92–94, 118–20,
194–95, 211
intermediate goods, 18, 92–94, 118–20,
194–95, 211
investment expenditures, 77–79, 78*f*
per capita incomes and, 143–47
productivity growth in, 70–72, 71*f*, 82
skill intensity in, 221–22, 222*t*–223*t*
terms of trade, 144–45, 146*f*
trade deficits in, 4–5, 11, 15–16, 31,
57–58
employment and, 79–84, 81*f*–83*f*
manufacturing jobs
benefits of trade for, 83–84, 236
decline in, 14–16, 57–58, 58*f*, 63–67, 85
deindustrialization and, 67–79

international comparisons, 66*f*, 66–67,
67*t*
labor market closure and, 60–63
multiplier, 59*b*–60*b*
offshoring and, 67, 84
policy implications, 31
productivity growth and, 11, 15, 17–18,
31, 58, 68–72, 69*t*, 71*f*, 82, 85
public's concerns about, 4, 30
trade deficits and, 11, 79–84, 81*f*–83*f*
wage inequality, 54
mass-layoff separations, 48, 48*n*
Mass Layoff Statistics (BLS), 48, 48*n*
migration, 27
monetary policy
employment and, 31, 42–43
study implications for, 24–25, 238
multilateral trading system, 25
multinational companies, employment data
on, 84
multiplier framework, 38, 39*b*–40*b*, 43
manufacturing employment, 59*b*–60*b*

National Association of Manufacturing
(NAM), 59*b*
national savings, 23, 31, 239
natural gas, 182
newly industrialized economies (NIEs),
specialization patterns in, 140–41
nontradable sectors, employment in, 60
North American Free Trade Agreement
(NAFTA), 4, 42, 54, 54*n*, 143, 202
North American Industry Classification
System (NAICS)
Chinese exports, 111*b*
industry payroll shares, 223*t*, 223–25
productivity data, 213, 214*t*
skill intensity, 206, 208*f*
worker classification, 207*b*

Obama administration, 3, 9
offshoring
conclusions, 238
employment growth and, 11
firm stability and, 49*n*
intermediate inputs, 194*n*, 194–95
lost jobs and, 48, 51
manufacturing jobs and, 67, 84
obstacles to, 238*n*
price effects, 72–73
productivity and, 84
of services, 51–52
tradability and, 61–62
wage inequality and, 198, 216–17

Ohlin, Bertil, 158n, 187. *See also* Heckscher-
    Ohlin theory
oil prices, 171–83
    overview of, 20–21
    boom in, 174–79
    conclusions, 183
    economic effects of, 172–74, 173f
    as exceptional case, 12
    future scenarios, 179–83, 180t
    policy implications, 10, 25, 238, 250–51
    terms of trade and, 148
    trade balance and, 155, 163
    welfare effects, 178–79
oil speculators, 174
Organization of Petroleum Exporting
    Countries (OPEC), 174, 177
output, manufacturing jobs and, 58, 68–72,
    69t

per capita incomes
    export similarity and, 92, 97, 97n, 103
    manufactured goods and, 143–47, 144f
    specialization patterns and, 140–42, 141t
petroleum industry. *See* oil prices
policy implications, 238–51. *See also specific
        topic*
    overview of, 8–10, 23–25, 31
    foreign absorption, 240
    foreign growth, 239–40
    income inequality, 54–55, 249
    innovation, 241–44
    oil, 10, 25, 238, 250–51
    trade policy, 244–49
    US products, 240–41
    worker dislocation, 249–50
political factors, 26, 63
prices
    analysis of, 212–18
        measurement error, 216, 227–30
    Chinese trade shares and, 111b–113b
    of computers and electronic products,
        227
    data on, 202–203, 203f
    dispersion by technology classification,
        115–18, 116f
    factors of production and, 188 (*See also*
        Stolper-Samuelson theory)
    head-to-head competition and, 92–94
    of high-technology products, 92, 144–45
    import-share-weighted, 213–14, 214t
    intermediate inputs versus finished
        goods, 118–20, 194–95
    manufactured imports, 144–45,
        145f–146f

oil (*See* oil prices)
    productivity growth and, 71f, 71–73,
        189–90, 212–13, 215–16
    product quality and, 92–93, 120–22,
        121f, 125, 129–31
    of services versus goods, 75–76, 76f
    skill-share-weighted, 214–16, 215f
    terms of trade and, 166–68
processing trade, product quality and, 131,
    131n
product(s). *See also* export(s)
    categories of, competitiveness concerns
        and, 16–17, 92
    export similarity indices, 95–97, 96t
    factor intensity of, 94, 188n, 223
    high-tech (*See* high-technology
        products)
    noncompeting, specialization patterns,
        191
    prices of (*See* prices)
    quality of (*See* product quality)
    skill intensity of, 193, 205–209, 208f,
        218
    technology classification of, 104–107,
        105t–106t
product-cycle theory, 93–94
production costs
    product quality and, 120
    wages and, 52–53
productivity growth
    in China, 136–37, 148–49
    in developing countries, 237n
    intermediate inputs and, 194–95
    manufactures versus services, 70–72
    manufacturing jobs and, 11, 15, 17–18,
        31, 58, 68–72, 69t, 71f, 82, 85
    offshoring and, 84
    prices and, 71f, 71–73, 189–90, 212–13,
        215–16
    sector-biased, 190
    specialization patterns and, 159–60
    wages and, 52–53, 74b
    welfare effects, 136
product quality, 120–22, 209
    at country level, 129–31, 130f
    identification of, 121f, 121–22
    measurement of, 125–31
    prices and, 92–93, 120–22, 121f, 125,
        129–30
    production costs and, 120
    production process and, 131, 131n
    quality ladders, 128
    by technology classification, 122, 123f,
        128–29, 128t–129t

protectionism, 8, 9
public's concerns
    overview of, 2–6, 29–31, 87, 235
    good jobs, 30–31 (*See also* manufacturing
        jobs)
    lost jobs (*See* lost jobs)
    policy implications, 31
    total jobs (*See* total jobs)

quality. *See* product quality

Rand Corporation, 236
recessions. *See also* global financial crisis
    manufacturing jobs and, 82
    public's concerns and, 29
    trade deficit after, 40–42
relative unit values. *See* unit values
resource allocation, 139
Ricardo, David, 6
    trade model
        of trade performance, 159–61
        of welfare effects, 6, 17, 136, 139–40,
            153
Rodrik, Dani
    on elasticity of labor demand, 49n
    on free trade theory, 187n
    on productivity growth, 88
    on specialization patterns, 140
    on technological sophistication, 103,
        104, 106n, 110n
    on wage inequality, 196
Rybczynski effect, 189n

Samuelson, Paul
    competitiveness concerns, 16, 87–89
    on gains from trade, 133–34, 238
    on income inequality, 10
    on skill intensity, 193
    on specialization, 124
    on terms of trade, 185
    trade models used by, 11–12, 17, 19,
        153, 157 (*See also* Stolper-
        Samuelson theory)
    welfare concerns, 6–7, 17–18, 87–89,
        124, 135, 136–39, 165
savings, domestic, 23, 31
scale economies, 138n, 138–39
sectoral trade balances, 83–84
services
    demand for, versus goods, 75–76, 76f, 85
    income elasticity of, 73
    investment expenditures, 77–79, 78f
    offshoring of, 51–52
    productivity growth in, 70–72

terms of trade, 147–48
    tradability of, 61–62
similarity indices for exports, 95–97, 96t
skilled labor, 187–88, 196–99
    definition of, 207b
    simulation models, 210–12
    skill intensity measures, 205–209, 208f
    wage behavior, 203–205, 204f
skill intensity, 193, 205–209
    of developing-country imports, 221–25
    import share by, 206, 208f
    specialization and, 209, 212, 218–19
    US manufacturing industries by, 221–
        22, 222t–223t
skill premiums, 22, 199–219
    conclusions, 218–19
    factor content, 210, 218–19
    price analysis, 212–18
    recent developments, 202–209
        wage behavior, 203–205, 204f
    simulation models, 210–12
skill-share-weighted prices, 214–16, 215f
solar energy, 88, 236, 251
specialization
    across-product, 91–92, 120
    assumptions about, in trade theories,
        62–63, 190–95
    changes in, 192–94
    classical models of, 159–60
    factor endowments and, 187–88
    gains from trade and, 136
    incomplete, 237n
    patterns of, 92
        competitiveness and, 16–17
        income levels and, 140–42, 141t
        wage inequality and, 21–22
        welfare effects, 18
    product technology classification and,
        104–107
    skill intensity and, 209, 212, 218–19
    vertical, 110–11, 118
    within-product, 107, 117, 131
specific-factor theories, 196–98
Stolper, Wolfgang, 188
Stolper-Samuelson theory, 188
    factor prices, 62–63, 214
    as general equilibrium theory, 198
    Heckscher-Ohlin theory merged with,
        189
    import substitution, 124
    intermediate inputs, 194–95
    magnification effect, 188, 215
    skill premium, 200–201, 202n
    worker heterogeneity, 197n

substitution. *See* import substitution
Summers, Lawrence
    on oil prices, 12, 171, 183
    on value added per worker, 242n
    welfare and inequality concerns, 6–8, 7n
supply
    labor, 34, 194–95
    manufacturing jobs and, 67–79
    oil, 174–79, 175t, 177t
supply chains, 93, 209

tariffs, 25, 162, 231–32
tax policy, 24–25, 242n, 243–44, 249
technological diffusion, 26, 138n, 160
technological sophistication, 103–15
    conclusions, 236–38
    deindustrialization and, 67
    product classification, 104–107,
        105t–106t
        price dispersion by, 115–18, 116f
        product quality by, 122, 123f,
            128–29, 128t–129t
        unit values by, 110, 114t
        US-China disaggregated analysis,
           111b–113b
    vertical specialization, 110–11, 118
terms of trade
    behavior of, 18, 135–36, 142f, 142–47,
        147f
    competitiveness concerns and, 94
    exchange rates and, 166–68
    foreign growth and, 138
    gains from trade and, 133–34
    manufacturing, 144–45, 146f
    oil prices and, 148
    other goods and services, 147–48
    policy implications, 242–43
    trade balance and, 19–20, 153–54, 158
        graphical analysis of, 162–65,
            163f–164f
    US-China, 145, 146f
    wage inequality and, 185
    welfare effects, 17–18, 135, 149
Törnqvist index, 149
total employment, 13–14
    sector share in, 60–61, 61f
total factor productivity (TFP), 69–72, 71f
total jobs, 33–43
    defined, 29
    demand and, 34–42
    policy implications, 31
tradability
    lost jobs and, 49, 49n
    of manufactured products, 57

    manufacturing jobs and, 60–61
    of services, 61–62
Trade Adjustment Assistance (TAA)
        Program, 48
trade barriers, 25
trade deficits, 153–69
    causes of, 13
    competitiveness and, 156–57
    correcting for, 157–62
        trade performance assessment,
            160–62
    data on, 154–57, 155f–156f
    employment and, 35–42
    in high-tech goods, 88, 157, 236
    impact of, 19–20, 152
    import growth and, 33–34, 40–42
    in manufacturing, 5, 11, 15–16, 31, 57–58
        employment and, 11, 79–84, 81f–83f
    oil prices and, 155, 163
    policy implications, 24
    terms of trade and, 19–20, 153–54, 158,
        162
        graphical analysis of, 162–65,
            163f–164f
    US growth performance and, 2
    welfare effects
        simulation models, 165–67
        trade models, 167–69
trade equation framework, 154
trade gains
    from developing-country growth, 9–12,
        23–25, 42, 133–34, 149–52
    estimation of, 136, 149–52, 151t
    sources of, 136–39
    specialization and, 136
trade liberalization
    economist's support for, 8
    policy implications, 244
    wage inequality and, 189
trade performance, assessment of, 160–62
trade policy
    guideline for, 12
    manufacturing trade, 5
    during Obama administration, 3, 9
    study implications for, 24–25, 244–49
trade volume, wage inequality and, 202
transfer problem, 158, 158n
transfer system
    for displaced workers, 25, 249–50
    for income distribution, 249
transfer theory, of trade performance,
        160–62, 161f
Trans-Pacific Partnership, 25, 248–49
transportation costs, 127, 127n

unemployment. *See also* employment
  during global financial crisis, 42
  involuntary, 34, 47
  structural rate of, 34
United Kingdom, 139, 217*n*
United Nations Classification by Broad
      Economic Categories (BEC), 119*n*
United States
  development pattern in, 58
  global position of, 25–27
US Census Bureau, product classification,
      104, 110*n*
US Department of Commerce, high-
      technology products report, 88,
      124
US Department of Labor surveys, 46–47
US Department of Trade, Trade Adjustment
      Assistance (TAA) Program, 48
US Energy Information Administration
      (EIA), future scenarios, 172,
      179–83, 180*t*
US International Trade Commission, 94
  End-Use Classification, 119*n*
  product classification, 104
US National Science Foundation (NSF),
      Science Indicators, 88
unit values
  export overlap by, 99–103, 101*t*–102*t*,
      107*f*–109*f*, 107–10
  intermediate inputs versus finished
      goods, 118–20, 119*t*
  measurement of, 118
  by technology classification, 110, 114*t*,
      129*t*, 129–30
unskilled labor, 187–88, 196–99
  definition of, 207*b*
  developing-country imports, 221–25
  simulation models, 210–12
  skill intensity measures, 205–209, 208*f*
  wage behavior, 203–205, 204*f*
Uruguay Round, 4

vertical specialization, 110–11, 118

wage inequality, 187–98
  overview of, 7–8, 21, 185
  competitiveness concerns, 16–17
  effects of trade on, 11–12
  evidence for, 22–23
  at firm and industry levels, 53–54, 196
  indicators of, 205

labor market imperfections, 195–96
labor mobility, 53, 189–95
lost jobs, 52–54
mandated wage changes, 216–17, 231–33
policy implications, 54–55
productivity growth, 74*b*
skill premiums (*See* skill premiums)
specialization, 190–95
specific factors, 196–98
trade balance, 159–60
wage distribution, 217–18
worker classification and, 203–205, 204*f*
worker heterogeneity, 196–98, 211
wage polarization hypothesis, 218
welfare, 135–52. *See also* trade gains
  overview of, 17–18, 87–89
  aggregate, 6–7, 22–23
  Hicks' conjecture, 139–49
    developing-country impact, 148–49
    evidence, 141–42, 142*f*
    first two phases (1950–80), 143
    manufactured goods (1980–2009),
      143–47, 144*f*–147*f*
    other goods and services (1980–
      2009), 147–48
  oil prices and, 178–79
  theory on, 136–39
  trade balance and (*See* trade deficits)
worker(s). *See also* employment; labor market
  classification of, 187–88, 196–99
    definitions, 207*b*
    developing-country imports, 221–25
    simulation models, 210–12
    skill intensity measures, 205–209,
      208*f*
    wage behavior by, 203–205, 204*f*
    wage distribution, 217–18
  displacement of (*See* lost jobs)
  heterogeneity of, 196–98, 211
  insecurity of, 49–50
  mobility of, 53, 189–95
World Trade Organization (WTO), 25, 42
  alternative energy products, 88
  Chinese accession, 42, 245
  dispute settlement system, 245–46
  Doha Round, 3, 25, 246
  Information Technology Agreement,
      115*n*
  oil tariffs, 251, 251*n*
  role of, 245–49
  Uruguay Round, 4

Other Publications from the
Peterson Institute for International Economics

WORKING PAPERS

94-1 APEC and Regional Trading Arrangements in the Pacific   Jeffrey A. Frankel with Shang-Jin Wei and Ernesto Stein

94-2 Towards an Asia Pacific Investment Code   Edward M. Graham

94-3 Merchandise Trade in the APEC Region: Is There Scope for Liberalization on an MFN Basis? Paul Wonnacott

94-4 The Automotive Industry in Southeast Asia: Can Protection Be Made Less Costly?   Paul Wonnacott

94-5 Implications of Asian Economic Growth   Marcus Noland

95-1 APEC: The Bogor Declaration and the Path Ahead   C. Fred Bergsten

95-2 From Bogor to Miami...and Beyond: Regionalism in the Asia Pacific and the Western Hemisphere   Jeffrey J. Schott

95-3 Has Asian Export Performance Been Unique?   Marcus Noland

95-4 Association of Southeast Asian Nations and ASEAN Free Trade Area: Chronology and Statistics Gautam Jaggi

95-5 The North Korean Economy Marcus Noland

95-6 China and the International Economic System   Marcus Noland

96-1 APEC after Osaka: Toward Free Trade by 2010/2020   C. Fred Bergsten

96-2 Public Policy, Private Preferences, and the Japanese Trade Pattern Marcus Noland

96-3 German Lessons for Korea: The Economics of Unification Marcus Noland

96-4 Research and Development Activities and Trade Specialization in Japan Marcus Noland

96-5 China's Economic Reforms: Chronology and Statistics Gautam Jaggi, Mary Rundle, Daniel H. Rosen, and Yuichi Takahashi

96-6 US-China Economic Relations Marcus Noland

96-7 The Market Structure Benefits of Trade and Investment Liberalization Raymond Atje and Gary Clyde Hufbauer

96-8 The Future of US-Korea Economic Relations   Marcus Noland

96-9 Competition Policies in the Dynamic Industrializing Economies: The Case of China, Korea, and Chinese Taipei Edward M. Graham

96-10 Modeling Economic Reform in North Korea   Marcus Noland, Sherman Robinson, and Monica Scatasta

96-11 Trade, Investment, and Economic Conflict Between the United States and Asia   Marcus Noland

96-12 APEC in 1996 and Beyond: The Subic Summit   C. Fred Bergsten

96-13 Some Unpleasant Arithmetic Concerning Unification Marcus Noland

96-14 Restructuring Korea's Financial Sector for Greater Competitiveness Marcus Noland

96-15 Competitive Liberalization and Global Free Trade: A Vision for the 21st Century   C. Fred Bergsten

97-1 Chasing Phantoms: The Political Economy of USTR   Marcus Noland

97-2 US-Japan Civil Aviation: Prospects for Progress   Jacqueline McFadyen

97-3 Open Regionalism   C. Fred Bergsten

97-4 Lessons from the Bundesbank on the Occasion of Its 40th (and Second to Last?) Birthday   Adam S. Posen

97-5 The Economics of Korean Unification Marcus Noland, Sherman Robinson, and Li-Gang Liu

98-1 The Costs and Benefits of Korean Unification   Marcus Noland, Sherman Robinson, and Li-Gang Liu

98-2 Asian Competitive Devaluations Li-Gang Liu, Marcus Noland, Sherman Robinson, and Zhi Wang

98-3 Fifty Years of the GATT/WTO: Lessons from the Past for Strategies or the Future   C. Fred Bergsten

98-4 NAFTA Supplemental Agreements: Four Year Review Jacqueline McFadyen

98-5 Local Government Spending: Solving the Mystery of Japanese Fiscal Packages   Hiroko Ishii and Erika Wada

98-6 The Global Economic Effects of the Japanese Crisis   Marcus Noland, Sherman Robinson, and Zhi Wang

98-7 The Relationship Between Trade and Foreign Investment: Empirical Results for Taiwan and South Korea Li-Gang Liu, The World Bank, and Edward M. Graham

99-1 Rigorous Speculation: The Collapse and Revival of the North Korean Economy   Marcus Noland, Sherman Robinson, and Tao Wang

99-2 Famine in North Korea: Causes and Cures   Marcus Noland, Sherman Robinson, and Tao Wang

99-3 Competition Policy and FDI: A Solution in Search of a Problem? Marcus Noland

99-4 The Continuing Asian Financial Crisis: Global Adjustment and Trade
Marcus Noland, Sherman Robinson, and Zhi Wang

99-5 Why EMU Is Irrelevant for the German Economy Adam S. Posen

99-6 The Global Trading System and the Developing Countries in 2000
C. Fred Bergsten

99-7 Modeling Korean Unification
Marcus Noland, Sherman Robinson, and Tao Wang

99-8 Sovereign Liquidity Crisis: The Strategic Case for a Payments Standstill
Marcus Miller and Lei Zhang

99-9 The Case for Joint Management of Exchange Rate Flexibility
C. Fred Bergsten, Olivier Davanne, and Pierre Jacquet

99-10 Does Talk Matter After All? Inflation Targeting and Central Bank Behavior
Kenneth N. Kuttner and Adam S. Posen

99-11 Hazards and Precautions: Tales of International Finance Gary C. Hufbauer and Erika Wada

99-12 The Globalization of Services: What Has Happened? What Are the Implications?
Gary Clyde Hufbauer and Tony Warren

00-1 Regulatory Standards in the WTO
Keith Maskus

00-2 International Economic Agreements and the Constitution Richard M. Goodman and John M. Frost

00-3 Electronic Commerce in Developing Countries Catherine L. Mann

00-4 The New Asian Challenge
C. Fred Bergsten

00-5 How the Sick Man Avoided Pneumonia: The Philippines in the Asian Financial Crisis Marcus Noland

00-6 Inflation, Monetary Transparency, and G-3 Exchange Rate Volatility
Kenneth N. Kuttner and Adam S. Posen

00-7 Transatlantic Issues in Electronic Commerce Catherine L. Mann

00-8 Strengthening the International Financial Architecture: Where Do We Stand? Morris Goldstein

00-9 On Currency Crises and Contagion
Marcel Fratzscher

01-1 Price Level Convergence and Inflation in Europe John H. Rogers, Gary Clyde Hufbauer, and Erika Wada

01-2 Subsidies, Market Closure, Cross-Border Investment, and Effects on Competition: The Case of FDI on the Telecommunications Sector
Edward M. Graham

01-3 Foreign Direct Investment in China: Effects on Growth and Economic Performance Edward M. Graham and Erika Wada

01-4 IMF Structural Conditionality: How Much Is Too Much? Morris Goldstein

01-5 Unchanging Innovation and Changing Economic Performance in Japan
Adam S. Posen

01-6 Rating Banks in Emerging Markets
Liliana Rojas-Suarez

01-7 Beyond Bipolar: A Three-Dimensional Assessment of Monetary Frameworks
Kenneth N. Kuttner and Adam S. Posen

01-8 Finance and Changing US-Japan Relations: Convergence Without Leverage — Until Now Adam S. Posen

01-9 Macroeconomic Implications of the New Economy Martin Neil Baily

01-10 Can International Capital Standards Strengthen Banks in Emerging Markets?
Liliana Rojas-Suarez

02-1 Moral Hazard and the US Stock Market: Analyzing the "Greenspan Put"?
Marcus Miller, Paul Weller, and Lei Zhang

02-2 Passive Savers and Fiscal Policy Effectiveness in Japan
Kenneth N. Kuttner and Adam S. Posen

02-3 Home Bias, Transaction Costs, and Prospects for the Euro: A More Detailed Analysis Catherine L. Mann and Ellen E. Meade

02-4 Toward a Sustainable FTAA: Does Latin America Meet the Necessary Financial Preconditions? Liliana Rojas-Suarez

02-5 Assessing Globalization's Critics: "Talkers Are No Good Doers???"
Kimberly Ann Elliott, Debayani Kar, and J. David Richardson

02-6 Economic Issues Raised by Treatment of Takings under NAFTA Chapter 11
Edward M. Graham

03-1 Debt Sustainability, Brazil, and the IMF
Morris Goldstein

03-2 Is Germany Turning Japanese?
Adam S. Posen

03-3 Survival of the Best Fit: Exposure to Low-Wage Countries and the (Uneven) Growth of US Manufacturing Plants
Andrew B. Bernard, J. Bradford Jensen, and Peter K. Schott

03-4 Falling Trade Costs, Heterogeneous Firms, and Industry Dynamics
Andrew B. Bernard, J. Bradford Jensen, and Peter K. Schott

03-5 Famine and Reform in North Korea
Marcus Noland

03-6 Empirical Investigations in Inflation Targeting Yifan Hu

03-7 Labor Standards and the Free Trade Area of the Americas Kimberly Ann Elliott

03-8 Religion, Culture, and Economic Performance Marcus Noland

03-9 It Takes More than a Bubble to Become Japan Adam S. Posen

03-10 The Difficulty of Discerning What's Too Tight: Taylor Rules and Japanese Monetary Policy Adam S. Posen and Kenneth N. Kuttner

04-1 Adjusting China's Exchange Rate Policies Morris Goldstein

04-2 Popular Attitudes, Globalization, and
Risk   Marcus Noland
04-3 Selective Intervention and Growth: The
Case of Korea   Marcus Noland
05-1 Outsourcing and Offshoring: Pushing
the European Model Over the Hill,
Rather Than Off the Cliff!
Jacob Funk Kirkegaard
05-2 China's Role in the Revived Bretton
Woods System: A Case of Mistaken
Identity   Morris Goldstein and Nicholas
R. Lardy
05-3 Affinity and International Trade
Marcus Noland
05-4 South Korea's Experience with
International Capital Flows
Marcus Noland
05-5 Explaining Middle Eastern
Authoritarianism   Marcus Noland
05-6 Postponing Global Adjustment: An
Analysis of the Pending Adjustment of
Global Imbalances   Edwin M. Truman
05-7 What Might the Next Emerging Market
Financial Crisis Look Like?
Morris Goldstein, assisted by Anna Wong
05-8 Egypt after the Multi-Fiber Arrangement:
Global Approval and Textile Supply
Chains as a Route for Industrial
Upgrading   Dan Magder
05-9 Tradable Services: Understanding the
Scope and Impact of Services Offshoring
J. Bradford Jensen and Lori G. Kletzer
05-10 Importers, Exporters, and Multinationals:
A Portrait of Firms in the US that Trade
Goods   Andrew B. Bernard, J. Bradford
Jensen, and Peter K. Schott
05-11 The US Trade Deficit: A Disaggregated
Perspective   Catherine L. Mann and
Katharina Plück
05-12 Prospects for Regional Free Trade in Asia
Gary Clyde Hufbauer and Yee Wong
05-13 Predicting Trade Expansion under FTAs
and Multilateral Agreements
Dean A. DeRosa and John P. Gilbert
05-14 The East Asian Industrial Policy
Experience: Implications for the Middle
East   Marcus Noland and Howard Pack
05-15 Outsourcing and Skill Imports: Foreign
High-Skilled Workers on H-1B and L-1
Visas in the United States
Jacob Funk Kirkegaard
06-1 Why Central Banks Should Not Burst
Bubbles   Adam S. Posen
06-2 The Case for an International Reserve
Diversification Standard
Edwin M. Truman and Anna Wong
06-3 Offshoring in Europe — Evidence of a
Two-Way Street from Denmark
Peter Ørberg Jensen, Jacob Funk
Kirkegaard, and Nicolai Søndergaard
Laugesen
06-4 The External Policy of the Euro Area:
Organizing for Foreign Exchange
Intervention   C. Randall Henning

06-5 The Eurasian Growth Paradox
Anders Åslund and Nazgul Jenish
06-6 Has EMU Had Any Impact on the Degree
of Wage Restraint?   Adam S. Posen and
Daniel Popov Gould
06-7 Firm Structure, Multinationals, and
Manufacturing Plant Deaths   Andrew B.
Bernard and J. Bradford Jensen
07-1 The Trade Effects of Preferential
Arrangements: New Evidence from the
Australia Productivity Commission
Dean A. DeRosa
07-2 Offshoring, Outsourcing, and Production
Relocation—Labor-Market Effects in the
OECD Countries and Developing Asia
Jacob Funk Kirkegaard
07-3 Do Markets Care Who Chairs the Central
Bank?   Kenneth N. Kuttner and Adam S.
Posen
07-4 Industrial Policy, Innovative Policy,
and Japanese Competitiveness: Japan's
Pursuit of Competitive Advantage
Marcus Noland
07-5 A (Lack of) Progress Report on China's
Exchange Rate Policies   Morris Goldstein
07-6 Measurement and Inference in
International Reserve Diversification
Anna Wong
07-7 North Korea's External Economic
Relations   Stephan Haggard and Marcus
Noland
07-8 Congress, Treasury, and the
Accountability of Exchange Rate Policy:
How the 1988 Trade Act Should Be
Reformed   C. Randall Henning
07-9 Merry Sisterhood or Guarded
Watchfulness? Cooperation Between the
International Monetary Fund and the
World Bank   Michael Fabricius
08-1 Exit Polls: Refugee Assessments of North
Korea's Transitions   Yoonok Chang,
Stephan Haggard, and Marcus Noland
08-2 Currency Undervaluation and Sovereign
Wealth Funds: A New Role for the WTO
Aaditya Mattoo and Arvind Subramanian
08-3 Exchange Rate Economics
John Williamson
08-4 Migration Experiences of North Korean
Refugees: Survey Evidence from China
Yoonok Chang, Stephan Haggard, and
Marcus Noland
08-5 Korean Institutional Reform in
Comparative Perspective   Marcus Noland
and Erik Weeks
08-6 Estimating Consistent Fundamental
Equilibrium Exchange Rates
William R. Cline
08-7 Policy Liberalization and FDI Growth,
1982 to 2006   Matthew Adler and
Gary Clyde Hufbauer
08-8 Multilateralism Beyond Doha
Aaditya Mattoo and Arvind Subramanian
08-9 Famine in North Korea Redux?
Stephan Haggard and Marcus Noland

08-10 Recent Trade Patterns and Modes of Supply in Computer and Information Services in the United States and NAFTA Partners   Jacob Funk Kirkegaard

08-11 On What Terms Is the IMF Worth Funding?   Edwin M. Truman

08-12 The (Non) Impact of UN Sanctions on North Korea   Marcus Noland

09-1 The GCC Monetary Union: Choice of Exchange Rate Regime   Mohsin S. Khan

09-2 Policy Liberalization and US Merchandise Trade Growth, 1980–2006   Gary Clyde Hufbauer and Matthew Adler

09-3 American Multinationals and American Economic Interests: New Dimensions to an Old Debate   Theodore H. Moran

09-4 Sanctioning North Korea: The Political Economy of Denuclearization and Proliferation   Stephan Haggard and Marcus Noland

09-5 Structural and Cyclical Trends in Net Employment over US Business Cycles, 1949–2009: Implications for the Next Recovery and Beyond Jacob F. Kirkegaard

09-6 What's on the Table? The Doha Round as of August 2009   Matthew Adler, Claire Brunel, Gary Clyde Hufbauer, and Jeffrey J. Schott

09-7 Criss-Crossing Globalization: Uphill Flows of Skill-Intensive Goods and Foreign Direct Investment   Aaditya Mattoo and Arvind Subramanian

09-8 Reform from Below: Behavioral and Institutional Change in North Korea   Stephan Haggard and Marcus Noland

09-9 The World Trade Organization and Climate Change: Challenges and Options   Gary Clyde Hufbauer and Jisun Kim

09-10 A Tractable Model of Precautionary Reserves, Net Foreign Assets, or Sovereign Wealth Funds   Christopher D. Carroll and Olivier Jeanne

09-11 The Impact of the Financial Crisis on Emerging Asia   Morris Goldstein and Daniel Xie

09-12 Capital Flows to Developing Countries: The Allocation Puzzle   Pierre-Olivier Gourinchas and Olivier Jeanne

09-13 Mortgage Loan Modifications: Program Incentives and Restructuring Design   Dan Magder

09-14 It Should Be a Breeze: Harnessing the Potential of Open Trade and Investment Flows in the Wind Energy Industry   Jacob Funk Kirkegaard, Thilo Hanemann, and Lutz Weischer

09-15 Reconciling Climate Change and Trade Policy   Aaditya Mattoo, Arvind Subramanian, Dominique van der Mensbrugghe, and Jianwu He

09-16 The International Monetary Fund and Regulatory Challenges   Edwin M. Truman

10-1 Estimation of De Facto Flexibility Parameter and Basket Weights in Evolving Exchange Rate Regimes   Jeffrey Frankel and Daniel Xie

10-2 Economic Crime and Punishment in North Korea   Stephan Haggard and Marcus Noland

10-3 Intra-Firm Trade and Product Contractibility   Andrew B. Bernard, J. Bradford Jensen, Stephen J. Redding, and Peter K. Schott

10-4 The Margins of US Trade   Andrew B. Bernard, J. Bradford Jensen, Stephen J. Redding, and Peter K. Schott

10-5 Excessive Volatility in Capital Flows: A Pigouvian Taxation Approach   Olivier Jeanne and Anton Korinek

10-6 Toward a Sunny Future? Global Integration in the Solar PV Industry   Jacob Funk Kirkegaard, Thilo Hanemann, Lutz Weischer, Matt Miller

10-7 The Realities and Relevance of Japan's Great Recession: Neither Ran nor Rashomon   Adam S. Posen

10-8 Do Developed and Developing Countries Compete Head to Head in High Tech?   Lawrence Edwards and Robert Z. Lawrence

10-9 US Trade and Wages: The Misleading Implications of Conventional Trade Theory   Lawrence Edwards and Robert Z. Lawrence

10-10 Wholesalers and Retailers in US Trade   Andrew B. Bernard, J. Bradford Jensen, Stephen J. Redding, and Peter K. Schott

10-11 The Design and Effects of Monetary Policy in Sub-Saharan African Countries   Mohsin S. Khan

10-12 Managing Credit Booms and Busts: A Pigouvian Taxation Approach   Olivier Jeanne and Anton Korinek

10-13 The G-20 and International Financial Institution Governance   Edwin M. Truman

10-14 Reform of the Global Financial Architecture   Garry J. Schinasi and Edwin M. Truman

10-15 A Role for the G-20 in Addressing Climate Change?   Trevor Houser

10-16 Exchange Rate Policy in Brazil   John Williamson

10-17 Trade Disputes Between China and the United States: Growing Pains so Far, Worse Ahead?   Gary Clyde Hufbauer and Jared C. Woollacott

10-18 Sovereign Bankruptcy in the European Union in the Comparative Perspective   Leszek Balcerowicz

11-1 Current Account Imbalances Coming Back   Joseph Gagnon

11-2 Too Big to Fail: The Transatlantic Debate   Morris Goldstein and Nicolas Véron

11-3 Foreign Direct Investment in Times of Crisis   Lauge Skovgaard Poulsen and Gary Clyde Hufbauer

11-4   A Generalized Fact and Model of Long-
       Run Economic Growth: Kaldor Fact as a
       Special Case   Daniel Danxia Xie
11-5   Integrating Reform of Financial
       Regulation with Reform of the
       International Monetary System
       Morris Goldstein
11-6   Capital Account Liberalization and the
       Role of the RMB   Nicholas Lardy and
       Patrick Douglass
11-7   Capital Controls: Myth and Reality — A
       Portfolio Balance Approach
       Nicolas E. Magud, Carmen M. Reinhart,
       and Kenneth S. Rogoff
11-8   Resource Management and Transition in
       Central Asia, Azerbaijan, and Mongolia
       Richard Pomfret
11-9   Coordinating Regional and Multilateral
       Financial Institutions
       C. Randall Henning
11-10 The Liquidation of Government Debt
       Carmen M. Reinhart and M. Belen
       Sbrancia
11-11 Foreign Manufacturing Multinationals
       and the Transformation of the Chinese
       Economy: New Measurements, New
       Perspectives   Theodore H. Moran
11-12 Sovereign Wealth Funds: Is Asia
       Different?   Edwin M. Truman
11-13 Integration in the Absence of
       Institutions: China-North Korea Cross-
       Border Exchange   Stephan Haggard,
       Jennifer Lee, and Marcus Noland
11-14 Renminbi Rules: The Conditional
       Imminence of the Reserve Currency
       Transition   Arvind Subramanian
11-15 How Flexible Can Inflation Targeting Be
       and Still Work?   Kenneth N. Kuttner and
       Adam S. Posen
11-16 Asia and Global Financial Governance
       C. Randall Henning and Mohsin S. Khan
11-17 India's Growth in the 2000s: Four Facts
       Utsav Kumar and Arvind Subramanian
11-18 Applying Hubbert Curves and
       Linearization to Rock Phosphate
       Cullen S. Hendrix
11-19 Delivering on US Climate Finance
       Commitments   Trevor Houser and Jason
       Selfe
11-20 Rent(s) Asunder: Sectoral Rent
       Extraction Possibilities and Bribery by
       Multinational Corporations
       Edmund Malesky, Nathan Jensen, and
       Dimitar Gueorguiev
11-21 Asian Regional Policy Coordination
       Edwin M. Truman
11-22 China and the World Trading System
       Aaditya Mattoo and Arvind Subramanian
12-1   Fiscal Federalism: US History for
       Architects of Europe's Fiscal Union
       C. Randall Henning and Martin Kessler
12-2   Financial Reform after the Crisis: An
       Early Assessment   Nicolas Véron

12-3   Chinese Investment in Latin American
       Resources: The Good, the Bad, and the
       Ugly   Barbara Kotschwar, Theodore H.
       Moran, and Julia Muir
12-4   Spillover Effects of Exchange Rates: A
       Study of the Renminbi   Aaditya Mattoo,
       Prachi Mishra, and Arvind Subramanian
12-5   Global Imbalances and Foreign Asset
       Expansion by Developing-Economy
       Central Banks   Joseph Gagnon
12-6   Transportation and Communication
       Infrastructure in Latin America: Lessons
       from Asia   Barbara Kotschwar
12-7   Lessons from Reforms in Central and
       Eastern Europe in the Wake of the Global
       Financial Crisis   Anders Åslund
12-8   Networks, Trust, and Trade: The
       Microeconomics of China-North Korea
       Integration   Stephan Haggard and
       Marcus Noland
12-9   The Microeconomics of North-South
       Korean Cross-Border Integration
       Stephan Haggard and Marcus Noland
12-10 The Dollar and Its Discontents
       Olivier Jeanne
12-11 Gender in Transition: The Case of North
       Korea   Stephan Haggard and Marcus
       Noland
12-12 Sovereign Debt Sustainability in Italy
       and Spain: A Probabilistic Approach
       William R. Cline
12-13 John Williamson and the Evolution of
       the International Monetary System
       Edwin M. Truman
12-14 Capital Account Policies and the Real
       Exchange Rate   Olivier Jeanne
12-15 Choice and Coercion in East Asian
       Exchange Rate Regimes
       C. Randall Henning
12-16 Transactions: A New Look at Services
       Sector Foreign Direct Investment in Asia
       Jacob Funk Kirkegaard
12-17 Prospects for Services Trade
       Negotiations   Jeffrey J. Schott, Minsoo
       Lee, and Julia Muir
12-18 Developing the Services Sector
       as Engine of Growth for Asia: An
       Overview   Marcus Noland, Donghyun
       Park, and Gemma B. Estrada
12-19 The Renminbi Bloc Is Here: Asia Down,
       Rest of the World to Go?
       Arvind Subramanian and Martin Kessler
12-20 Performance of the Services Sector in
       Korea: An Empirical Investigation
       Donghyun Park and Kwanho Shin
12-21 The Services Sector in Asia: Is It an
       Engine of Growth?
       Donghyun Park and Kwanho Shin
12-22 Assessing Potential Inflation
       Consequences of QE after Financial
       Crises   Samuel Reynard
12-23 Overlooked Opportunity: Tradable
       Business Services, Developing Asia, and
       Growth   J. Bradford Jensen

13-01 The Importance of Trade and Capital Imbalances in the European Debt Crisis Andrew Hughes Hallett and Juan Carlos Martinez Oliva

POLICY BRIEFS

98-1 The Asian Financial Crisis Morris Goldstein

98-2 The New Agenda with China C. Fred Bergsten

98-3 Exchange Rates for the Dollar, Yen, and Euro Simon Wren-Lewis

98-4 Sanctions-Happy USA Gary Clyde Hufbauer

98-5 The Depressing News from Asia Marcus Noland, Sherman Robinson, and Zhi Wang

98-6 The Transatlantic Economic Partnership Ellen L. Frost

98-7 A New Strategy for the Global Crisis C. Fred Bergsten

98-8 Reviving the "Asian Monetary Fund" C. Fred Bergsten

99-1 Implementing Japanese Recovery Adam S. Posen

99-2 A Radical but Workable Restructuring Plan for South Korea Edward M. Graham

99-3 Crawling Bands or Monitoring Bands: How to Manage Exchange Rates in a World of Capital Mobility John Williamson

99-4 Market Mechanisms to Reduce the Need for IMF Bailouts Catherine L. Mann

99-5 Steel Quotas: A Rigged Lottery Gary Clyde Hufbauer and Erika Wada

99-6 China and the World Trade Organization: An Economic Balance Sheet Daniel H. Rosen

99-7 Trade and Income Distribution: The Debate and New Evidence William R. Cline

99-8 Preserve the Exchange Stabilization Fund C. Randall Henning

99-9 Nothing to Fear but Fear (of Inflation) Itself Adam S. Posen

99-10 World Trade after Seattle: Implications for the United States Gary C. Hufbauer

00-1 The Next Trade Policy Battle C. Fred Bergsten

00-2 Decision-Making in the WTO Jeffrey J. Schott and Jayashree Watal

00-3 American Access to China's Market: The Congressional Vote on PNTR Gary Clyde Hufbauer and Daniel H. Rosen

00-4 Third Oil Shock: Real or Imaginary? Consequences and Policy Alternatives Philip K. Verleger, Jr.

00-5 The Role of the IMF: A Guide to the Reports John Williamson

00-6 The ILO and Enforcement of Core Labor Standards Kimberly Ann Elliott

00-7 "No" to Foreign Telecoms Equals "No" to the New Economy! Gary C. Hufbauer and Edward M. Graham

01-1 Brunei: A Turning Point for APEC? C. Fred Bergsten

01-2 A Prescription to Relieve Worker Anxiety Lori G. Kletzer and Robert E. Litan

01-3 The US Export-Import Bank: Time for an Overhaul Gary Clyde Hufbauer

01-4 Japan 2001—Decisive Action or Financial Panic Adam S. Posen

01-5 Fin(d)ing Our Way on Trade and Labor Standards? Kimberly Ann Elliott

01-6 Prospects for Transatlantic Competition Policy Mario Monti

01-7 The International Implications of Paying Down the Debt Edwin M. Truman

01-8 Dealing with Labor and Environment Issues in Trade Promotion Legislation Kimberly Ann Elliott

01-9 Steel: Big Problems, Better Solutions Gary Clyde Hufbauer and Ben Goodrich

01-10 Economic Policy Following the Terrorist Attacks Martin Neil Baily

01-11 Using Sanctions to Fight Terrorism Gary Clyde Hufbauer, Jeffrey J. Schott, and Barbara Oegg

02-1 Time for a Grand Bargain in Steel? Gary Clyde Hufbauer and Ben Goodrich

02-2 Prospects for the World Economy: From Global Recession to Global Recovery Michael Mussa

02-3 Sovereign Debt Restructuring: New Articles, New Contracts—or No Change? Marcus Miller

02-4 Support the Ex-Im Bank: It Has Work to Do! Gary Clyde Hufbauer and Ben Goodrich

02-5 The Looming Japanese Crisis Adam S. Posen

02-6 Capital-Market Access: New Frontier in the Sanctions Debate Gary Clyde Hufbauer and Barbara Oegg

02-7 Is Brazil Next? John Williamson

02-8 Further Financial Services Liberalization in the Doha Round? Wendy Dobson

02-9 Global Economic Prospects Michael Mussa

02-10 The Foreign Sales Corporation: Reaching the Last Act? Gary Clyde Hufbauer

03-1 Steel Policy: The Good, the Bad, and the Ugly Gary Clyde Hufbauer and Ben Goodrich

03-2 Global Economic Prospects: Through the Fog of Uncertainty Michael Mussa

03-3 Economic Leverage and the North Korean Nuclear Crisis Kimberly Ann Elliott

03-4 The Impact of Economic Sanctions on US Trade: Andrew Rose's Gravity Model Gary Clyde Hufbauer and Barbara Oegg

03-5 Reforming OPIC for the 21st Century Theodore H. Moran and C. Fred Bergsten

03-6 The Strategic Importance of US-Korea Economic Relations Marcus Noland

03-7 **Rules Against Earnings Stripping: Wrong Answer to Corporate Inversions** Gary Clyde Hufbauer and Ariel Assa

03-8 **More Pain, More Gain: Politics and Economics of Eliminating Tariffs** Gary Clyde Hufbauer and Ben Goodrich

03-9 **EU Accession and the Euro: Close Together or Far Apart?** Peter B. Kenen and Ellen E. Meade

03-10 **Next Move in Steel: Revocation or Retaliation?** Gary Clyde Hufbauer and Ben Goodrich

03-11 **Globalization of IT Services and White Collar Jobs: The Next Wave of Productivity Growth** Catherine L. Mann

04-1 **This Far and No Farther? Nudging Agricultural Reform Forward** Tim Josling and Dale Hathaway

04-2 **Labor Standards, Development, and CAFTA** Kimberly Ann Elliott

04-3 **Senator Kerry on Corporate Tax Reform: Right Diagnosis, Wrong Prescription** Gary Clyde Hufbauer and Paul Grieco

04-4 **Islam, Globalization, and Economic Performance in the Middle East** Marcus Noland and Howard Pack

04-5 **China Bashing 2004** Gary C. Hufbauer and Yee Wong

04-6 **What Went Right in Japan** Adam S. Posen

04-7 **What Kind of Landing for the Chinese Economy?** Morris Goldstein and Nicholas R. Lardy

05-1 **A Currency Basket for East Asia, Not Just China** John Williamson

05-2 **After Argentina** Anna Gelpern

05-3 **Living with Global Imbalances: A Contrarian View** Richard N. Cooper

05-4 **The Case for a New Plaza Agreement** William R. Cline

06-1 **The United States Needs German Economic Leadership** Adam S. Posen

06-2 **The Doha Round after Hong Kong** Gary Clyde Hufbauer and Jeffrey J. Schott

06-3 **Russia's Challenges as Chair of the G-8** Anders Åslund

06-4 **Negotiating the Korea–United States Free Trade Agreemen** Jeffrey J. Schott, Scott C. Bradford, and Thomas Moll

06-5 **Can Doha Still Deliver on the Development Agenda?** Kimberly Ann Elliott

06-6 **China: Toward a Consumption Driven Growth Path** Nicholas R. Lardy

06-7 **Completing the Doha Round** Jeffrey J. Schott

06-8 **Choosing Monetary Arrangements for the 21st Century: Problems of a Small Economy** John Williamson

06-9 **Can America Still Compete or Does It Need a New Trade Paradigm?** Martin Neil Baily and Robert Z. Lawrence

07-1 **The IMF Quota Formula: Linchpin of Fund Reform** Richard N. Cooper and Edwin M. Truman

07-2 **Toward a Free Trade Area of the Asia Pacific** C. Fred Bergsten

07-3 **China and Economic Integration in East Asia: Implications for the United States** C. Fred Bergsten

07-4 **Global Imbalances: Time for Action** Alan Ahearne, William R. Cline, Kyung Tae Lee, Yung Chul Park, Jean Pisani-Ferry, and John Williamson

07-5 **American Trade Politics in 2007: Building Bipartisan Compromise** I. M. Destler

07-6 **Sovereign Wealth Funds: The Need for Greater Transparency and Accountability** Edwin M. Truman

07-7 **The Korea-US Free Trade Agreement: A Summary Assessment** Jeffrey J. Schott

07-8 **The Case for Exchange Rate Flexibility in Oil-Exporting Economies** Brad Setser

08-1 **"Fear" and Offshoring: The Scope and Potential Impact of Imports and Exports of Services** J. Bradford Jensen and Lori G. Kletzer

08-2 **Strengthening Trade Adjustment Assistance** Howard F. Rosen

08-3 **A Blueprint for Sovereign Wealth Fund Best Practices** Edwin M. Truman

08-4 **A Security and Peace Mechanism for Northeast Asia: The Economic Dimension** Stephan Haggard and Marcus Noland

08-5 **World Trade at Risk** C. Fred Bergsten

08-6 **North Korea on the Precipice of Famine** Stephan Haggard, Marcus Noland, and Erik Weeks

08-7 **New Estimates of Fundamental Equilibrium Exchange Rates** William R. Cline and John Williamson

08-8 **Financial Repression in China** Nicholas R. Lardy

09-1 **Did Reagan Rule In Vain? A Closer Look at True Expenditure Levels in the United States and Europe** Jacob F. Kirkegaard

09-2 **Buy American: Bad for Jobs, Worse for Reputation** Gary Clyde Hufbauer and Jeffrey J. Schott

09-3 **A Green Global Recovery? Assessing US Economic Stimulus and the Prospects for International Coordination** Trevor Houser, Shashank Mohan, and Robert Heilmayr

09-4 **Money for the Auto Industry: Consistent with WTO Rules?** Claire Brunel and Gary Clyde Hufbauer

09-5 **The Future of the Chiang Mai Initiative: An Asian Monetary Fund?** C. Randall Henning

09-6 **Pressing the "Reset Button" on US-Russia Relations** Anders Åslund and Andrew Kuchins

09-7 **US Taxation of Multinational Corporations: What Makes Sense, What Doesn't** Gary Clyde Hufbauer and Jisun Kim

09-8 Energy Efficiency in Buildings: A Global Economic Perspective   Trevor Houser

09-9 The Alien Tort Statute of 1789: Time for a Fresh Look   Gary Clyde Hufbauer

09-10 2009 Estimates of Fundamental Equilibrium Exchange Rates   William R. Cline and John Williamson

09-11 Understanding Special Drawing Rights (SDRs)   John Williamson

09-12 US Interests and the International Monetary Fund   C. Randall Henning

09-13 A Solution for Europe's Banking Problem   Adam S. Posen and Nicolas Véron

09-14 China's Changing Outbound Foreign Direct Investment Profile: Drivers and Policy Implication   Daniel H. Rosen and Thilo Hanemann

09-15 India-Pakistan Trade: A Roadmap for Enhancing Economic Relations   Mohsin S. Khan

09-16 Pacific Asia and the Asia Pacific: The Choices for APEC   C. Fred Bergsten

09-17 The Economics of Energy Efficiency in Buildings   Trevor Houser

09-18 Setting the NAFTA Agenda on Climate Change   Jeffrey J. Schott and Meera Fickling

09-19 The 2008 Oil Price "Bubble"   Mohsin S. Khan

09-20 Why SDRs Could Rival the Dollar   John Williamson

09-21 The Future of the Dollar   Richard N. Cooper

09-22 The World Needs Further Monetary Ease, Not an Early Exit   Joseph E. Gagnon

10-1 The Winter of Their Discontent: Pyongyang Attacks the Market   Stephan Haggard and Marcus Noland

10-2 Notes on Equilibrium Exchange Rates: William R. Cline and John Williamson

10-3 Confronting Asset Bubbles, Too Big to Fail, and Beggar-thy-Neighbor Exchange Rate Policies   Morris Goldstein

10-4 After the Flop in Copenhagen   Gary Clyde Hufbauer and Jisun Kim

10-5 Copenhagen, the Accord, and the Way Forward   Trevor Houser

10-6 The Substitution Account as a First Step Toward Reform of the International Monetary System   Peter B. Kenen

10-7 The Sustainability of China's Recovery from the Global Recession   Nicholas R. Lardy

10-8 New PPP-Based Estimates of Renminbi Undervaluation and Policy Implications   Arvind Subramanian

10-9 Protection by Stealth: Using the Tax Law to Discriminate against Foreign Insurance Companies   Gary C. Hufbauer

10-10 Higher Taxes on US-Based Multinationals Would Hurt US Workers and Exports   Gary Clyde Hufbauer and Theodore H. Moran

10-11 A Trade Agenda for the G-20   Jeffrey J. Schott

10-12 Assessing the American Power Act: The Economic, Employment, Energy Security and Environmental Impact of Senator Kerry and Senator Lieberman's Discussion Draft   Trevor Houser, Shashank Mohan, and Ian Hoffman

10-13 Hobbling Exports and Destroying Jobs   Gary Clyde Hufbauer and Theodore H. Moran

10-14 In Defense of Europe's Grand Bargain   Jacob Funk Kirkegaard

10-15 Estimates of Fundamental Equilibrium Exchange Rates, May 2010   William R. Cline and John Williamson

10-16 Deepening China-Taiwan Relations through the Economic Cooperation Framework Agreement   Daniel H. Rosen and Zhi Wang

10-17 The Big U-Turn: Japan Threatens to Reverse Postal Reforms   Gary Clyde Hufbauer and Julia Muir

10-18 Dealing with Volatile Capital Flows   Olivier Jeanne

10-19 Revisiting the NAFTA Agenda on Climate Change   Jeffrey J. Schott and Meera Fickling

10-20 Renminbi Undervaluation, China's Surplus, and the US Trade Deficit   William R. Cline

10-21 The Road to a Climate Change Agreement Runs Through Montreal   Richard J. Smith

10-22 Not All Financial Regulation Is Global   Stéphane Rottier and Nicolas Véron

10-23 Prospects for Implementing the Korea US Free Trade Agreement   Jeffrey J. Schott

10-24 The Central Banker's Case for Doing More   Adam S. Posen

10-25 Will It Be Brussels, Berlin, or Financial Markets that Check Moral Hazard in Europe's Bailout Union? Most Likely the Latter!   Jacob Funk Kirkegaard

10-26 Currency Wars?   William R. Cline and John Williamson

10-27 How Europe Can Muddle Through Its Crisis   Jacob Funk Kirkegaard

10-28 KORUS FTA 2.0: Assessing the Changes   Jeffrey J. Schott

10-29 Strengthening IMF Surveillance: A Comprehensive Proposal   Edwin M. Truman

10-30 An Update on EU Financial Reforms   Nicolas Véron

11-1 Getting Surplus Countries to Adjust   John Williamson

11-2 Corporate Tax Reform for a New Century   Gary Clyde Hufbauer and Woan Foong Wong

11-3 The Elephant in the "Green Room": China and the Doha Round   Aaditya Mattoo, Francis Ng, and Arvind Subramanian

11-4   The Outlook for International Monetary
        System Reform in 2011: A Preliminary
        Report Card   Edwin M. Truman
11-5   Estimates of Fundamental Equilibrium
        Exchange Rates, May 2011
        William R. Cline and John Williamson
11-6   Revitalizing the Export-Import Bank
        Gary Clyde Hufbauer, Meera Fickling,
        and Woan Foong Wong
11-7   Logistics Reform for Low-Value
        Shipments   Gary Clyde Hufbauer and
        Yee Wong
11-8   What Should the United States Do about
        Doha?   Jeffrey J. Schott
11-9   Lessons from the East European
        Financial Crisis, 2008–10   Anders Åslund
11-10   America's Energy Security Options
        Trevor Houser and Shashank Mohan
11-11   Keeping the Promise of Global
        Accounting Standards   Nicolas Véron
11-12   Markets vs. Malthus: Food Security and
        the Global Economy   Cullen S. Hendrix
11-13   Europe on the Brink   Peter Boone and
        Simon Johnson
11-14   IFSWF Report on Compliance with the
        Santiago Principles: Admirable but
        Flawed Transparency   Sarah Bagnall and
        Edwin M. Truman
11-15   How Flexible Can Inflation Targeting Be
        and Still Work?   Kenneth N. Kuttner and
        Adam S. Posen
11-16   US Tax Discrimination Against Large
        Corporations Should Be Discarded
        Gary Clyde Hufbauer & Martin Vieiro
11-17   Debt Relief for Egypt?   John Williamson
        and Mohsin Khan
11-18   The Current Currency Situation
        William R. Cline and John Williamson
11-19   G-20 Reforms of the International
        Monetary System: An Evaluation
        Edwin M. Truman
11-20   The United States Should Establish
        Normal Trade Relations with Russia
        Anders Åslund and Gary Clyde Hufbauer
11-21   What Can and Cannot Be Done about
        Rating Agencies   Nicolas Véron
12-1   The Coming Resolution of the European
        Crisis   C. Fred Bergsten and
        Jacob Funk Kirkegaard
12-2   Japan Post: Retreat or Advance?
        Gary Clyde Hufbauer and Julia Muir
12-3   Another Shot at Protection by Stealth:
        Using the Tax Law to Penalize Foreign
        Insurance Companies   Gary C. Hufbauer
12-4   The European Crisis Deepens
        Peter Boone and Simon Johnson
12-5   Interest Rate Shock and Sustainability of
        Italy's Sovereign Debt   William R. Cline
12-6   Using US Strategic Reserves to Moderate
        Potential Oil Price Increases from
        Sanctions on Iran   Philip K. Verleger, Jr.
12-7   Projecting China's Current Account
        Surplus   William R. Cline

12-8   Does Monetary Cooperation or
        Confrontation Lead to Successful Fiscal
        Consolidation?   Tomas Hellebrandt,
        Adam S. Posen, and Marilyne Tolle
12-9   US Tire Tariffs: Saving Few Jobs at High
        Cost   Gary Clyde Hufbauer and
        Sean Lowry
12-10   Framework for the International Services
        Agreement   Gary Clyde Hufbauer,
        J. Bradford Jensen, and Sherry Stephenson.
        Assisted by Julia Muir and Martin Vieiro
12-11   Will the World Trade Organization Enjoy
        a Bright Future?   Gary C. Hufbauer and
        Jeffrey J. Schott
12-12   Japan Post: Anti-Reform Law Clouds
        Japan's Entry to the Trans-Pacific
        Partnership   Gary Clyde Hufbauer and
        Julia Muir
12-13   Right Idea, Wrong Direction: Obama's
        Corporate Tax Reform Proposals
        Gary Clyde Hufbauer and Martin Vieiro
12-14   Estimates of Fundamental Equilibrium
        Exchange Rates, May 2012
        William R. Cline and John Williamson
12-15   Restoring Fiscal Equilibrium in the
        United States   William R. Cline
12-16   The Trans-Pacific Partnership and Asia-
        Pacific Integration: Policy Implications
        Peter A. Petri and Michael G. Plummer
12-17   Southern Europe Ignores Lessons from
        Latvia at Its Peril   Anders Åslund
12-18   The Coming Resolution of the European
        Crisis: An Update   C. Fred Bergsten and
        Jacob Funk Kirkegaard
12-19   Combating Widespread Currency
        Manipulation   Joseph E. Gagnon
12-20   Why a Breakup of the Euro Area Must
        Be Avoided: Lessons from Previous
        Breakups   Anders Åslund
12-21   How Can Trade Policy Help America
        Compete?
        Robert Z. Lawrence
12-22   Hyperinflations Are Rare, but a Breakup
        of the Euro Area Could Prompt One
        Anders Åslund
12-23   Updated Estimates of Fundamental
        Equilibrium Exchange Rates
        William R. Cline and John Williamson
13-1   The World Needs a Multilateral
        Investment Agreement   Anders Åslund

* = out of print

POLICY ANALYSES IN INTERNATIONAL
ECONOMICS Series

1   The Lending Policies of the International
     Monetary Fund*   John Williamson
     August 1982   ISBN 0-88132-000-5
2   "Reciprocity": A New Approach to World
     Trade Policy?*   William R. Cline
     September 1982   ISBN 0-88132-001-3
3   Trade Policy in the 1980s*   C. Fred Bergsten
     and William R. Cline
     November 1982   ISBN 0-88132-002-1

4   International Debt and the Stability of the
    World Economy*   William R. Cline
    September 1983   ISBN 0-88132-010-2
5   The Exchange Rate System,* 2d ed.
    John Williamson
    Sept. 1983, rev. June 1985   ISBN 0-88132-034-X
6   Economic Sanctions in Support of Foreign
    Policy Goals*   Gary Clyde Hufbauer and
    Jeffrey J. Schott
    October 1983   ISBN 0-88132-014-5
7   A New SDR Allocation?*   John Williamson
    March 1984   ISBN 0-88132-028-5
8   An International Standard for Monetary
    Stabilization*   Ronald L. McKinnon
    March 1984   ISBN 0-88132-018-8
9   The Yen/Dollar Agreement: Liberalizing
    Japanese Capital Markets*   Jeffrey Frankel
    December 1984   ISBN 0-88132-035-8
10 Bank Lending to Developing Countries:
    The Policy Alternatives*   C. Fred Bergsten,
    William R. Cline, and John Williamson
    April 1985   ISBN 0-88132-032-3
11 Trading for Growth: The Next Round of
    Trade Negotiations*   Gary C. Hufbauer and
    Jeffrey J. Schott
    September 1985   ISBN 0-88132-033-1
12 Financial Intermediation Beyond the Debt
    Crisis*   Donald R. Lessard and
    John Williamson
    September 1985   ISBN 0-88132-021-8
13 The United States-Japan Economic
    Problem*   C. Fred Bergsten and William R.
    Cline, Oct. 1985, 2d ed. January 1987
                            ISBN 0-88132-060-9
14 Deficits and the Dollar: The World
    Economy at Risk*   Stephen Marris
    Dec. 1985, 2d ed. November 1987
                            ISBN 0-88132-067-6
15 Trade Policy for Troubled Industries*
    Gary Clyde Hufbauer and Howard F. Rosen
    March 1986   ISBN 0-88132-020-X
16 The United States and Canada: The Quest
    for Free Trade*   Paul Wonnacott, with an
    appendix by John Williamson
    March 1987   ISBN 0-88132-056-0
17 Adjusting to Success: Balance of Payments
    Policy in the East Asian NICs*   Bela
    Balassa and John Williamson
    June 1987, rev. April 1990
                            ISBN 0-88132-101-X
18 Mobilizing Bank Lending to Debtor
    Countries*   William R. Cline
    June 1987   ISBN 0-88132-062-5
19 Auction Quotas and United States Trade
    Policy*   C. Fred Bergsten, Kimberly Ann
    Elliott, Jeffrey J. Schott, and Wendy E. Takacs
    September 1987   ISBN 0-88132-050-1
20 Agriculture and the GATT: Rewriting the
    Rules*   Dale E. Hathaway
    September 1987   ISBN 0-88132-052-8
21 Anti-Protection: Changing Forces in United
    States Trade Politics*   I. M. Destler and
    John S. Odell
    September 1987   ISBN 0-88132-043-9

22 Targets and Indicators: A Blueprint for the
    International Coordination of Economic
    Policy   John Williamson and Marcus Miller
    September 1987   ISBN 0-88132-051-X
23 Capital Flight: The Problem and Policy
    Responses*   Donald R. Lessard and
    John Williamson
    December 1987   ISBN 0-88132-059-5
24 United States-Canada Free Trade: An
    Evaluation of the Agreement*
    Jeffrey J. Schott
    April 1988   ISBN 0-88132-072-2
25 Voluntary Approaches to Debt Relief*
    John Williamson
    Sept. 1988, rev. May 1989
    ISBN 0-88132-098-6
26 American Trade Adjustment: The Global
    Impact*   William R. Cline
    March 1989   ISBN 0-88132-095-1
27 More Free Trade Areas?*   Jeffrey J. Schott
    May 1989   ISBN 0-88132-085-4
28 The Progress of Policy Reform in Latin
    America*   John Williamson
    January 1990   ISBN 0-88132-100-1
29 The Global Trade Negotiations: What Can
    Be Achieved?*   Jeffrey J. Schott
    September 1990   ISBN 0-88132-137-0
30 Economic Policy Coordination: Requiem
    for Prologue?*   Wendy Dobson
    April 1991   ISBN 0-88132-102-8
31 The Economic Opening of Eastern Europe*
    John Williamson
    May 1991   ISBN 0-88132-186-9
32 Eastern Europe and the Soviet Union in the
    World Economy*   Susan Collins and
    Dani Rodrik
    May 1991   ISBN 0-88132-157-5
33 African Economic Reform: The External
    Dimension*   Carol Lancaster
    June 1991   ISBN 0-88132-096-X
34 Has the Adjustment Process Worked?*
    Paul R. Krugman
    October 1991   ISBN 0-88132-116-8
35 From Soviet DisUnion to Eastern Economic
    Community?*   Oleh Havrylyshyn and
    John Williamson
    October 1991   ISBN 0-88132-192-3
36 Global Warming: The Economic Stakes*
    William R. Cline
    May 1992   ISBN 0-88132-172-9
37 Trade and Payments after Soviet
    Disintegration*   John Williamson
    June 1992   ISBN 0-88132-173-7
38 Trade and Migration: NAFTA and
    Agriculture*   Philip L. Martin
    October 1993   ISBN 0-88132-201-6
39 The Exchange Rate System and the IMF: A
    Modest Agenda   Morris Goldstein
    June 1995   ISBN 0-88132-219-9
40 What Role for Currency Boards?
    John Williamson
    September 1995   ISBN 0-88132-222-9
41 Predicting External Imbalances for the
    United States and Japan*   William R. Cline
    September 1995   ISBN 0-88132-220-2

42 Standards and APEC: An Action Agenda*
John S. Wilson
October 1995   ISBN 0-88132-223-7

43 Fundamental Tax Reform and Border Tax
Adjustments*   Gary Clyde Hufbauer
January 1996   ISBN 0-88132-225-3

44 Global Telecom Talks: A Trillion Dollar
Deal*   Ben A. Petrazzini
June 1996   ISBN 0-88132-230-X

45 WTO 2000: Setting the Course for World
Trade   Jeffrey J. Schott
September 1996   ISBN 0-88132-234-2

46 The National Economic Council: A Work in
Progress*   I. M. Destler
November 1996   ISBN 0-88132-239-3

47 The Case for an International Banking
Standard   Morris Goldstein
April 1997   ISBN 0-88132-244-X

48 Transatlantic Trade: A Strategic Agenda*
Ellen L. Frost
May 1997   ISBN 0-88132-228-8

49 Cooperating with Europe's Monetary
Union   C. Randall Henning
May 1997   ISBN 0-88132-245-8

50 Renewing Fast Track Legislation*
I. M. Destler
September 1997   ISBN 0-88132-252-0

51 Competition Policies for the Global
Economy   Edward M. Graham and
J. David Richardson
November 1997   ISBN 0-88132-249-0

52 Improving Trade Policy Reviews in the
World Trade Organization Donald Keesing
April 1998   ISBN 0-88132-251-2

53 Agricultural Trade Policy: Completing the
Reform   Timothy Josling
April 1998   ISBN 0-88132-256-3

54 Real Exchange Rates for the Year 2000
Simon Wren Lewis and Rebecca Driver
April 1998   ISBN 0-88132-253-9

55 The Asian Financial Crisis: Causes, Cures,
and Systemic Implications
Morris Goldstein
June 1998   ISBN 0-88132-261-X

56 Global Economic Effects of the Asian
Currency Devaluations   Marcus Noland,
LiGang Liu, Sherman Robinson, and Zhi
Wang
July 1998   ISBN 0-88132-260-1

57 The Exchange Stabilization Fund: Slush
Money or War Chest? C. Randall Henning
May 1999   ISBN 0-88132-271-7

58 The New Politics of American Trade: Trade,
Labor, and the Environment   I. M. Destler
and Peter J. Balint
October 1999   ISBN 0-88132-269-5

59 Congressional Trade Votes: From NAFTA
Approval to Fast Track Defeat
Robert E. Baldwin and Christopher S. Magee
February 2000   ISBN 0-88132-267-9

60 Exchange Rate Regimes for Emerging
Markets: Reviving the Intermediate Option
John Williamson
September 2000   ISBN 0-88132-293-8

61 NAFTA and the Environment: Seven Years
Later   Gary Clyde Hufbauer, Daniel Esty,
Diana Orejas, Luis Rubio, and Jeffrey J.
Schott
October 2000   ISBN 0-88132-299-7

62 Free Trade between Korea and the United
States?   Inbom Choi and Jeffrey J. Schott
April 2001   ISBN 0-88132-311-X

63 New Regional Trading Arrangements in
the Asia Pacific?   Robert Scollay and
John P. Gilbert
May 2001   ISBN 0-88132-302-0

64 Parental Supervision: The New Paradigm
for Foreign Direct Investment and
Development   Theodore H. Moran
August 2001   ISBN 0-88132-313-6

65 The Benefits of Price Convergence:
Speculative Calculations
Gary Clyde Hufbauer, Erika Wada, and
Tony Warren
December 2001   ISBN 0-88132-333-0

66 Managed Floating Plus   Morris Goldstein
March 2002   ISBN 0-88132-336-5

67 Argentina and the Fund: From Triumph to
Tragedy   Michael Mussa
July 2002   ISBN 0-88132-339-X

68 East Asian Financial Cooperation
C. Randall Henning
September 2002   ISBN 0-88132-338-1

69 Reforming OPIC for the 21st Century
Theodore H. Moran
May 2003   ISBN 0-88132-342-X

70 Awakening Monster: The Alien Tort
Statute of 1789   Gary Clyde Hufbauer and
Nicholas Mitrokostas
July 2003   ISBN 0-88132-366-7

71 Korea after Kim Jong-il   Marcus Noland
January 2004   ISBN 0-88132-373-X

72 Roots of Competitiveness: China's Evolving
Agriculture Interests   Daniel H. Rosen,
Scott Rozelle, and Jikun Huang
July 2004   ISBN 0-88132-376-4

73 Prospects for a US-Taiwan FTA
Nicholas R. Lardy and Daniel H. Rosen
December 2004   ISBN 0-88132-367-5

74 Anchoring Reform with a US-Egypt Free
Trade Agreement   Ahmed Galal and
Robert Z. Lawrence
April 2005   ISBN 0-88132-368-3

75 Curbing the Boom-Bust Cycle: Stabilizing
Capital Flows to Emerging Markets
John Williamson
July 2005   ISBN 0-88132-330-6

76 The Shape of a Swiss-US Free Trade
Agreement   Gary Clyde Hufbauer and
Richard E. Baldwin
February 2006   ISBN 978-0-88132-385-6

77 A Strategy for IMF Reform
Edwin M. Truman
February 2006   ISBN 978-0-88132-398-6

78 US-China Trade Disputes: Rising Tide,
Rising Stakes   Gary Clyde Hufbauer,
Yee Wong, and Ketki Sheth
August 2006   ISBN 978-0-88132-394-8

79 Trade Relations Between Colombia and the United States   Jeffrey J. Schott, ed.
August 2006   ISBN 978-0-88132-389-4

80 Sustaining Reform with a US-Pakistan Free Trade Agreement   Gary Clyde Hufbauer and Shahid Javed Burki
November 2006   ISBN 978-0-88132-395-5

81 A US–Middle East Trade Agreement: A Circle of Opportunity?   Robert Z. Lawrence
November 2006   ISBN 978-0-88132-396-2

82 Reference Rates and the International Monetary System   John Williamson
January 2007   ISBN 978-0-88132-401-3

83 Toward a US-Indonesia Free Trade Agreement   Gary Clyde Hufbauer and Sjamsu Rahardja
June 2007   ISBN 978-0-88132-402-0

84 The Accelerating Decline in America's High-Skilled Workforce Jacob F. Kirkegaard
December 2007   ISBN 978-0-88132-413-6

85 Blue-Collar Blues: Is Trade to Blame for Rising US Income Inequality?   Robert Z. Lawrence
January 2008   ISBN 978-0-88132-414-3

86 Maghreb Regional and Global Integration: A Dream to Be Fulfilled   Gary C. Hufbauer and Claire Brunel, eds.
October 2008   ISBN 978-0-88132-426-6

87 The Future of China's Exchange Rate Policy Morris Goldstein and Nicholas R. Lardy
July 2009   ISBN 978-0-88132-416-7

88 Capitalizing on the Morocco-US Free Trade Agreement: A Road Map for Success Gary Clyde Hufbauer and Claire Brunel, eds
September 2009   ISBN 978-0-88132-433-4

89 Three Threats: An Analytical Framework for the CFIUS Process   Theodore H. Moran
August 2009   ISBN 978-0-88132-429-7

90 Reengaging Egypt: Options for US-Egypt Economic Relations Barbara Kotschwar and Jeffrey J. Schott
January 2010   ISBN 978-088132-439-6

91 Figuring Out the Doha Round   Gary Clyde Hufbauer, Jeffrey J. Schott, and Woan Foong Wong
June 2010   ISBN 978-088132-503-4

92 China's Strategy to Secure Natural Resources: Risks, Dangers, and Opportunities   Theodore H. Moran
June 2010   ISBN 978-088132-512-6

93 The Implications of China-Taiwan Economic Liberalization   Daniel H. Rosen and Zhi Wang
January 2011   ISBN 978-0-88132-501-0

94 The Global Outlook for Government Debt over the Next 25 Years: Implications for the Economy and Public Policy   Joseph E. Gagnon with Marc Hinterschweiger
June 2011   ISBN 978-0-88132-621-5

95 A Decade of Debt   Carmen M. Reinhart and Kenneth S. Rogoff
September 2011   ISBN 978-0-88132-622-2

96 Carbon Abatement Costs and Climate Change Finance   William R. Cline
July 2011   ISBN 978-0-88132-607-9

97 The United States Should Establish Permanent Normal Trade Relations with Russia   Anders Åslund and Gary Clyde Hufbauer
April 2012   ISBN 978-0-88132-620-8

98 The Trans-Pacific Partnership and Asia-Pacific Integration: A Quantitative Assessment   Peter A. Petri, Michael G. Plummer, and Fan Zhai
November 2012   ISBN 978-0-88132-664-2

99 Understanding the Trans-Pacific Partnership   Jeffrey J. Schott, Barbara Kotschwar, and Julia Muir
January 2013   ISBN 978-0-88132-672-7

BOOKS

IMF Conditionality*   John Williamson, ed.
1983   ISBN 0-88132-006-4

Trade Policy in the 1980s*   William R. Cline, ed.
1983   ISBN 0-88132-031-5

Subsidies in International Trade*   Gary Clyde Hufbauer and Joanna Shelton Erb
1984   ISBN 0-88132-004-8

International Debt: Systemic Risk and Policy Response*   William R. Cline
1984   ISBN 0-88132-015-3

Trade Protection in the United States: 31 Case Studies*   Gary Clyde Hufbauer, Diane E. Berliner, and Kimberly Ann Elliott
1986   ISBN 0-88132-040-4

Toward Renewed Economic Growth in Latin America*   Bela Balassa, Gerardo M. Bueno, Pedro Pablo Kuczynski, and Mario Henrique Simonsen
1986   ISBN 0-88132-045-5

Capital Flight and Third World Debt* Donald R. Lessard and John Williamson, eds.
1987   ISBN 0-88132-053-6

The Canada-United States Free Trade Agreement: The Global Impact*   Jeffrey J. Schott and Murray G. Smith, eds.
1988   ISBN 0-88132-073-0

World Agricultural Trade: Building a Consensus*   William M. Miner and Dale E. Hathaway, eds.
1988   ISBN 0-88132-071-3

Japan in the World Economy*   Bela Balassa and Marcus Noland
1988   ISBN 0-88132-041-2

America in the World Economy: A Strategy for the 1990s*   C. Fred Bergsten
1988   ISBN 0-88132-089-7

Managing the Dollar: From the Plaza to the Louvre*   Yoichi Funabashi
1988, 2d ed. 1989   ISBN 0-88132-097-8

United States External Adjustment and the World Economy*   William R. Cline
May 1989   ISBN 0-88132-048-X

Free Trade Areas and U.S. Trade Policy* Jeffrey J. Schott, ed.
May 1989   ISBN 0-88132-094-3

Dollar Politics: Exchange Rate Policymaking
in the United States*   I. M. Destler and
C. Randall Henning
September 1989   ISBN 0-88132-079-X
Latin American Adjustment: How Much Has
Happened?*   John Williamson, ed.
April 1990   ISBN 0-88132-125-7
The Future of World Trade in Textiles and
Apparel*   William R. Cline
1987, 2d ed. June 1999   ISBN 0-88132-110-9
Completing the Uruguay Round: A Results-
Oriented Approach to the GATT Trade
Negotiations*   Jeffrey J. Schott, ed.
September 1990   ISBN 0-88132-130-3
Economic Sanctions Reconsidered (2 volumes)
Economic Sanctions Reconsidered:
Supplemental Case Histories Gary C. Hufbauer,
Jeffrey J. Schott, and Kimberly Ann Elliott
1985, 2d ed. Dec. 1990   ISBN cloth 0-88132-115-X
                         ISBN paper 0-88132-105-2
Economic Sanctions Reconsidered: History
and Current Policy   Gary C. Hufbauer, Jeffrey
J. Schott, and Kimberly Ann Elliott
December 1990   ISBN cloth 0-88132-140-0
                         ISBN paper 0-88132-136-2
Pacific Basin Developing Countries: Prospects
for the Future*   Marcus Noland
January 1991   ISBN cloth 0-88132-141-9
                         ISBN paper 0-88132-081-1
Currency Convertibility in Eastern Europe*
John Williamson, ed.
October 1991   ISBN 0-88132-128-1
International Adjustment and Financing: The
Lessons of 1985-1991*   C. Fred Bergsten, ed.
January 1992   ISBN 0-88132-112-5
North American Free Trade: Issues and
Recommendations*   Gary Clyde Hufbauer and
Jeffrey J. Schott
April 1992   ISBN 0-88132-120-6
Narrowing the U.S. Current Account Deficit*
Alan J. Lenz
June 1992   ISBN 0-88132-103-6
The Economics of Global Warming
William R. Cline
June 1992   ISBN 0-88132-132-X
US Taxation of International Income:
Blueprint for Reform   Gary Clyde Hufbauer,
assisted by Joanna M. van Rooij
October 1992   ISBN 0-88132-134-6
Who's Bashing Whom? Trade Conflict in High-
Technology Industries   Laura D'Andrea Tyson
November 1992   ISBN 0-88132-106-0
Korea in the World Economy*   Il SaKong
January 1993   ISBN 0-88132-183-4
Pacific Dynamism and the International
Economic System*   C. Fred Bergsten and
Marcus Noland, eds.
May 1993   ISBN 0-88132-196-6
Economic Consequences of Soviet
Disintegration*   John Williamson, ed.
May 1993   ISBN 0-88132-190-7
Reconcilable Differences? United States-Japan
Economic Conflict*   C. Fred Bergsten and
Marcus Noland
June 1993   ISBN 0-88132-129-X

Does Foreign Exchange Intervention Work?
Kathryn M. Dominguez and Jeffrey A. Frankel
September 1993   ISBN 0-88132-104-4
Sizing Up U.S. Export Disincentives*
J. David Richardson
September 1993   ISBN 0-88132-107-9
NAFTA: An Assessment   Gary Clyde Hufbauer
and Jeffrey J. Schott, *rev. ed.*
October 1993   ISBN 0-88132-199-0
Adjusting to Volatile Energy Prices
Philip K. Verleger, Jr.
November 1993   ISBN 0-88132-069-2
The Political Economy of Policy Reform
John Williamson, ed.
January 1994   ISBN 0-88132-195-8
Measuring the Costs of Protection in the United
States   Gary Clyde Hufbauer and
Kimberly Ann Elliott
January 1994   ISBN 0-88132-108-7
The Dynamics of Korean Economic
Development*   Cho Soon
March 1994   ISBN 0-88132-162-1
Reviving the European Union*
C. Randall Henning, Eduard Hochreiter, and
Gary Clyde Hufbauer, eds.
April 1994   ISBN 0-88132-208-3
China in the World Economy Nicholas R. Lardy
April 1994   ISBN 0-88132-200-8
Greening the GATT: Trade, Environment,
and the Future   Daniel C. Esty
July 1994   ISBN 0-88132-205-9
Western Hemisphere Economic Integration*
Gary Clyde Hufbauer and Jeffrey J. Schott
July 1994   ISBN 0-88132-159-1
Currencies and Politics in the United States,
Germany, and Japan   C. Randall Henning
September 1994   ISBN 0-88132-127-3
Estimating Equilibrium Exchange Rates
John Williamson, ed.
September 1994   ISBN 0-88132-076-5
Managing the World Economy: Fifty Years
after Bretton Woods   Peter B. Kenen, ed.
September 1994   ISBN 0-88132-212-1
Reciprocity and Retaliation in U.S. Trade Policy
Thomas O. Bayard and Kimberly Ann Elliott
September 1994   ISBN 0-88132-084-6
The Uruguay Round: An Assessment*   Jeffrey J.
Schott, assisted by Johanna Buurman
November 1994   ISBN 0-88132-206-7
Measuring the Costs of Protection in Japan*
Yoko Sazanami, Shujiro Urata, and Hiroki Kawai
January 1995   ISBN 0-88132-211-3
Foreign Direct Investment in the United States,
3d ed. Edward M. Graham and Paul R. Krugman
January 1995   ISBN 0-88132-204-0
The Political Economy of Korea-United States
Cooperation*   C. Fred Bergsten and
Il SaKong, eds.
February 1995   ISBN 0-88132-213-X
International Debt Reexamined*
William R. Cline
February 1995   ISBN 0-88132-083-8
American Trade Politics, 3d ed.   I. M. Destler
April 1995   ISBN 0-88132-215-6

Managing Official Export Credits: The Quest for a Global Regime*   John E. Ray
July 1995   ISBN 0-88132-207-5
Asia Pacific Fusion: Japan's Role in APEC*
Yoichi Funabashi
October 1995   ISBN 0-88132-224-5
Korea-United States Cooperation in the New World Order*   C. Fred Bergsten and Il SaKong, eds.
February 1996   ISBN 0-88132-226-1
Why Exports Really Matter!*
ISBN 0-88132-221-0
Why Exports Matter More!*   ISBN 0-88132-229-6
J. David Richardson and Karin Rindal
July 1995; February 1996
Global Corporations and National Governments
Edward M. Graham
May 1996   ISBN 0-88132-111-7
Global Economic Leadership and the Group of Seven   C. Fred Bergsten and C. Randall Henning
May 1996   ISBN 0-88132-218-0
The Trading System after the Uruguay Round*
John Whalley and Colleen Hamilton
July 1996   ISBN 0-88132-131-1
Private Capital Flows to Emerging Markets after the Mexican Crisis*   Guillermo A. Calvo, Morris Goldstein, and Eduard Hochreiter
September 1996   ISBN 0-88132-232-6
The Crawling Band as an Exchange Rate Regime: Lessons from Chile, Colombia, and Israel   John Williamson
September 1996   ISBN 0-88132-231-8
Flying High: Liberalizing Civil Aviation in the Asia Pacific*   Gary Clyde Hufbauer and Christopher Findlay
November 1996   ISBN 0-88132-227-X
Measuring the Costs of Visible Protection in Korea*   Namdoo Kim
November 1996   ISBN 0-88132-236-9
The World Trading System: Challenges Ahead
Jeffrey J. Schott
December 1996   ISBN 0-88132-235-0
Has Globalization Gone Too Far?   Dani Rodrik
March 1997   ISBN paper 0-88132-241-5
Korea-United States Economic Relationship*
C. Fred Bergsten and Il SaKong, eds.
March 1997   ISBN 0-88132-240-7
Summitry in the Americas: A Progress Report
Richard E. Feinberg
April 1997   ISBN 0-88132-242-3
Corruption and the Global Economy
Kimberly Ann Elliott
June 1997   ISBN 0-88132-233-4
Regional Trading Blocs in the World Economic System   Jeffrey A. Frankel
October 1997   ISBN 0-88132-202-4
Sustaining the Asia Pacific Miracle: Environmental Protection and Economic Integration   Andre Dua and Daniel C. Esty
October 1997   ISBN 0-88132-250-4
Trade and Income Distribution
William R. Cline
November 1997   ISBN 0-88132-216-4

Global Competition Policy   Edward M. Graham and J. David Richardson
December 1997   ISBN 0-88132-166-4
Unfinished Business: Telecommunications after the Uruguay Round   Gary Clyde Hufbauer and Erika Wada
December 1997   ISBN 0-88132-257-1
Financial Services Liberalization in the WTO
Wendy Dobson and Pierre Jacquet
June 1998   ISBN 0-88132-254-7
Restoring Japan's Economic Growth
Adam S. Posen
September 1998   ISBN 0-88132-262-8
Measuring the Costs of Protection in China
Zhang Shuguang, Zhang Yansheng, and Wan Zhongxin
November 1998   ISBN 0-88132-247-4
Foreign Direct Investment and Development: The New Policy Agenda for Developing Countries and Economies in Transition
Theodore H. Moran
December 1998   ISBN 0-88132-258-X
Behind the Open Door: Foreign Enterprises in the Chinese Marketplace   Daniel H. Rosen
January 1999   ISBN 0-88132-263-6
Toward A New International Financial Architecture: A Practical Post-Asia Agenda
Barry Eichengreen
February 1999   ISBN 0-88132-270-9
Is the U.S. Trade Deficit Sustainable?
Catherine L. Mann
September 1999   ISBN 0-88132-265-2
Safeguarding Prosperity in a Global Financial System: The Future International Financial Architecture, Independent Task Force Report Sponsored by the Council on Foreign Relations
Morris Goldstein, Project Director
October 1999   ISBN 0-88132-287-3
Avoiding the Apocalypse: The Future of the Two Koreas   Marcus Noland
June 2000   ISBN 0-88132-278-4
Assessing Financial Vulnerability: An Early Warning System for Emerging Markets
Morris Goldstein, Graciela Kaminsky, and Carmen Reinhart
June 2000   ISBN 0-88132-237-7
Global Electronic Commerce: A Policy Primer
Catherine L. Mann, Sue E. Eckert, and Sarah Cleeland Knight
July 2000   ISBN 0-88132-274-1
The WTO after Seattle   Jeffrey J. Schott, ed.
July 2000   ISBN 0-88132-290-3
Intellectual Property Rights in the Global Economy   Keith E. Maskus
August 2000   ISBN 0-88132-282-2
The Political Economy of the Asian Financial Crisis   Stephan Haggard
August 2000   ISBN 0-88132-283-0
Transforming Foreign Aid: United States Assistance in the 21st Century   Carol Lancaster
August 2000   ISBN 0-88132-291-1
Fighting the Wrong Enemy: Antiglobal Activists and Multinational Enterprises
Edward M. Graham
September 2000   ISBN 0-88132-272-5

Globalization and the Perceptions of American Workers Kenneth Scheve and Matthew J. Slaughter
March 2001 ISBN 0-88132-295-4

World Capital Markets: Challenge to the G-10 Wendy Dobson and Gary Clyde Hufbauer, assisted by Hyun Koo Cho
May 2001 ISBN 0-88132-301-2

Prospects for Free Trade in the Americas Jeffrey J. Schott
August 2001 ISBN 0-88132-275-X

Toward a North American Community: Lessons from the Old World for the New Robert A. Pastor
August 2001 ISBN 0-88132-328-4

Measuring the Costs of Protection in Europe: European Commercial Policy in the 2000s Patrick A. Messerlin
September 2001 ISBN 0-88132-273-3

Job Loss from Imports: Measuring the Costs Lori G. Kletzer
September 2001 ISBN 0-88132-296-2

No More Bashing: Building a New Japan–United States Economic Relationship C. Fred Bergsten, Takatoshi Ito, and Marcus Noland
October 2001 ISBN 0-88132-286-5

Why Global Commitment Really Matters! Howard Lewis III and J. David Richardson
October 2001 ISBN 0-88132-298-9

Leadership Selection in the Major Multilaterals Miles Kahler
November 2001 ISBN 0-88132-335-7

The International Financial Architecture: What's New? What's Missing? Peter B. Kenen
November 2001 ISBN 0-88132-297-0

Delivering on Debt Relief: From IMF Gold to a New Aid Architecture John Williamson and Nancy Birdsall, with Brian Deese
April 2002 ISBN 0-88132-331-4

Imagine There's No Country: Poverty, Inequality, and Growth in the Era of Globalization Surjit S. Bhalla
September 2002 ISBN 0-88132-348-9

Reforming Korea's Industrial Conglomerates Edward M. Graham
January 2003 ISBN 0-88132-337-3

Industrial Policy in an Era of Globalization: Lessons from Asia Marcus Noland and Howard Pack
March 2003 ISBN 0-88132-350-0

Reintegrating India with the World Economy T. N. Srinivasan and Suresh D. Tendulkar
March 2003 ISBN 0-88132-280-6

After the Washington Consensus: Restarting Growth and Reform in Latin America Pedro-Pablo Kuczynski and John Williamson, eds.
March 2003 ISBN 0-88132-347-0

The Decline of US Labor Unions and the Role of Trade Robert E. Baldwin
June 2003 ISBN 0-88132-341-1

Can Labor Standards Improve under Globalization? Kimberly Ann Elliott and Richard B. Freeman
June 2003 ISBN 0-88132-332-2

Crimes and Punishments? Retaliation under the WTO Robert Z. Lawrence
October 2003 ISBN 0-88132-359-4

Inflation Targeting in the World Economy Edwin M. Truman
October 2003 ISBN 0-88132-345-4

Foreign Direct Investment and Tax Competition John H. Mutti
November 2003 ISBN 0-88132-352-7

Has Globalization Gone Far Enough? The Costs of Fragmented Markets Scott C. Bradford and Robert Z. Lawrence
February 2004 ISBN 0-88132-349-7

Food Regulation and Trade: Toward a Safe and Open Global System Tim Josling, Donna Roberts, and David Orden
March 2004 ISBN 0-88132-346-2

Controlling Currency Mismatches in Emerging Markets Morris Goldstein and Philip Turner
April 2004 ISBN 0-88132-360-8

Free Trade Agreements: US Strategies and Priorities Jeffrey J. Schott, ed.
April 2004 ISBN 0-88132-361-6

Trade Policy and Global Poverty William R. Cline
June 2004 ISBN 0-88132-365-9

Bailouts or Bail-ins? Responding to Financial Crises in Emerging Economies Nouriel Roubini and Brad Setser
August 2004 ISBN 0-88132-371-3

Transforming the European Economy Martin Neil Baily and Jacob Funk Kirkegaard
September 2004 ISBN 0-88132-343-8

Chasing Dirty Money: The Fight Against Money Laundering Peter Reuter and Edwin M. Truman
November 2004 ISBN 0-88132-370-5

The United States and the World Economy: Foreign Economic Policy for the Next Decade C. Fred Bergsten
January 2005 ISBN 0-88132-380-2

Does Foreign Direct Investment Promote Development? Theodore H. Moran, Edward M. Graham, and Magnus Blomström, eds.
April 2005 ISBN 0-88132-381-0

American Trade Politics, 4th ed. I. M. Destler
June 2005 ISBN 0-88132-382-9

Why Does Immigration Divide America? Public Finance and Political Opposition to Open Borders Gordon H. Hanson
August 2005 ISBN 0-88132-400-0

Reforming the US Corporate Tax Gary Clyde Hufbauer and Paul L. E. Grieco
September 2005 ISBN 0-88132-384-5

The United States as a Debtor Nation William R. Cline
September 2005 ISBN 0-88132-399-3

NAFTA Revisited: Achievements and Challenges Gary Clyde Hufbauer and Jeffrey J. Schott, assisted by Paul L. E. Grieco and Yee Wong
October 2005 ISBN 0-88132-334-9

US National Security and Foreign Direct Investment   Edward M. Graham and David M. Marchick
May 2006   ISBN 978-0-88132-391-7
Accelerating the Globalization of America: The Role for Information Technology   Catherine L. Mann, assisted by Jacob Funk Kirkegaard
June 2006   ISBN 978-0-88132-390-0
Delivering on Doha: Farm Trade and the Poor   Kimberly Ann Elliott
July 2006   ISBN 978-0-88132-392-4
Case Studies in US Trade Negotiation, Vol. 1: Making the Rules   Charan Devereaux, Robert Z. Lawrence, and Michael Watkins
September 2006   ISBN 978-0-88132-362-7
Case Studies in US Trade Negotiation, Vol. 2: Resolving Disputes   Charan Devereaux, Robert Z. Lawrence, and Michael Watkins
September 2006   ISBN 978-0-88132-363-2
C. Fred Bergsten and the World Economy   Michael Mussa, ed.
December 2006   ISBN 978-0-88132-397-9
Working Papers, Volume I   Peterson Institute
December 2006   ISBN 978-0-88132-388-7
The Arab Economies in a Changing World   Marcus Noland and Howard Pack
April 2007   ISBN 978-0-88132-393-1
Working Papers, Volume II   Peterson Institute
April 2007   ISBN 978-0-88132-404-4
Global Warming and Agriculture: Impact Estimates by Country   William R. Cline
July 2007   ISBN 978-0-88132-403-7
US Taxation of Foreign Income   Gary Clyde Hufbauer and Ariel Assa
October 2007   ISBN 978-0-88132-405-1
Russia's Capitalist Revolution: Why Market Reform Succeeded and Democracy Failed   Anders Åslund
October 2007   ISBN 978-0-88132-409-9
Economic Sanctions Reconsidered, 3d ed.   Gary Clyde Hufbauer, Jeffrey J. Schott, Kimberly Ann Elliott, and Barbara Oegg
November 2007
    ISBN hardcover 978-0-88132-407-5
    ISBN hardcover/CD-ROM 978-0-88132-408-2
Debating China's Exchange Rate Policy   Morris Goldstein and Nicholas R. Lardy, eds.
April 2008   ISBN 978-0-88132-415-0
Leveling the Carbon Playing Field: International Competition and US Climate Policy Design   Trevor Houser, Rob Bradley, Britt Childs, Jacob Werksman, and Robert Heilmayr
May 2008   ISBN 978-0-88132-420-4
Accountability and Oversight of US Exchange Rate Policy   C. Randall Henning
June 2008   ISBN 978-0-88132-419-8
Challenges of Globalization: Imbalances and Growth   Anders Åslund and Marek Dabrowski, eds.
July 2008   ISBN 978-0-88132-418-1
China's Rise: Challenges and Opportunities   C. Fred Bergsten, Charles Freeman, Nicholas R. Lardy, and Derek J. Mitchell
September 2008   ISBN 978-0-88132-417-4

Banking on Basel: The Future of International Financial Regulation   Daniel K. Tarullo
September 2008   ISBN 978-0-88132-423-5
US Pension Reform: Lessons from Other Countries   Martin Neil Baily and Jacob Funk Kirkegaard
February 2009   ISBN 978-0-88132-425-9
How Ukraine Became a Market Economy and Democracy   Anders Åslund
March 2009   ISBN 978-0-88132-427-3
Global Warming and the World Trading System   Gary Clyde Hufbauer, Steve Charnovitz, and Jisun Kim
March 2009   ISBN 978-0-88132-428-0
The Russia Balance Sheet   Anders Åslund and Andrew Kuchins
March 2009   ISBN 978-0-88132-424-2
The Euro at Ten: The Next Global Currency?   Jean Pisani-Ferry and Adam S. Posen, eds.
July 2009   ISBN 978-0-88132-430-3
Financial Globalization, Economic Growth, and the Crisis of 2007–09   William R. Cline
May 2010   ISBN 978-0-88132-4990-0
Russia after the Global Economic Crisis   Anders Åslund, Sergei Guriev, and Andrew Kuchins, eds.
June 2010   ISBN 978-0-88132-497-6
Sovereign Wealth Funds: Threat or Salvation?   Edwin M. Truman
September 2010   ISBN 978-0-88132-498-3
The Last Shall Be the First: The East European Financial Crisis, 2008–10   Anders Åslund
October 2010   ISBN 978-0-88132-521-8
Witness to Transformation: Refugee Insights into North Korea   Stephan Haggard and Marcus Noland
January 2011   ISBN 978-0-88132-438-9
Foreign Direct Investment and Development: Launching a Second Generation of Policy Research, Avoiding the Mistakes of the First, Reevaluating Policies for Developed and Developing Countries   Theodore H. Moran
April 2011   ISBN 978-0-88132-600-0
How Latvia Came through the Financial Crisis   Anders Åslund and Valdis Dombrovskis
May 2011   ISBN 978-0-88132-602-4
Global Trade in Services: Fear, Facts, and Offshoring   J. Bradford Jensen
August 2011   ISBN 978-0-88132-601-7
NAFTA and Climate Change   Meera Fickling and Jeffrey J. Schott
September 2011   ISBN 978-0-88132-436-5
Eclipse: Living in the Shadow of China's Economic Dominance   Arvind Subramanian
September 2011   ISBN 978-0-88132-606-2
Flexible Exchange Rates for a Stable World Economy   Joseph E. Gagnon with Marc Hinterschweiger
September 2011   ISBN 978-0-88132-627-7
The Arab Economies in a Changing World, 2d ed.   Marcus Noland and Howard Pack
November 2011   ISBN 978-0-88132-628-4
Sustaining China's Economic Growth After the Global Financial Crisis   Nicholas R. Lardy
January 2012   ISBN 978-0-88132-626-0

Who Needs to Open the Capital Account?
Olivier Jeanne, Arvind Subramanian, and John
Williamson
April 2012   ISBN 978-0-88132-511-9
Devaluing to Prosperity: Misaligned Currencies
and Their Growth Consequences Surjit S. Bhalla
August 2012   ISBN 978-0-88132-623-9
Private Rights and Public Problems: The Global
Economics of Intellectual Property in the 21st
Century   Keith Maskus
September 2012   ISBN 978-0-88132-507-2
Global Economics in Extraordinary Times:
Essays in Honor of John Williamson
C. Fred Bergsten and C. Randall Henning, eds.
November 2012   ISBN 978-0-88132-662-8
Rising Tide: Is Growth in Emerging Economies
Good for the United States?
Lawrence Edwards and Robert Z. Lawrence
February 2013   ISBN 978-0-88132-500-3

SPECIAL REPORTS

1   Promoting World Recovery: A Statement on
    Global Economic Strategy*
    by 26 Economists from Fourteen Countries
    December 1982   ISBN 0-88132-013-7
2   Prospects for Adjustment in Argentina,
    Brazil, and Mexico: Responding to the Debt
    Crisis*   John Williamson, ed.
    June 1983   ISBN 0-88132-016-1
3   Inflation and Indexation: Argentina, Brazil,
    and Israel*   John Williamson, ed.
    March 1985   ISBN 0-88132-037-4
4   Global Economic Imb alances*
    C. Fred Bergsten, ed.
    March 1986   ISBN 0-88132-042-0
5   African Debt and Financing*   Carol
    Lancaster and John Williamson, eds
    May 1986   ISBN 0-88132-044-7
6   Resolving the Global Economic Crisis:
    After Wall Street*
    by Thirty-three Economists from Thirteen
    Countries
    December 1987   ISBN 0-88132-070-6
7   World Economic Problems*   Kimberly Ann
    Elliott and John Williamson, eds.
    April 1988   ISBN 0-88132-055-2
    Reforming World Agricultural Trade*
    by Twenty-nine Professionals from
    Seventeen Countries
    1988   ISBN 0-88132-088-9
8   Economic Relations Between the United
    States and Korea: Conflict or Cooperation?*
    Thomas O. Bayard and Soogil Young, eds.
    January 1989   ISBN 0-88132-068-4
9   Whither APEC? The Progress to Date and
    Agenda for the Future* C. Fred Bergsten, ed.
    October 1997   ISBN 0-88132-248-2
10 Economic Integration of the Korean
    Peninsula   Marcus Noland, ed.
    January 1998   ISBN 0-88132-255-5
11 Restarting Fast Track*   Jeffrey J. Schott, ed.
    April 1998   ISBN 0-88132-259-8

12 Launching New Global Trade Talks: An
    Action Agenda   Jeffrey J. Schott, ed.
    September 1998   ISBN 0-88132-266-0
13 Japan's Financial Crisis and Its Parallels to
    US Experience   Ryoichi Mikitani and
    Adam S. Posen, eds.
    September 2000   ISBN 0-88132-289-X
14 The Ex-Im Bank in the 21st Century: A New
    Approach   Gary Clyde Hufbauer and
    Rita M. Rodriguez, eds.
    January 2001   ISBN 0-88132-300-4
15 The Korean Diaspora in the World
    Economy   C. Fred Bergsten and
    Inbom Choi, eds.
    January 2003   ISBN 0-88132-358-6
16 Dollar Overvaluation and the World
    Economy   C. Fred Bergsten and
    John Williamson, eds.
    February 2003   ISBN 0-88132-351-9
17 Dollar Adjustment: How Far? Against
    What?   C. Fred Bergsten and
    John Williamson, eds.
    November 2004   ISBN 0-88132-378-0
18 The Euro at Five: Ready for a Global Role?
    Adam S. Posen, ed.
    April 2005   ISBN 0-88132-380-2
19 Reforming the IMF for the 21st Century
    Edwin M. Truman, ed.
    April 2006   ISBN 978-0-88132-387-0
20 The Long-Term International Economic
    Position of the United States
    C. Fred Bergsten, ed.
    May 2009   ISBN 978-0-88132-432-7
21 Resolving the European Debt Crisis
    William R. Cline and Guntram B. Wolff, eds.
    February 2012   ISBN 978-0-88132-642-0
22 Transatlantic Economic Challenges in an
    Era of Growing Multipolarity
    Jacob Funk Kirkegaard, Nicolas Véron, and
    Guntram B. Wolff, eds.
    June 2012   ISBN 978-0-88132-645-1

WORKS IN PROGRESS

Launching a Comprehensive US Export Strategy
Howard F. Rosen and C. Fred Bergsten, editors
Banking System Fragility in Emerging
Economies   Morris Goldstein and Philip Turner
The Future of the World Trade Organization
Gary Clyde Hufbauer and Jeffrey J. Schott
China's Rise as Global Direct Investor:
Policy Implications   Daniel H. Rosen and
Thilo Hanemann
Fueling Up: The Economic Implications of
America's Oil and Gas Boom   Trevor Houser
Foreign Direct Investment in the United States:
Benefits, Suspicions, and Risks with Special
Attention to FDI from China
Theodore H. Moran and Lindsay Oldenski
Dereliction of Duties: The Rise, Fall, and
Possible Rebound of US Trade Policy
Craig VanGrasstek

DISTRIBUTORS OUTSIDE THE UNITED STATES

**Australia, New Zealand,
and Papua New Guinea**
D. A. Information Services
648 Whitehorse Road
Mitcham, Victoria 3132, Australia
Tel: 61-3-9210-7777
Fax: 61-3-9210-7788
Email: service@dadirect.com.au
www.dadirect.com.au

India, Bangladesh, Nepal, and Sri Lanka
Viva Books Private Limited
Mr. Vinod Vasishtha
4737/23 Ansari Road
Daryaganj, New Delhi 110002
India
Tel: 91-11-4224-2200
Fax: 91-11-4224-2240
Email: viva@vivagroupindia.net
www.vivagroupindia.com

**Mexico, Central America, South America,
and Puerto Rico**
US PubRep, Inc.
311 Dean Drive
Rockville, MD 20851
Tel: 301-838-9276
Fax: 301-838-9278
Email: c.falk@ieee.org

Asia (*Brunei, Burma, Cambodia, China,
Hong Kong, Indonesia, Korea, Laos, Malaysia,
Philippines, Singapore, Taiwan, Thailand,
and Vietnam*)
East-West Export Books (EWEB)
University of Hawaii Press
2840 Kolowalu Street
Honolulu, Hawaii 96822-1888
Tel: 808-956-8830
Fax: 808-988-6052
Email: eweb@hawaii.edu

Canada
Renouf Bookstore
5369 Canotek Road, Unit 1
Ottawa, Ontario KlJ 9J3, Canada
Tel: 613-745-2665
Fax: 613-745-7660
www.renoufbooks.com

Japan
United Publishers Services Ltd.
1-32-5, Higashi-shinagawa
Shinagawa-ku, Tokyo 140-0002
Japan
Tel: 81-3-5479-7251
Fax: 81-3-5479-7307
Email: purchasing@ups.co.jp
*For trade accounts only. Individuals will find
Institute books in leading Tokyo bookstores.*

Middle East
MERIC
2 Bahgat Ali Street, El Masry Towers
Tower D, Apt. 24
Zamalek, Cairo
Egypt
Tel. 20-2-7633824
Fax: 20-2-7369355
Email: mahmoud_fouda@mericonline.com
www.mericonline.com

United Kingdom, Europe
(*including Russia and Turkey*)**, Africa,
and Israel**
The Eurospan Group
c/o Turpin Distribution
Pegasus Drive
Stratton Business Park
Biggleswade, Bedfordshire
SG18 8TQ
United Kingdom
Tel: 44 (0) 1767-604972
Fax: 44 (0) 1767-601640
Email: eurospan@turpin-distribution.com
www.eurospangroup.com/bookstore

**Visit our website at:
www.piie.com
E-mail orders to:
petersonmail@presswarehouse.com**